THE CRIMINALIZATION OF ABORTION IN THE WEST

T0334857

THE
CRIMINALIZATION
OF ABORTION
IN THE WEST

Its Origins in Medieval Law

WOLFGANG P. MÜLLER

CORNELL UNIVERSITY PRESS
Ithaca and London

First published 2012 by Cornell University Press
First printing, Cornell Paperbacks, 2017

Library of Congress Cataloging-in-Publication Data

Müller, Wolfgang P., 1960–
    The criminalization of abortion in the West : its origins in medieval law / Wolfgang P. Müller.
        p. cm.
    Includes bibliographical references and index.
    ISBN 978-0-8014-5089-1 (cloth : alk. paper)
    ISBN 978-1-5017-1365-1 (pbk. : alk. paper)
    1. Abortion—Law and legislation—Europe, Western.
    2. Abortion—Law and legislation—History.   3. Law, Medieval.   I. Title.
        KJC8377.M85   2012
        345′.02850940902—dc23   2011051733

Contents

ACKNOWLEDGMENTS

Work on what would become the present book started in the spring of 2002, when Anne Lefebvre-Teillard (Institut Catholique de Paris) and Frank Roumy (Université de Paris XI, now at Paris II) invited me to present my vision of medieval canon law over the course of four seminar sessions to their graduate students. Left subsequently with a considerable stack of lecture notes, I developed the idea of writing a short introduction to the subject, which would point to omissions and shortcomings in scholarship apart from the conventional summary of previous historiography. The principal outcome of this initial work phase was my essay "Church Law as a Field of Historical Inquiry," which my coeditor, Mary E. Sommar, and I placed at the beginning of our 2006 essay collection in honor of Kenneth Pennington.

By 2005 I had realized that my original attempt to add proper historical dimension to the study of medieval church law had been too narrow in scope. The twelfth-century rise of canon law schools, systematized canonical doctrine, and uniform judicial procedures could not be isolated from parallel developments in the secular and penitential spheres; and my methodological critique of legal historiography risked excessive abstraction without continuous reference to concrete examples and original source material. To mend the situation, I decided to fold into the narrative the results of my earlier research on the criminalization of abortion from 1140 to 1650, conducted between 1992 and 1999 and published in 2000 as a monograph under the German title of *Die Abtreibung*.

In the fall of 2006 an outline of the definitive nine chapters was in place, and the draft stage got under way. It continued uninterrupted until the spring of 2009 and still required two substantive revisions thereafter, one in the spring of 2010 and another in May–June of 2011. Undoubtedly, the process would have taken even longer had it not been for the generous financial and logistical support of several institutions. My gratitude returns yet again to my Parisian hosts of 2002, without whom there might not have been a prime mover for the project. Moreover, significant monetary help in the form of a research fellowship was offered by the Gerda–Henkel Stiftung in Düsseldorf, Germany, during my sabbatical year of 2004–5, which in turn had been granted by my academic home, Fordham University, and was to be supplemented by another Fordham Faculty Fellowship in the spring of 2010. Fordham also provided me with a semester-long leave of absence for the spring of 2007, allowing me to write and bask in the hospitality of Sverre Bagge and Torstein Jørgensen at the Centre for Medieval Studies in Bergen, Norway.

Among those who lent their expertise and particular energy to the making of this book, I find for the third time reason to include Franck Roumy, who went far out of his way to invite and accommodate me in France in 2002. I am also grateful to Mary E. Sommar (now at the University of Pennsylvania in Millersville) for having been the first native to confront this foreigner's infelicities of expression over the whole length of my earliest manuscript version. Idiomatic alerts came from many others as well, of whom I wish to name Ken Pennington (Catholic University of America), my adviser, once and always. Ken's enduring support over the years has been rivaled only by Ludwig Schmugge (Zurich and Rome), who as director of the Repertorium Poenitentiariae Germanicum never stopped looking out for me from the beginnings of our collaboration in the Vatican Archives some fifteen years ago. Meanwhile, the most thoroughgoing suggestions for improvement of the book came from Monica Green (Arizona State University), who not only helped me with the chapter dedicated to medical matters, her main area of expertise, but also used her scarce time as leader of the 2009 National Endowment for the Humanities summer seminar, "Disease in the Middle Ages," in London to read the entire text and scrutinize it for clarity and soundness. The introduction below consists in large part of my responses to her perceptive criticism.

Abbreviations

AC	Archivio Capitolare, Archivo Capitular
AD	Archives Départmentales
AN	Archives Nationales
APA	Archivio della Penitenzieria Apostolica, Rome
AS	Archivio di Stato
BAV	Biblioteca Apostolica Vaticana, Vatican City
BL	British Library, London
BM	Bibliothèque Municipale
BMCL	*Bulletin of Medieval Canon Law,* new series 1–(1971–)
BN	Bibliothèque Nationale / Biblioteca Nazionale / Biblioteca Nacional
BSB	Bayerische Staatsbibliothek
C.	Causa, see *Decretum* (subdivision of part two)
c.	*capitulum* (chapter)
can.	canon
cap.	*capitulum*
CCL	*Corpus Christianorum, Series Latina* 1–(Turnhout: Brepols, 1953–); with *CCL* cont. med. 1–(Turnhout: Brepols, 1973–)
CCR	*Calendar of Close Rolls (1216–1485),* 66 vols. (London: HMSO, 1883–1916)
Clem.	*Clementinae,* ed. Emil Friedberg, *Corpus iuris canonici,* vol. 2 (Leipzig: Tauchnitz, 1881), part 4
Cod.	*Codex,* see *Corpus iuris civilis* (part 3)
1(–5) Comp.	*Compilatio prima (–quinta),* ed. Emil Friedberg, *Quinque Compilationes antiquae necnon Collectio canonum Lipsiensis* (Leipzig: Tauchnitz, 1882)
cont. med.	continuatio medievalis, see *CCL*
Councils & Synods	*Councils and Synods with Other Documents Relating to the English Church,* ed. Maurice Powicke and

	Christopher Cheney, 2 vols. (Oxford: Oxford University Press, 1964)
CPR	*Calendar of Patent Rolls (1216–1485)*, 59 vols. (London: HMSO, 1891–1916)
D.	*Distinctio*, see *Decretum* (subdivision of parts 1, 3)
DA	*Deutsches Archiv für Erforschung des Mittelalters* 1–(1943–)
DBI	*Dizionario biografico degli italiani* 1–(1960–)
Decretum	*Decretum Gratiani*, ed. Emil Friedberg, *Corpus iuris canonici,* vol. 1 (Leipzig: Tauchnitz, 1879)
Die Abtreibung	Wolfgang P. Müller, *Die Abtreibung. Anfänge der Kriminalisierung 1140–1650* (Cologne: Böhlau, 2000)
Dig.	*Digesta*, see *Corpus iuris civilis* (part 2)
d.p.c.	*dictum post capitulum* (Gratian's comment after chapter), see *Decretum*
fol.	*folium (folia)*, in a manuscript
HRG	*Handwörterbuch zur deutschen Rechtsgeschichte*, 5 vols. (Berlin: Schmidt, 1971–1998)
Inst.	*Institutiones*, see *Corpus iuris civilis* (part 1)
LL	*Leges* (publication series, see *MGH*)
m.	membrane
Mansi	Gian Domenico Mansi, *Sacrorum conciliorum nova et amplissima collectio*, 31 vols. (Florence: Zatta, 1759–98)
MGH	*Monumenta Germaniae Historica*
pl.	*placitum*, or plea, a legal excerpt included in Anthony Fitzherbert, *La Graunde Abridgement*
pr.	*proemium*, the introductory portion of legal texts in the Corpus iuris civilis
q.	*quaestio*, see *Decretum* (subdivision of part 2)
QFIAB	*Quellen und Forschungen aus italienischen Archiven und Bibliotheken* 1–(1943–)
Reg.	Registrum, Register, Registro, Registre
RHDFE	*Revue historique de droit français et étranger* 1–(1922–)
RIDC	*Rivista internazionale di diritto comune* 1–(1990–)
RPG	*Repertorium Poenitentiariae Germanicum*, ed. Ludwig Schmugge et al., vol. 1–(Tübingen: Niemeyer, 1996–)

SB	*Settimane di studio del Centro italiano di studi sull'alto medioevo* 1–(1956–)
SG	*Studia Gratiana* 1–(1953–)
s.v.	*sub verbo*, medieval commentary "on the words"
Tanner	*The Decrees of the Ecumenical Councils*, trans. Norman Tanner, 2 vols. (Washington, DC: Catholic University of America Press, 1990)
TNA	The National Archives, Kew (England)
TRG	*Tijdschrift voor Rechtsgeschiedenis* 1–(1918–)
Typologie	*Typologie des sources du moyen âge occidental* 1–(Turnhout: Brepols, 1972–)
UL	University Library
Vulgata	*Bibliorum sacrorum iuxta Vulgatam Clementinam nova editio*, ed. Alois Gramatica (Vatican City: Polyglotta Vaticana, 1929), or any later edition
X	*Liber extra* (*Decretales Gregorii IX*), ed. Emil Friedberg, *Corpus iuris canonici,* vol. 2 (Leipzig: Tauchnitz, 1881), part 3

THE CRIMINALIZATION OF
ABORTION IN THE WEST

Introduction

This book is concerned with the historical processes by which, over the course of the High and later Middle Ages, abortion as such—or what in American English denotes the termination of a pregnancy at the will of the pregnant woman herself—came to be treated as worthy of criminal punishment. To find the act for the first time identified as a "crime" in the modern sense of the word one has to go back to the writings of twelfth-century teachers at the emerging schools of ecclesiastical (or canon) and Roman law in the northern Italian city of Bologna. It was there that the present-day notion of crime was differentiated systematically and in wholly unprecedented fashion from other forms of wrong such as "sin" and "tort." And since then a theoretical consensus as to the proper meaning of these terms was perpetuated institutionally at centers of jurisprudence housed in so-called universities.

Jurists who worked during the formative phase of academic (or scholastic) law were quick to agree with Gratian, the author of the oldest canonistic textbook (ca. 1140), that the killing of a human fetus would constitute homicide and warrant identical punitive measures. They also followed another of Gratian's suggestions to the effect that the humanity of unborn life was not the immediate result of conception but rather occurred subsequently, that is, when embryonic existence acquired limbs and human shape with the infusion of an immortal soul. In prevailing lawyerly opinion, this decisive event

1

came about sometime early during gestation if not, according to the civilian Azo Porticus (fl. 1190), either forty or eighty days into the pregnancy, depending on whether the expected baby was a boy or a girl.

The basic outline of this theory soon enjoyed wide circulation with its insistence on the complete equation of abortion and homicide as long as the slain victim possessed human form. By 1250 it must have been known all across the Latin Christian world, from Portugal and Ireland in the extreme west to Poland and Hungary in the east. Its thoroughgoing dissemination was secured by church officials whose hierarchy adopted the teachings of academic jurisprudence from the outset as its general law. Where lay jurisdictions, on the other hand, were slow to embrace the doctrine (in Germany, for example), or failed altogether to do so (as in England), the rules provided by Gratian, Azo, and their colleagues were nevertheless preached in the ecclesiastical sphere and insisted upon in sermons, private confessions, and courts of spiritual adjudication.

The road from theory to practical implementation was a very long and arduous one. The oldest known trial from Italy that fully adheres to the significance of the terms "criminal" and "abortion" in modern parlance was recorded in Venice during the month of June 1490, some three hundred years after Bolognese theorists had placed the offense on a par with homicide. Similarly, instances of actual sentencing from the kingdom of France do not seem to trace back far beyond the fifteenth century. This compels us to look for earlier evidence at a different set of criminal prosecutions that also centered on charges of manslaughter in the maternal womb.[1]

Having established the parallel between death of a human fetus and homicide, Azo and Gratian exerted influence on judicial practice of their own time not so much by offering legal protection to unwanted children as by threatening criminal punishment for those who had killed an unborn child against the will of the pregnant mother. Over the course of the thirteenth and fourteenth centuries, records alluding to prenatal manslaughter as a capital offense regularly reported incidents in which the defendant was said to have caused "miscarriage by assault." From 1200 to the early 1300s, English common-law courts dealt with dozens of unborn children killed by external aggressors and granted women aggrieved by the violent termination of their

---

1. Early French cases of criminal abortion proper appear in two royal *lettres de remission*, dating respectively to February 1392 and July 1399; see Paris, AN, JJ 142, no. 103, in Jean-Claude Bologne, *La naissance interdite. Sterilité, avortement, contraception au moyen âge* (Paris: Orban, 1988), 287–288; and Paris, AN, JJ 154, no. 310. The Italian incident of 1490 is documented in Venice, AS, Reg. 3657, fol. 41r, and printed in *Die Abtreibung*, 245n429; cf. below, chap. 8, note 7.

pregnancies the right to press felony charges against perpetrators. In one case of 1283 or 1284, proceedings even resulted in the convict's execution by hanging, proving that summonses of this kind had to be taken seriously.[2]

Miscarriage by assault, then, figured prominently among homicide trials on account of unborn victims at least until the second half of the fourteenth century. Royal judges in France referred to it with a term of its own, *encis,* and Latin sources employed the noun *percussio* and its derivatives to describe the offense. Moreover, modern scholarship on normative sources dating from biblical to ancient times has noted that the connection between concern for the life of the human fetus and assault cases was commonplace long before twelfth-century jurists went about forging criminal law into coherent doctrine. Historians of late medieval crime have further explained the tight correlation between the two by pointing to insufficient capabilities of law enforcement on the part of investigating judges. Downward justice as it came to be wielded in monopolistic fashion by Western judiciaries after 1500 was alien to the preceding period, when inquiries into alleged crime still depended to a high degree on the private initiative of accusers. If mothers were unwilling to pursue in court injury caused to them by the premature end of a pregnancy, prosecutors possessed few practical means to safeguard the unborn baby and its right to survival as proposed by academic theorists.

Common opinion among Bolognese lawyers consistently embraced Gratian and Azo's view that homicide and the abortion of a human fetus should be subject to identical judicial standards, further implying that these were to encompass the crime of infanticide as well. The criterion of birth was of no significance to twelfth-century law teachers, who rather presented the moment of animation and formation, between forty and eighty days after conception, as the decisive prerequisite for charges of punishable manslaughter. Given the importance of scholastic jurisprudence as one of the principal agents of criminalization in the West, the following treatment will reflect these juristic parameters and discuss all medieval crime cases involving fatal attacks on "animated" life, regardless of their timing before, during, or instantly after delivery. In keeping with the same approach and again inspired by the influential doctrines of Gratian and Azo, I will omit from consideration contraception as a legal offense. Academic discourse soon reached a

---

2. Kew, TNA, Just. 1/547A, m. 20d; in *Die Abtreibung*, 291n497, translated by Sir John Baker in Philip Rafferty, "Roe v. Wade: The Birth of a Constitutional Right" (Ann Arbor, MI: University Microfilms International, 1992), 530–531 (under the wrong date of 1318); cf. Sara M. Butler, "Abortion by Assault: Violence against Pregnant Women in Thirteenth and Fourteenth Century England," *Journal of Women's History* 17 (2005): 9–31.

consensus whereby recourse to contraceptives as such was excluded from crime strictly speaking, and debated punishment for harm caused by sterilizing potions under several separate categories of (not necessarily intended) poisoning.[3]

In many ways, late medieval scholastic notions of what was meant by criminal abortion run counter to our modern understanding of the term. Theory fused the crime with homicide overall and infanticide in particular, and judicial practice treated miscarriage by assault as the prototypical allegation of prenatal manslaughter well into the fourteenth century. Additional signs of otherness emerge, moreover, from an examination of how jurists and courts at the time employed the Latin concept of *crimen* and what mental associations it triggered. Issues of juristic nomenclature and procedure, for that matter, loom especially large in the present book. The nature and contents of the original source material render the retrieval of lived circumstances difficult if not impossible, and a thick layer of formulaic language exposes readers to narratives shaped by normative requirements and at the expense of what actually happened on the ground, be it in the privacy of homes or during interrogations. Abortion in medieval practice remains enigmatic and for the most part eludes our modern curiosity. Its vicissitudes as an offense, however, provide an excellent marker for the slow and uneven advance of academic law and its application in Western society, as it was only in conjunction with the jurisprudence of Azo and Gratian that Latin Christianity learned to regard the willful slaying of a human fetus as deserving of legal punishment.

Central to the following analysis is certainly the word "crime," which will be used consistently in the way it is invoked in everyday language today, namely, as wrongdoing requiring lawful retribution from the hands of publicly appointed officials. The closest synonym in the language of Bolognese jurisprudence would have been the Latin noun *reatus*. All the same, modern historiography has treated the English expression routinely as a rendering of its etymological ancestor, crimen, in spite of the fact that for jurists from the period prior to 1500 the latter had a much wider range of possible connotations. For depending on context, trained lawyers would have referred to crimen in not one but up to four different senses. First, they would have

---

3. Though rich in primary source material, the studies of John Noonan, *Contraception: A History of Its Treatment by the Catholic Theologians and Canonists,* 2nd ed. (Cambridge, MA: Harvard University Press, 1986), and John Boswell, *The Kindness of Strangers: The Abandonment of Children in Western Europe from Late Antiquity to the Renaissance* (New York: Pantheon, 1988), do not distinguish sufficiently between late medieval references to sin, crime, and tort or different forms of court proceedings.

spoken of it in now familiar fashion in order to denote a punishable crime; second, as a variety of misconduct leading to *irregularitas*, or ineligibility to higher (sacramental) rank within the ecclesiastical hierarchy; third, as sin (*peccatum*) in the modern Catholic understanding of the term—that is, as a wrong redeemable through private confession and secretly imposed works of penance (*penitentia*); and fourth, as another form of peccatum against God's justice, perpetrated publicly and worthy of atonement before everyone's eyes.

Perhaps most conspicuous, albeit barely studied by scholars, is the last-mentioned type of crimen that came to be investigated by way of public penitential proceedings. In 1995, an inquiry by the American historian Mary Mansfield challenged older work for having assumed that *penitentia publica* had quickly withered in Western Christendom after the Fourth Lateran Council of 1215 had universally obliged Christians to confess sins to their parish priest in secret and for a minimum of once a year. In liturgical sources from northern France, Mansfield had discovered that openly performed penance persisted until 1300 and possibly far beyond. Her findings were further corroborated by Friederike Neumann, whose monograph of 2008 highlights widespread application of the same disciplinary tool at the hands of fifteenth-century officials from the southern German diocese of Constance. The two authors, moreover, did not refer to earlier research by R. H. Helmholz, who in articles of the 1970s and 1980s had already observed that well-advertised rites of spiritual redemption formed a vital institution in English ecclesiastical courts until the very end of the Middle Ages. The available evidence, in short, made each author realize that in many places and for the longest time, procedures for the detection and repression of notorious or commonly known spiritual wrongs occupied a vast gray area between the domains of judicial prosecution proper and sacramental confession with its absolute insistence on privacy.[4]

While focusing on abortion, miscarriage by assault, and infanticide, the following discussion of late medieval legal realities challenges previous assumptions about the gray area and its purported intractability. Public penance, it will be argued, was subject to uniform procedural rules that canon lawyers from Gratian to Hostiensis (d. 1271) defined and systematized alongside the better-studied judicial formats of criminal accusation

---

4. Richard H. Helmholz, "Index: Penance, Public," in Richard H. Helmholz, *Canon Law and the Law of England* (London: Hambledon Press, 1987), 361; Mary Mansfield, *The Humiliation of Sinners: Public Penance in Thirteenth-Century France* (Ithaca: Cornell University Press, 1995); Friederike Neumann, *Öffentliche Sünder in der Kirche des Spätmittelalters. Verfahren—Sanktionen—Rituale* (Cologne: Böhlau, 2008); see also note 13 below.

and inquisition. Individuals suffering from a reputation tainted by crimen were often required to appear before their ecclesiastical judges and answer charges brought by way of anonymous denunciation (*via denuntiationis*). The process promised restoration of one's good name through (sometimes collective) oaths of innocence, or the denounced person had to submit to works of spiritual satisfaction after failing to perform sworn (com)purgation or confessing voluntarily. Strictly speaking, the late medieval church administered no more than five types of punishment: exclusion from Christian worship through personal excommunication or the interdict placed upon entire communities and regions, suspension, deposition, and degradation from clerical orders. Every other corrective means fell under the category of penitentia, a fact that historians of medieval crime have frequently overlooked.[5] The consequences of such disregard are neither trivial nor merely technical in character. To begin with, acts of atonement for those found in need of them not only comprised prayer, fasting, and other pious exercises like pilgrimage but also allowed for elaborate shaming rituals, flogging, commutation to monetary payment, and imprisonment of uncertain duration and duress. Any resemblance of the latter to criminal punishment is grossly misleading, however, given that in a penitential setting suspects had to carry the burden of proof themselves, whereas in ordinary penal proceedings they were to be considered innocent until proven guilty.[6] In addition, scholars today would be ill advised if they mistook cases of fetal or infant death recorded in the form of canonical denuntiationes as reliable indicators of an underlying fatality, because hearsay rather than solid physical and testimonial evidence was at the root of investigations into public penitential *crimina*. In other words, entries in ecclesiastical registers relating to our subject were mostly prompted by defamation (*mala fama*) and not by tangible traces of a crime.

In the twelfth and thirteenth centuries, the Latin West embarked on a path that was to distinguish it from all other civilizations by associating abortion with the new concept of criminal behavior in current parlance. Firsthand investigations into the stages of this process and its late medieval ramifications have been fairly sporadic and visibly peaked in the 1970s, when modern

---

5. Accordingly, the distinction highlighted by Heinz Schilling, "History of Crime or History of Sin? Some Reflections on the Social History of Early Modern Church Discipline," in *Politics and Society in Reformation Europe: Essays for Sir Geoffrey Elton on His Sixty-Fifth Birthday*, ed. Erkki Kouri and Tom Scott (New York: St. Martin's, 1987), 289–310, is applicable from the twelfth century onward.

6. Richard H. Helmholz, "The Law of Compurgation," in Richard H. Helmholz, *The Ius Commune in England: Four Studies* (Oxford: Oxford University Press, 2001), 90–124, assumes to the contrary that church and secular courts were governed by comparable standards of culpability.

legislation and a legal reform movement across the hemisphere—inspiring, among other things, the decision of the U.S. Supreme Court in *Roe v. Wade* (1973)—liberalized abortion decisively in the face of older court precedent and crime statutes.[7] With regard to significant work published by earlier generations of historians, mention must be made of Siegfried Schultzenstein's article on the normative situation in premodern and early modern France (1904–5) and of Franz Dölger's essay on antiquity (1934).[8] There is also the doctoral dissertation (1942) of Roger John Huser, who tracked pertinent sources in church law, and Giuseppe Palazzini's substantive survey of the medieval evidence (1943), which for the remainder of the century furnished numerous authors with an important data mine.[9] More recent studies steering clear of political partisanship and aiming instead at an improved knowledge of the medieval documentation include the inquiries of Yves Brissaud for France (1972) and Giancarlo Garancini for Italy (1975) and the discussion of ecclesiastical church registers from England by R. H. Helmholz (1975).[10] The fullest analysis of any legal system and its handling of abortion prior to the year 1500 is available for the common law of the English crown.[11]

7. List of United States Supreme Court Decisions, 410 U.S. 113, 113–179 (1973).

8. Siegfried Schultzenstein, "Das Abtreibungsverbrechen in Frankreich," *Zeitschrift für vergleichende Rechtswissenschaft* 17 (1904): 360–421; ibid. 18 (1905): 266–312; Franz Dölger, "Das Lebensrecht des ungeborenen Kindes und die Fruchtabtreibung in der Bewertung der heidnischen und christlichen Antike," in *Antike und Christentum. Kultur-und religionsgeschichtliche Studien,* vol. 4 (Münster: Aschendorff, 1934), 1–61.

9. Roger J. Huser, *The Crime of Abortion in Canon Law: An Historical Synopsis and Commentary,* Collected Study Series 162 (Washington, DC: Catholic University of America Press, 1942); Giuseppe Palazzini, *Ius fetus ad vitam eiusque tutela in fontibus ac doctrina canonica usque ad saeculum xvi* (Urbania: Bramantes, 1943). Both are consulted by John Noonan, "An Almost Absolute Value in History," in *The Morality of Abortion: Legal and Historical Perspectives,* ed. John Noonan (Cambridge, MA: Harvard University Press, 1970), 1–59.

10. Yves Brissaud, "L'infanticide à la fin du moyen âge," *RHDFE* 50 (1972): 229–256; Giancarlo Garancini, "Materiali per la storia del procurato aborto nel diritto intermedio," *Jus* 22 (1975): 395–528; Richard H. Helmholz, "Infanticide in the Province of Canterbury during the Fifteenth Century," *Journal of Psychohistory* 2 (1975): 379–390 (reprinted in Helmholz, *Canon Law and the Law of England,* 157–168).

11. Harold Schneebeck, "The Law of Felony in Medieval England from the Accession of Edward I until the Mid-Fourteenth Century" (PhD diss., University of Iowa, 1973), 232–243; cf. Barbara Kellum, "Infanticide in England in the Later Middle Ages," *Journal of Psychohistory* 1 (1973): 367–388. John Baker's translations and historical commentary are presented by Rafferty, "Roe v. Wade," 461–765.

In August of 2000, my own monograph on the criminalization of abortion (and infanticide) in the Middle Ages appeared under the German title *Die Abtreibung*. The book treats the subject comprehensively and for the whole Latin West, covering judicial practice until 1500 and juristic theory until 1650. Based on printed as well as manuscript materials, *Die Abtreibung* is divided into one section dedicated to prescriptive sources and another that deals with court records and the actual handling of ecclesiastical and secular cases by papal officials in the Vatican, municipal administrators in Florence and Venice, and agents of royal jurisdiction in Paris and London.[12] Briefly put, the German version of 2000 provides an account that is for the most part source-driven, while emphasis here is placed on interpretive issues of causation and change. In *Die Abtreibung*, discussion of the evidence is structured along the lines of literary genre and questions of prescriptive versus pragmatic intent. Original sources are ordered according to their appearance in specific runs of records compiled by church or lay authority. In what follows, on the other hand, special attention is paid to the divergence between modern and premodern realities of crime, as well as to the challenge of having to capture normative developments of a distant past in language that is informed by the legal and social exigencies of our own era. In light of prosecution being centered for centuries on cases of miscarriage by assault, for example, jurists and judges must have understood authoritative rhetoric demanding from them the repression of prenatal manslaughter differently from the spontaneous associations it provokes in the modern mind. To address the issue, the ensuing analysis is primarily concerned with the difficulty of presenting wrong as it was perceived and prosecuted before 1500 to Westerners of the twenty-first century. The hazards of miscommunication are far greater than scholarship on medieval crime and abortion has conceded. The absence from the Middle Ages of state-run justice monopolies, the persistent weakness of top-down law enforcement, and the mentioned coexistence of penitential and punitive crimina in the same realm of public order all intimate that current notions may be inadequate for an accurate assessment of criminal phenomena and abortion during the period.

Habits of thinking about justice today appear to be incompatible with premodern attitudes. Thus we are told in the first of nine chapters that apart from the criminalization of abortion, criminalization itself was an innovation of the twelfth century. In chapter 2 we learn that the Latin noun *crimen* covered multiple offenses besides those we consider crimes today and that

---

12. Wolfgang P. Müller, *Die Abtreibung. Anfänge der Kriminalisierung 1140–1650* (Cologne: Böhlau, 2000), cited hereafter as *Die Abtreibung*; see also Abbreviations.

canonical jurisprudence of the later Middle Ages devised a minimum of three different avenues to remedy them. Chapter 3 opposes the widespread assumption that societal trends toward criminal sentencing were greatly dependent on legislative or political intervention, arguing instead that the process relied on the success of law professors in promoting their ideas, characterized by systematic logical coherence and by the institutional reach and permanence universities were able to project. Chapters 4 and 5 go on to illustrate that the deep rift between those who favor abortion rights and others who defend the unborn unconditionally perpetuates a disagreement that is at least as old and continuous as the legal tradition of the West. Chapter 6 examines references in judicial sources from before 1500 to the medical side of induced miscarriages and abortion without, however, finding remnants of what might have been a consolidated body of clinical knowledge among midwives or other (academically trained) health practitioners. Chapter 7 discusses trials of prenatal manslaughter as crime properly speaking and suggests that actual condemnations as well as the infliction of specific punishments treated in chapter 8 were rare and nearly impossible to obtain unless the convicts were marginalized persons such as foreign maidservants or adulterous or older single women. Chapter 9, finally, expresses reservations with regard to late medieval court registers and their utility for crime statistics, given that intricate rules associated with each type of proceeding and restrictions placed on the admissibility of cases in terms of proof render most of the surviving data unsuitable for quantitative study beyond the ascertainment of prosecutorial patterns.

Because this book puts particular emphasis on modern questions about abortion and on the difficulty of answering them without distorting late medieval social and legal realities, alternative strategies of ordering the historical data are precluded by necessity. Readers who favor a presentation according to literary genre will continue to find *Die Abtreibung* more accommodating. For those who seek information organized into geographical or jurisdictional units, the general index at the end of this book may prove helpful. The eminently topical orientation of the following chapters, however, defies other trajectories of investigation and, perhaps most important, the appreciation of criminal abortion as a phenomenon traceable along chronological lines. To alleviate the situation, let it be stated succinctly that our story begins in late antiquity and during the early medieval period with compilations of church law (*canones*), Roman jurisprudence and legislation, tribal custom (*Leges*), and manuals of penance (penitentials), which later provided twelfth-century lawyers with their authoritative materials. From the canones Gratian and his successors took the equation between fetal manslaughter and homicide and notions of their incompatibility with the exercise of priestly functions from the rank of subdeacon upward. The principal contribution on the part of the penitentials was their long-standing insistence on the absolute wrongfulness of abortion regardless of who had committed the act or for what reason. This instead had been the principal concern of customary Leges that came into existence after 500 and attached monetary compensation to various manifestations of prenatal death. Tariffs typically depended on the social status of mothers, victims, and perpetrators, whereas women who willingly ended their own pregnancies formed a neglected topic of regulation outside church discipline.

As discussed in the final section of chapter 1, the Leges became the first casualty of the Western turn toward jurisprudence over the course of the long twelfth century. Extremely popular between 500 and 1050, they fell into obsolescence not only because they foresaw payment according to someone's station in local society rather than embracing the new ideal of equal justice for all; the Leges also propagated modes of judicial proof that were increasingly regarded with suspicion and treated as mockery of the truth. Ordeals and compurgation had been the perfect bargaining tools for litigation in tight-knit communities, given that they hinged on measuring the support and loyalty adversaries could muster during dispute processing. Somebody with many friends did not have to dread purgatory oaths, sworn alongside character witnesses known as "oath-helpers" or the proper healing of his hands after the carrying of a hot iron or the outcome of duels to learn whether or not right was on his side: few arbitrators would have dared to find a similarly resourceful and "honorable" defendant liable, especially if he appeared surrounded by an impressive entourage. After 1050, however, the rise of systematic law was coupled with the advance of societal groups in favor of definitive sentencing on the basis of "forensic" fact-finding techniques. Reliant for their well-being on social and spatial mobility, they were destined to gain from the new juristic culture insofar as it promised uniform adjudication from place to place and to the relative disadvantage of those aided traditionally (along with the Leges) by family roots and the rationality of "communal" preferment. Traders, merchants, artisans, and townspeople in general, it is argued at the end of chapter 3, were among the first to assist in the demise of solidarity tests such as *ordalia* and collective oaths and conversely benefited from the shift toward "objective" eyewitness testimony, written proof, and confession. The growing appeal of categorical standards, with the implied capability of undercutting self-regulation in neighborhoods and their opaque peacekeeping arrangements, facilitated as well the definition of wrongful behavior in the abstract and prompted, through Gratian and Azo (introduced in the opening parts of chapter 1), the swift discovery of both crime and criminal abortion.

A pioneering force in the process of criminalization was undoubtedly the Western church, which rapidly took advantage of scholastic jurisprudence to streamline its normative teachings, carry them deep into ecclesiastical court activity, and encourage full lay compliance on the basis of Azo's influential reinterpretation and "canonization" of the Roman law on abortion as equivalent, for the human fetus, to homicide. Clerical judges can be shown to have applied canonistic rules insofar as record keeping, again stimulated by new academic approaches to right and wrong, permits modern scholars to peer into the day-to-day workings of justice. As early as in a letter Pope Innocent III dispatched in 1211, an ordained priest accused of fetal death by assault was to face suspension from his altar duties provided the victim had been formed and alive, precisely as it had been prescribed by Gratian and his commentators (see chapter 2). Manuals of private sacramental penance prepared by canon lawyers and theologians afford mass-produced, if indirect, evidence for the utilization of Bolognese canon law in individual and secret confessions, which was specifically designed to leave no traces in writing and allow for no distinction between abortion proper and violently induced miscarriages. The consolidation and spread of these guidelines in adjudication can be safely assumed from the late 1100s onward, and the same must be true for the investigation of public peccata by way of denuntiationes. Actual documentation of the latter seems to anchor proceedings only in the fifteenth century, when a modest number of reputed sinners were summoned on account of infanticide or prenatal manslaughter by officials in England. In addition to wide-ranging circumstantial clues, however, a persistent focus on prescholastic proof by compurgation clearly points to the great antiquity of the practice, just as it is more than likely that reliance on penitential denunciations until the end of the Middle Ages extended to both northern and Mediterranean areas.[13]

Paradoxically, the sole jurisdiction in the West to escape the reception of Bolognese standards by forging simultaneously its own systematized legal doctrine, the common law of the English monarchy, became the first to subject its laity to criminal prosecution in the modern sense of the word. It was

13. Richard Trexler, "Infanticide in Florence: New Sources and First Results," *History of Childhood Quarterly* 1 (1973): 107–108, counts (in note 69) fifty-seven instances of public penance, enjoined by the bishop of Fiesole between 1531 and 1540, for couples found guilty of "overlaying," or child suffocation in bed (cf. below, chap. 9, note 4), further assuming that this type of prosecution formed a sixteenth-century novelty.

barely six years after the start of the surviving crown plea rolls, in 1200, that the oldest case of miscarriage by assault was included among charges and followed in due course by a steady succession of similar entries all through the thirteenth century (treated in the concluding section of chapter 2). The incidents in question were regularly classified as "felonious," by which common lawyers meant capital offenses worthy of the death penalty. For whenever an unborn victim possessed human shape, fatal interference with it amounted in their minds to *homicidium*. Azo and Gratian's criteria of manslaughter, that is to say, were again adopted by the royal justices of England. Moreover, although their attitude was unusually timely, it reflected trends that asserted themselves with comparable vigor far and wide across Latin Christianity. On both sides of the British Channel, criminalization was inspired by the model of ecclesiastical justice; it originally met with concrete application in the lay sphere when a woman used threats of execution as leverage against someone she accused of having killed a baby in her womb; and it advanced in a process that was governed by the consensus of legal experts and laid down in writings emanating from the leading professional schools, whether at Bologna for canonists and continental jurists or, for insular ones, at the Inns of Court in London. Before the end of the Middle Ages, legislation passed by popes, kings, and princes (partly surveyed in chapter 3) had little effect on the spread of norms stipulating punishment for abortion either in jurisprudence or in judicial realities on the ground.

After forming the absolute vanguard in the criminal prosecution of miscarriage by assault among secular jurisdictions, English common law radically redefined its position toward fetal existence from 1307, the beginning of Edward II's reign, until 1348. By the end of the period, royal justices had concluded that babies did not possess human quality unless they had been born and were extant "in the nature of things" (*in rerum natura*), a view colleagues seem to have adhered to with remarkable consistency until the death of the last Tudor, Queen Elizabeth I, in 1603 (see chapter 5). Notwithstanding, however, that the complete normative turnaround was a phenomenon uniquely restricted to England, it coincided with a moment of crisis in juristic opinion and practice felt equally on the Continent. In core areas of Bolognese jurisprudence such as the kingdoms of France and Aragon, for example, punitive action against miscarriages brought on by assault (chapter 7) also faded as access to civil damage suits was facilitated. In the second half of the fourteenth century, French judges handled ever-dwindling numbers of defendants who risked capital punishment for having killed a woman's child in the womb. Conversely, prosecutors were still hesitant to launch proceedings without being prompted to do so by the presence of an interested private party and did not investigate autonomously and from above many abortions or infanticides. In the independent urban jurisdictions of northern Italy, on the other hand, it appears that crime inquiries involving the death of (unborn) offspring never really focused on anything but allegations against mothers of unwanted children, given that inquisitions of *infanticidium* and (in a place like Venice) willfully terminated pregnancies alone are known to have been registered among penal charges, and perhaps increasingly so from the 1300s onward.

The very decades of the fourteenth century that witnessed the rejection of Gratian and Azo's criminal doctrine by English common law likewise accounted for attempts by leading Bolognese teachers to depart from the original positions their predecessors had propagated since the twelfth century. Everything suggests that the acceptance of "creatianist" doctrine by the earliest canonists and Roman lawyers was inspired by contemporary scholastic theologians who taught that formation marked the instant when God "created" an immortal human soul and infused it into the fetus (hence "creatianism"). In the formulation of Gratian's most prolific commentator, Huguccio (fl. 1190), this theory was transmitted by "catholic faith" and amounted to a matter of orthodoxy.[14] Azo and other glossators of Justinian's *Corpus iuris civilis*, the fundamental textbook of their school, wrote in the same spirit and in spite of the fact that their authoritative source embraced ancient Stoic philosophy with regard to prenatal development, which to the contrary denied the fetus humanity at any time prior to its delivery and presence in rerum natura. Confronted with lack of support from his own teaching materials, Azo was obliged to cite, in unison with his peers from the faculties of theology and church law, a single passage from the Ordinary Gloss on the Old Testament (Exodus 21:22–23) in order to add weight to the creatianist viewpoint, effectively silencing and glossing over assertions he found in the Justinianic pages directly in front of him. Mainstream juristic opinion agreed with his interpretive maneuver for the rest of the Middle Ages (details in chapter 4) and beyond.

Shortly before English common lawyers came upon the Roman formula of in rerum natura and used it to strike fetal manslaughter from their list of felonies in 1348, two Bolognese professors, Signorolus de Homodeis and

---

14. "Non ergo nascitur [sc. anima] ut dicunt heretici cum semine id est ex semine. Nam ut fides catholica tradit cotidie creat Deus novas animas quas infundendo creat et creando infundit," Huguccio, *Summa,* C. 32, q. 2, c. 9, s.v. *cottidie* (Paris, BN, lat. 15397, fol. 84vb). Intellectual historians use "creatianist" and "creatianism" to refer to the position of Huguccio and others on ensoulment. The two terms must not be confused with "creationism" and "creationist."

Jacobus de Butrigariis, had begun questioning the creatianist leanings of their predecessors for exactly the same reason. As they pointed out, their principal textual authority, the *Corpus iuris civilis,* contained nothing to bolster the normative position scholasticism had held from the days of Azo. Around 1342, Signorolus wrote a notable piece of legal advice (*consilium*) in which he examined a host of quotations from Justinian's compilation that clearly denied the fetus participation in human nature. On the strength of his findings, he determined that at least by the standards of what he named "municipal" law (or *Ius civile*), based solely on the *Corpus iuris* and in opposition to canon law and academic consensus, abortion and miscarriage could not be treated as equivalent to homicide. According to Signorolus, northern Italian town statutes that imposed the death penalty for murder consequently obliged urban magistrates to abstain from application whenever an unborn baby, formed or unformed, had been killed. Later generations of jurists would always include those who produced their own version of what Signorolus had first suggested, with Baldus de Ubaldis (d. 1400) being arguably the most celebrated among them. They eventually came to be seen as partisans of a respectable minority viewpoint, whose dissent (tracked in chapter 3) was widely publicized in late medieval legal literature alongside Azo's *communis opinio.*

While it was obviously a simple operation for Bolognese theorists of the twelfth century to impose on their legal textbooks an embryology that would render abortion subject to punishment in court, it is equally clear that toward the middle decades of the 1300s certain challenges in criminal practice complicated the issue of fetal killings for scholastic teachers. Their renewed intellectual effort is again visible in the publication of *consilia* and commentary on the question of therapeutic intervention by representatives of the three university disciplines of theology, canon law, and medicine. Are medical doctors permitted to procure the death of an unborn baby for the sake of saving the mother's life? Around 1320, the theologian Johannes de Regina from Naples responded in the negative, assuming that the victim was formed and had been infused with a human soul. Toward 1365, the canonist Simon de Bursano reached the same conclusion but tentatively suggested that perhaps doctors could be excused from having caused fetal death because the casualty was merely an unintended side effect of attempts to save the pregnant woman. For the physician Gentile da Foligno, writing about 1340, preservation of the patient's life was the sole concern, which allowed him to view the child in the womb as a health threat in need of active removal. All three authors (discussed in chapters 4 and 6), moreover, were lecturing in important Italian cities that, as mentioned earlier, were simultaneously at the forefront of endeavors to investigate prenatal death beyond traditional allegations of miscarriage by assault. It may not be implausible to discern a link between, on the one hand, town magistrates who were better equipped to prosecute willfully terminated pregnancies and, on the other, writers who sought to assess potential repercussions of the intensifying prosecutorial fervor for (academic) health professionals.

When at some point in the 1300s the condemnation of abortion as a crime entered a critical phase marked by widespread elimination of violent miscarriages from the criminal caseload, English common lawyers, as noted, reacted most drastically by stripping prenatal existence altogether of its previously assumed humanity. The definitive formula of 1348 stated that felonious homicide presupposed a victim already born and in the nature of things, in what further implied that the offense of infanticide was still considered worthy of inclusion among the capital crown pleas. Curiously, however, modern legal historians have yet to discover accusations or indictments concerned with the slaying of infants in the abundance of felony charges recorded after the year 1348. To say the least, the sentencing of parents who had killed their own offspring at birth was thoroughly unpopular among lay jurors, given the extreme rarity of judicial interventions registered over the course of the thirteenth and early fourteenth centuries.[15] There is reason to believe that ordinary men and women frequently felt resentful toward court interference with their procreative choices and often rejected it as an unwarranted intrusion into family life. The impulse to protect the privacy of respectable people in the neighborhood seems to have found its most congenial outlet in procedural settings that were heavily reliant on juries. Outside England, they were especially common in Germany and adjacent areas to the north and east (surveyed in chapter 5). Around 1353, a panel of townspeople from Brno in southern Moravia put reservations against the criminalization of infanticide most succinctly. Although the verdict acknowledged the arrival of Azo and Gratian's teachings, its readers were also reminded that, customarily, a woman who did away with her baby was not to be punished at all, for "having delivered the child and owning it rightfully, she can suppress and kill it at will."[16]

---

15. Barbara Hanawalt, *The Ties That Bound: Peasant Families in Medieval England* (New York: Oxford University Press, 1986), 154–157, lists from the judicial records a total of four felony pleas alleging infanticide; *Die Abtreibung*, 315n535, adds another one from the York eyre, 1348.

16. "Dicebant enim quidam cum quibus concordabant iurati ad iudicium Antique Brunne spectantes quod ipsa mulier non esset aliqualiter punienda ex eo quod cum infantem genuisset et proprium ius in eum habuisset ipsum perimere potuit et necare," in *Právní knih města Brna z poloviny 14. století*, ed. Miroslav Flodr, 3 vols. (Brno: Blok, 1990–1993), 1:328 (no. 520); Emil Rössler, ed., *Die Stadtrechte von Brünn aus dem 13. und 14. Jahrhundert* (Prague: Calve, 1852), 252 (no. 536).

Proof that points to the perseverance of notions of collective honor is plentiful in normative texts from across the Latin West and far into the early modern period. Legislators and jurists of Bolognese inspiration, for example, repeatedly tackled the problem of whether an abortion or infanticide committed for the sake of preserving the reputation and *fama* of one's family merited full or reduced retribution, or none at all. Moreover—and unlike the juries of English common law—the criminal courts of continental Europe were expected to conform their decisions to the guidelines (*ordines iudiciarii*) of university jurisprudence. Otherwise known as manuals of Romano-canonical procedure, these ordines contain many rules that seem to have been crafted in anticipation of judges who would have been unable to assert their will against local groups and resourceful individuals. Trials for abortion proper, to begin with, permitted maximum punishment only when suspects confessed or had acted in the presence two well-regarded eyewitnesses (chapter 8). Proceedings did not start unless a dead body had been found and there was similar confirmation of a concealed pregnancy or delivery. A unique alternative to concealment that also rendered corroboration of murderous intent superfluous existed in the admission of recourse to abortifacient potions or prescriptions aside from the verified death of a fetus (chapter 7). Weaker forms of evidence stood no chance of leading to capital charges.

Whereas the ordines gave lay judges little discretion during the opening and closing phases of criminal trials, they endowed them with considerable powers while investigations were in full swing. Summonses threatened instant confiscation of one's property for nonappearance in court. Preliminary imprisonment could last for indefinite periods so as to break the resolve of defendants and have them confirm suspicions by admission. Torture was arguably allowed in nearly every case, as proceedings were not permitted to go forward except on the basis of criteria warranting forcible questioning—namely, concealment of gestation or the use of abortifacients (see chapter 8). The rationale behind this wide range of options for investigators in the middle of inquiries must be seen in the need to create ample space for ongoing party negotiations. Incarceration, torture, and the endless postponement of a final decision all helped set the stage for a screening process at the conclusion of which only those who lacked sympathy in the community risked suffering judicial hardship in both person and belongings. Allegations concerned with the punishment of abortion did not arise until the 1300s and in places where the coercive capabilities of prosecutors were strongest, that is, in the communes of northern Italy (and probably Aragon). Their agents were especially prone to inflicting retribution short of physical injury upon those who partly confessed to having concealed a pregnancy. French royal officials were typically content to keep women faced with the same predicament in custody for a calculated duration before releasing them, and did so very likely because of uneasiness with the idea of imposing themselves by way of definitive sentencing. In the meantime, late medieval jurisdictions on the whole did not possess the instruments of enforcement that would have been necessary to accuse women of honorable status or couples well entrenched in the neighborhood.

The present book ends chronologically with the Middle Ages, and the question arises of whether criminalization of abortion witnessed any fundamental change in the 1500s. For at least three different reasons, the answer seems to be yes. A decisive break occurred, for one thing, in the realm of ecclesiastical jurisdiction, which over the course of the 1500s lost its last vestiges of competency over the crimina of abortion, infanticide, and miscarriage by assault to lay authorities determined to subject every possible allegation of crime to their own and exclusive scrutiny. There is evidence that the counts and dukes of Savoy in the Italian Alps effected this transfer, which usually took the form of prosecutions for slander on the secular side, as early as in the late 1200s; but in England and many German territories, steps in the same direction had to await the first few decades of the sixteenth century.[17] Second, conviction rates for those who had killed unwanted offspring before, during, or after birth rose dramatically from 1500 until about 1650, mostly because of the elimination of procedural safeguards that late medieval lawyers had not circumvented. Imperial legislation of 1532 stipulated, for example, that the concealment of a pregnancy or of delivery entitled prosecutors to torture suspects automatically and without prior confession of guilt, and in 1556 a royal statute from France went as far as to legitimate execution on the basis of prenatal death and secret gestation alone. As a result, the number of criminal investigations soared. In individual German cities, it soon exceeded the known total of recorded instances for the entire Latin West from 1200 to 1500, in addition to the fact that Azo's doctrine, with its classification

---

17. From Germany, a penitential denunciation (as in note 4 above) for miscarriage by assault is recorded as late as 1516; cf. chap. 9, note 6; on the demise of crime allegations in English ecclesiastical courts, see Richard H. Helmholz, ed., *Select Cases of Defamation to 1600* (London: Selden Society, 1985), xxxvi–xlii, with implications for infanticide. Pierre Dubuis, "Enfants refusés dans les Alpes occidentales (XIVe–XVe siècles)," in *Enfance abandonnée et société en Europe* (Rome: Ecole française de Rome, 1991), 586–590, cites fiscal registers from Savoy that, between 1279 and 1465, mention (in my count) one abortion and six miscarriage cases based on mala fama and in language reminiscent of (if not competing with) public penitential jurisdiction; also Prisca Lehmann, *La repression des délits sexuels dans les états savoyards. Châtellenies des diocèses d'Aoste, Sion et Turin, fin XIIIe–XVe siècle* (Lausanne: University of Lausanne, 2006), 36, 128–130, 163–171.

of abortion and infanticide among the capital offenses, usually did not reach secular courts in Germany, Bohemia, Poland, and Hungary until after 1450.[18] Finally, the parameters for criminal prenatal manslaughter in the intellectual realm grew ever more intransigent as well (chapter 4). Originally inspired, it appears, by Protestant theologians, continental jurisprudence from 1600 onward gradually abandoned twelfth-century embryology in favor of a position that pushed infusion of the fetus with a human soul all the way back to the moment of conception.

Whether one looks at the criminalization of abortion primarily as a process that unfolded over time or prefers a topical approach structured around overarching themes such as region, jurisdiction, institutional agency, and historical causation, appreciation of the argument depends above all on a series of terminological distinctions. Apart from the two mutually exclusive categories of abortion and miscarriage by assault and in line with the previous definition of crime, I have avoided nominal derivatives such as "criminal" and "criminalization" except where the context endows them with the general meaning they have in Western legal language today. "Felony" and "felonious crime" in turn refer more narrowly to capital offenses and their treatment in English secular courts from 1200 to 1500. The word *crimen* has been applied only in its broader medieval meaning, permitting specification with the help of adjectives like "penitential" (as opposed to "punitive") and "ecclesiastical" (i.e., not "secular"). Given, moreover, that my examination cuts across different jurisdictional spheres and explores their manifold interconnectedness, I have sought to prevent confusion through the use of gratuitous homonyms. The noun and the attribute "civilian," for instance, are regularly invoked to denote scholastic jurisprudence as it was based on the ancient Roman *Corpus iuris civilis*, or for professors imparting it at late medieval law schools of the Bolognese type. In addition, I have employed "civil" as the equivalent of "noncriminal."

What is, in sum, the nature of the source material investigated here? First of all, the focus rests on cases and normative texts that treat prenatal manslaughter as *crimen*. Because for scholastic theorists who promoted criminalization of the act, the moment of birth was not a relevant dividing line, the scope of the book extends to infanticide charges as well. Since, in addition,

---

18. See chapters 3 and 5; Ulinka Rublack, "The Public Body: Policing Abortion in Early Modern Germany," in *Gender Relations in German History: Power, Agency, and Experience from the Sixteenth to the Nineteenth Century*, ed. Lynn Abrams and Elizabeth Harvey (Durham, NC: Duke University Press, 1997), 57–79.

actual accusations in court frequently framed miscarriages by assault as allegations of intentional fetal homicide, they are also addressed in the chapters that follow. Simultaneously, the inquiry does not cover incidents of abortion, infanticide, or miscarriage mentioned in any historical context other than that of wrongdoing subject to retribution as such. Proceedings concerned, for example, with poisonous abortifacients that, in the event, killed both the mother and her unborn or newborn child have been left out of consideration. While certainly of interest from many legal perspectives and as testimony to practices of birth control and their popularity in the later Middle Ages, they do not deal with induced fetal or infant death as autonomous and distinct offenses that by themselves called for intervention on the part of publicly appointed judges.

CHAPTER 1

The Earliest Proponents of Criminalization

From a modern Western perspective, it may appear as if present-day notions of crime existed at all times. The need to prosecute particularly heinous acts must have been felt throughout history, sustained by sentiments that transcended specific cultural contexts. What changed in between periods was at best the desire to exclude lesser forms of deviant behavior from criminal retribution, whereas public authority never ceased to demand accountability for wrongdoing serious enough to threaten the foundations of any social order. Hence the constant reiteration of age-old norms such as the biblical Ten Commandments (Exodus 20:2–17; Deuteronomy 5:6–21), categorically imposing upon generation after generation the seemingly iron rules of "You shall not kill" and "You shall not steal."

The historical record proves otherwise. In exploring the legal past, scholars have come to the realization that the elaboration of crime as a concept similar to the one now in use in the West did not get under way until the second half of the twelfth century. During the preceding half millennium of the early Middle Ages, from about 600 to 1100, nobody in Latin Christendom would have employed the term in the sense commonly attached to it today. Among those responsible for the watershed event—that is, the beginnings in Western history of crime properly speaking—was a group of specialists known as the teachers and practitioners of scholastic jurisprudence. Before the 1100s, professional jurists were not to be found.[1] By 1200 they had established themselves alongside full-time theologians and medical doctors at burgeoning schools of higher learning in Bologna, Paris, Montpellier, Oxford, and elsewhere. In response to an increasing demand for doctrinal expertise of unprecedented sophistication, jurists also started to offer advice and service to courts and adjudicating panels across the continent. With opportunities for lucrative employment in ecclesiastical administration and in urban and royal lay governments constantly on the rise, intellectual endeavors to create coherent normative constructs, and especially a system of church law, were key to the invention of crime as a distinct category of human conduct. Terminological clarification forged standards of right and wrong that academic circles and judicial tribunals have expanded upon ever since.

To credit high-medieval university professors of law and theology with groundbreaking contributions to the criminalization of certain behaviors does not imply that, as leading intellectuals, they were reshaping societal attitudes single-handedly. Quite to the contrary, scholastic thinkers were swept into the limelight by a massive cultural transformation affecting many areas of the Latin West. The so-called Peace Movement, gaining traction in the years after 1000, attests to incipient formulations of a political agenda aimed at the suppression of arbitrary violence and private feuding. In due time, its leaders were able to mobilize a substantial following, united by the idea that homicide constituted the worst possible disturbance of order among Christians. The categorical condemnation of bloodshed and killings, combined with the praise of peace as the normal state of public affairs, forcefully emerged from the indifference of previous ages, which had been dominated by endless cycles of warlord rivalry. People now rallied against endemic recourse to murder and mayhem as ordinary means of conflict management and became the principal clientele of those who, soon enough, were catapulted into positions of great prestige as figureheads of the systematic study of ecclesiastical and lay, or secular, law. By assuming, in line with the Peace Movement, that violent attacks on fellow human beings were intolerable and called for punitive action, an ever greater number of Westerners inquired about possibilities of judicial intervention. The search for abstract norms regulating the behavior of every individual was on.

---

1. Manlio Bellomo, *The Common Legal Past of Europe, 1000–1800*, trans. Lydia Cochrane (Washington, DC: Catholic University of America Press, 1995), 34–54; James Brundage, *The Medieval Origins of the Legal Profession. Canonists, Civilians, and Courts* (Chicago: University of Chicago Press, 2008), 46–74, assigns "law without lawyers" to the early Middle Ages as well.

The twelfth century was decisive in distinguishing punishable acts from other forms of human misconduct. For the first time in Western history, scholastic teachers systematically explored the difference between crime and tort, between litigation in pursuit of material compensation and, alternatively, penal consequences for delinquents found to have disturbed the public peace and offended the common good. Jurists also defined criteria of sin and spiritual satisfaction so as to set them apart from mechanisms governing wrong and its retribution in this world. To speak in modern parlance about criminalization in Latin Christendom prior to the formative phase of terminological reflection from about 1150 to 1200 would, as a result, be anachronistic and in disregard of contemporary conceptual capabilities. It was during the same period, moreover, that courts and judges seized the opportunity of drawing abortion into the orbit of punitive justice. A closer look at the two events—the origins of a coherent crime language on the one hand and the criminalization of attacks on unborn human life on the other—reveals that both were intimately connected. Efforts by the learned to rank prenatal killings among allegations in need of punishment grew together with the ability to express ideas of this nature accurately and adequately. Or to put it differently, abortion figured as a crime in medieval Western jurisprudence for as long as there was crime, given that, up to the later 1100s, laws did not subscribe to a streamlined and logically consistent understanding of the term.

The Scholastic Origins of Criminal Abortion

Social and economic conditions calling for reliance on professional legal expertise had been wanting before the twelfth-century rise of "universities," urban centers of higher education that offered students the prototypes of a "scholastic" study program. Gratian belonged to an ensemble of intellectual "Founding Fathers" who placed the emerging theological, medical, and juristic disciplines on sound scholarly foundations. As it turned out, he put together a textbook for lectures on church, or canon, law that was comprehensive, systematic, and methodically compelling at the same time. In classrooms throughout Latin Christendom, the final version of his *Decretum,* assembled around 1140, quickly eclipsed all of the older canon law collections.[2] While preserving most of the authoritative

---

2. Gratian, *Decretum Gratiani,* in *Corpus iuris canonici,* vol. 1, ed. Emil Friedberg (Leipzig: Tauchnitz, 1879). The discovery of a "first recension," preceding Friedberg's vulgate version, by Anders Winroth, *The Making of Gratian's Decretum* (Cambridge: Cambridge University Press, 2000), has provoked dissent as to its exact historical significance; see Carlos Larrainzar, "La ricerca attuale sul

source material compiled and transmitted over the centuries, Gratian displayed the normative tradition in an unprecedented dialectic arrangement, juxtaposing canones in support (*pro*) as well as against (*contra*) propositions thought to reveal the canonical truth. In addition, he supplied a running commentary (*dicta*) of his own, expressly inviting readers to identify contradictions between "discordant canons." Through informed reasoning, they were to be reduced to the "concordance" of real—that is to say coherent—canonistic doctrine. For many generations, concern about internal inconsistencies between ecclesiastical norms had been minimal, limited to single-handed corrections or rhetorical exercises in the prefaces of early medieval canonical collections. The greatest "turning point" in the history of canon law was reached when scholastic teachers, sustained by a rapidly growing trend, established the elimination of logical "dissonances" for the sake of overall doctrinal "harmony" as the principal assignment of academic professionals. Along with them, canonists, juristic experts trained in the canons, and the "science" of canonistic jurisprudence became permanent features of the educational landscape.[3]

Late medieval students attending introductory lectures on the law of the church were unlikely to hear about the issue of fetal killings in extensive detail. From the appearance of the Decretum onward, canonistic textbooks displayed but a handful of references to the subject, which typically figured as brief remarks tied to more comprehensive legal queries. For Gratian, this meant that he once cited a letter (*epistola decretalis*) of Pope Pelagius I (556–561) discussing the case of a woman who had miscarried when she found herself squeezed between two suddenly startled horses (D. 50, c. 48). The author of the Decretum invited his audience to ponder whether the scenario amounted to veritable criminal homicide. In a

Decretum Gratiani," in *La cultura giuridico-canonica medioevale*, ed. Enrique de León and Nicholas Álvarez des las Asturias (Milan: Giuffrè, 2003), 45–88; Javier Viejo Ximénez, "La composicion del Decreto di Graciano," *Ius canonicum* 45 (2005): 431–485; Atria Larson, "The Influence of the School of Laon on Gratian: The Usage of the Glossa Ordinaria and Anselmian Sententie in De Penitentia (Decretum, C. 33 q. 3)," *Mediaeval Studies* 72 (2010): 197–244.

3. The quoted expressions are taken from important studies of Gratian's achievement by Stephan Kuttner, *Harmony from Dissonance: An Interpretation of Medieval Canon Law* (Latrobe, PA: Archabbey Press, 1960), reprinted in Stephan Kuttner, *The History of Ideas and Doctrines of Canon Law in the Middle Ages*, 2nd ed. (Aldershot, UK: Ashgate, 1992), no. 1; Paul Fournier, "Un tournant de l'histoire du droit 1060–1140," *Nouvelle Revue historique de droit français et étranger* 41 (1917): 129–180, reprinted in *Paul Fournier. Mélanges de droit canonique*, ed. Theo Kölzer, 2 vols. (Aalen, Ger.: Scientia, 1983), 2:373–424 (no. 17); Stephan Kuttner, "Urban II and the Doctrine of Interpretation: A Turning Point?" *SG* 15 (1972): 53–85, reprinted in Kuttner, *History of Ideas and Doctrines*, no. 4.

second and equally fleeting passage (C. 2, q. 5, d.p.c. 20), he again suggested that there existed a close correspondence between homicidium and abortion. The text reproduces a rhetorical question originally posed by Pope Stephen VI (886–889). Presuming that someone causing the death of a fetus was called *homicida*, the pope had speculated, would not he who had killed a one-day-old infant possess even less of an excuse from similar charges? The obvious answer notwithstanding, scholastic writers preferred as their principal "seat" (*sedes materiae*), or point of departure, for learned reflections one last mention of abortion in a cluster of canons (C. 32, q. 2, c. 8–10) Gratian had assembled under his own leading *quaestio* (d.p.c. 7): "Concerning those who procure an abortion, the question is whether they are to be judged as homicides, or not." The response is presented immediately afterward, in a rubric (to c. 8) that precedes several pieces of additional authoritative justification: "He who procures an abortion before the soul is infused into the body is not a homicide." In support of his conclusion, Gratian quoted three excerpts from the normative tradition. A pair of texts (c. 8–9) he ascribed to the authority of Saint Augustine (d. 431). A third and final passage (c. 10) came from the pen of another patristic writer, Jerome (d. 429).[4]

Readers consulting the Decretum for guidance in academic lectures and courtroom activities seem to have met with little difficulty when trying to understand the doctrine of abortion that Gratian had drawn from older church norms. Over the next century, his immediate successors, the decretists, built a strong consensus to the effect that what the author of their textbook had intended by speaking about ensoulment as the necessary prerequisite for charges of homicide was that, before the incriminating act, the aborted fetus had to have acquired human shape. On the basis of the chapters attributed to Saints Augustine and Jerome, it was agreed that physical formation marked the entry of an immortal soul into the conceived body. Following the lead of their "master," commentators also considered it superfluous to advance more elaborate explanations, apart from reiterating, tirelessly, the crucial equation of homicide with killings of the formed fetus (*puerperium formatum*). Having distinguished abortions amounting to actual homicidium from others that did not qualify as such, canonistic theorists at schools across Latin Christendom went on to debate other legal implications in treatments they devoted to

---

4. Huser, *The Crime of Abortion in Canon Law*, 41–43, and Noonan, "An Almost Absolute Value in History," 33–37, have analyzed Gratian's remarks on abortion. According to Winroth, *The Making*, 223, C. 32, q. 2, d.p.c. 7–c.10 was not included in the first recension of the *Decretum*.

the broader topic of manslaughter. It was understood, though rarely rendered explicit, that teachings under the heading of *De homicidio* would likewise extend to cases involving the death of "ensouled," "formed," or "animated" life in the maternal womb.[5]

Modern observers who investigate the doctrinal attitudes of canonists in the earliest, formative period of their discipline, from around 1140 to 1234, may be led to believe that in the minds of Gratian and his students, abortion formed on the whole a rather marginal concern. By the time the decretists had placed the matter in the larger framework of crime and homicide, it appears as though quests for systematic coherence had been satisfied and interest in the argument subsided. Similar impressions are evoked by the circumstance that when canon lawyers of the 1170s began to supplement the Decretum with additional canonical material and more recent papal decretals circulating outside Gratian's work as *extravagantes*, the problem of fetal death did not figure very prominently. Only two new chapters mentioning abortion made their way into the *Liber extra*, the second definitive textbook adopted by canon law schools in 1234. The companion volume to Gratian, promulgated by Pope Gregory IX under the title of *Decretales Gregorii IX*, was seen by decretalist commentators as scarcely adding to the conclusions of previous canonistic thought. Both extravagantes were positioned under the familiar rubric of *De homicidio voluntario* (X 5.12) and corroborated long-held assumptions according to which certain abortions warranted equation with voluntary homicide. The first text (X 5.12.5) was understood to reiterate the crucial difference between actual killings of a formed fetus (*in actu*) and merely virtual slayings, "as if" of a human being (*ut homicida*), becoming manifest, for example, in the death of a shapeless and barely conceived embryo. The second (X 5.12.20), originally issued by Pope Innocent III in 1211, affords apostolic confirmation of the idea that bodily formation separates homicidal abortions from nonhomicidal ones. Whereas the former necessitate criminal canonical sentencing, the latter call only for penitential intervention and appeal to Christian conscience in view of the afterlife and future salvation. Other decretal collections law professors lectured on—the *Liber sextus* authorized by Pope Boniface VIII in 1298, the *Clementinae* of 1317, and the *Extravagantes Iohannis XXII* of 1322—make no reference to abortion at all, which again seems to indicate that questions relating to the

---

5. Garancini, "Materiali per la storia del procurato aborto," 451–472; Bonifacio Honings, "L'aborto nei decretisti e nei decretalisti," *Apollinaris* 50 (1977): 246–273; and *Die Abtreibung*, 13–52, have provided surveys of early canonistic discussion on abortion.

protection of unborn existence represented but a collateral aspect of more pressing legal issues.[6]

As soon as attention is extended beyond the confines of canonistic debate to the neighboring field of Roman law studies, however, any thought of scholastic indifference toward abortion turns out to be unfounded. Medieval attempts to formulate abstract and generally binding principles of conduct and effect their amalgamation into a single and coherent system of norms for the laity were doubtlessly animated by the same cultural transformation that led to the establishment of the canonistic curriculum. It was not by accident that both branches of Western jurisprudence, one to be applied in the secular and the other in the ecclesiastical sphere, found their first permanent home in a single location, the northern Italian city of Bologna, and that they assumed contours almost contemporaneously, about the middle of the twelfth century. Yet unlike Gratian, their counterpart, the earliest exponents of legal sources grounded in the ancient imperial rather than canonical tradition did not have to distill their authoritative materials from widely disparate excerpts and bring them into a suitable textbook format. What they needed to accomplish was to reassemble, after half a thousand years of obsolescence, the long extant *Corpus iuris civilis,* the late ancient synthesis of Roman law originally pieced together by a commission of jurists working under Emperor Justinian I (527–565). The recovery, set into motion by the generations of Pepo (fl. 1070) and Irnerius (fl. 1120), the alleged founders of the Bolognese civilian school, appears to have reached completion by 1150, when manuscripts attest to continuous teaching activities in the form of marginal glosses that accumulated, in layer upon layer, around Justinian's now fully reconstituted Latin text.[7]

Twelfth-century glossators found in the Roman source material several statements concerning abortion and the juristic approach to nascent life. Each was imbued with a decidedly pagan spirit, untouched by the Christian

6. The four "official" decretal collections, promulgated by popes between 1234 and 1322, have been edited by Emil Friedberg, *Corpus iuris canonici*, vol. 2 (Leipzig: Tauchnitz, 1881).

7. Stephan Kuttner, "The Revival of Jurisprudence," in *Renaissance and Renewal in the Twelfth Century*, ed. Robert Benson and Giles Constable (Cambridge, MA: Harvard University Press, 1982), 299–323, reprinted in Stephan Kuttner, *Studies in the History of Medieval Canon Law* (Aldershot, UK: Ashgate, 1990), no. 3; Winroth, *The Making*, 146–174; Michael Hoeflich and Jasonne Grabher, "The Establishment of Normative Legal Texts. The Beginnings of the Ius Commune," in *The History of Medieval Canon Law in the Classical Period 1140–1234*, ed. Wilfried Hartmann and Kenneth Pennington (Washington, DC: Catholic University of America Press, 2008), 1–21.

sensibilities of Jerome and Saint Augustine and younger proponents including, as noted, the figure of Gratian. The imperial laws (*leges*) of the *Corpus
iuris civilis* in effect retained the same embryological teachings of Stoic origin
that classical Roman jurists of the second and third centuries had embraced.
The viewpoint favored by them had denied to the unborn (*partus*) any participation in human nature. As long as birth was pending, they had conceded
that citizens would be free to appoint unborn and "future" children as heirs,
and act "as though a fetal existence were already present in the human
sphere" (Dig. 1.5.7). But juristic opinion had also agreed that should death
occur before the moment of delivery, this would instantly cancel hereditary
claims on behalf of the partus, which, according to the formulation of the
most famous lawyer of Roman Antiquity, Ulpian (Dig. 35.2.9.1), constituted
nothing but "a part of the mother's womb and her entrails" (*mulieris portio
est vel viscerum*). Ulpian and his pagan colleagues, in other words, had created
a legal fiction by assuming that the fetus possessed individual rights for purposes of hereditary succession only.[8]

Stoic indifference toward arguments admitting the possibility of prenatal
human life affected as well the treatment of abortion in the Roman *Corpus*,
which mentions the act as a potential offense on a total of four occasions.
Three leges, or legal "fragments," concern, historically, the same scenario
of an ex-wife who aborted the child of her recently divorced husband. To
protect the father's stake in a legitimate heir, two of the fragments, attributed to the ancient jurists Marcian (Dig. 47.11.4) and Tryphoninus (Dig.
48.19.39), specify that an imperial decision had ordered the willfully miscar-
rying woman to be relegated into "temporary" exile. In a fourth and final
lex touching upon fetal death, the Roman lawyer Paul detailed the treatment awaiting those who administered love potions or abortifacient beverages (Dig. 48.19.38.5). Paul's text stated that regardless of their good or evil
intentions, perpetrators of lower social standing were to be sent to the mines,
whereas more honorable delinquents would endure banishment to an island
and lose part of their property. "If," on the other hand, "a man or woman
died from it" (*si ex hoc homo aut mulier perierit*), those found responsible would,
in the words of Paul, "suffer capital execution" (*ultimo supplicio adficiuntur*).[9]

---

8. The full text of Justinian's compilation is available in the edition of Theodor Mommsen, Paul
Krüger, Wilhelm Schöll, and Wilhelm Kroll, *Corpus iuris civilis*, 4 vols. (Berlin: Weidmann, 1872–95).

9. Enzo Nardi, *Procurato aborto nel mondo greco-romano* (Milan: Giuffrè, 1971), 431–441, 605–618,
provides a comprehensive dossier of the ancient source material on abortion.

As a result and by taking their authoritative textbook literally, Bolognese glossators might have identified temporary exile as the proper form of punishment for abortion and supplemented it with a warning to those who were experimenting with abortifacients, given that they risked capital execution for any ensuing fatality, whether proof of malicious intent was available against them or not. Especially the third text of the *Corpus* addressing abortion performed in defiance of a pregnant woman's former spouse (Dig. 48.8.8) makes it look as though Roman lawyers had proposed exile as the proper legal consequence not just for recalcitrant divorcees but for willingly aborting women in general. The passage, placed by Justinian's commissioners under a rubric ominously entitled *About the Cornelian Law on Murderers and the Makers of Poison* (Dig. 48.8), quotes Ulpian as having said that "if it is made manifest that a female has used force against her own entrails and miscarried a fetus, the provincial governor will order her to go into exile." The original context of Ulpian's words can still be inferred from an inscription placed atop the fragment, which attributes the remark to his "Thirty-Third Book on the Edict." Not until the eighteenth century, however, did juristic scholarship working toward the full reconstruction (palingenesis) of Ulpian's writings realize that the Edict in question had exclusively dealt with marital issues.[10] When, more than half a millennium earlier, scholastic glosses started to fill the blank spaces surrounding the text of Justinian's *Corpus* in the manuscripts, the obvious link—proposed by Marcian, Thryphoninus, and Ulpian—between abortion and the punishment of *exilium* came to serve very different interpretive ends.

Regardless of uncertainties in the wording, it seems as if teachers at the nascent schools of Roman law quickly agreed on how to expound the authoritative *leges* on abortion. The oldest preserved comments, possibly dating back as far as to the 1170s, already exhibit the core of doctrinal opinion as it would prevail among lawyers for the rest of the Middle Ages. The first glossators also anticipated later habits of presenting the chief tenets of civilian jurisprudence in the form of brief annotations to Dig. 47.11.4, the

---

10. First in an anonymous dissertation defended at the University of Halle in Saxony on April 29, 1732, in *Exercitationes ad Pandectas*, 99, secs. 14–15, ed. Johann Heinrich Boehmer (Hannover: Schmid, 1764), 386–388, 415; the discovery was made possible by centuries of humanist palingenesis; cf. *Die Abtreibung*, 141–152; see also Judith Evans Grubbs, *Women and the Law in the Roman Empire: A Sourcebook on Marriage, Divorce, and Widowhood* (London: Routledge, 2002), 202: "Abortion . . . was not per se against the law"; whereas Konstantinos Kapparis, *Abortion in the Ancient World* (London: Duckworth, 2002), 182–184, seems unaware of Ulpian's rubric when he concludes: "Abortion was criminalized, and that was it."

above-mentioned fragment that cites the ancient jurist, Marcian, as follows:[11] "The deified Severus and Antoninus wrote in a rescript that she who intentionally aborted ought to be sent into temporary exile by the governor. For it can appear shameful for her to have defrauded her husband of children with impunity." Contrary to the way they edited Ulpian's excerpt on the subject (Dig. 48.8.8), the original compilers of Justinian's *Corpus,* working around 530, quoted Marcian at sufficient length to inform readers about the exact historical reason for the imposition of exile. Two Antonine co-emperors, Severus and Caracalla (198–211), had framed the rule expressly so as to safeguard spousal claims of paternity. Neither the original imperial rescript nor the Stoic viewpoint cherished by the ancient jurists would have led to the introduction of repressive means for the sole sake of protecting unborn life. And yet, a millennium afterward, Bolognese glossators pondering the passage reached precisely the opposite conclusion. Their particular stance is apparent from the earliest efforts to explain Marcian's words "must be sent into temporary exile" to twelfth-century academic audiences: "Before the fortieth day, because until then [the partus] is not a human being. Otherwise, she [who has intentionally aborted] will be charged with homicide according to the Mosaic Law."[12] Circulating anonymously in the 1170s, the comment was eventually associated with the authorship of the Bolognese *doctor legum* Azo Porticus (d. 1202), and then carried, along with Azo's set (or apparatus) of annotations, into the *Glossa ordinaria* of Accursius, whose standard commentary filled the margins of practically every manuscript copy of Justinian's *Corpus* from about 1250 to the end of the medieval period.[13] Albeit succinct, the text successfully encapsulated key features of what developed into common opinion among civilian lawyers in that it proposed a first phase, up to the fortieth day after conception, of nonhuman existence in the maternal womb. Equation of the following stage, extending to the moment of birth, with complete possession of humanity on the part of the fetus, was used to justify full protection under the law of homicide, whereas the initial period of gestation, lasting five to six weeks, warranted no more than temporary banishment for the termination of a pregnancy.

---

11. Alan Watson, ed., *The Digest of Justinian,* 2 vols. (Philadelphia: University of Pennsylvania Press, 1998); the translation here is taken from Grubbs, *Women and the Law,* 202.

12. *Glossa ad* Dig. 47.11.4, s.v. *exilium dandam* (Olomouc, Státní okresní archiv, C. O. 273, fol. 123va; ascribed to "az." in both, Bamberg, SB, Jur. 19, fol. 163va; and Vatican, BAV, Pal. lat. 748, fol. 134va).

13. Accursius, *Glossa ordinaria ad* Dig. 47.11.4, s.v. *exilium,* printed in *Corpus iuris Iustiniani,* 6 vols (Lyon: Societas Typographica, 1612), 3:1386.

We do not have to look far for the source inspiring the radical departure of "pre-Azonian" glosses from provisions to be found in Justinian's normative guidelines. The *Corpus iuris civilis* does not contain excerpts alluding to the presence of human nature in the unborn, nor does the compilation ever suggest that abortion might be deserving of homicide charges. Instead, the only textbook at twelfth-century law schools to advance such ideas was Gratian's Decretum. It turns out that canonists and interpreters of the Roman leges (*legiste*) approached the issue in perfect alignment, a fact further highlighted by the appeal they both made to the Mosaic Law for authoritative support of their positions. One of the central canonical chapters on abortion, attributed in Gratian's work to Saint Augustine (C. 32, q. 2, c. 9), starts off with the name of Moyses, the biblical prophet said to have stated (in Exodus 21:22–23) that "should someone strike a pregnant woman who later miscarries, he must give soul for soul if the fetus had been formed; had the fetus not been formed, however, he must offer monetary compensation." By way of the purportedly Augustinian quote and in line with the leading theologians of their own day, medieval decretists and civilians relied on the *Septuagint*, an expanded Greek translation of the Old Testament dating back to the third century before Christ. An alternative rendering of the passage, undertaken by Jerome around 380 and adopted throughout the medieval Western church as the "vulgate" version of the Hebrew Bible, rather speaks of a violent blow to the detriment of the expecting mother, whose physical injury would call for a damage payment, or in the case of her death, for full retaliation. Unlike the Greek *Septuagint*, Jerome's *Vulgata* as well as the underlying, original version of the Jewish *Torah* do not envision penal consequences for fetal injury.[14]

Forms of Sentencing in Medieval Jurisprudence

The criminalization of abortion in the West had its point of departure in the lecture halls of Roman and canon law at Bologna and occurred during a time span historians have defined as the "formative phase" of medieval juristic thought. The period was marked at one end by the appearance of the Decretum (around 1140) and at the other by the consolidation of doctrine in

---

14. Compare the *Septuaginta,* ed. Alfred Rahlfs (Stuttgart: Württembergische Bibelanstalt, 1935), 122 (English version, chap. 4, note 1), with Jerome's *Vulgata* (Exodus 21:22–23), *Bibliorum sacrorum iuxta vulgatam Clementinam versio Latina,* ed. Aloisius Gramatica (Vatican City: Polyglotta Vaticana, 1951); ancient translations of the biblical text have been juxtaposed and examined by Nardi, *Procurato aborto,* 161–180.

the form of civilian and canonistic standard commentaries, or glossae ordinariae, which routinely accompanied scholastic textbooks from the 1230s
onward. Following Gratian's accomplishment and the recovery of Justinian's
leges, canonists and civilians, or legists, integrated the offense of abortion
within decades into a coherent theory of wrong. Invoking Moyses as their
primary authority, they placed the beginning of human existence neither at
the moment of conception nor at birth. They rather embraced the embryological concept of "successive animation" (*animatio successiva*), whereby the
immortal soul enters as the fetus assumes appropriate bodily features. The
same line of reasoning further persuaded jurists to treat willful miscarriage
of a formed fetus on a par with infanticide and homicide, as opposed to killings committed at an earlier stage of pregnancy. Acceptance of this construct
put legists completely at odds with the treatment of the partus in the ancient
Roman leges while furnishing an illustration of twelfth-century intellectual
efforts to harmonize textbook materials not just internally but in accordance
with fundamental tenets of Christian orthodoxy. In the process, canonistic teachings informed interpretations of Justinian's *Corpus,* especially with
regard to assumptions about moral behavior, and canonists borrowed heavily
from their civilian colleagues when it came to legal technicalities and procedural matters. The result was a synthesis that thoroughly permeated the
two disciplines. Before long, it obtained recognition under the label of *Ius
commune,* an overarching framework of rules common to university jurisprudence in general.[15]

Although church lawyers, guided by Gratian, paved the way for the theoretical equation of abortion with attempted and actual homicide, Bolognese civilians first associated the offense with punishments that nowadays are
clearly recognizable as criminal ones. Legists agreed that persons guilty of the
intended killing of a fetus younger than forty days, as well as of the nonfatal
attack on a formed partus, were to be threatened with temporary exile. Full-
fledged homicide of an articulated creature in the maternal womb instead
demanded the death penalty. Because twelfth-century canonists for their part
wrote little specifically devoted to abortion, legal historians have had to delve
deeply into decretist and decretalist glosses on homicidium for information
about the nature of ordinary ecclesiastical sentencing. Further complicating
the picture is that outcomes for the guilty envisaged by classical canon law
defy, from a modern terminological standpoint, straightforward classification
as "punitive." In 1211, for example, Pope Innocent III was faced with an

---

15. Bellomo, *Common Legal Past,* 55–118; Helmholz, *Ius Commune in England,* 1–11.

urgent judicial question. It involved a monk who had terminated the existence of his own offspring by hitting his pregnant lover on the lower body. The apostolic response was unequivocal. If the victim of the miscarriage had been "alive," Innocent wrote, the accused had "to abstain from altar services" and do so without delay.[16]

Innocent's choice of words, *debet ab altaris officio abstinere*, highlighted the applicability of canonical irregularity (*irregularitas*), which among other things barred "criminous" laymen and clerics guilty of homicide in principle from the exercise of priestly functions. As a personal condition, it entailed suspension from sacramental duties and the loss of ordinary ecclesiastical income by way of a benefice, which most churchmen received, along with their appointed pastoral positions, to support themselves economically. The risk of becoming irregular particularly affected clerics in the higher, or "major," sacred orders (*ordines maiores*), from subdeacon through deacon and priest to bishop and all candidates intent on joining their ranks. Given, moreover, that irregularitas operated as an automatic impediment or routine injunction upon discovery of a crime, present-day habits of expression would probably categorize Innocent III's judicial reply of 1211, recommending withdrawal of the prerogative to administer at the altar, as something more akin to a disciplinary measure. By the same token, our current notions would regard temporary imprisonment or money payments, which ecclesiastical tribunals of the later Middle Ages also meted out against homicidal clergy and laymen, as perfectly adequate judicial responses to violent misconduct. Canonists of the period, however, viewed incarceration and monetary impositions not as instruments of vindictive action or punishment (*pena*), but as forms of penance (penitentia), devised to alleviate the burden of sin.[17]

Exclusion from the performance of sacramental rites, tied intrinsically to the predicament of canonical irregularitas, did not always figure as a penalty. The sons of priests, the physically impaired, or women for that matter, were subject to disqualification from the ordines maiores notwithstanding the fact that they had incurred no culpability of their own. Canon law plainly

---

16. Innocent III, *Sicut ex litterarum* (4 Comp. 5.6.4; X 5.12.20), translated in chap. 2, note 12.

17. For the central distinction between penance and punishment, between crime, tort, and sin, and the definition of irregularity, see the classical treatment of Stephan Kuttner, *Kanonistische Schuldlehre von Gratian bis auf die Dekretalen Gregors IX. (1140–1234)* (Vatican City: Polyglotta Vaticana, 1935), 11–34, 42–48; Richard Fraher, "The Theoretical Justification for the New Criminal Law of the High Middle Ages: 'Rei publicae interest, ne crimina remaneant impunita,'" *University of Illinois Law Review* 3 (1984): 577–595; and Lotte Kéry, *Gottesfurcht und irdische Strafe. Der Beitrag des mittelalterlichen Kirchenrechts zur Entstehung des Strafrechts* (Cologne: Böhlau, 2006), 114–161.

viewed them as being ineligible for admission to the sacerdotal dignity, which explains why Innocent III in 1211 was prepared to impose suspension short of any attempt to establish criminal intent. The narrative of the papal letter leaves no doubt that the suspect had provided the material cause for his lover's miscarriage, proving him to be a homicide as long as the slain victim had been human. Following late medieval canonical standards, this degree of homicidal involvement was sufficient to place defendants on the same level of responsibility as judges rendering a capital sentence, or soldiers inflicting death in battle, whose activities, while legitimate, nevertheless equaled homicidium and barred sacred ordination.[18] In substance, therefore, the pope's decision of 1211 was not about punishment. It merely signaled apostolic approval of the idea that, in the ecclesiastical courts, abortion amounted to actual manslaughter from the moment the fetus assumed form and became alive.[19]

If clerical judges also imposed imprisonment, physical pain short of bloodshed and enduring harm, public humiliation, or monetary payments on clerics or laypersons, the rationale behind their ruling was, according to common legal opinion, penitential and not punitive and provided medicine for the spiritual survival of sinners. Together with the scant treatment of abortion in decretist and early decretalist literature, unwillingness to apply the rigor of civilian punishment—that is, temporary exile or death—to defendants appearing before the church courts again seems to suggest that canonistic doctrine was not interested in the offense beyond assigning it a place within the general scholastic theory of crimen. Such a conclusion, however, would distort historical reality, as canon lawyers played an instrumental role in classifying abortion as a secular crime in the modern sense of the word. Early on, legists of Azo's generation had been content to offer vague cross-references (allegationes) to the Mosaic Law when pointing to the ultimate source of their interpretation of the Roman law, without acknowledging any greater indebtedness to contemporary canonical doctrine. It is nonetheless evident that their ecclesiastical colleagues were decisive in bringing the

---

18. In addition to the literature cited in the previous note, cf. Vito Piergiovanni, *La punibilità degli innocenti nel diritto canonico dell'età classica*, vol. 1, *La discussione del problema in Graziano e nella decretalistica* (Milan: Giuffrè, 1971).

19. The point was still disputed in Innocent's time, with canonists such as Huguccio (ca. 1190), *Summa*, C. 32, q. 2, c. 9, s.v. *mulctetur pecunia* (Paris, BN, lat. 15397, fol. 84vb), and Laurentius Hispanus (ca. 1215), see *Glossa Palatina*, C. 32, q. 2, c. 9, s.v. *mulctetur pecunia* (Vatican, BAV, Pal. lat. 658, fol. 82ra), arguing that irregularitas should likewise extend to the abortion of unformed embryos; cf. *Die Abtreibung*, 26n48, 29n56.

views of Moyses to bear on pertinent passages from Justinian's textbook. In effect, the decretists first extended the concept of successive animation to the exposition of Dig. 48.19.38.5, a fragment in which the ancient lawyer Paul had proposed a set of "extraordinary" penalties for the use of abortifacient or love potions (*abortionis aut amatorium poculum*).

A commentary, written around 1209 and known as the *Glossa Palatina*, records the single-handed attempt of Laurentius, a Spanish canonist, to "canonize" Paul's excerpt as it was read at the neighboring Roman law schools. The Spaniard maintained that the original meaning of the lex, submitting purveyors of *abortionis pocula* to execution "should a man or woman die from it," was phrased to cover as well the fatal poisoning of ensouled fetuses. For centuries to come, the glossa ordinaria on the Decretum, composed around 1215 by Johannes Teutonicus, would perpetuate the idea that "dynamic" abortion, procured with the help of herbal concoctions, warranted easier conviction in the lay courts than ordinary killings, given that Paul had proposed death or, for failed intoxication, the lesser penalty of forced labor in the mines as appropriate even where malicious intent had not been proven.[20] Civilians, to be sure, failed to integrate Paul's fragment for a long time into their own discussions of abortion. When, perhaps as late as in the 1400s, they started to follow the interpretive lead of Laurentius Hispanus, they did so without admitting to canonistic inspiration, in the same way that anonymous authors of the oldest, "pre-Azonian" allegationes to Marcian's Dig. 47.11.4, had concealed, behind approximate citations of the Mosaic Law, just how profoundly their understanding of criminal abortion depended on explanations offered by Gratian and the early decretists.[21]

Crimen in "An Age without Lawyers" (500–1050)

Although the criminalization of abortion began chronologically in the formative years of scholastic jurisprudence between 1140 and 1240 and

---

20. *Glossa Palatina*, C. 32, q. 2, c. 9, s.v. *pro anima* (Vatican, BAV, Pal. lat. 658, fol. 82ra), printed in *Die Abtreibung*, 34n68; cf. Johannes Teutonicus, *Glossa ordinaria*, C. 32, q. 2, c. 9, s.v. *det animam* (Munich, BSB, lat. 14024, fol. 166va); and the updated version of the Ordinary Gloss by Bartholomeus Brixiensis (ca. 1236), in *Corpus iuris canonici* (Venice: Magna Societas, 1584), col. 2112.

21. The commentary of Bartolus de Saxoferrato (d. 1356), on Dig. 48.19.38.5 (Munich, BSB, lat. 3634, 251vb), contains no reference yet to the Laurentian exposition of Paul's lex. Acceptance of the canonistic reading by civilians may not predate the 1400s, when its widespread adoption is evident from four consultations written around 1459 by different Italian lawyers about a single criminal case; see chap. 9, note 25.

geographically at the schools of canonistic and Roman legal studies in the northern Italian city of Bologna, this does not imply that during the earlier Middle Ages the slaying of nascent life in a woman's body was nowhere addressed as crimen or that nobody considered it a wrongful act. Documentary evidence from the period between 500 and 1050 includes many mentions of the subject in a variety of prescriptive contexts, with the procurement of miscarriage figuring among offenses in no less than three important strands of normative literature. Whereas one of them, the collections of church law (canones) prior to Gratian's Decretum, constituted a textual tradition with deep roots in late antiquity, the other two, compilations of tribal customs (Leges Barbarorum) and manuals of penance (Libri penitentiales), were both of post-Roman descent and owed their existence, as did the canon law books, to clerical authorship.[22] Whether the intended audiences were priestly, monastic, or lay, literary production always involved individuals whose education relied on authoritative ecclesiastical sources from the ancient period and on Latin readings steeped in the moral, administrative, and legal terminologies of bygone imperial society and long-defunct Roman jurisprudence.

Modern Westerners investigating the original meaning of early medieval norms must be aware of the enormous cultural distance that separates them from the people who once generated the extant source material. To illustrate the abyss, there is agreement among historians today that the period resolved tensions between persons and groups without recourse to professional lawyers or to a body of systematic legal thought. Justinian's Digest, containing four references to abortion that would intrigue scholastic jurists from the twelfth century onward, was never quoted by anyone in the Latin world between the years 603 and 1076. For more than half a millennium, specialized teachers and institutions giving permanence to clear-cut and widely accepted juristic concepts did not exist. Concurrently, the clerical writers of canonical collections, of penitentials and customary Leges for the laity, went on to employ former Roman expressions and named certain phenomena of their own living environment with words that in ancient Latin would have been the equivalents of "law" (lex), "judges" (judices), "sin" (peccatum), "crime" (crimen), "proof" (probatio), "guilt" (culpa), and so forth. It is obvi-

---

22. Comprehensive guides to the sources are provided by Cyrille Vogel, Les "Libri Paenitentiales," Typologie 27 (Turnhout, Belg.: Brepols, 1978), with a supplement by Allen Frantzen (1985); Lotte Kéry, Canonical Collections of the Early Middle Ages (ca. 400–1140): A Bibliographical Guide to the Manuscripts and Literature (Washington, DC: Catholic University of America Press, 1999). For the Leges, see Patrick Wormald, The Making of English Law: King Alfred to the Twelfth Century, vol. 1, Legislation and Its Limits (Oxford: Oxford University Press, 1999), 29–70.

ously not easy to determine what represents a historically adequate rendering of these and similar terms, one that reflects most accurately the way in which inherited juridical concepts were understood by men and women of the early Middle Ages.

The canonical collections from Roman times (about 400) until Gratian (around 1140) cite abortion for the most part in connection with what lawyers today would call "material" norms. Compilers of canones ranked the act in close proximity to homicide as a serious failing before God and the Christian faithful. On occasion, the equation with homicidium is even rendered explicit. In the oldest and, prior to the Decretum, most assiduously copied ecclesiastical condemnation by the Council of Ancyra (314), for example, specifications in line with the theory of successive animation are lacking, while other ancient canons, circulating nearly as widely, already anticipate the scholastic distinction between prehuman and human life in the maternal womb.[23] At times, conciliar decrees also echo the harsher treatment Roman jurists like Paul had reserved for dynamic abortion, that is, miscarriage brought on by abortifacient or love potions independent of foul play, and frequently with the added mention of contraceptive beverages. For the rest, early medieval canon law texts from the ninth century onward offer terse statements as to the exact length of penance awaiting confessed sinners. Exclusion from church services and submission to works of atonement (penitentia) are typically prescribed for seven versus three years, depending on whether the killing involved a formed or an unformed fetus. In rare cases the duration is made longer and, more commonly, somewhat shorter.[24] It is instead very difficult to gauge what is now defined as the "procedural" law underlying these substantive provisions and to discern standards that permitted ecclesiastical authorities to assess whether and how the indicated quotas of spiritual satisfaction were to be administered. One firm assumption regards the basic format of penitential exercises. It presupposed annual seasons of fasting and food restrictions especially during Lent, the forty-day span (quadragesima) leading up to the week of Easter.

The next category of sources to emerge historically was that of early medieval Germanic and Celtic customs. Over the course of the sixth century,

23. As in Lérida (546), can. 2 (Mansi 8.612); cf. Ancyra (314), can. 21 (Mansi 2.519). The early medieval transmission of canonical texts can be traced with the help of Linda Fowler-Magerl, *Clavis canonum: Selected Canon Law Collections before 1140* (Hannover: Hahn, 2005).

24. Huser, *The Crime of Abortion*, 30–40; Nardi, *Procurato aborto*, 669–682; Garancini, "Materiali," 411–445; and Heinz Schwarz, *Der Schutz des Kindes im Recht des frühen Mittelalters* (Bonn: Röhrscheid, 1993), 35–68, discuss early medieval canons; Noonan, *Contraception*, 14–50, looks at the evidence from a different perspective.

literacy was rapidly monopolized by churchmen. Appreciation of the need to put rules of proper conduct into writing was fading beyond ecclesiastical circles, whose members began to produce lists of so-called *compositiones*, damage payments tribal groups were supposed to make in attempts to secure the peaceful settlement of their disputes. The texts were often transmitted under the resounding title of "Laws" (Leges). As the English legal historian Patrick Wormald has observed, there are hints of the ancient Roman order in the way clerical collectors sought to bestow an authoritative ring on their works. While authors from former regions of the empire presented the Leges as issued by superior command, those living in areas never subjected to Rome were more likely to introduce the rules as customary and approved by local and communal consensus.[25] Apart from differences of formal presentation, however, they all shared many fundamental traits. The Salic Law, first compiled under the reign of the Merovingian king Clovis (d. 511), furnishes an apt illustration of how cases of abortion characteristically occupied the attention of secular courts and assemblies. In a late sixth-century version of the original, the violent death of a fetus is treated in conjunction with homicide:

> If someone kills a child in the mother's womb or an unnamed newborn within the first nine nights, he shall be liable to pay 100 *solidi* or 4,000 denars.
>
> If someone kills a free girl under age before she can bear children, he shall be liable to pay 200 *solidi* or 8,000 denars.
>
> If someone kills a free woman of childbearing age, he shall be liable to pay 600 *solidi* or 24,000 denars.
>
> If someone kills a [free] woman past childbearing age, he shall be liable to pay 200 *solidi* or 8,000 denars.[26]

The excerpt is representative of the Leges in general in that it places paramount importance on considerations of personal status. Monetary estimates, commonly known as *wergeld*, are juxtaposed with specific categories of victims, whose individual worth is measured on the basis of social rank and utility. The violent death of a free woman is said to warrant monetary compensation, or composition, in accordance with her ability to give birth. If the

---

25. Patrick Wormald, "Inter cetera bona . . . genti suae: Law-Making and Peace-Keeping in the Earliest English Kingdoms," in *La giustizia nell'alto medioevo (secoli v–viii)*, Settimane 42 (Spoleto: Centro italiano di studi sull'alto medioevo, 1995), 967–968.

26. *Pactum Legis Salicae*, 24.5–6, 8–9, ed. Karl Eckhard, *MGH LL* 1.4.1 (Hannover: Hahn, 1962), 91–92 (version K); cf. also ibid., 41.15–21, ed. Eckhard, 160–161, translated by Katherine Fischer-Drew, *The Laws of the Salian Franks* (Philadelphia: University of Pennsylvania Press, 1991), 86, 105–106.

slain female is not of childbearing age, her valuation drops to one-third of what would be considered appropriate in the opposite case. Following the same logic, the loss of an infant or child about to be born free is viewed as meriting satisfaction by way of wergeld, or at least as long as the blame can be laid on an adversarial party. Equally important to note, the verdicts for homicide listed in the Lex Salica fall short of physical punishment and limit themselves to the offering of damage payments.

At the time when constituents of the third group of prescriptive writings on behalf of abortion—the penitential manuals—finally advanced from remote origins in the Anglo-Irish Church of the sixth and seventh centuries toward the Continent and into core regions of the former Roman Empire, canon law collections and early medieval tribal customs displayed rules that suggest a sharp contrast to the modern eye. The ancient canones, on the one hand, embraced impersonal principles of conduct to which every sinner was supposed to submit. Tribal Leges, on the other hand, subscribed to diametrically opposed notions of personal status and social acceptance as central to assessments of accountability. By necessity, therefore, early medieval Celtic and Germanic clerics must have felt like people living in a divided world, with religious communities shaped by individually binding and permanent written standards and societal habits marked by the need to demonstrate, in the face of entrenched local enmities and threats of revenge, unflinching solidarity with family and adherence to ever-shifting friendship alliances. In due course, however, a synthesis was achieved between ancient individualist and customary perceptions of deviant behavior. It found its fullest expression in the new guidelines for confessors that, arriving out of Ireland and England, reached the mainland of western Europe during the ascent of the Carolingians to the Frankish throne in the 700s.

In trying to understand the original purpose and function of penitentials and early medieval norms, two German scholars, Hubertus Lutterbach and Ludger Körntgen, have expressed conflicting views about the ways in which confessors evaluated degrees of sin.[27] To Lutterbach, it seemed clear that Anglo-Irish and Frankish manuals were progressively exposed to collectivist and post-Roman concepts of liability, a trend he considered evident not only

---

27. Hubertus Lutterbach, "Intentions- oder Tathaftung? Zum Bussverständnis in den frühmittelalterlichen Bussbüchern," *Frühmittelalterliche Studien* 34 (1995): 120–43, critically reviewed by Ludger Körntgen, *DA* 52 (1996): 754. See also Wilfried Hartmann, *Kirche und Kirchenrecht um 900. Die Bedeutung der spätkarolingischen Zeit für Tradition und Innovation im kirchlichen Recht* (Hannover: Hahn, 2008), 228–235.

in the pervasive use of penitential tariffs mimicking the compensatory payments of the Salic Law and other tribal Leges but also in tendencies to reduce penance for offenses that had been committed in the interest of one's own family or clan. The wrong of, say, homicide was consequently treated as a less serious infraction if it had occurred in defense of a close relative or if monetary compensation had been paid to the victim's side. Ludger Körntgen, for his part, has argued that the penitential sources quoted by Lutterbach refer just as often to individualistic and purportedly Roman modes of guilt assessment and scrutinize the inner responsibility of sinners for their misdeeds in juxtaposition with Lutterbach's Germanic criteria. Accordingly, the length of fasting and other forms of spiritual redemption often fluctuates within a single list of penitential tariffs, depending upon the penitent's usefulness to his group or, alternatively, the intrinsic nature of the sinful act, with killings out of negligence, for instance, drawing reduced penances if compared with those for intentional manslaughter. Körntgen complemented his observations with the significant reminder that Lutterbach's neat divide between individual and impersonal notions of penitential responsibility in antiquity versus status-based and collective ones during the early Middle Ages remains questionable as there existed no ancient forerunners of the *Libri penitentiales*, with tariffs of spiritual satisfaction, to permit conclusions on the basis of parallel data.

Partial confirmation of Körntgen's contention that the Libri penitentiales were as much a mouthpiece of Roman insistence on the categorical sinfulness of voluntary homicide as they were an accommodation of Germanic views of intended yet somehow "honorable" violence for the sake of one's personal relations can be found, among other things, in the way the texts deal with abortion. From the eighth century onward, the distinctiveness and novelty of their approach to issues of manslaughter were recognized by ecclesiastical and secular elites who saw in the penitentials a welcome canonical supplement to legal arrangements prevailing in the lay sphere. The Leges were designed to compensate women of free status monetarily for miscarriages suffered through the hands of an outsider. By the same logic, mothers who wished to terminate their own pregnancy could do so without risk of payment, as killings perpetrated within a group rather than between two factions did not form a constellation envisioned by Celtic, Germanic, or early Carolingian Laws. Tribal lay society, quite unlike the ancient Roman state, did not condemn homicidium as such but merely assessed the possibilities of financial settlement between rivaling alliances, to be reached with the help of impartial arbiters. Members of a single solidarity network or family would not have turned to an external mediator for resolution of their internal disputes, nor would they have traded wergeld with one another, given that the sum had to be drawn from a pool of shared resources.[28] The situation was different, however, when episodes of violent slaying by a close relative, such as parental infanticide or abortion, were brought to the attention of priestly confessors relying on post-Roman penitential manuals, in that these imposed on the sinner, in truly revolutionary fashion, unprecedented and highly detailed quotas of fasting and praying. In the canon law of antiquity, differentiated spiritual retribution for attacks on nascent life depending on the culprit's identity had been unknown. Toward 800, it began to spread across the West as part of the Libri penitentiales, highlighting a process that appears to have been inspired ultimately by Germanic rationales of compensation. Redemptive tariffs were now being extended to any conceivable type of wrong, whether it offended a feuding warlord and his entourage or God and his clerical *familia*. Penitential exercises, including the seven years of periodic abstention from certain foods for the death of a human fetus, allowed for conversion into monetary payments, in imitation of practices long recommended by tribal custom.[29]

Ludger Körntgen has rightly pointed out that penitential manuals furnish no more than ambiguous proof for claims according to which early medieval application of penance was increasingly "Germanized." At the same time, though, sufficient evidence suggests that Hubertus Lutterbach's characterization of normative developments during the era is, globally speaking, not just insightful but essentially correct. After all, modern experts including both Körntgen and Lutterbach are in agreement about yet another development, illustrated by the advance of legal institutions that, without doubt, first enter the historical record as part of Germanic and Celtic customary Leges. The laws of late ancient Rome had favored judicial methods of ascertaining guilt and innocence through accurate "fact finding," that is, by aiming at the reconstruction of whether or not an alleged and incriminating act, such as the killing of a fetus against spousal will, had indeed been

---

28. Scholarship has noted the absence from the Leges of murder committed within families. Inspired by the *Libri penitentiales*, Charlemagne became the first medieval lay ruler to promote liability for the offense in statutes (*capitularia*) of the early 800s; cf. Hartmann, *Kirche und Kirchenrecht*, 222–228, and note 32, below.

29. The analysis of penitentials from a historical rather than philological or theological perspective has been pioneered by Raymund Kottje, *Die Bussbücher Halitgars von Cambrai und des Hrabanus Maurus* (Berlin: de Gruyter, 1980), esp. 9–12; for surveys in English of "revisionist" work inspired by Kottje, cf. Rob Meens, "The Frequency and Nature of Early Medieval Penance," in *Handling Sin: Confession in the Middle Ages*, ed. Peter Biller and Alastair Minnis (Woodbridge, NY: York Medieval Press, 1998), 35–61; Sarah Hamilton, *The Practice of Penance 900–1050* (Oxford: Oxford University Press, 2001), 1–11.

committed. In addition, juristic scrutiny had concentrated on the evaluation of extenuating circumstances that centered on the defendant's intent to behave criminally and ranged from pure accident to neglect and, more serious still, to malice aforethought. After the demise of the empire in the West, the surviving canon law collections certainly preserved, via continuous copying, manifold literary traces of these typically Roman ideas about penal responsibility. Simultaneously, however, canonical sources started to incorporate and adapt for their own purposes distinctly tribal techniques of discerning "truth." Most prominent among them were the so-called ordeals (*ordalia*) and recourse to compurgation.[30]

Briefly put, compurgationes obliged the accused, along with a specific number of oath helpers, to swear to his innocence. Co-jurors were selected from among the defendant's personal acquaintances and asked to vouch for his good reputation and standing in the community. They performed their task as character witnesses and did not have to possess knowledge of the purported offense. Procedures involving ordalia instead assumed multiple formats, such as that of a duel between two litigants or their substitutes or, alternatively, hot-water tests in which one of the adversaries would try to prove his claim through submersion of a hand in a cauldron of boiling water. Within days, the burnt flesh would be inspected by arbiters who announced their opinion as to whether the healing process had gone forward favorably. If the wound was discovered to have festered, courts concluded that God had abandoned the ailing man's case in a manifest sign of his culpability. Regardless of formalities, Germanic customs preferred to establish guilt in ways that led away from the reconstruction of past facts and favored evidence capable of being enacted, rather than reenacted, before the eyes of everyone present. Whereas Roman procedures asked if someone had physically and intentionally performed a wrong, the Leges framed investigations as an ongoing verification of social support. Would swearing parties be able to muster the agreed number of respectable oath helpers? Would one side enjoy sufficient backing to recruit the strongest champion for an impending trial by battle? Or, again, would bystanders embrace judicial decisions based upon inspection of a scorched palm and turn them into enduring marks of conflict resolution?

---

30. The increasing presence of proof by ordalia and oaths in canonical collections from 847 onward is emphasized by Hartmann, *Kirche and Kirchenrecht*, 261–267, 320; for references to the source material, Robert Bartlett, *Trial by Fire and Water: The Medieval Judicial Ordeal* (Oxford: Oxford University Press, 1986), 32–47. Compurgation persisted in church proceedings until the end of the Middle Ages; see the bibliographic references in chap. 2, note 22.

Modern historiography has coined the expression "communal justice" to describe the environment in which ordeals, oath helpers, duels, and other varieties of Germanic procedure thrived during the earlier Middle Ages. The adjective "communal" refers to tight-knit communities epitomizing the extremely fragmented political situation of the West in the years between 500 and 1050, when power was wielded primarily on the local level and informed by intensely personal relationships, with landowning warrior dynasties and their protection-seeking clienteles being surrounded by likeminded competitors. Order and peace were predicated upon the possibility of feud and vendetta, which constantly threatened to disrupt an intricate web of alliances. Stability did not necessarily flow from written norms but required continuous effort by leaders accustomed to determining questions of right and wrong in light of fleeting and bipartisan sentiment. What today constitutes an autonomous judicial sphere remained undetached from other forms of dispute processing. The procedures and outcomes tribal Leges recommended as lawful revolved around status and were designed to test the inner cohesiveness of groups and their resolve to rally behind individual members.[31] At the height of his reign in 802, the greatest conqueror of the age, Charlemagne, was content to urge aristocrats in conflict with neighboring clans to desist, after the violent death of a relative or friend, from ingrained habits of revenge taking and accept monetary compensation as stipulated by the Leges. Unflinching submission to the law seemed beyond the imagination of contemporary lay rulers. The loss of face it implied was considered automatic, unless someone's obedience to impersonal norms could be presented to fellows and foes as having been inspired by honorable motivations such as Christian deference toward the Lord and His commandments.[32] Similarly, abortion in the modern sense of the word, performed with the consent of pregnant mothers, was seen as meriting adverse consequences

---

31. For the distinction between "communal" and "downward" justice, see Peter Brown, "Society and the Supernatural: A Medieval Change," *Daedalus* 104 (1975): 137, revised in *Society and the Holy in Late Antiquity*, ed. Peter Brown (Berkeley: University of California Press, 1982), 310–311. Despite the objections raised by Bartlett, *Trial by Fire*, 155–168, Brown's generalizations retain much of their validity; cf. Paul Hyams, *Rancor and Reconciliation in Medieval England* (Ithaca: Cornell University Press, 2003), 3–33; Stephen White, *Feuding and Peace-Making in Eleventh-Century France* (Aldershot, UK: Ashgate, 2005), 4–12.

32. "Wishing ourselves to act against those who have dared to commit the evil of homicide and lest sin flourishes and great hostilities among Christians occur, the accused shall, whenever, through insinuation of the devil, a homicide occurs, make amends and speedily pay composition for the committed wrong to the relatives of the slain person." Charlemagne, *Capitulare de missis* 32, in *Capitularia regum Francorum*, ed. Alfred Boretius, *MGH*, LL 2.1 (Hannover: Hahn, 1883), 97, translated by Paul Dutton, *Carolingian Civilization: A Reader* (Peterborough, ON: Broadview, 1993), 67.

only if circumstances pertained to the sacred and where sinners sought other-worldly reward while voluntarily undergoing penitential exercises of fasting, money payments or—in cases carried to the extreme—public humiliation in front of peers and bystanders.

At the other end of the spectrum, historians have adopted the label "downward justice" to denote modes of adjudication diametrically opposed to the small-scale mechanisms of communal dispute settlement prevalent during the early Middle Ages. From about 1050 at the latest, ideas concerning the peaceful redress of wrongdoing in downward fashion seem to have exerted an increasing fascination among the people of western Europe. The growth of this new mentality presupposed, to begin with, fundamental societal change in that it called for judges capable of imposing their will "unilaterally" and endowed with authority superior to the mediating role of traditional arbiters who in keeping with the Leges assisted litigants in pursuing monetary compensation or in stalling ulterior rounds of reciprocal and collective revenge. For this transformation to come about, political leadership had to gain enough strength to appropriate key functions of self-rule in matters of peacekeeping and channel them toward centralized administrative structures. Beneficiaries of the power transfer had to challenge long-cherished habits of adjudication and implement standards that favored abstract and impersonal criteria of liability over preferment of status and nearby family or friendship networks. They further needed to draw on support from people disadvantaged by older, face-to-face arrangements and anxious to embrace procedural safeguards placing everybody on a par with locally entrenched adversaries. The spread of universally binding principles also required an intellectual and educational mobilization of unprecedented proportions, so as to create and disseminate normative knowledge both widely held and logically compelling.

Historical research has identified several early advocates of downward prosecution in Western society. They all figured as leading representatives of the ecclesiastical hierarchy who incidentally left a number of highly influential canonical writings. One penitential manual entitled the *Corrector* and circulated by Burchard of Worms (ca. 1020), for example, has been credited with the first consistent attempt at eliminating discrepancies from among the penitential tariffs. Intolerance toward internal contradictions, to be sure, provides the cornerstone for any systematic investigation of normative materials.[33] In the

---

33. Greta Austin, *Shaping Church Law around the Year 1000: The Decretum of Burchard of Worms* (Aldershot, UK: Ashgate, 2008); Ludger Körntgen, "Canon Law and the Practice of Penance: Burchard of Worms's Penitential," *Early Medieval Europe* 14 (2006): 103–117.

years after 1060, moreover, so-called reform collections of canon law started to put emphasis on specific authoritative sources (*auctoritates*) to legitimize political centralization within the church and bolster extravagant claims of papal monarchy. And while reformers endeavored to weed out texts now perceived as inappropriate—that is, of lay origin—a triad of experts in the tradition of canones—Bernold of Constance (d. 1100), Ivo of Chartres (d. 1116), and Alger of Liege (fl. 1123)—marked in their works the crucial advance of interpretive techniques for the harmonization of seemingly irreconcilable auctoritates. The theoretical instructions of Bernold, Ivo, and Alger would soon inspire Gratian's Concordance of Discordant Church Norms (*Concordia discordantium canonum*), as his Decretum was originally named.[34] In a gradual buildup, their contributions facilitated the rise of scholastic jurisprudence, which in turn established, uniformly and lastingly, not only jurisdictional categories such as crime but precise legal definitions for individual charges like abortion as well.

---

34. See the literature cited above, note 3; John Gilchrist, *Canon Law in the Age of Reform, 11th–12th Centuries* (Aldershot, UK: Ashgate, 1993), xi–xvi; Robert Somerville and Bruce Brasington, *Prefaces to Canon Law Books in Latin Christianity: Selected Translations, 500–1245* (New Haven, CT: Yale University Press, 1998), 105–169; Christof Rolker, *Canon Law and the Letters of Ivo of Chartres* (Cambridge: Cambridge University Press, 2010), 290–302.

CHAPTER 2

Early Venues of Criminalization

When twelfth-century intellectuals in the wake of Gratian transformed the refinement of ecclesiastical and secular law into successful professional pursuits, they took advantage of an opportunity for which there had been insufficient promise just a hundred years earlier. What allowed them to prosper was that they could act in alliance with newly emerging political forces that also drew on ideas of downward justice as the central tenet of their reasoning. After half a millennium of relative dormancy, interest in absolute and nonnegotiable punishment such as exile or death for abstract categories of wrongdoing including homicide rapidly gained in popularity and advanced especially in core areas of the so-called economic take-off, which greatly affected western Europe in the period from 1050 onward. Spurred by the explosive development of trade, many people moved back to the long-neglected towns of ancient Roman times. Poorly maintained bridges and highways underwent repairs to accommodate increasing travel activity and contributed logistically to the complex process of urbanization. In due course, markets, focal points of population and infrastructure, and centers of artisanship and scholastic learning converged and overlapped. Bologna, the alma mater of medieval jurists, was, and still is, situated at the intersection of the four most important Italian traffic arteries. On the other side of the Alps, Paris provided the principal destination for theologians and traders who hailed from cities and commercially viable regions along the rivers Loire in the south, Rhine in the east, and Thames across the English Channel to the north, if not beyond.[1]

To illustrate the common cultural ground shared by academic lawyers, theologians, and townspeople, fundamental changes in the realm of judicial procedure may serve as a case in point. Following their protracted prevalence in the legal affairs of early medieval laity and churchmen, communal modes of proof measuring a defendant's ability to mobilize local solidarity groups in formal rituals like the ordeal started to lose their former credibility and faded with particularly alarming speed in regions of strong urban growth. After 1100 and within a matter of generations, one city council after another adopted regulations to exempt inhabitants from the now unwelcome practice of hot iron and water tests, in line with canonists who increasingly denounced them as superstitious nonsense and unwarranted temptations of God. Clerical rejection eventually culminated in the general prohibition of priestly participation decreed by the Fourth Lateran Council of 1215.[2] With older methods of verification becoming obsolete and uncanonical, clergy and citizens found a welcome substitute in techniques of evidence gathering that allowed judges to determine single-handedly whether wrong had been committed as alleged. Germanic ordeals had given procedural and protective advantage to people who stayed close to their home base, surrounded by friends and family, and to individuals of local esteem and status who easily accepted the burden of liability by sharing compensatory wergeld payments for, say, an adversary's miscarriage with a large household or allied peers and dependents. To those who, on the other hand, assembled in ever more substantial numbers at trading posts and in walled settlements next to important navigable rivers and roads, mobility was paramount and required safe passage over long distances. True justice for traders and their urban business partners implied that the power of insiders in deciding the outcome of legal conflict had to be curtailed in favor of investigations that examined incriminating behavior regardless of a suspect's origins and treated persons from afar no differently than respected neighbors or relatives living nearby. Scholastic jurisprudence responded to the demands of free trade and travel by converting assessments of penal responsibility from ritualized manifestations of loyalty into reconstructions of fact.

---

1. The classic account of the economic turnaround in the West is by Robert Lopez, *The Commercial Revolution of the Middle Ages, 950–1350* (Englewood Cliffs, NJ: Prentice-Hall, 1971).

2. Lateran IV, can. 18 (Tanner 1:244). Cf. Bartlett, *Trial by Fire and Water*, 77–92; and, for urban agency in the rejection of ordalia, Raoul van Caeneghem, "Reflexions on Rational and Irrational Modes of Proof in Medieval Europe," *TRG* 58 (1990): 263–279.

Apart from adjustments in terms of scale, it seems appropriate to compare the mission of Gratian, his scholastic successors, and their clientele with that of modern Western jurists and political groupings eager to promote a single global agenda in favor of human rights and due process against multiple normative arrangements sustained by local elites and customary decision making. In either case, the imposition of abstract and uniform written rules facilitates above all the unimpeded exchange of goods and free movement of strangers otherwise vulnerable to exploitation by people embedded in networks of neighborly self-help. In both scenarios, the success of Western jurisprudence depends ultimately on the degree to which legal doctrine garners support from leaders capable of endowing downward techniques of judicial sentencing with coercive strength and powers of implementation. With the advancement of criminal laws being tied to the presence of agencies effectively centralizing governmental functions, economies particularly conducive to trade and commerce, and literate cultures promoting submission to impersonal principles of conduct, it is unsurprising to find that the earliest records attesting to actual application in court of the scholastic equation between homicide and abortion originated from places and authorities renowned for their exceptional administrative reach and timely hierarchical consolidation. Prenatal manslaughter soon appeared in a variety of cases brought before the ecclesiastical tribunals. Among lay jurisdictions, on the other hand, felonious accusations centering on fetal death first incurred punishment from the hands of royal justices in England, where they remained, throughout the 1200s, a frequently documented charge.

Crimen in Sacramental Confession

From antiquity, canonical authorities had regarded the willful ending of prenatal life as a serious offense and threatened perpetrators with permanent exclusion from the sacred rites and with eternal damnation. According to canones that circulated centuries before Gratian, a sinner's reconciliation would depend on his readiness to perform penance as imposed by the ecclesiastical hierarchy. The exercise of priestly functions and access to related income for persons found guilty of homicidal miscarriage was deemed impossible except, perhaps, by way of apostolic dispensation. When, as a result, canonists and theologians active during the formative period of their disciplines, between 1140 and 1234, began to assemble and interpret relevant norms from the preceding millennium, they did not have to invent new rules as much as they had to forge older regulations for the first time into a coherent construct. In their quest for doctrinal consistency, they created a distinct format of secret sacramental penance that is the direct ancestor of the penitential order for Catholic Christians today. In 1215 a famous decree of the Fourth Lateran Council obliged every baptized believer to confess sinful acts at least once a year to his ordinary parish priest. The conciliar pronouncement followed intense elaboration of confessional theory by early scholastic teachers, who in dissecting the canonical tradition had come to define central aspects of spiritual redress with a mentality that reflected radically novel, twelfth-century ideas about individual intent as the principal measurement of accountability.[3]

Sin, theologians and canon lawyers had agreed, resided exclusively in the sinner's disregard for divine and mandatory precepts. For the discerning priest who listened to the secret revelations of his parishioners, the main challenge lay in the proper ascertainment of external clues for one's internal resolve to commit wrong, as well as in the detection, during confession, of deep sorrow (*contritio*) and sincere inner disposition to repent. Priestly evaluation, proponents of penitential doctrine had further concluded, would greatly depend on subtle psychological insight into endless gradations of liability, to the effect that confessors were encouraged to use free discretion in their assignment of penitential duties, contrary to the earlier medieval reliance on fixed tariffs, listed in mechanical juxtaposition with individual and itemized failings. Again in recognition of the fact that prescholastic interest in quantified compensation—for instance, fasting for a specific length of time—was to be considered less essential to the process of purification than the penitent's heartfelt desire to find relief, learned consensus abandoned assumptions according to which final absolution needed to be postponed until fasts and other exercises of self-mortification and humiliation had been completed. Henceforth, sacramental cleansing conferred through the words "I absolve you" was to be granted before works of satisfaction, or penance, had been carried out.[4]

Meandering distinctions from the pen of Petrus Cantor, a celebrated Parisian master of theology who died in 1197, convey a sense of the difficulties

---

3. Lateran IV, can. 21 (Tanner 1.245); as to scholastic discussions leading up to the decree of 1215, see the literature cited by Joseph Goering, "The Internal Forum and the Literature of Penance and Confession," *Traditio* 59 (2004): 181–186.

4. The precise origins of this reversal have not been identified, although the reordering of *absolutio* and *satisfactio* corresponded to concerns that were key to the scholastic analysis of liablity; see Peter Biller, "Confession in the Middle Ages: Introduction," in Biller and Minnis, *Handling Sin*, 3–33; and the bibliographical references in chap. 1, notes 22, 29. On the beginnings of the legal and theological distinction between sin and crime, Kéry, *Gottesfurcht und irdische Strafe*; Johannes Gründel, *Die Lehre von den Umständen der menschlichen Handlung im Mittelalter* (Münster: Aschendorff, 1963).

that the new penitential standards of early scholasticism posed for priestly practitioners. In his voluminous manual of confessional casuistry (*Liber casuum conscientiae*) written toward the close of the twelfth century, Petrus dwelled at great length on incidents of homicide, not failing to address the specific problem of how to assign culpability to various occurrences of sinful abortion. In passing, the author of the *Liber* reminded academic audiences of the crucial distinction between formed and human versus unformed and nonhuman life in the uterus, which scholastic teachers such as Gratian, by citing the biblical version of the *Septuagint* (Exodus 21:22–23), had attributed directly to Moses and his Ten Commandments. In addition, the *Liber casuum* puts forth a string of circumstances that from a confessor's perspective made certain cases of prenatal death appear more serious than other ones:

> It is often said that a bad superior kills by his bad example. If, however, two people are said to be equally bad while one of them somehow through his example kills more people than the other, many consider them equally guilty of homicide.
>
> Contrary to this it seems that Moses assigns harsher punishment to the person who eliminates [*excutit*] a formed and alive fetus than to someone who eliminates while [the fetus] is still unformed, whereas, according to the above scenario, it is clear that each of the two sinned to the same extent because they both did the same, regardless of whether the fetus had been formed or not, and also because they neither knew nor could have known easily whether the fetus had been formed or not.
>
> But perhaps Moses presumed that there had been greater contempt in the person who eliminated the formed fetus and therefore assigned harsher punishment out of this presumption or due to the greater horror. Because, indeed, if someone knew that the fetus was already alive, he would not beat a pregnant woman as readily.
>
> Although, if one abstained from the beating because he knew the fetus to be alive and the other did not abstain, the latter would sin more.[5]

Petrus Cantor may have been an exciting lecturer. In considering his remarks on the manifold complexities awaiting priests who wished to assign suitable penance to killers of fetuses, it is important to note that, as rather halting

---

5. Petrus Cantor, *Summa de sacramentis et animae consiliis*, vol. 3, *Liber casuum conscientiae* 369, ed. Jean-Albert Dugauquier, Analecta mediaevalia Namurcensia 21 (Louvain: Nauwelaerts, 1967), 561–562.

reflections, they attest to a historic moment in time when elements of confessional conduct were still in the process of conceptual and practical refinement. In order to establish the main criteria of sinful intent, Petrus insisted over and over again that confessors not only had to evaluate why presumably sinful actions such as violent miscarriage occurred but also had to ponder the tangible effects. He and his fellow theologians viewed circumstances and outcomes as decisive indicators of spiritually deviant behavior. Comparable to visible branches growing from an invisible root, they helped pinpoint motivations that otherwise remained hidden in the recesses of a sinner's soul.

Attempts undertaken by Peter the Chanter and his circle to establish, around 1200, an academic subfield of theology primarily devoted to pastoral concerns produced, in the short run, several instructive guidebooks for confessors, among which Thomas of Cobham's *Summa* (1216) achieved wider circulation and longer-lasting acclaim than the Summae of his Parisian colleagues, Robert of Flamesborough (pub. 1208–1213) and Peter of Poitiers (pub. 1215).[6] By concentrating on a casuistic approach and offering questions rather than answers so as to encourage discretionary thinking about nearly intractable episodes of sinning, the authors promoted a form of confessional discourse that ultimately did not prevail against juristic treatments originating from the schools of canon law at Bologna. The strong dependency of theologians in Paris and elsewhere on imported models of canonistic orientation had already become apparent when Peter Lombard, compiler of the principal scholastic textbook for theological studies, the *Summa sententiarum* (1160), copied his treatment of the sacraments in large part from the Decretum, including Gratian's passages on the question of abortion (C. 32, q. 2, d.p.c. 7–10).[7] In the same vein, modern scholarship investigating the penitential Summae is unanimous in its conclusion that from the 1230s at the latest, confessional doctrine started to grow rigid, repetitive, and highly legalistic in outlook, displaying a conformity of teachings and terminology that persisted until the age of the Catholic Reformation in the second half of the sixteenth century. An instrumental role in this process of theoretical consolidation has been attributed to the handbook of penance written, shortly after 1220, by

---

6. See the fundamental study of James W. Baldwin, *Masters, Princes, and Merchants: The Social Views of Peter the Chanter and His Circle* (Princeton, NJ: Princeton University Press, 1970); more recent literature on the subject in Goering, "Internal Forum," 188–191.

7. *Sententiae* 4.31.4, ed. *Magistri Petri Lombardi Parisiensis episcopi sententiae in quatuor libris distinctae* (Grottaferrata, It.: Collegium Sancti Bonaventurae ad Claras Aquas, 1981), 445–446; author and textbook are presented by Giulio Silano in the introduction to his translation of Peter Lombard, *The Sentences*, vol. 1 (Toronto, ON: University of Toronto Press, 2007), vii–xxx.

the famous Bolognese canonist and papal confessor Raymond of Penyafort. As is commonly known, Raymond later assembled the *Decretales Gregorii IX* (1234), which, in tandem with the Decretum, served as one of the fundamental normative authorities for medieval canon lawyers. By revising and updating his *Summa de penitentia* in 1236, Raymond was able to supply a set of compatible guides for both judicial church tribunals and the court of conscience.[8]

Raymond's confessional work represented a veritable watershed and impacted future literary treatments of sinful behavior in decisive ways. Experts in the administration of penance across Latin Christendom considered his teachings particularly important. Their attitude is manifest, above all, in the appearance of an Ordinary Gloss by William of Rennes (about 1241), a feature normally reserved to foundational works of academic lecturing such as Gratian's, Justinian's *Corpus*, Peter Lombard's *Sentences*, or Raymond's own collection of *Decretales*. Certainly, no other scholastic work on confession could boast a standard marginal commentary. Likewise illustrating the exceptional role of the *Summa de penitentia* in advancing an internally coherent model of penance throughout the West, the section Raymond devoted to the subject of abortion proved highly popular with subsequent writers on confession. Late medieval readers of Raymond's handbook received the following advice on the matter, accompanied by William's gloss, which is shown below in italics:

What about someone who beats a pregnant woman or poisons her? And what if she takes the poison in order to abort or not to conceive? Would someone like that not be considered irregular and a homicide?

My answer is: if the fetus was already formed and animated, he is truly a homicide if the woman suffered a miscarriage through the beating* or through the potion, because he killed a human being.

If he killed, however, [a fetus] not yet animated, he shall not be called a homicide insofar as irregularity is concerned, but he shall rather be considered a "quasi-homicide" [*ut homicida*] with regard to penance. And the same applies to someone who gives or takes poison or the like to avoid generation or conception.

---

8. *Summa de penitentia*, ed. Xavier Ochoa and Aloysio Diaz (Rome: Insitutum iuridicum Claretianum, 1976); cf. Stephan Kuttner, "Raymond of Peñafort as an Editor," *BMCL* 12 (1982): 65–80, reprinted in Kuttner, *Studies in the History*, no. 12; Erik A. Reno III, "The Authoritative Text: Raymond of Penyafort's Editing of the Decretals of Gregory IX" (PhD diss., Columbia University, 2011).

*What if there is doubt whether or not a death or a miscarriage has been caused through the beating, or whether [the killed being] was animated or not? I respond: If he who beat has doubts or believes so with probability, he must abstain from [altar] service and promotion lest he risk [salvation] while he remains in this belief. If, however, his doubt is minor and approximate, he may disregard it if he can and administer and receive promotion.[9]

The clarification offered by Raymond and his annotator greatly inspired successive penitential authors, who copied or adapted what they found in textual variations revealing a bewildering scope of didactic purposes. Although modern research has barely charted the proliferation of works produced in the wake of the *Summa de penitentia*, investigators have tried to categorize the multiplicity of formats late medieval *confessionalia* used to target specific audiences. Large and encyclopedic Summae, for example, provided tools for centers of clerical instruction, whether knowledge was transmitted to aspiring "ordinary" parish priests in cathedral schools or in *studia* of the mendicant orders, founded from the 1220s onward to train itinerant Franciscans and Dominicans in their prospective capacity as "extraordinary" confessors. Meanwhile, handbooks of minor or pocket size, often translated into the vernacular languages, carried confessional guidelines to remote rural churches and into the homes of the laity, informing almost everyone, it seems, about elementary definitions of spiritual wrongs like abortion.[10] Over time, the average believer must have encountered in annual, or at least occasional, rites of sacramental confession Raymond's reminder that, for church authorities, the procurement of fetal death entailed two different outcomes. If the unborn had been human in form and hence animated or alive, its killing was an actual homicide. Alternatively, the killing of an unformed fetus constituted "virtual homicide" and merely called for correction as a sin. Instructors also produced manuals with questionnaires for more detailed interrogation. Churchmen were encouraged to use them proactively, popularizing the concept of divine condemnation even among Christians who had never lent their hands to an abortion or ever thought of doing so.

---

9. Ochoa and Diaz, *Summa de penitentia* 2.1 (*De homicidio*), 448; the original Latin comment by William of Rennes (on 2.1.6, s.v. *ex illa percussione*) is printed in *Summa sancti Raymundi de Penyafort* (Rome: Tallini, 1603; repr., Farnborough, UK: Gregg, 1967), 153a.

10. Leonard Boyle, "Summae Confessorum," in *Les genres littéraires dans les sommes théologiques et philosophiques médiévales* (Louvain: Institut d'études médiévales, 1982), 271–80; Michelle Mulchahey, *First the Bow Is Bent in Study: Dominican Education before 1350* (Toronto, ON: University of Toronto Press, 1998), 527–552.

Raymond of Penyafort embraced common opinion among canonists by stating that the line of separation between the killing of an unformed and that of a formed fetus coincided with the boundary between infractions pertaining to the disciplinary sphere of church jurisdiction and those requiring only penitential satisfaction. To terminate the life of an unborn child still lacking human shape would demand penitentia by way of fasts, pilgrimages, or other exercises of discretionary duration and rigor. Ending the existence of a fetus with the physical contours of a being already in possession of an immortal soul implied in addition that perpetrators had to endure the administrative consequences of manslaughter, with the ordinary canonical pena amounting to irregularity (irregularitas) and permanent exclusion from priestly rights and duties. Raymond further referred to the related sin of contraception, which prevented, as did lesser abortion, natural growth into an "animated" and "alive" person. The remarks of the *Summa* were complemented by William of Rennes, whose glossa resolved with juristic pragmatism a problem that had caused theologians like Peter the Chanter and his circle to indulge in prolonged and speculative ruminations. Shunning all psychological subtlety, William limited the obligation of penitents to assume responsibility for an abortion. Whenever the evidence was insufficient to establish guilt "with probability," the glossator believed that the whole matter could be left to the sinner's own determination. The gloss employed the Latin term *probabiliter*, which the legally educated among William's readers would have recognized as a reference to proof hard enough to hold up in openly prosecuted cases.[11]

Judicial Crimen in the Ecclesiastical Courts

In the context of secret confession, late medieval canonists and theologians did not deal with issues that could be construed into something other than crimina of the mind. The constant broadcasting of penance in theory and practice contributed nevertheless decisively to the process of criminalization. By 1250, confessors everywhere in the West probed into the consciences of their Christian flock, reminding them with identical words and uniform admonitions of God's commandment not to impede procreation in order to avoid eternal punishment in the afterlife and, possibly, retribution from the hands of church ministers. When it came to prosecuting the canonical

---

11. Richard Fraher, "Conviction According to Conscience: The Medieval Jurists' Debate Concerning Judicial Discretion and the Law of Proof," *Law and History* 7 (1989): 23–88; Kenneth Pennington, "Torture in the Ius Commune," in *Mélanges en l'honneur d'Anne Lefebvre-Teillard*, ed. Bernard d'Alteroche et al. (Paris: Presses universitaires, 2009), 818–830.

offense publicly, moreover, clerics and clerical institutions were again quick to proceed from rhetoric to action. The papal registers, beginning with the pontificate of Innocent III in 1198, are the oldest continuous and still extant record of the sacerdotal hierarchy. Students today do not have to go through many of the chronologically arranged volumes to encounter a judicial case that concentrated on the forcible death of a fetus. A decretal of 1211, soon inserted into collections for use at the canon law schools, contains Innocent's reply to the legal query of an unidentified abbot. "As we have read in your letter," the pope wrote,

> a priest from your order who had been a black monk once play-fully grabbed a pregnant woman by her belt; the same priest had an improper relationship with the woman, who also claimed that he was the father of the child in her womb and that, hurt by his playful behav-ior, she had suffered a miscarriage.
>
> Now the priest, following the advice of respectable men, believes that he must cease to say mass.
>
> After due consultation with our advisers, we as the pope tell you that the priest is entitled to administer if the aborted fetus was not alive; otherwise, the priest will have to abstain from celebrating the holy office.[12]

Church lawyers who placed the papal pronouncement in the framework of canonistic jurisprudence seem to have welcomed the text especially because it helped them settle a long-standing dispute concerning the applicabil-ity of *irregularitas*. Was the suspension from priestly duties dependent on whether the killed unborn had been alive and formed? Eminent teachers including Huguccio and Laurentius Hispanus had given a negative response and extended the disciplinary measure to include abortion committed prior to animation. After Innocent's authoritative intervention, support for their opinion quickly waned.

Most perplexing from a modern perspective is the incriminating scenario depicted by Innocent, which fails to correspond to what Westerners now accept as prototypical instances of abortion. By current standards, a priest who casually drags his pregnant girlfriend by her belt, causing a miscarriage, would at best qualify as someone faced with charges of negligence. In the narrative of 1211, however, excuses of neglect are nowhere to be found.

---

12. *Sicut ex litterarum* (Reg. 14.107; X 5.12.20); cf. chap. 1, notes 16–19. The original and the definitive textbook versions of 1216 and 1234 included Innocent's letter under the rubric "On Voluntary Homicide" (4 Comp. 5.6 and X 5.12).

Should the unborn victim turn out to be human in shape, irregularity is said to apply automatically, regardless of the presence or absence of volition to kill. In addition, it seems incompatible with present notions that Bolognese canonists of the early 1200s put the pope's intervention on behalf of the former black monk under the label of "voluntary homicide" (*De homicidio voluntario*) in textbook collections. Clearly, canonistic reasoning during the period rested on premises that are not immediately comprehensible eight hundred years later. What canon lawyers at the time focused on when they discussed ordinary incidents of manslaughter brought to the attention of ecclesiastical judges was not so much the act of killing itself but rather the problem of how such occurrences affected the sacramental dignity and integrity of the priesthood.

Church law made permission to receive ordination and join sacerdotal ranks dependent on multiple moral and spiritual criteria. Convicted murderers were automatically considered ineligible or, in technical terms, irregular. Canonical precepts also established that inadmissibility to the holy orders did not have to rest on punishable behavior. Access was equally denied to the criminal judges of the laity, for example, or to notaries supplying written documentation in a capital case, as both assumed a role in the shedding of human blood whenever they assisted in a lawful execution. Because of their sex, women figured among the *irregulares* as well, and many children fell under the condition because of illegitimate birth, with canonistic opinion being keenly aware that their exclusion was valid despite the state of innocence assigned to them by divine and human justice. Irregularitas, in other words, was not punishment. It only provided a rationale for assessing which candidate or incumbent was canonically fit to celebrate mass and the sacraments and who, by extension, would be entitled to reap the material rewards of priestly endowments, or benefices (*beneficia*).

There was yet another reason for Innocent's indifference toward excuses based on negligence. In agreement with the canonists who placed the letter of 1211 under the rubric of voluntary homicide, the pope's response reflected general scholastic understanding as it tied the institution of canonical irregularity to deeper and more stringent theological concerns about divine judgment and eternal salvation. Suspension from, or denial of admission to, the office of priest was rigorously enforced against those who had tainted themselves with actual, as opposed to attempted, homicidium. When ordained or future clergy had been sentenced and decided to pursue their rehabilitation through dispensation, they first had to show that allegations against them were completely unfounded. In what renders the interpretation of the source material especially difficult, late medieval assessments of canonical culpability adopted standards that seem exceedingly harsh to our present-day minds. Innocent's lack of interest in varying degrees of criminal guilt would fall squarely within the scope of ecclesiastical routine over the course of the next three centuries. We can cite at random a number of letters reaching the Apostolic Court of Penance (Sacra Penitentiaria Apostolica) and requesting a *dispensatio*, or declaration of innocence, in relation to charges of abortion. What, for instance, caused an unnamed churchman in the lower orders around 1350 to come forward and depict events leading up to a violent miscarriage in the following fashion? The anonymous petitioner had spent a night with his pregnant lover when suddenly they both heard her husband knock at the bedroom door. Frightened, the cleric helped the woman escape by lowering her to the ground through an open window. Upon returning home, she received a beating (*percussio*) from her enraged spouse and delivered a dead child shortly thereafter. Was the awkwardness of her improvised flight to be blamed for the fetal death, or had the husband provoked the fatal outcome? The supplicant concluded his text with the plea that the pope grant him the desired canonical remedy.[13]

Or what are we to make of the parson Mathias Jacobi of Godkow, from the diocese of Cracow, whose *supplicatio* informed apostolic officials in 1461 that he had once ordered his servant Helena to fix his bed? Because Helena had refused to do so, the priest had pulled her by the sleeves until his grip, forced by Helena's adamant resistance, inadvertently loosened and released her to fall backward against a wooden vessel. The next morning, the maid felt ill and soon miscarried, to the great surprise of Mathias, who believed her to be a virgin. Why, under the circumstances, was he compelled to seek the assistance of the Sacra Penitentiaria in order to overcome accusations of homicidal death and be permitted to continue in the exercise of his sacred duties? And again, why did Matheus Michaelis, a deacon from the nearby diocese of Poznan, have to obtain apostolic confirmation of his integrity as an ordained minister in 1450? In his presentation of the facts, Matheus admitted that he had been playful with a young woman, imitating to an extent the behavior of the former black monk reported to Innocent III in 1211. As Matheus told the story, though, he and the woman had not been lovers. Rather, she was his sister, whose pregnancy he had not been able to notice at the time. Additionally, their wrestling match had occurred in the presence of her husband, who incidentally kicked his wife with one foot just as Matheus pushed her down

---

13. The text has been edited by Paul Lecacheux, "Une formulaire de la Pénitencerie Apostolique au temps du Cardinal Albornoz (1357–1358)," *Mélanges d'archéologie et d'histoire* 18 (1898): 42.

to the floor. Matheus, in sum, could plead ignorance of his sibling's physical condition; he was unsure of whether he or his brother-in-law had triggered the subsequent miscarriage, and he had not acted maliciously. Still, church law pressed him to appease fears that he might have incurred the stain of priestly inability. He appealed for judicial aid to the highest ecclesiastical court in Western Christendom, empowered to issue declarations of canonical conformity and *dispensationes* from impediments of irregularity.[14]

For an adequate interpretation of irregular status, it is important to note that the modern procedural principle known as presumption of innocence, *in dubio pro reo*, did not apply. As Stephan Kuttner pointed out long ago, medieval jurists established two different standards of accountability, with lines of demarcation being drawn between the court of penance on the one hand and punitive church jurisdiction on the other. The distinction was due to the divergent goals of the two fora. When criminal suspects faced judicial sentencing, proof of guilt had to be clearer than daylight. Something like the presumption of innocence was certainly in place. The situation differed in the sphere of confession, which was informed by ideas of God's ultimate justice, capable of pursuing traces of guilt into the remotest corners of a sinner's heart. Killers who had successfully eluded the exacting tests of legal responsibility would nevertheless be held liable at Christ's return on Judgment Day. To cure the ills of sin while there was still time, confessors had to scrutinize their penitents like doctors sensing a serious but hidden ailment. Absolution was not to be imparted generously. A telling illustration of this pastoral attitude can be seen in the rigorous conception of guilt referred to by canonists as *in re illicita*, which penitents incurred when acting "under illicit conditions." Confessional judges would weigh in accumulative manner every consequence flowing from illicit behavior. Committing adultery, for instance, constituted a grave sin in its own right. If it preceded spousal drama and led, however unrelated, to violent miscarriage, the incident would automatically be charged to the adulterer's account. Likewise, priests were not supposed to indulge in gratuitous physical contact with women, either inside or outside their homes. If they did so in defiance of canonical norms, any homicidal abortion, provoked wittingly or unwittingly, would instantly burden their conscience with manslaughter.[15]

---

14. Transcriptions of the two requests are available in *Bullarium Poloniae* 6:81 (no. 333, 10 September 1461), cf. *RPG* 4:47–48 (no. 1803); *Bullarium Poloniae* 5:355 (no. 1656, 16 January 1450), cf. *RPG* 2:261. For literature concerning the pardoning powers of the Papal Penitentiary see below, note 19.

15. Kuttner, *Kanonistische Schuldlehre*, 61–68; Kéry, *Gottesfurcht und irdische Strafe*, 114–122; additional cases implying maximum fault in re illicita are mentioned by Wolfgang P. Müller, "Violence

The above-cited declaratory letters and Innocent's remarks of 1211 do not refer to confessional proceedings, although each appeals to the stricter standards of responsibility spiritual courts applied for the sake of a sinner's soul. The pope's primary concern was, after all, not whether an individual had actually committed homicide but whether someone would meet priestly qualifications. Determination depended on the candidate's eligibility for office, the lack of which canonists called irregularitas. God's ordained ministers on earth needed to be selected in accordance with the most stringent criteria, thought to coincide among other things with the rigorous notions of culpability applying in the penitential realm. Only those eventually entering heaven were seen as truly pure. Admission to the sacred orders (ordines maiores), ranging from subdeacon and deacon to priest and bishop, had to be governed by comparable measures of impeccability. As a result, late medieval judicial sources informing us about clerics accused of miscarriage or abortion are steeped in language designed to fend off suspicions of guilt incurred in re illicita. Eventually, this rhetoric affected juristic excuses far beyond the orbit of ecclesiastical justice.[16]

The origins of abortion as a crime can be located from an intellectual standpoint in the twelfth-century schools of scholastic jurisprudence at Bologna, culturally among the literate members of the clergy, economically in areas of the most intense urban and mercantile development, politically in advanced efforts to centralize government, and institutionally within the jurisdiction of the Latin church. Still, the search for early instances of judicial implementation in line with current notions has thus far been frustrated. Ecclesiastical court records from the early 1200s attest to the crimen of fetal homicide in private penitential and public prosecutorial contexts. However, the actual cases they report of irregular homicidal priests do not warrant modern qualification as criminal offenses, given that their most dreaded outcome—the loss of priestly office and income—is now understood in terms of professional ineligibility rather than punishment. With regard to the penitential exercises of fasting, pilgrimage, and prayer imposed on late medieval sinners who admitted to abortion in the context of confession, moreover, there is again no compelling reason to speak of sanctions that resemble punitive measures today. One feature in particular renders the distinctive character of the sacramental

---

et droit canonique. Les enseignements de la Pénitencerie Apostolique (XIIIe–XVIe siècle)," *Revue historique* 131 (2007): 773n12.

16. It is unclear to what extent pardons for homicide issued by the French and English crowns derived from the exculpatory language of the canonists; cf. Müller, "Violence et droit canon," 793n37; Helen Lacey, *The Royal Pardon: Access to Mercy in Fourteenth-Century England* (Woodbridge, NY: York Medieval Studies, 2009), 26–43, 59–73.

rite evident. Penitential works enjoined by a confessor were part of formalities pertaining to the sphere of voluntary justice. It was left to the penitent to decide whether he wished to reveal his transgressions to a priest, express sorrow for them, and accept the burden of satisfaction.

Public Penitential Crimen

The survey of ecclesiastical procedures investigating the crimen of prenatal homicide remains incomplete without mention of yet another judicial instrument at the disposal of late medieval clerical authorities. Legal historians have noticed that scholastic jurisprudence provided four distinct formats for the initiation of "ordinary" church proceedings. Cases could be brought either by way of sacramental confession (*via confessionis*), private accusation (*via accusationis*), public inquest (*via inquisitionis*), or finally, in response to anonymous denunciations (*via denuntiationis*).[17] There are reasons why penitential denuntiationes have barely been examined by modern scholarship. Trials starting with a sinner's confession, with an aggrieved accuser, or through intervention by state officials have survived as part of the Western legal experience. They have attracted the interest of experts trained in schools of law and theology, who characteristically trace to their historical roots modes of adjudication that continue to be practiced today. By contrast, late medieval penitential denuntiationes have neither an equivalent nor a derivative in current justice systems and present an institution that faded into obscurity long ago. The obsolescence of the suits is further accentuated by two facts: first, that denuntiationes, according to canonical theory, did not necessarily have to be recorded in writing, and second, that their general purpose defies easy classification in now-familiar juristic and canonistic terms. On the one hand, the procedure in question belonged to the spiritual sphere in that it combated wrong with penitential injunctions; on the other, the most typical method of gathering proof, based on (collective) purgatory oaths, turned inquiries into a highly visible, communal undertaking.[18]

---

17. The triple distinction of public court prosecutions (as opposed to penitential confessiones) was famously expressed by canon 8 (Tanner 1:237–239) of the Fourth Lateran Council (1215), later incorporated into X 5.1.24; cf. Richard Fraher, "IV Lateran's Revolution in Criminal Procedure: The Birth of Inquisitions, the End of Ordeals and Innocent III's Vision of Ecclesiastical Politics," in *Studia in honorem eminentissimi cardinalis Alphonsi M. Stickler*, ed. Rosalio I. Card. Castillo Lara (Vatican City: LAS, 1992), 91–111; Markus Hirte, *Papst Innozenz III., das IV. Laterankonzil und die Strafverfahren gegen Kleriker. Eine registergestützte Untersuchung zur Entwicklung der Verfahrensarten zwischen 1198 und 1215* (Tübingen: Diskord, 2005).

18. Most documented penitential denuntiationes currently known to historians are of English origin; cf. Richard H. Helmholz, "Crime, Compurgation and the Courts of the Medieval Church,"

Dispensations and declaratory letters from the Sacra Penitentiaria confirming the absence or removal of irregularity attest to looming denuntiationes as an important reason for clerical candidates and men in holy orders to come forward and seek apostolic clearance. Apart from occasional petitions said to have been motivated by personal scruples of conscience and the desire to exercise priestly functions while remaining "on the safer side of salvation" (*ad maiorem cautelam salvationis*), the majority of supplications recording incidents of abortion employ a second explanatory formula stating that "out of envy toward the petitioner it is asserted by some that he is guilty of homicide in ways rendering him permanently unfit for the sacred ministry and altar service."[19] The envious instigators of incriminating rumors were frequently unknown. Regardless, they entailed for the denounced an acute risk of being officially branded as infamous. Canonical procedures provided a remedy for the debilitating effects of a tarnished reputation in trials to be opened via denuntiationis. Their sole prerequisite was evidence, confirmed by respectable members of the community, that defamatory gossip concerning a criminal act like homicide or abortion was circulating to the detriment of a named individual. The existence of anonymous denuntiationes could be formally ascertained by neighbors, local prelates, or the discredited person himself, all of whom were entitled to initiate proceedings in the church courts. The purpose of intervention was spiritual in nature because the soul of a suspect needed to be redeemed or because the potentially divisive impact of slanderous speech on peaceful relations within the parish had to be kept from infecting everybody.

The outcome of denunciatory suits depended, for example, on whether the defamed was prepared to acknowledge his guilt in confession. Those sorrowfully admitting to fault swore never to repeat their error (*abjuratio*) and received sacramental absolution as well as a salutary penance from church officials who also enjoined silence on future detractors under pain of excommunication. The community was purged from the poisonous rumors of *mala fama*. If instead the imputed wrongdoer refused to confess, courts often demanded that he clear himself by swearing an oath of innocence along with

---

Law and History Review 1 (1983): 1–26, reprinted in Helmholz, *Canon Law and the Law of England*, 119–144; Lawrence R. Poos, *Lower Ecclesiastical Jurisdiction in Late Medieval England* (Oxford: Oxford University Press, 2001), 43–55; records of the archpresbyterate Wetzlar in central Germany for the years 1459–1520 offer a rare parallel from the European mainland, see chap. 9, note 6.

19. The two phrases are recurrent in petitions for *literae declaratoriae*, cf. *RPG*, vols. 1–6, index, s.v. *emulus* and *cautela*. Introductory information on the operations of the *Sacra Penitentiaria Apostolica* can be found in Kirsi Salonen and Ludwig Schmugge, *A Sip from the Well of Grace: Medieval Texts from the Apostolic Penitentiary* (Washington, DC: Catholic University of America Press, 2009), 13–83.

a specified number of oath helpers. Because the peculiar nature of the cases has not been recognized sufficiently, modern research has been slow to examine court records containing information about how this judicial mechanism was actually implemented. All too rarely, scholars have investigated judicial initiatives against detracting voices that threatened to strike aspirant or ordained clergy with the impediment of irregularity. Scattered among the anecdotal evidence available in print, there is one mention in 1347 of a cleric, Gerard Halegrin de Chasseny, denounced for murder and two violent miscarriages. In the end, Gerard was found not guilty by the episcopal court at Soissons after having successfully countered the charge with the aid of two co-jurors.[20]

Especially important for present purposes, denunciatory suits also affected the laity. In a series of articles, the American legal historian R. H. Helmholz has explored fifteenth-century registers of English diocesan tribunals and found that they often contain notices concerning the fate of ordinary Christians exposed to anonymous imputations of wrongdoing. Among his references, Helmholz has cited several cases in which individuals, denounced on account of miscarriages caused by percussiones, potions, or other means, appeared before their ordinary spiritual judges, whose intervention consisted of imposing compurgation in attempts to restore the defendants' good names. In two instances from London and Rochester recorded during the early 1490s, final clearance required an oath "by six hands" (*a sexta manu*), that is, swearing by the defamed and five additional compurgators. In similar mentions of proceedings at Canterbury in 1416, 1469, and 1471, as well as one occurrence from London in 1487, there is no information about procedural outcomes. To appreciate what would have happened to suspects who failed the test of collective oath taking or simply confirmed the veracity of mala fama, it is necessary to rely on the story of Joan Rose. In 1470, the young woman from the diocese of Canterbury ruefully confessed to having killed her newborn child. Given that canon law from Gratian onward placed the violent death of an animated fetus on a par with infanticide and homicide, the penance imposed on Joan and described below must have differed little from the way contemporary ecclesiastical courts would have treated those convicted of hearsay abortion charges:

---

20. Paris, AN, JJ 76, no. 95; cf. *Registres du Trésor des chartes. Inventaire analytique* 3.3, ed. Aline Vallée (Paris, Archives Nationales, 1984), 16 (no. 6241, August 1347). Firenze, AS Diplomatico. Atti del vescovo di Pistoia, vols. 1–4 (from 1287 to 1301), contains numerous depositions by witnesses relating to the fama of priests and priestly candidates; my thanks to Dr. Giuseppe Biscioni (Florence, State Archives) for help in identifying the material.

The judge ordered her to walk, dressed only in a long shirt, . . . in procession through her parochial church of Hyth on three Sundays, carrying a half-pound wax candle in her right hand and the knife, with which she killed the little boy, or a similar one, in her left; and to circle in similar fashion the market place at Canterbury twice; and again twice the market at Feversham and twice the market of Ashford.[21]

Laypersons found to be public sinners were oftentimes compelled to face shaming rituals in the presence of gleeful onlookers. The Middle Ages witnessed many instances of openly performed penance, but the display of penitentia in connection with denuntiationes attested to an especially symmetrical relationship between judicial cause and effect. Procedural logic required ill repute to be removed through mobilization of sworn testimony by people of good reputation, or, alternatively, by way of unrestrained abandonment to the voices of contempt, albeit for a limited time only. When abjuration and exercises of atonement had been completed, slander was to cease and penitents regained their lost standing by way of ceremonial readmission to the church, with pastors admonishing everyone to honor the restoration of harmony and respect.

The known examples of English denunciatory proceedings date without exception to the 1400s and thereafter. On the other side of the Channel, information about laity investigated by church officials for mala fama remains very scarce, as case material and the procedure itself have received little scrutiny on the part of modern scholarship. It is obvious, however, that the trial format was deeply rooted in early medieval court practices, which subsequent scholastic jurisprudence merely systematized and fitted into twelfth-century canonistic doctrine. As mentioned earlier, Innocent III became the first pope to subsume the results of learned effort under the label of proceedings launched via denuntiationis. The expression stood for a type of prosecution that straddled the judicial divide between the secret forum of voluntary penance and public tribunals enforcing punishment, in that it combined full visibility with penitential retribution and spiritual atonement with mandatory sentencing (see figure 1).[22]

---

21. Translated from the Latin version in Helmholz, "Infanticide in the Province of Canterbury," 383n30, reprinted in Helmholz, *Canon Law and the Law of England*, 163n30; also ibid., 380n10–13, 159n10–13, for the other references cited in this paragraph.

22. Wolfgang P. Müller, "The Internal Forum of the Later Middle Ages: A Modern Myth?," *Law and History Review* 33 (2015): 887–913, discusses penitential denuntiationes in greater detail; Helmholz, "The Law of Compurgation," 90–124, on the other hand, views their central element of proof, compurgation, as incompatible with late medieval canonical procedure.

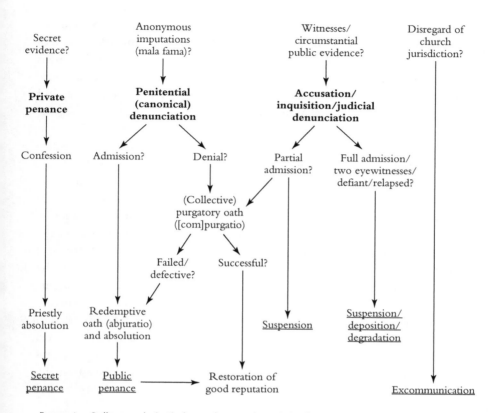

FIGURE 1.   Ordinary ecclesiastical procedures against crimina (1200–1500)

To ensure the silencing of mala fama, lawyers perpetuated communal elements of justice that had been dominant before the advent of Gratian and university jurisprudence. As an alternative to the nonpartisan, factual reconstruction of incriminating events emphasized by scholastic theoreticians in inquisitorial and accusatorial proceedings, penitential denuntiationes investigated truth by relying on collective oaths that greatly favored well-entrenched individuals. Sworn testimony was not admitted to demonstrate that an anonymous allegation lacked substance. Oath helpers rather served as character witnesses, expected to act in support of the denounced. The decisive evidentiary function was attributed to traditional, prescholastic tests of group solidarity, reminiscent of standards that church tribunals had employed from the time when Regino, abbot of Prüm, described the workings of episcopal *Sendgerichte* (lower synodal courts) in his native Middle Rhine region around 906.[23] In using compurgation, denunciations marked the continued reliance in normative thinking on solemn and exhibitionist rites of penitential inquiry, working at the expense of people on the fringes of local society and playing into the hands of those with many friends in the neighborhood.

Public penance, which modern historiography often assumes to have survived the establishment of sacramental penance only in remote places and in opposition to the general teachings of the church, persisted as a regular feature of denunciatory proceedings in England and elsewhere from the early 1200s until the age of the Reformation.[24] Despite the mandatory infliction of public penance upon persons unable to purge themselves of ill fame, however, a closer look at the canonical rationale for denunciatory proceedings prevents identification of their outcome in the form of *penitentia publica* with something akin to criminal sanctions in our current understanding. By relying on group-based oaths and local reputation as key criteria for the establishment of guilt or innocence, canonists never lost sight of the principal purpose animating investigations by way of denuntiatio. In their eyes, the ultimate prosecutorial goal lay in the elimination of mala fama and its pernicious effects on the spiritual health of Christians. Questions about whether rumors pointing to, say, miscarriage really corresponded to actual fact had to be left to other types of judicial inquiry. In the given context, vague criminal imputations constituted the sole wrong to be targeted, a fact that explains why many of the cases recorded in fifteenth-century England were brought, voluntarily and out of concern for their communal respectability, by the discredited individuals themselves.[25]

Cursory evidence of abortion cases indicates, moreover, that rules linking manifest sins to penitentia publica and secret ones to penitentia privata did not always apply in late medieval canonistic doctrine, notwithstanding asser-

---

23. Regino Prumensis, *Liber de synodalibus causis et disciplinis ecclesiasticis*, ed. Friedrich Wasserschleben (Leipzig: Engelmann, 1840), partly translated by Wilfried Hartmann, *Das Sendhandbuch des Regino von Prüm* (Darmstadt: Wissenschaftliche Buchgesellschaft, 2004); John McNeill and Helena Gamer, *Medieval Handbooks of Penance: Translations from the Principal 'Libri Poenitentiales' and Selections from Related Documents* (New York: Columbia University Press, 1938), 289–345. The fundamental procedural analysis is by Albert Koeniger, *Die Sendgerichte in Deutschland*, vol. 1 (Munich: Lentner, 1907), 11–34.

24. The pioneering study is by Mansfield, *The Humiliation of Sinners*, 7–23; confirmed on the basis of sources from medieval Germany by Neumann, *Öffentliche Sünder*, 7–27.

25. For illustrations of judicial routine, see *The Courts of the Archdeaconry of Buckingham, 1484–1523*, ed. Elizabeth Elvey (Aylesbury, UK: Buckinghamshire Record Society, 1975); Richard Wunderli, *London Church Courts and Society on the Eve of the Reformation* (Cambridge, MA: Harvard University Press, 1981); Poos, *Lower Ecclesiastical Jurisdiction*.

tions by numerous historians that the dichotomy between public and private spiritual retribution turned into an absolute principle following the Fourth Lateran Council of 1215. In reality, the supreme administrative authority in penitential matters throughout Latin Christendom, the Sacra Penitentiaria, informed officials as late as in 1503 that the killing of priests (*presbytericidium*) would regularly necessitate atonement through visible acts of humiliation unless safety considerations (*si tutus pateat*) warranted the issuance of a special apostolic voucher.[26] When confessors dealt with offenses other than presbytericidium, the discretionary power they wielded in determining proper injunctions for wrongdoing again afforded the canonical possibility of sacramental satisfaction in the presence of spectators. In 1456, for example, the Papal Penitentiary registered a request submitted by Ursula, wife of Blasius Litteratus, a citizen from the Hungarian town of Pecz. Ursula's written account stated that she had expected a child from her lawful husband until "without any scheming, cause, or guilt on her part," the pregnancy ended in a spontaneous miscarriage. As a true worshiper of Christ (*ut vera christicola*), Ursula went to tell her confessor, who "perhaps not knowing the law," ordered her to line up, according to custom, with others who were obliged to repent their failings in public. Although she was prepared to accept her penitential duties, Ursula was afraid of embarrassing herself and family in front of peers and onlookers. She decided to turn to the Roman Curia, seeking apostolic permission to have her penance converted into a different mode of pious self-mortification. "By special mandate," her petition was granted, providing a reminder that late medieval secret and sacramental penance could, at the confessor's discretion, still result in shameful exposure.[27]

The initial push toward criminalization of abortion in the West undoubtedly came from the church. Twelfth-century canon lawyers created uniform doctrine out of clearly formulated premises and logically deduced norms. They became the first to operate with well-defined juridical concepts, preparing the ground for modern ways of thinking about right and wrong. By 1234, the notion of sin had been relegated to the realm of God's justice, tort consistently described legal complaints aiming at the restitution of damages, and crime regularly referred to behavior deemed punishable as such, with prosecutions often being supplemented by "civil" proceedings in pursuit of compensatory claims. Ecclesiastical courts embraced the new canonical

---

26. In a tax list for scribes and proctors compiled at the Curia between 1503 and 1513; see Wolfgang P. Müller, "Die Taxen der päpstlichen Pönitentiarie, 1338–1569," *QFIAB* 78 (1998): 260, lines 379–381.

27. Rome, APA Reg. div. 5, fol. 187r (2 January 1456), printed in *Die Abtreibung*, 181n313.

theory in day-to-day practice, associating *abortiones* with *homicidia* in the confessional forum, demanding public penance from laymen who failed to silence rumors about their involvement in the violent death of unborn life, and threatening clergy guilty of the charge with permanent removal from spiritual office. Somewhat paradoxically, though, none of the consequences envisioned by late medieval ecclesiastical tribunals coincide with modern notions of punitive sentencing. Sacramental *penitentia* was voluntary. Penitential works performed in the open allowed defamed individuals to overcome a bad reputation and frequently followed unsuccessful attempts at compurgation rather than proof establishing truth beyond reasonable doubt. And while suspension and deposition from the sacred ministry still await priests for the willful killing of a fetus, such repercussions are now regarded as disciplinary measures and not as criminal punishment.

Royal Jurisdiction in Thirteenth-Century England

Clerical culture was also instrumental in carrying the theoretical equation of abortion and homicide beyond the limits of church administration. When we look for early signs of criminalization in the lay sphere, it is apparent that scholastic doctrine reached one branch of secular justice with particular rapidity, offering, from a modern perspective, the oldest instances of fetal death's being treated as a veritable crime. In more specific terms, pertinent judicial activity predicated upon ideas of mandatory prosecution and sentencing first came to be associated with the royal jurisdiction of thirteenth-century England. Legal historians are in agreement that decades before the onset of consistently recorded criminal documentation around 1200, the Anglo-Norman monarchy had started to promote growth of a unified English common law that, apart from the name, shared but a few traits with the Bolognese *Ius commune* shaped simultaneously by jurisprudence on the European mainland. Angevin rulers realized independently that maintenance of peace within their realm was guaranteed most effectively by a centralized system of justice enforcement. Their subsequent policies fostered regular persecution of robbery, rape, and manslaughter under the category of "felonious" offenses (*feloniae*). As "crown pleas" (*placita coronae*), they required handling by the king's officials and warranted the maximum penalty of execution.

To detect behavior amounting to felony, administrators tapped into traditional networks of self-help. Neighborhood representatives would report violent acts to so-called justices (*justitiarii*), itinerant members of the king's court in London who in turn collected and prepared allegations for adjudication at various stops along their circuit. Upon convening judicial sessions known as *eyres*, the justitiarii admitted private accusations (appeals) as well as investigations set into motion by way of public indictment. From the beginning, a panel of at least twelve jurors, recruited from the locality in which a crime was believed to have been committed, assumed critical functions in determining whether charges had to be considered true or false. When, after a momentous decision of the Fourth Lateran Council in 1215, the church ended priestly participation in hot-water tests reliant on God's interference rather than human decision making, the powers of final sentencing also devolved to English lay juries. At this point at the latest, the path had been cleared for the development of an insular common-law culture that maintained its distinctiveness in relation to Romano-canonical modes of secular litigation in areas across the British Channel. Although it is important to keep in mind that because of the work of the ecclesiastical judges, familiarity with and daily recourse to Bolognese legal procedures in England were nearly as pervasive as elsewhere in the West, their full-scale adoption by royal jurisdiction was no longer feasible. The examination of criminal wrong now rested on the division of tasks between centrally appointed agents overseeing the lawful conduct of proceedings and jurors from the vicinity wielding the exclusive right of finding defendants guilty or not guilty.[28]

The formal constraints of English common law did not rule out the possibility that in tackling specific issues members of the king's judiciary were still prepared to apply rules and doctrines with obvious origins in the continental Ius commune. Extensive reliance on canonistic teachings is manifest, for example, in the most famous literary monument produced by a medieval common lawyer, the Latin treatise *On the Laws and Customs of England*, traditionally ascribed to Crown Justice Henry Bracton (d. 1268). The brief passage Bracton (or one of his colleagues) dedicated to the legal treatment of abortion is not only placed under the rubric of felonious crown pleas but also copies almost word for word passages from Raymond of Penyafort's *Summa de penitentia*. Readers of Bracton thus learn about the canonical equation between violent fetal death and homicide as if it had been a firm component of lay justice. In addition, the treatise reiterates that homicide presupposes a victim infused with a soul and shaped like a human being. The result of Bracton's intervention was that criminal condemnation of attacks on prenatal

---

28. Hyams, *Rancor and Reconciliation*, 166–212; Roger Groot, "The Early Thirteenth-Century Jury," in *Twelve Good Men and True: The Criminal Trial Jury in England, 1200–1800*, ed. James Cockburn and Thomas Green (Princeton, NJ: Princeton University Press, 1988), 3–35.

existence gained great visibility in English lawyerly circles.[29] Meanwhile, a second juristic manual carrying the title of *Fleta*, inspired by Bracton and surviving in a single manuscript written toward 1290, supplemented Raymond's instructions with a text that seems to reflect the realities of crime prosecution in the kingdom far more accurately than what Bracton had culled from his penitential informant. In elaborating on private accusations to be brought by women (*De appello feminae*), the anonymous author of Fleta observed that those who had lost an animated fetus as a result of battery were allowed to sue their attackers as felons provided that fetal death had ensued within three days after the violent incident. Earlier on, the royal Magna Carta of 1215, with Bracton in its wake, had limited female appellants to rape and abduction cases and accusations by wives who had witnessed the killing of their own husbands. In 1290, Fleta instead suggested that procedural restrictions had loosened somewhat to accommodate felonious charges on account of wrongful miscarriage as well.[30] In any event, the theoretical statements of Bracton and Fleta support impressions that criminal protection of unborn human life as defined by Gratian and the canonists received a warm welcome among thirteenth-century common-law practitioners.

Early records of crown pleas, going back to the sixth year of King Richard I's reign in 1194, repeatedly attest to women who pursued as felony the violent termination of a pregnancy. Most of them claimed to have been battered by someone who did not belong to the family. The oldest case of culpable miscarriage is mentioned for 1200, when Agnes, the daughter of Saxus, brought an appeal of homicidal aggression against John of Paris, a citizen from the town of Lincoln. In the second half of the century, judicial rolls compiled by justices returning from the eyre further allude to the existence of a procedural rule allowing female plaintiffs to initiate a criminal trial in each of the three instances of spousal murder, rape, and fetal death. The legal prerogative seems to have been reserved to the aggrieved themselves, as

29. Bracton, *De legibus et consuetudinibus Angliae*, ed. George Woodbine (New Haven, CT: Yale University Press, 1922); Samuel Thorne, trans., *Bracton: On the Laws and Customs of England*, 2 vols. (Cambridge, MA: Harvard University Press, 1968), 2:341, inspired by Raymond's *Summa*, above note 19.

30. *Fleta*, ed. Henry Richardson and George Sayles, 4 vols. (London: Selden Society, 1955–1984), 1:23, 1:33; in Thorne, *Bracton*, 2:418–419, fetal death is absent from the list of crown pleas open to women; for the doctrinal underpinnings, see Cecil Meekings, *Crown Pleas of the Wiltshire Eyre 1249* (Devizes, UK: Wiltshire Archeological and Natural History Society, 1961), 88–90; Margaret Kerr, "Husband and Wife in Criminal Proceedings in Medieval England," in *Women, Marriage, and Family in Medieval Christendom: Essays in Memory of Michael M. Sheehan C.S.B.*, ed. Michael Sheehan et al. (Kalamazoo, MI: Medieval Institute Publications, 1998), 222–234.

charges brought by John Boleheveds in Cornwall 1284 against John Hobba for having provoked a fatality in the womb of Mabel of Trethyas met with instant rejection on the part of the presiding judges. The appeal could not be lodged by anyone, the official explanation stated, except the appellant's immediately affected wife, Mabel. For the same reason, Stephen of Saint Albans was not admitted during the London eyre of 1244 to prosecute a deadly attack on the unborn child of his spouse, Alicia. Because Alicia was still alive, the court informed Stephen, she had to come forward by herself. The remarks explain why fathers and husbands hurt by the loss of nascent offspring rarely presented felonious complaints to the jurors alone and unaccompanied.[31]

Crown pleas addressing the willful killing of a human fetus commenced as well ex officio and by court indictment. If suspicions in the neighborhood could be backed up by hard evidence, jury members were entitled to accuse individuals publicly. Serious investigative efforts did not get under way unless tangible traces of a crime had been uncovered. Where residents had come across a dead body within the confines of their community, they were obliged to raise the "hue and cry" and loudly alert people nearby to the gruesome discovery. Finders also needed to summon the local crown official, or coroner, whose duty it was to examine dubious casualties on the spot. While conducting his forensic analysis, the "coronator" would assemble a committee of sworn local witnesses ("jury of inquest") to inspect the deceased and give testimony about probable causes leading up to the fatal incident. Results of the preliminary inquiry were documented in the primary examiner's coroner roll, written with the intent of briefing itinerant justices before their arrival at the next provincial eyre.[32] The claim of English monarchs to act as supreme guardians of the public order was again made manifest in connection with accusations launched by a private party. Had a criminal appeal been abandoned by the plaintiff or compromised because of

---

31. The fullest accounts in English of judicial material dealing with felonious abortion are those of Schneebeck, "The Law of Felony," 232–243; Rafferty, "Roe v. Wade," 119–195; *Die Abtreibung*, 283–297; Joseph Dellapenna, *Dispelling the Myths of Abortion History* (Durham, NC: Carolina Academic Press, 2006), 125–211. As to the cases mentioned, cf. Agnes filia Saxi v. Johannes de Paris, in *Select Pleas of the Crown, 1200–1225*, ed. Frederick Maitland (London: Quaritch, 1888), 39 (no. 82; King's Bench, 1200); Johannes Boleheveds v. Johannes Hobba, Shropshire eyre of 1284, Kew, TNA, Just. 1/112, m. 9d; Galfridus de Sancto Albano v. Stephanus de Tulbuche (1234), in *The London Eyre of 1244*, ed. Helena Chew and Martin Weinbaum (London: London Record Society, 1970), 35–36 (no. 84).

32. Roy F. Hunnisett, *The Medieval Coroner* (Cambridge: Cambridge University Press, 1961); Smith, "Medieval Coroner Rolls: Legal Fiction or Historical Fact?" in *Courts, Counties, and the Capital*, ed. Diana Dunn (New York: St Martin's, 1996), 93–115.

a formal error of his, the case was by no means considered closed. The justices rather assumed the initiative, especially when the allegations turned out to be of some substance. Granted that the incriminating offense constituted, in principle, a breach of everyone's commitment to peace in the realm, the idea that offenders might escape proper retribution was wholly unacceptable to prosecutors.[33]

Formulaic entries in the eyre rolls characterize induced fetal death as an infringement of the general ban on violence or brand charges as generic and unspecified acts of slaying (*occisio*). The main reason justifying classification of the offense as a felony is hardly ever mentioned by name. Still, there are indirect clues showing that the equation with homicidium recommended by Bracton ultimately inspired thirteenth-century common-law prosecutions. At times, the proof is hidden in small procedural details. In October 1247, for instance, Philip of Andover found himself imprisoned by the bishop of Salisbury upon accusations of having caused a miscarriage. In order to be freed until the day of the final verdict, he needed to secure a special mandate ("writ") calling for the town sheriff to convoke a jury and have Philip's innocence ascertained through issuance of a preliminary sentence. Once jurors had furnished a formal statement confirming that suspicions rested merely on personal spite and enmity (*de odio et atia*), Philip could move on to request a second "writ of bail," enabling him to offer the necessary sureties for his temporary release from jail. Asking for a letter de odio et atia before seeking permission to give warranties was not supposed to occur in private pleas other than those amounting to accusations of homicide.[34]

Along the same lines, the mention of town privileges proves revelatory. In the earliest days of English common law, citizenries had successfully bargained with the king for judicial exemptions, so that a certain Robert of Hakeney, for example, could ask at the London eyre of 1276 that his allegedly felonious involvement in a percussio be adjudged by a jury consisting of the mayor and a group of Londoners. According to the court roll, the justices followed Robert's wish "because suspicions against him were slight" and "although he came from the liberty of the city [*de libertate civitatis*]." What

---

33. One case is the official inquest started after dismissal of Galfridus de Sancto Albano's private plea at the London eyre of 1244 (above, note 31).

34. The letter de odio et atia is preserved in Kew, TNA, C. 144/3, m. 55 (10 October 1247); the writ of bail, TNA, C. 54/16, m. 15 (cf. *CCR* [31 Hen. III] 16, 12 December 1247). The case eventually came before the Wiltshire eyre of 1249, TNA, Just. 1/996, m. 40; see the comprehensive analysis by Meekings, *Crown Pleas*, 78–79, 276 (no. 562); and Stuart Jenks, "The Writ and the Exception de odio et atia," *Journal of Legal History* 23 (2002): 1–22.

was meant by the latter remark can be gleaned from a longer passage recorded at the previous eyre of 1244, where another man, William Bertone, had been sued by Isabelle, the wife of Serlo, in an identical case of fetal death tied to violent beatings. Like Robert a generation afterward, William wanted his guilt or innocence to be determined by the mayor and a panel of co-jurors. But the attempt was in vain. Burdened by strongly incriminating evidence, William was compelled to invoke the "great law" of the city, which pre-scribed that a purgatory oath be taken by at least thirty-six hands, since the matter was, as the entry notes, "about the death of a human being [*de morte hominis*]." Marginal commentary left by justices perusing the documenta-tion of eyre sessions or scribbles added during registration of royal pardons confirm that contemporary lawyers put fetal existence automatically on a par with born life.[35]

Common law received manifold inspiration from the canonistic treat-ment of abortion that culminated in the adoption of scholastic animation theory. As a matter of fact, it did not happen very frequently that writers of plea rolls referred to casualties without detailing the stage of the victim's physical development. Reflecting terminology present in both Bracton and Fleta, express recognition of the fetus as "alive" implied that the court was confronted with the death of a human being. At times, descriptions of the bodily state grew more elaborate, with indications of sex obliquely acknowl-edging previous formation and ensoulment. Some records even include exact measurements of the aborted remains, always calculated in multiples of a thumb's length. The crucial significance of fetal shape was, in other words, beyond doubt, finding confirmation, for example, at the Southampton eyre of 1280, where the case of Walter Gode must have weighed on people's minds. A previous appeal had charged Walter and others in his company with the beating of Alicia, wife of Adam le Prest, causing her to deliver just one month into the pregnancy. Although the woman accused Walter and his accomplices of intentional killing, the panel of jurors refused to accept her claim and declined to have defendants face the maximum penalty. Jury members argued on embryological grounds to justify their leniency, observ-ing that they had been unable to determine whether the unborn baby, eight

35. Naomi Hurnard, *The King's Pardon for Homicide before A.D. 1307* (Oxford: Oxford University Press, 1969), 106–107; and *CCR* (18 Edw. II) 100, provide illustrations of the equation. Also London, BL, Additional Charter 5153, m. 11d (Willelmus Sorel v. Robertus de Hakeney, 1271), translated by Martin Weinbaum, in *The London Eyre of 1276* (London: London Record Society, 1976), 61 (no. 222); Isabella uxor Serlonis v. Willelmus Bertone (1242), in Chew and Weinbaum, *The London Eyre of 1244*, 62–64 (no. 157–158).

digits tall, was a boy or a girl. Under the circumstances, the felonious nature of the incident could not be established. Apart from a prison term imposed on account of Alicia's injury, Walter and his fellows managed to escape the proceedings unharmed.[36]

That treating abortion as a capital offense did not pose an empty threat can be surmised from the way the accused reacted. Many defendants ignored summons that ordered them to stand trial. In response, their belongings were confiscated, whether or not juries arrived at a guilty verdict. Those discharged obtained assurances encouraging them to return home, although their movable property was permanently kept by the crown to punish previous contumacious behavior. Clearly, the legal consequences of manslaughter in the womb were greatly dreaded, as fear for life persuaded more than just a few to prefer outlawry and loss of cattle to the prospect of appearing in the king's court. And indeed, should the panel of sworn men confirm felonious accusations, those convicted were sent to the gallows. Looming particularly large in this context was the fate of Maude de Haule, who in 1283 or 1284 was said to have struggled with Joan of Hallynghurst, then pregnant. Joan had tried to intervene in a fight between Maude and Agnes la Converse, whereupon the angry Maude drove the uninvited mediator out of the house. Joan tumbled down the stairs and, four days later, bore a dead child, about ten weeks before it was due. The accused Maude was thrown into prison at Newgate and remained locked up until justices, commissioned to investigate inmates ("gaol delivery") arrived on the scene. In the end, a board of twelve peers condemned Maude to execution by hanging. Notwithstanding the fact that in cases of percussio the actual infliction of capital punishment was exceedingly rare, many seem to have anticipated it and absconded immediately.[37]

Justices conducting eyre sessions could not implement juristic theories of homicide in person. Their influence on the decision-making process ended right before the passing of the final verdict. English royal courts reserved sentencing not to trained lawyers but to a jury assembled from ordinary local men. Jurors often functioned as witnesses in the same case they eventually came to rule on. They would possess inside knowledge of the crime or of the identity and habits of a defendant. Legal expertise, let alone impartiality, was not expected of them. They did not have to justify their final determination

---

36. Kew, TNA, Just. 1/786, m. 1 (Alicia uxor Ade le Prest v. Walterus Gode et al.), cited by Schneebeck, "The Law of Felony," 239–240; the full text is in *Die Abtreibung*, 290n495.

37. Kew, TNA, Just. 1/547A, m. 20d, translated by John Baker in the appendix of Rafferty, "Roe v. Wade," 530–531, where the text, recorded at the Middlesex eyre 1320/21, bears the wrong date of 1318; cf. Schneebeck, "The Law of Felony," 241n59; for the Latin version, *Die Abtreibung*, 291n497.

in favor of life or death, and relegation of their judgment to higher judicial authority was not allowed. In the eyes of the justitiarii, therefore, the painstaking analysis of available evidence was less of a priority than the obligation to gather information within narrowly defined parameters of lawfulness. Eyre rolls repeatedly document official efforts to protect the suspect from malicious accusations by, for example, making sure that the originally chosen procedural path was pursued scrupulously. The appeal of Mabel, Warner of Wenlok's daughter, at the Shropshire eyre of 1292 did not hold up to closer scrutiny. Her charges specified neither the date at which Hugh of Walle was supposed to have beaten the pregnant Mabel nor where exactly her unborn child had died under the impact of Hugh's percussiones. In view of these deficiencies, the case was declared null and void. Cancellation followed the basic principle that private criminal suits were compromised if they rested on assertions lacking factual accuracy in any of the details. For failure to frame criminal allegations properly, appellants like Mabel were put in jail to await a royal letter of pardon or be released upon payment of a fine. They shared their situation with those whose crown pleas had not convinced jurors and produced an outcome in favor of the accused.[38] In order to avoid irreversible judicial mistakes, justices also sought to obtain satisfactory answers with regard to the concrete effects of criminal misconduct. The formulary of an appeal in *Fleta* outlines the hypothetical case of a percussio that "within three days" resulted "in a dead delivery at least three weeks premature." By contrast, most court records limit quantitative information to the lapse of time occurring between battery and stillbirth. If indictments spoke of a couple of weeks separating the two events, nobody seems to have minded the discrepancy. At the London eyre of 1244, justices were not even surprised to learn that purported blows against the stomach of Sara, wife of Albin le Portour, did not provoke a miscarriage until fifteen weeks afterward. Despite objections, jurors were urged to pass their verdict all the same.[39]

If juries did not produce a definitive sentence, justices again wondered about the rationale. Because many private appeals were brought in hopes of settling out of court with the adversary, royal officials continuously worried

---

38. Kew, TNA, Just. 1/739, m. 81 (Mabilia filia Warneri de Wenlok v. Hugo de Walle, 1292). Parallel instances of formal mistakes nullifying the accuser's plea are in *Select Pleas of the Crown*, 32 (no. 73, Norfolk eyre of 1203); Doris Stenton, ed., *The Earliest Lincolnshire Assize Rolls A.D. 1202–1209* (Lincoln, UK: Lincoln Record Society, 1926), 111 (no. 629, eyre of 1202).

39. Chew and Weinbaum, *The London Eyre of 1244*, 50–51 (no. 124); a lapse of two weeks features in the appeal of Alicia uxor Ade filii Ivonis (1248), Kew, TNA, Just. 1/176, m. 27d (Shropshire eyre, 1249); cf. Richardson and Sayles, *Fleta*, 1:33.

about financial agreements reached behind their backs. At Kent in 1241, the jury informed the court that the appellant, William Swayn, had amicably settled with the defendant, Henry Fratard, accused of battery and ensuing felonious miscarriage. Sensing that they had been deceived, the justices ordered the plaintiff's arrest for what in procedural terms meant that he had suffered legal defeat by being unable to show the truthfulness of his charges. William was not dismissed until he had paid half a mark in fines to the crown. To persuade justices, *juratores* (jurors) also had the possibility of challenging the outcome of an alleged beating. During the Gloucestershire eyre of 1248, for instance, they tried to minimize complaints against Adam Wayne and his companions. While deliberating panel members conceded that Adam and his accomplices had struck Amicia, Eadmer Gundewine's pregnant wife, the miscarriage she had endured after nine days was reportedly the result of toilsome work and Amicia's own "stupid behavior."[40]

To ensure even-handed justice, crown officials attentively scrutinized jury conduct in favor of milder punitive treatment. They noted with special care instances in which panel members had failed to fulfill their judicial duties. Plea rolls often contain language to the effect that court personnel had disregarded procedural formalities or that communities had colluded with defendants and permitted them to evade arrest. In 1256, the villagers of Northcharleston were penalized at the Northumberland eyre for not having imprisoned William Messor in connection with charges of felonious percussio, and in 1243 the inhabitants of Stoke Curcy were at the king's mercy after sheltering John of Rechich, an outlaw for having avoided royal investigation on account of a violent miscarriage. Among prosecutors of the crown, Richard of Ewell was suspected in 1276 of having released the draper Richard Scharp all too quickly. In his capacity as sheriff, Ewell had accepted sureties from six rather than the twelve men required by London law. Judges presiding over the city eyre further observed that Scharp's alleged provocation of a premature delivery (by his own wife?) called for a higher number of pledges, as the severity of the offense equaled manslaughter (*occisio hominis*). After incidents of administrative neglect, culprits were subjected to the discretion of the king, who ordinarily received them back into his grace upon payment of a stipulated sum.[41]

---

40. Kew, TNA, Just. 1/274, m. 14d (Alicia uxor Eadmer de Gundewine v. Adam Wayne et al.); English translation in Dellapenna, *Dispelling the Myths*, 137; Kew, TNA, 1/359, m. 36 (William Swayn v. Henricus Fratard), transcribed in *Die Abtreibung* 290n496.

41. London, BL, Additional Charter 5153, m. 4d (Uxor eius [?] v. Ricardus Scharp), translated in Weinbaum, *The London Eyre of 1276*, 23 (no. 76); Kew, TNA, Just. 1/756, m. 25d (Juliana filia Maynardi v. Johannes de Rechich), translated by Charles Chadwyck-Healey in *Somersetshire*

Court rolls were kept to demonstrate the conformity of proceedings with rules established by the common law and to document the proper collection of legal fees accruing to the royal treasury. As administrators and jurors performed their judicial tasks, the reasons for stricter or less stringent adherence to the norms remained, on the whole, unrecorded. Perhaps most intriguing in this regard is the case of Thomas, identified as an educated man (*magister*) with the indicative surname of "the Surgeon." At the Kent eyre of 1279, Thomas was presented as having triggered, with punches, the death of Agnes le Deyster's unborn child. In the definitive verdict, however, jurors tersely stated that they did not wish to convict the defendant of the alleged felony, a decision that leaves the modern observer, confronted with a highly exceptional case scenario, perplexed as to why Thomas was found not guilty.[42] Against common procedural habit, he had been indicted notwithstanding the fact that neither the mother nor the father of the victim had come forward to press charges. Did the *juratores*, as a result, rule in a way that intentionally safeguarded the special relationship between Agnes and Thomas as her physician? Or did the jury plainly refuse to pronounce a condemnation under circumstances implying the invasion of parental autonomy, with Agnes herself being unwilling to pursue the matter in court? Official sources do not yield a response. At the same time, subsequent developments in the common law, to be treated below in chapter 5, show that the prosecution of violent miscarriages in royal tribunals suffered a dramatic loss of popularity from the 1280s onward. By 1350, cases of fetal death through battery had ceased to be part of the English crown pleas. It is all the more important to remember that procurement of abortion in the modern acceptance of the term, performed with the consent of the pregnant mother, had never held a place among thirteenth-century appeals and indictments. Adjudication of criminal *percussiones* had been the sole concern.

Pleas, Civil and Criminal, from the Rolls of the Itinerant Justices, Close of the Twelfth Century—41 Henry III ([London,] 1897), 321 (no. 1243); Sibilla v. Willelmus Messor (1256), in *The Early Assize Rolls for the County of Northumberland*, ed. William Page (Durham, UK: Andrews, 1891), 121.

42. Kew, TNA, Just. 1/369, m. 37d (Crown v. Thomas le Surgien); first pointed out by Schneebeck, "The Law of Felony," 238n52, printed in *Die Abtreibung*, 297n506.

CHAPTER 3

Chief Agents of Criminalization

Recent textual discoveries by Anders Winroth and his colleagues have shed much light on the inconspicuous and workman-like atmosphere in which Gratian put together his compilation of sources for the scholarly study of church law. The founding father of the new academic discipline certainly envisioned his Decretum to be a homemade pedagogical tool, introducing students more effectively than previous canonical collections to the art of adjudicating ecclesiastical court cases. Still, the idea of presenting the normative tradition comprehensively and within an organizational scheme that would instruct readers how to establish, through intellectual effort, harmony and concordance between seemingly discordant canons did not enter Gratian's mind by a single stroke of genius. It is now apparent that he began by aiming at a much smaller collection of legal distinctions and questions. This prompted him to assemble a "first recension," subsequently expanded to absorb overlooked materials, borrowings from Roman law, and a topical treatise on the sacraments (*De consecratione*). After a period of gestation that may have lasted for many years, the final product in the form of a stable, vulgate version of the Decretum did not emerge until the 1140s. Further authorial intervention on the part of Gratian's successors assumed written permanence far into the next generation of Bolognese schoolmen.

The oldest canonistic textbook was not composed by a man who worked in isolation. Gratian must have lectured at the city of Bologna, where contemporary juristic experts like Bulgarus tried to interpret Justinian's *Corpus* of Roman law by following the same dialectic method that canonists down the street—and slightly before them, theologians in northern France—had begun to apply to authoritative statements of their own discipline. In refashioning age-old sources in his scribal atelier, Gratian was quickly joined by imitators. In the classroom he shared with students his growing appreciation for the need to distinguish concepts like crime from lesser varieties of wrong and for adding precision to doctrinal pronouncements on the exact juncture between homicide and abortion. Gratian, in other words, successfully seized the moment by being active in the right place, embracing the latest scholarly trends, defining his particular area of inquiry, and honing his skills through constant and groundbreaking research in the primary sources. The original format and lasting fame of his Decretum reveal him as an intellectual pioneer of great magnitude. He belonged to a select group of thinkers who forged the didactic instruments that have allowed academic professionals in the West to thrive publicly ever since.

Modern scholarship has treated the historical circumstances of Gratian's epochal achievement in ways that often betray incredulity or indifference. Early biographers have sought to place him high in the ecclesiastical hierarchy among bishops and cardinals, and some accounts have attempted to explain the rapid adoption of his Decretum in schools of canon law across the Latin hemisphere by postulating an official, twelfth-century papal approbation of the text. With John Noonan's revisionist account of 1979, on the other hand, it has become accepted opinion that practically nothing is known about Gratian's life.[1] Apart from certainty with regard to his name, recollections by his immediate followers, the decretists, treat him as an obscure figure. The author of the first standard reading in canonistic classrooms was perhaps a monk and probably active in or around Bologna. He doubtlessly worked as one teacher among many. His endeavor as a canonical compiler constituted, in current terms, an eminently private undertaking and succeeded because of spontaneous proliferation rather than authoritative imposition from above. And yet historians, while confronted with a scholastic model of justice that permeated society mostly sideways and through academic institutions, have generally insisted in their reconstructions of the past on anachronistic ideas

---

1. John Noonan, "Gratian Slept Here: The Changing Identity of the Father of the Systematic Study of Canon Law," *Traditio* 35 (1979): 145–172, reprinted in John Noonan, *Canons and Canonists in Context* (Goldbach, Ger.: Keip, 1997), no. 4; but cf. Francesco Reali, "Magister Gratianus e le origini del diritto civile europeo," in *Graziano da Chiusi e la sua opera*, ed. Francesco Reali (Chiusi, It.: Edizioni Lui, 2009), 17–130; for additional bio-bibliographical information, see chap. 1 notes 2–3.

about legislation and governmental initiative as primary instigators of late medieval legal development.

Students seeking orientation in the field will find an array of papal and royal decrees available in editions and translations. Simultaneously, they will struggle to access juristic treatises and court manuals from the pen of canonists and civilians, whose learned works have rarely been printed in modern times or rendered in modern languages. To cite a conspicuous example, the Latin version of the Ordinary Gloss, consulted by canon lawyers from about 1250 as a routine marginal supplement to Gratian's remarks on, say, the formed fetus, was last sent to the press in the 1620s.[2] An excessive focus on normative acts issued by the political leadership has created interpretive distortions that often obscure the functioning of law in its original medieval context. Episodes of governmental interference in matters relating to the criminalization of abortion illustrate that, in contrast with current Western assumptions about power arrangements, initiative in the shaping of legal doctrine and court practice always remained with the university teachers. In historical reality, medieval law professors, graduates, and trained legal practitioners never ceased to dominate the relationship between legislation and learning.

To contend that law school teachers shaped and disseminated essential doctrines of jurisprudence autonomously and without significant or effective supervision by outside agencies does not, of course, imply that academics did not seek alliances with ruling elites or acknowledge considerable areas of mutual interest. Ultimately, however, their affinity with the powerful formed a necessary and almost automatic extension of the normative construct they tried to propagate, which unfailingly extolled the virtues of clearly defined premises, transparent procedures, and logically predictable outcomes. The success or failure of legal theories rested in particular on the perfect compatibility between rules and required their harmonious accommodation in a fully explicated hierarchy of religious and social values. Lawyers postulated a set of fundamental rights and obligations they found divinely manifested either in nature, in the main articles of Christian faith, or in other provisions safeguarding the general state of the church. Uniform and lawful application

---

2. Rudolf Weigand, "The Development of the Glossa Ordinaria to Gratian's Decretum," in Hartmann and Pennington, *The History of Medieval Canon Law*, 55–97; only the opening portion (on D. 1–20) of the standard decretist commentary by Johannes Teutonicus (1215) and Bartholomaeus Brixiensis (1236) is translated; see James Gordley and Augustine Thompson, *The Treatise on Law (Decretum DD. 1–20)* (Washington, DC: Catholic University of America Press, 1993).

of these "constitutional" norms in practice counted among the chief duties of God's leading representatives on earth, while there was never any clear identification as to who among existing human rulers was to be endowed with supreme legislative and judicial authority. Theorists merely established the rightfulness of claims to exercise superior and centralized control over subjects, clerical and lay, in what made their pronouncements and services attractive to those vying for independent governance across domains and territories. In the end, though, the commonality of concerns, with systematic law bolstering the legitimacy of sovereign rule and sovereigns lending political authority in return, did not put the juristic establishment in a position of outright dependency on princely or even papal will.

This chapter examines the relationship between jurists and legislators from three different perspectives. To begin with, late medieval ecclesiastical and royal statutes concerned with abortion as crimen are shown to have been treated as less than literally binding texts. The glossing activities of law professors freely modified their legislative content in light of prevailing juristic doctrine and proposed restriction or outright rejection whenever academic theory and its systematic appeal seemed compromised. Innovative normative impulses were expected to come instead from the law schools themselves, where, for example, two Bolognese teachers working in the 1340s intervened heavy-handedly in previous learned discourse and denied humanity to the fetus altogether. The absence of interference in momentous legal change on the part of political leaders is further discussed as a reminder of how the criminalizing trends of the twelfth century did not depend on coercive imposition from above but rather occurred spontaneously and in response to the specific needs of a new force in society, the townspeople. Jurisprudence spread from important centers of urbanization outward and did so with or without the assistance of top-down command.

Legislation versus Juristic *Communis Opinio*

In the later Middle Ages, there was not a single place in the West where abortion was made into a punishable offense by way of statutory decree, mandated from the top. Criminalization proceeded through the activity of teachers and intellectuals such as Gratian and successive generations of canonists, who based their condemnation as well as the crucial distinction between animated and inanimate fetal existence on texts attributed not to conciliar or apostolic authority but to the church fathers, Jerome and Saint Augustine, and to a clearly interpolated translation of the Bible. As noted earlier, the relevant passages from the Decretum were swiftly incorporated into

Peter Lombard's textbook for studies in scholastic theology and profoundly affected the understanding of Justinian's *Corpus iuris civilis*. In the days of Azo Porticus (d. 1202), the statements of ancient Roman lawyers and emperors were thoroughly canonized in disregard of the fact that, historically speaking, the authoritative laws of Rome had never considered abortion to be a crime in itself and evidently ignored stages of animation. Individual voices within the scholastic community—observing, for instance, that the vulgate version of the Old Testament used in Western churches lacked all reference to the dividing line between formed and unformed human life—went unheeded, as did occasional juristic remarks suggesting that unborn life might not have enjoyed imperial protection in antiquity. The formation of common lawyerly opinion went on undisturbed, with the effect that Innocent III's ruling on prenatal existence of 1211 barely modified views among the learned. Bolognese canonists invoked the pope's letter only for the purpose of arguing against a minority of colleagues who maintained that the canonical sanction of irregularity encompassed both actual homicide and killings of unformed life in the uterus.[3]

Upon clarification of a technicality leaving academic canonists in controversy with one another, active participation of the Apostolic See in defining abortion as an ecclesiastical crime ended right where it had started, with Innocent's judicial response and its inclusion in the second scholastic textbook for canon law studies, the *Decretales*, or *Liber extra*, promulgated by Pope Gregory IX in 1234. It is well known, moreover, that on a macroscopic level, canonistic development witnessed a very limited phase of normative intervention from the top of the sacerdotal hierarchy. After a century and a half in which the growth of doctrine was accompanied by a steady output of decretal collections supplementing and updating Gratian's groundbreaking effort as standard teaching tools, scholastic recourse to new compilations bearing the stamp of papal approval definitively subsided in 1322. For the rest of the Middle Ages, canon lawyers pursued different paths of juristic refinement, no longer securing for themselves official recognition each time they wished to

---

3. Chap. 1, notes 16–17. Doubts concerning the civilian equation of abortion with homicide (cf. chap. 1, notes 12–13) in the Ordinary Gloss on the *Lombarda* by Carolus de Tocco (1208–10), *in Lombardam* 1.9.4, s.v. *apprecietur,* ed. *Leges Langobardorum* (Venice: Sessa, 1537), fol. 20rb; and in the decretist *Summa Bambergensis* (1206–10), C. 32, q. 2, c. 9, s.v. *pro anima* (Liège, BM, 127E, fol. 252va); both printed in *Die Abtreibung*, 35n71, 97n177, quickly faded from early scholastic debate. Jerome's biblical rendering of Exodus 21:22–23 (chap. 1, note 14), was treated in the same way; inserted as 1 Comp. 5.10.2 into the Bolognese decretalist collection of 1191, the passage did not reappear when *Compilatio prima* was superseded by the *Liber extra* in 1234.

expand their reservoir of authoritative texts for use in the classroom. Modern historians have tried to explain the abrupt end of cooperation between schoolmen and supreme leadership in the Western church by pointing out how canonists, to improve their arguments, increasingly relied on practical literature arising from day-to-day litigation. Alternatively, scholarship has surmised that theory was fundamentally complete by the early 1300s and did not require ulterior general legislation. Either explanation, to be sure, silently acknowledges the fundamental otherness of canon law in an age when adjudication and learning proved capable of forming and flourishing without previous or continuous directives from the highest political authorities.[4]

The fate of Innocent's letter, uniquely destined among papal decisions to inform the views of Bolognese jurisprudence on abortion, turns out to be equally exemplary and instructive when the wording of the text is considered. In 1211 the pope did not intend to issue a binding statute but was responding to the legal query of an unidentified Carthusian abbot. The discretionary scholastic editing that subsequently prepared the decretal for the lecture halls did not highlight which passages were to be considered important and innovative or where older canonical provisions were meant to undergo modification. Contrary to interpretive habits now prevalent in the West, late medieval lawyers did not seek to uncover loopholes and dwell in particular on ambiguous formulations. Interpreters took for granted that legislative dispositions would not make sense without knowledge of what juristic experts and "common opinion among the doctors" had said about the matter at hand. It was generally assumed that legislative acts did not treat juridical issues exhaustively. Key information about precise points of law would rather appear in lawyerly commentary, whence it is possible to assert that decretals, conciliar decrees, Roman leges, and lay statutes devoid of explication by university professors and legal practitioners did not possess a great amount of judicial or didactic value. On the whole, regulations lacking learned elaboration in the form of marginal glosses tacitly reveal their irrelevance for the building of consensus among the exponents of jurisprudence and suggest failure to inform court practice in areas of the continental Ius commune and of English common law.

---

4. Basic historical accounts, such as James Brundage, *Medieval Canon Law* (London: Longman, 1995), concentrate their attention on the high point of papal intervention between 1140 and 1322, whereas successive doctrinal development is briefly treated as belonging to an "Age of Consiliators"; cf. Mario Ascheri et al., eds., *Legal Consulting in the Civil Law Tradition* (Berkeley: University of California Press, 1999); another title, Martin Bertram, ed., *Stagnation oder Fortbildung? Aspekte des allgemeinen Kirchenrechts im 14. und 15. Jahrhundert* (Tübingen: Niemeyer, 2004), alludes to the fact that the period is often thought to have performed poorly in terms of legal innovation.

Meanwhile, statutory activity placing abortion among the most serious offenses grew all the more widespread at the provincial level of church administration. The multiplication of criminal norms at local councils and synods seems to have been geared especially toward priests and disseminated information that in structure and substance paralleled what confessors found in penitential works fashioned after Thomas of Cobham's and Raymond of Penyafort's pioneering *Summae*.[5] Inspired by their exhortations, bishops increasingly resorted to the promulgation of decrees that publicized in the parishes the canonistic condemnation of attacks on unborn life. As the inventory of pertinent statutes is far from complete, legal historians have supplied a number of provisional assessments, repeatedly emphasizing the striking absence in synodal legislation of Gratian's distinction between the formed and unformed fetus. Almost none of the printed *statuta*, modern scholars have indicated, mention the twofold nature of homicidium envisioned by Bolognese canonists, a fact that has led Italian legal historian Giancarlo Garancini and others to conclude that Western prelates frequently ignored general doctrine in favor of indiscriminate sanctions for every form of killing during gestation.[6] The silence of late medieval normative sources, however, cannot be construed as having implied the elimination from law of something they did not state expressly. Depending on circumstance, the omissions highlighted by Garancini were simply the side effect of an exclusive focus on questions of sacramental penance or resulted from a narrowly defined interest in problems of judicial implementation. Contemporaries did not consult episcopal decisions in isolation but tied them for further elucidation to standard academic commentary. It is therefore not by sheer accident that diocesan mandates often address procedural details for which established doctrine did not furnish hard-and-fast responses. Particular attention was paid, for instance, to the pastoral issue of absolution from abortion, which most stipulations reserved to the ordinary leader of the diocese. Restriction of spiritual pardoning powers to the pope alone was rarely conceded, save in cases where charges of prenatal homicide had been brought in connection with magic.[7]

---

5. Chap. 2, notes 8–10. For an overview of synodal *statuta*, Garancini, "Materiali," 469–477; *Die Abtreibung*, 76–81.

6. Garancini, "Materiali," 477; similarly Huser, *The Crime of Abortion*, 57–58; Palazzini, *Ius fetus ad vitam*, 144–147.

7. Details in chap. 7, notes 35, 37–39; regarding abortion as an episcopal *casus reservatus*, see *Die Abtreibung*, 72–73.

The previous observations suggest that against modern legal thinking, late medieval lawgivers exercised their formal juridical powers to meet the needs of scholastic jurisprudence rather than vice versa. In addition, the history of canon law on abortion shows in at least one conspicuous incident how the doctrinal autonomy of academic lawyers persisted well into the early modern period. The brief pontificate of Sixtus V from 1585 to 1590 was marked not only by energetic attempts to intensify rule over the city of Rome and papal territories in central Italy but also by sweeping architectural transformations that shaped several of the most famous Roman streets and squares in existence today. With equally fierce determination, the Franciscan pope pursued the task of enforcing basic demands of Christian morality. He issued a series of statutes that aimed in particular at the repression of sexual deviancy. Henceforth, adultery and certain accusations of incest were to be treated as outright capital crimes, revealing clear intent on the part of Sixtus to combine ethical and judicial standards into a single category of wrong.[8] Abortion was next on the legislator's agenda. On October 29, 1588, he promulgated a bull, known by its opening word as *Effraenatam*, in which he sought to put the long-standing canonical prohibition of prenatal killings on entirely new foundations. Gratian's distinction between formed and unformed fetal life was declared obsolete and maximum punishment was extended to include, apart from all intentionally provoked miscarriages, the successful administration of contraceptive herbs and potions as well. According to *Effraenatam*, convicted parties and their accomplices were to be held liable for murder in both the ecclesiastical and secular courts. Clerics were to be stripped automatically (ipso facto) and permanently of their ministry and income and shared the fate of instant excommunication with culprits from among the laity. Neither in public proceedings nor in secret sacramental confession could absolution or dispensation be granted if not by the Apostolic See.[9]

Sixtus V reserved his strongest legal antidote for cases within the competence of criminal secular and church jurisdiction. He insisted that clergy openly convicted of abortion or contraception were to face deposition and subsequent extradition to the lay authorities for execution, in what subjected them to punishments that were identical to those for unordained individuals

---

8. *Ad compescendam* (30 October 1586), in *Bullarium Romanum*, vol. 8, ed. Luigi Tomasetti (Turin: Dalmazzo, 1863), no. 70; *Volentes* (5 April 1587), in ibid., no. 80. Historiographical background is provided by Irene Polverini Fosi, "Justice and Its Image: Political Propaganda and Social Reality in the Pontificate of Sixtus V," *The Sixteenth-Century Journal* 24 (1993), 75–96.

9. *Effraenatam*, in *Bullarium Romanum*, vol. 9, ed. Luigi Tomasetti (Turin: Dolmazzo, 1865), 39–42b (no. 134); cf. *Die Abtreibung*, 134–140.

who "in actual fact" had been sentenced as homicides (*vere homicidae*). The pope must have been aware that *Effraenatam* constituted a revolutionary departure from more than four hundred years of canonistic teaching, given that in the concluding paragraphs of his statute he took care to prevent attempts at undercutting, through juristic commentary, the unprecedented rigor of his legislative act. Prosecutorial zeal also induced him to suspend ordinary criminal procedure by admitting testimony from people usually considered ineligible to serve as witnesses. Past practice, Sixtus explained, had revealed just how frequently crimes of this nature were improperly shielded by their privacy. In order to bring clandestine behavior impeding procreation or gestation in the womb to light and justice, *Effraenatam* places the accused on a par with the worst enemies of Western Christianity, the heretics, whose entitlement to what jurisprudence regarded as a full and fair trial had already been curtailed by the end of the thirteenth century.[10]

That the dependency of ecclesiastical legislation on scholastic doctrine persisted through the early days of the post-Tridentine period is confirmed by the unperturbed criticism with which canonists and judges greeted the promulgation of *Effraenatam*. In reaction to what must have been widespread disapproval, Gregory XIV, the immediate successor on the papal throne, revoked the bull just six months into his pontificate. The Gregorian statute, *Sedes Apostolica*, published in May 1591, offered a ringing formulation that subsequent generations of lawyers cited tirelessly and with enthusiasm, to the effect that what Sixtus had stipulated in relation to contraception and the murder of "inanimate" fetal life ought to be reduced, again and forever, "to the limits of general jurisprudence" *(ad terminos iuris communis)*, as though the contrary portions of *Effraenatam* had never emanated from the Curia.[11] Differently put, Gregory XIV fully restored Gratian's distinction between two phases of life in the maternal womb and varying penalties for each of them, ending a moment of apostolic rejection that had lasted for two and a half years, from 1588 to 1591. Within the same time span, moreover, a Neapolitan judge by the name of Jacobus de Grafiis produced a judicial decision in which he brought to bear on *Effraenatam*, then formally in force, the

---

10. On "extraordinary" *inquisitiones* of "heretical depravity," James B. Given, *Inquisition and Society: Power, Discipline, and Resistance in Languedoc* (Ithaca: Cornell University Press, 1997), 13–51; Jörg Feuchter, *Ketzer, Konsuln und Büßer* (Tübingen: Mohr-Siebeck, 2007), 9–24; and below, chapter 7.

11. *Sedes Apostolica* (31 May 1591), in *Bullarium Romanum*, 9:430b–431a (no. 21); in unison with many others, the celebrated criminalist Prosperus Farinaccius (d. 1606), *Praxis et theorica criminalis* 2.2 (Frankfurt/M.: Palthenius, 1610), 77a–86b, hailed Gregory's legislation for having brought the Sixtine *bulla* "back onto the path of lawfulness" *(redacta fuit ad viam iuris)*.

very interpretive attitudes his late medieval colleagues had cherished when confronting unwelcome legislative texts. The remarks of Jacobus show his resolve to make the radical innovations of 1588 look as compatible as possible with long-established learned opinion on the matter. In further discussing the Sixtine prohibition of legal regard for theories of successive animation in the uterus, the Neapolitan decision unflinchingly restates as correct the older canonistic view laid down in the glossa ordinaria. Stubborn lawyerly attachment to traditional academic jurisprudence rather than recent pontifical injunction certainly played an important part in persuading Gregory XIV to retract *Effraenatam* shortly after he took office.[12]

In dealing with legislation passed by political leaders outside the ecclesiastical orbit, juristic opinion again adhered to principles of exposition no different from the ones recommended in canonistic thought and practice. By the mid-fourteenth century, representatives of the academic Ius commune had set enduring interpretive parameters for legal practitioners who faced tensions or serious discrepancy between tenets of scholastic jurisprudence and stipulations contained in a secular statute. Learned advice favored the restrictive reading of all, or at least of so-called odious, norms while a third group of theorists preferred to use the term *statutum odiosum* only for laws that aimed at the infliction of bodily punishment. In any event, jurists wholeheartedly agreed on the fundamental premise that new legislative acts promulgated by late medieval emperors, kings, princes, or town governments did not possess juridical validity unless they fit neatly into the schemes of common doctrine.[13] It is, as a result, indicative of indifference at the schools and in the courts that for a long time the oldest royal enactment embracing Bolognese concepts of abortion as a capital offense failed to attract attention in the form of written commentary. In the mid-1200s, the famous Castilian king Alfonso X ordered the compilation of the *Libro des las leyes.* Better known under the title of *Las Siete Partidas,* the *Libro* is testimony to the strong influence of late medieval university law on the Iberian Peninsula. In their treatment of prenatal death (7.8.8) and on many other occasions, Alfonso's compilers borrowed heavily from decretist and civilian teachings first formulated by Gratian, Azo, and colleagues:

---

12. Jacobus de Grafiis, *Decisiones aureae* 1 (Venice: Giunta, 1609), fol. 206vb–210ra, bk. 2, *decisio* 63; the bulk of his text (first published in 1592) was completed before May 1591.

13. Laurent Mayali, "Le notion de 'statutum odiosum' dans la doctrine romaniste au moyen âge," *Ius commune* 12 (1984): 57–69; Wolfgang P. Müller, "Signorolus de Homodeis and the Late Medieval Interpretation of Statutory Law," *RIDC* 6 (1995): 221–228; Andrea Padovani, "La glossa di Odofredo agli statuti veneziani di Iacopo Tiepolo del 1242," *RIDC* 20 (2009): 89–111.

If a woman wittingly [*scienter*] drinks or eats something, or hits her own stomach with her fists, thereby causing an abortion, she is to be killed if the fetus was already alive; otherwise, she must be exiled to an island for five years. The same applies to the husband who wittingly beats his wife so that she miscarries. Should an outsider do this instead, he shall suffer death for a live [fetus] and five years of exile for one not yet alive.[14]

Premodern lawyers betrayed little awareness of the above regulations, despite their attribution to a legendary ruler like Alfonso the Wise. The persistent lack of interest was hardly caused by prolonged resistance from the aristocracy, who, according to current historical understanding, did not permit use of the *Siete Partidas* in royal Castilian tribunals until, in 1348, the Ordenamientos de Alcalá finally granted the necessary license in top-downward fashion.[15] As far as is known, juristic reaction from the bottom up did not produce significant glosses before about 1500, a sign either that Alfonso's catalog of measures against criminal abortion met with general disregard on the part of his judges or that standards of the continental Ius commune applied in central Castilian courts automatically and as a blueprint, never entering into serious conflict with the king's provisions. Much of the text reflects Bolognese teachings quite faithfully, by invoking, for instance, the same punishments of death and temporary exile that Azo had read into Justinian's *Corpus*; by referring to the fetus with the Roman expression of *partus* rather than the canonistic *puerperium*; and by insisting, in line with the ancient Lex Cornelia, on the need to act intentionally (*scienter*) as a key prerequisite of full legal responsibility. In addition, the Castilian legislator took the distinction from the canon law tradition between a partus that was alive and another that was not yet *vivificatus*. The term *vivificatus* is absent from Gratian's Decretum but figures visibly in Innocent III's decretal of 1211, which Alfonso's compatriot, Raymond of Penyafort, later incorporated into the *Liber extra*.[16]

Given the high degree of convergence between *Siete Partidas* 7.8.8 and academic doctrine, it may not come as a surprise that express recognition of

---

14. For the Latin text, see *Las Siete Partidas* 7.8.8 (Salamanca: Andrea de Portonariis, 1555), fol. 30vb–31ra; English introduction and translation by Samuel Scott and Robert Burns, *Las Siete Partidas*, 5 vols. (Philadelphia: University of Pennsylvania Press, 2001), 1:xxx–xlviii; 5:1346–1347.

15. José Garcia-Marín, *El aborto criminal en la legislación y la doctrina. Pasado y presente de una polemica* (Madrid: Ediciones de derecho reunidas, 1980), 25–26; Emma Montanos-Ferrín and José Arnilla-Bernál, *Estudios de historia del derecho criminal* (Madrid: Dykinson, 1990), 156–180.

16. As X 5.12.20; the parallel points of Bolognese doctrine, which set the stage for the *Siete Partidas* 7.8.8, are treated above, chapters 1 and 2.

a major disagreement had to await intervention by the celebrated Spanish jurist Gregorio Lopez, whose critical testimony in the form of a marginal glossa was first published with the authoritative text in 1555. Would it really be possible for a husband who had wittingly beaten his pregnant wife to get away with a reduced sanction of five years in exile, notwithstanding the fact that the ensuing miscarriage had killed a fetus endowed with a human soul? Being thoroughly trained in the traditions of scholastic jurisprudence, Gregorio Lopez could not help but wonder about the juxtaposition in the *Siete Partidas* of incriminating behavior and a spouse's resolve to proceed scienter and in awareness of homicidal implications. To overcome the interpretive difficulty, the Spanish commentator responded in the same way that his younger colleague Jacobus de Grafiis did a few decades later when confronted with *Effraenatam*. Each acted as if there were no serious discrepancy between the legislative mandate and common opinion of the lawyers. Faced with a law that proposed lesser retribution for fatal attacks on the unborn child of one's marital partner, Gregorio chose to start on a positive note, suggesting that, in truth, the envisioned perpetrator had resorted to battery not out of malice (*dolo*) but for purely disciplinary reasons, which, as the glossator omitted to mention, would have furnished other offenders, according to the Ius commune, with a valid excuse to escape capital punishment as well. In the opposite case of *dolus*, Gregorio continued, defendants involved in spousal conflict who intentionally provoked fetal death would, like any outsiders, suffer execution, turning the exception afforded by *Siete Partidas* on its head.[17]

At the time when Gregorio Lopez and Jacobus de Grafiis were active, the historical tide in the West had begun to turn against the deeply ingrained belief that legal norms were shaped above all by university teachers. The two sixteenth-century authors still shared older habits according to which the scholastic Ius commune would determine whether authoritative legislation was intrinsically aberrant and hence unlawful. Progressively, though, they relied on explanatory standards that looked ever more backward as the days went by. Certainly from the 1600s, a vastly different understanding of the lawyer's role in society was emerging. Instead of scholarly consensus, the will of the legislator gained ground in the common estimate as the sole source of valid law, a development illustrated, for example, by the rapid and permanent abandonment of the thirteenth-century glossae ordinariae in printed

---

17. Gregorius Lopez, *Glossa super* 7.8.8, s.v. *a su mujer*, in *Las Siete Partidas*, fol. 30vb–31ra; cf. Garcia-Marín, *El aborto criminal*, 132–141. On dolus as a prerequisite of full criminal liability in the Ius commune, see below note 25.

textbooks and court proceedings. Modern historians have characterized this thoroughgoing transformation of juridical culture as a process in which the administration of justice was gradually appropriated by the political leadership, with university teachers and judges reinventing themselves as state employees and with state legislation becoming the only binding definition of judicial right and wrong.[18] Meanwhile and for present purposes, it is important to note that the new mentality, presupposing rules that required formal establishment through governmental action from the top down, had possessed little or no significance during the later Middle Ages or, to be on the extreme side of cautiousness, at least not in connection with the criminalization of abortion. Prior to the 1500s, that is to say, the principal promoters of substantive doctrinal change were, always and across Latin Christendom, identical with those who had created criminal doctrine in the first place: the professors at the law schools and their graduates.

Communis Opinio and Peer Dissent

After completion of the final, vulgate redaction of the Decretum around 1140, canonistic interpreters found little reason to challenge the equation between abortion and the crimen of homicide. Unimpeded by major disagreement, learned discourse moved toward a single set of rules embraced by all doctors of the Ius commune. By the 1240s, their consensus had assumed written permanence in the form of glossae ordinariae on Gratian's compilation, the *Liber extra*, and Justinian's *Corpus iuris civilis*. Most remarkably, the standard commentary of Accursius on the Digest ignored the fact that Justinian's authoritative text did not adhere to Christian principles of protection for unborn life. To justify interpretations to the contrary, medieval civilians turned instead to the Septuagint, a Greco-Jewish translation of the

---

18. In the premodern era, "what must be qualified as 'law' had come into being and continued to exist outside of the 'state,' and not infrequently in opposition to the state"; state formation must be understood in terms of "progressive appropriation by the state of the task of administering the law in its various manifestations"; "full control over courts and law-making was only attained with the revolutions of the end of the eighteenth century," whereas previously, "no mere collection of legal writings, however authoritative, could have sufficed"; the practical impact of older jurisprudence conversely depended "on the method used in applying these texts," identifiable with "the specific technique introduced at the beginning of the twelfth century by the glossators of the University of Bologna": Antonio Padoa Schioppa, "Postface," in *The Origins of the Modern State in Europe, Thirteenth to Eighteenth Centuries*, vol. 4, *Legislation and Justice*, ed. Antonio Padoa Schioppa (Oxford: Oxford University Press, 1997), 337–338, 345–346; cf. also Dietmar Willoweit, "Programm eines Forschungsprojekts," in *Die Entstehung des öffentlichen Strafrechts. Bestandsaufnahme eines europäischen Forschungsproblems*, ed. Dietmar Willoweit (Cologne: Böhlau, 1999), 1–22.

Old Testament also cited, as mentioned, by the church lawyers. Concerted streamlining activities left scarcely any room for jurists who used the legal source material to demonstrate that their Roman predecessors had rejected the association of prenatal existence with human qualities. Before the fourteenth century, awareness that ancient jurisprudence had thought differently about embryological growth never transformed into more than casual and unheeded asides. They were instantly eclipsed by a barrage of commentary that insisted upon the absolute validity of established Bolognese opinion.

Against this background of scholastic routine in dogged pursuit of doctrinal uniformity, a rare marginal entry added around 1300 to the Accursian gloss in one among hundreds of surviving manuscripts is cast in a particularly glaring light. The anonymous author of this *additio* revealed a striking independence of mind in that he departed from otherwise uncontested legal views on abortion. Although he ultimately stopped short of challenging the general belief that successive stages of animation unfolded in the maternal womb, he did present a thorough reassessment, based on a fresh and highly idiosyncratic examination of the Roman *leges*, of how to summarize adequately the multiple gradations of punishment prescribed for fetal killings. As the point of departure for his explanations he selected a fragment of Tryphoninus, the second-century juristic expert, who in Dig. 48.19.39 speaks of different penalties for offenders, death and temporary exile:

> With regard to the meaning of this law we must distinguish: either the woman kills her offspring after birth, in which case she will be punished for parental murder [*parricidium*], as in Dig. 48.9.1 and Cod. 9.17.1; or she kills unborn offspring, for which she will receive capital punishment if she took money for the act; if she killed without taking money, she is punished with [temporary] exile provided she killed or rather destroyed life within forty days after conception; if she killed it after those forty days, she is punished with perpetual exile, as in Dig. 48.8.8. I understand Dig. 47.11.4 in the same fashion.[19]

The strongest statement of the *additor* contrary to the teachings of the glossa ordinaria was his attempt to limit the exposure of lay offenders to execution. According to his reasoning, death was inescapable only if the accused had been bribed to terminate a pregnancy, an aggravating circumstance that, perhaps in the eyes of the unknown author and definitely according to Bolognese

---

19. The Latin version of the gloss is printed in *Die Abtreibung*, 98n178; from *Additio ad* Dig. 48.19.39 (Vatican, BAV, lat. 1426, fol. 204ra); similarly *ad* Dig. 48.8.8, s.v. *si mulierem*, ibid., fol. 191va.

opinion from the period of Bartolus (d. 1357) onward, was considered decisive regardless of whether the unborn victim had possessed a human soul or not.[20] The additio further highlights a subtle difference in the punishment of abortion between Marcian's Dig. 47.11.4 (*temporale exilium*) and Ulpian's Dig. 48.8.8 (*exilium*), explaining that it attests to the presence of twofold penal retribution in the Roman law. The dualism supposedly acknowledged that fatalities in the womb could occur either before or after animation.

For the moment, mainstream lawyerly opinion remained unaware and unimpressed. Although the marginal supplement subjected to skeptical scrutiny views that were widely accepted as self-evident and part of the civilian glossa ordinaria, the additor did not oppose what surely represented the most invasive element of ordinary Bolognese interpretation, the canonistic distinction between nonhuman and human fetal life. In effect, the fundamental incompatibility of scholastic doctrine with the original position of Justinian's *Corpus* went unrecognized by yet another generation of lawyers until publication of a specific legal brief (*consilium*) on the matter signed by the Milanese jurist Signorolus de Homodeis (d. 1371). Written around 1340 and included in sixteenth-century editions of his works as the first (*primum*) in a series of cases for the instruction of judges, litigants, and students, the text offers an unprecedented treatment of abortion, guided not least by close inspection of pertinent passages from the Roman Digest. Signorolus obviously had a concrete situation in mind when he chose to reexamine the question of how the parallel in traditional Azonian and Accursian jurisprudence between induced miscarriages and homicide would find proper implementation at the hands of lay judges in the northern Italian city of Cremona:

> A Cremonese town statute stipulates that he who commits homicide shall be decapitated so that he dies. It recently happened that A and B fought with one another and that B's wife interfered in the fight. The aforementioned A struck B's wife with a shield just above her kidneys. Back home, the battery [percussio] caused the woman to abort, although she herself stayed alive.[21]

Fourteenth-century readers must have sensed the presence of an innovative approach as soon as they came across the following phrase, in which

---

20. Bartolus de Saxoferrato, *Commentaria, in* Dig. 47.11.4 (Munich, BSB, lat 3634, fol. 181rb). This rigorous interpretation survived well into the 1600s; cf. *Die Abtreibung*, 146n255.

21. Signorolus de Homodeis, *Consilia* (Lyon: Giunta, 1549), *Consilium* 1, fol. 1ra (no. 1); see Müller, "Signorolus," 226–230; *Die Abtreibung*, 99–105.

Signorolus announced that he would discuss the legal implications of B.'s percussio "first in terms of the Ius commune, and then from the standpoint of statutory law [*Ius proprium*]." Prior to the *Consilium primum*, few people would have thought of scholastic doctrine on abortion as consisting of more than a single set of rules. Signorolus instead presented himself as an advocate of greater interpretive freedom and supplemented general opinion with a second and wholly divergent line of reasoning.

Signorolus divided his argument into three main strands, two of which rested on long-reiterated academic assumptions. He started out by reviewing central notions of conventional Bolognese theory in favor of the death penalty. One by one, he cited the Ordinary Gloss on Marcian's pertinent lex (Dig. 47.11.4) as well as additional passages from Justinian's *Corpus* that dealt primarily with questions of hereditary succession. Together they were believed to place the fetus on a par with born children. The Milanese *consiliator* also provided references to ecclesiastical norms, so that by the end of his opening remarks he had covered the essentials of accepted juristic thinking. Next, Signorolus chose to traverse relatively uncharted territory by assembling considerations excusing A, the defendant in the Cremonese trial, from having to face capital punishment for the miscarriage endured by B's wife. The consilium dwells extensively on exceptions revolving around A's apparent lack of malice and finally culminates in the conclusion that decapitation is unwarranted since there is no positive proof establishing A's ability to identify the woman as pregnant before he thrust the shield into her side. A's aggression, furthermore, had not been aimed at the fetus but chiefly at the expectant mother; thus his case fell under the general maxim that without direct intent (*principalis intentio*), full liability was not to be presumed. In an intriguing aside, Signorolus went on to suggest that the Roman *Corpus* contained many phrases denying legal protection to unborn life and treated it merely as an extension of the mother's entrails (*pars viscerum matris*).[22] This likely had been A's impression as he turned against B's suddenly intervening spouse.

In moving forward, Signorolus embarked on a juristic investigation of his own, contending that the rules of the Ius commune did not necessarily apply to the Cremonese statute. The central premise behind his reflections was that the *Corpus iuris civilis* nowhere identified the fetus as a veritable human being (*homo*), whence the statutory infliction of death for homicidium did not

---

22. Echoing Ulpian's famous passage in Dig. 25.4.1.1; the present paraphrase is based on Signorolus, *Consilium* 1, fol. 1ra–b (no. 1, 3–6).

permit extension to the unborn. For the first time in Western legal history, Signorolus undertook an analysis that ignored church norms and defined the juridical nature of prenatal existence exclusively on the basis of Justinian's compilation:

> And this can be shown to be true in many ways. An etymological limitation, for example, implies the limitation of etymological derivatives, as in Dig. 12.1.2.2, Dig. 41.2.1, Dig. 16.1.1.1, and Inst. 1.14.5; which corresponds exactly to the above case, because before birth, the partus is not viewed as human properly speaking, as in Dig. 35.2.9.1 and Dig. 25.4.1.1. But if it is not referred to as human, we cannot use the term of homicide in the proper etymological sense, for the significance of the word implies its [legal] effect, as in Dig. 12.1.2.2, Cod. 3.12.3, and Cod. 1.3.26.[23]

Signorolus reinforced his conclusion with other citations from the leges, repeating that the attainment of humanity had to wait until birth. Apart from differences in terminology between partus and the Roman concept of homo, he believed he had found support for his position in a maxim admonishing Bolognese interpreters not to stretch the literal meaning of statutes beyond the limits set by Justinian's *Corpus*. By distinguishing the Ius commune from the Ius proprium and favoring a highly restrictive reading of statutory command, Signorolus appears to have looked for a way to display preconceived results in a technically sound format.[24]

In his final assessment, Signorolus reaffirmed the view that the statutes of Cremona did not condone punishment (*pena*) of abortion as homicide. At the same time, he left audiences speculating as to whether he understood the conclusion to mean partial or complete exemption of the offense from criminal prosecution both inside and outside town. His colleagues and successors were quick to remedy the omission and asserted that "arbitrary" and "extraordinary" sentencing short of mutilation or execution—usually temporary or permanent banishment—constituted the proper response. Signorolus for his part seemed content to recommend familiar judicial outcomes when he specified the treatment of convicted parties within the confines of the Ius commune and acknowledged the admissibility of differentiated

---

23. Signorolus, *Consilium* 1, fol. 1rb–va (no. 8–9); on partus and its meaning in Roman antiquity, see chap. 4, notes 4–5.

24. Signorolus, *Consilium* 1, fol. 1va (no. 10–12); concerning the rule *In statutis interpretatio non est amplianda*, Müller, "Signorolus," 226; Padovani, "La glossa di Odofredo," 94–97.

penalties depending on the stage of animation. This last concession, however, was not made without emphasis on the need to secure solid evidence for the presence of malice aforethought in the suspect's mind. Should judges harbor any residual doubt as to the exact degree of culpability, the author of the *Consilium primum* advised them to forgo execution and inflict only discretionary penae (*arbitrariae* or *extraordinariae*).[25]

In the long run, the method adopted by Signorolus of systematically separating the content of Justinian's leges from late medieval accretions in the form of scholastic glosses led to the realization that there was no necessary link between decretist and early civilian identifications of prenatal killing with homicide and the more lenient, classical Roman approach. As the findings of the Milanese doctor and nobleman began to proliferate, they were destined to challenge mainstream jurisprudence and cause a stir in both academic circles and the sphere of adjudication. As a matter of fact, *Consilium primum* was almost instantly transcribed and reedited for the literary needs of judicial personnel and university lecturers. By 1348, Jacobus de Butrigariis, a Bolognese teacher and colleague of Signorolus, had inserted a shorter version of the text into his own *Lectura* on Justinian's Codex, whereas Albericus de Rosate (d. 1360), a lay judge active at Bergamo, copied Signorolus twice, first into his *Quaestiones statutorum* and subsequently into a commentary on the Digest.[26] As a result of these interventions, a distinct, statutory understanding of abortion, defying the canonized interpretation of Roman law by the communis opinio, started to inform general juridical knowledge. Complete appropriation was, on the other hand, a slower and more haphazard process. Jacobus de Butrigariis, for example, professed adherence to the older categorization of abortion as a capital crime. Albericus de Rosate set a popular precedent through his noncommittal rendering of the contrary position, echoed especially by authors of fifteenth-century handbooks on criminal procedure. Conscientious repetition and abiding skepticism marked the writings of everyone following directly in the footsteps of Signorolus.

---

25. On lesser criminal retribution according to the Ius commune, cf. chapter 8; the scholastic discussion of dolus is surveyed by Woldemar Engelmann, *Die Schuldlehre der Postglossatoren* (Leipzig: Duncker & Humblodt, 1895); Marzia Lucchesi, *Siquis occidit occidetur. L'omicidio doloso nelle fonti consiliarie (secoli XIV–XVI)* (Padua: CEDAM, 1999).

26. Jacobus Butrigarius, *Lectura, super* Cod. 9.16.7, s.v. *Si quis necandi* (first recension: Lucca, Biblioteca Capitolare 372, fol. 183va–b; second recension, Paris: Parvus, 1516 [repr., Bologna: Formi, 1973], fol. 104vb–105ra); Albericus de Rosate, *Commentaria de statutis* (more commonly, *Quaestiones statutorum*) 3.59 (Frankfurt/M.: Richter, 1606), 245a–247a; Albericus de Rosate, *Commentarii, in* Dig. 1.5.7 (Venice: Societas Aquilae Renovantis, 1585; repr., Bologna: Formi, 1974), fol. 46vb–47rb (no. 3–10).

Nobody expressed himself fully in favor of the idea that municipal statutes excluded the death penalty as punishment for the slaying of a formed fetus.[27] Had it not been for Baldus de Ubaldis (1327–1400), a jurist of greatest prestige and stature, law professors might never have rallied around the opposite viewpoint in numbers large enough to earn them, until 1500, recognition as partisans of a respected minority opinion.

Although Baldus employed formulations and an argumentative logic that did not betray any dependency on Signorolus, the two jurists arrived at nearly identical conclusions. Baldus wished to exempt the fetus categorically from statutes referring to homo in a criminal context and was perhaps even prepared to restrict retribution of fetal killings to the ecclesiastical realm alone.[28] Notwithstanding doubts as to whether he and Signorolus contemplated statutory indemnity or just argued for the reduction of penal responsibility, the two interpreters and their most outspoken late medieval imitators—Paulus de Castro (d. 1419), Raphael Fulgosius (d. 1427), and Alexander Tartagnus (d. 1477)—became key instigators of several pathbreaking legal and intellectual developments.[29] They clearly anticipated explanatory techniques that early modern humanist jurisprudence would employ to reconstruct Roman law in its historicity and without the modifications resulting from centuries of scholastic commentary. Moreover and immediately after publication of the *Consilium primum* in the early 1340s, Signorolus, Baldus, and younger representatives of what eventually turned into an alternative Bolognese formula for the treatment of prenatal death in the lay courts seem to have prompted a wave of repressive action across northern Italy. It cannot be sheer coincidence that the oldest urban and communal statutes submitting abortion to retribution date from precisely the same period. Led by the communes of Biella (1345) and Prata (circa 1361–1366), a string of smaller towns in the Friuli region and along the

---

27. Tepid responses came from Angelus Aretinus (d. 1454), *Tractatus de maleficiis*, s.v. *Et ex intervallo dictus Titius, Quid si quis faciat* (Lyon: Giunta, 1555), 501b–502a; and Hippolytus de Marsiliis (d. 1529), *Commentaria, super* Dig. 48.8.8 (Lyon: Crespinus, 1531), fol. 33va; Hippolytus de Marsiliis, *in* Cod. 9.16.7 (Lyon: Crespinus, 1531), fol. 22vb–23ra. Angelus de Ubaldis (d. 1429), *Lectura, super* Cod. 9.16.7 (Lyon: Moylin, 1534), fol. 269rb, criticized Jacobus de Butrigariis for having extended the penalties of the Ius commune to fortuitous percussiones.

28. Baldus de Ubaldis, *Commentaria, in* Dig. 28.2.12, s.v. *in integrum* (Lyon: Societas Librariorum, 1551), fol. 42rb; for additional scholastic reactions, *Die Abtreibung*, 105–111.

29. Paulus de Castro, *Super Infortiato, in* Dig. 28.2.12 (Lyon: Trechsel, 1535), fol. 50va–b; Alexander Tartagnus, *Commentaria, super* Dig. 28.2.12 (Lyon: Freis, 1551), fol. 73vb–74va; the parallel view of Raphael Fulgosius, *in* Dig. 48.8.8, was cited by Prosperus Farinaccius, *Praxis et theorica criminalis* 2.2, q. 122 (Frankfurt/M.: Palthenius, 1610), 215b (no. 6), as available in print.

shores of the Lago Maggiore started to issue ordinances treating fetal man-slaughter as a capital crime.[30] Chronology suggests that municipal leaders did not step in to criminalize acts of this nature for the first time but rather felt that recent, learned criticism of the communis opinio threatened to undermine established ways of meting out punitive justice. Legal innovation arguably originated from the schools of jurisprudence, whence it spread and triggered local legislative responses. The unprecedented promulgation of Italian laws punishing fatal attacks on the unborn may have been aimed at preventing lawyers and teachers from further maintaining that the fetus, unlike human beings and regardless of bodily formation, did not deserve the highest degree of normative protection.

Systematic Law before the Rise of the Modern State

The criminalization of abortion in the later Middle Ages rested on the work of professional canonists and civilian lawyers at the emerging schools of jurisprudence. Being firmly rooted in Christian morality, scholastic thinkers were successful in clarifying vaguely perceived notions of right and wrong in society and in the normative tradition. Twelfth-century juristic thought, refined and imparted principally at Bologna, determined that specific forms of fetal death should be treated as equivalent to the crimen of homicide and merit execution as the maximum legal punishment. From the mid-1300s, Bolognese consensus weakened somewhat when a minority of professors began to challenge established views and concluded that the offense amounted to a lesser crime, calling for nonfatal retribution such as banishment. Meanwhile and from the modern perspective, it is important to keep in mind that popes, emperors, kings, princes, and other political leaders played but a minor role in the shaping of criminal concepts, procedures, and penalties. Jurists did welcome princely legislation because it added authoritative weight to their own doctrinal conclusions. Contrary to present-day expectations, however, they felt surprisingly free to bypass or modify legislative texts for the sake of accommodating internal debate and often highly partisan purposes. In the last analysis, common lawyerly opinion remained the sole standard legal

---

30. Biella (1345), cap. 21, in *Statuta communis Bugellae et documenta adiecta*, ed. Pietro Sella (Biella: Testa, 1904), 179; Prata (1361–1366), rubric 9, in *Comparazione analitica degli statuti di Prata con le loro derivazioni legislative*, ed. Egidio Zoratti (Udine: del Biano, 1908), discussed by Georg Dahm, *Das Strafrecht Italiens im ausgehenden Mittelalter* (Berlin: de Gruyter, 1931), 342–346; Garancini, "Materiali," 502–510; *Die Abtreibung*, 87–88. An earlier Italian statute from Siena (1309) reflects a different prosecutorial rationale, the fight against harmful magic; cf. below, chapter 7.

practitioners would always refer to. Until the 1500s, the mechanism of forging justice by way of learned discourse, through peer scrutiny, and collegial consent characterized the growth of legal systems everywhere in the West, be it the general law of the church, the royal English common law, or the Ius commune governing laity on the European mainland. With regard to the willful termination of pregnancies, the push toward punitive treatment and adjudication was surely a private undertaking and occurred quite removed from coercive and downward political interference.

Given a legal universe in which lawmakers represented an abstract and, as in the case of the ancient Roman *princeps*, rather fictitious entity postulated by law professors and judicial personnel, the description of late medieval juristic endeavor in adequate modern terms is greatly complicated. Notwithstanding the enormous distance between past and present, historiography has barely acknowledged the existence of a notable challenge. Scholarship typically persists in attributing to late medieval legislation priority over scholastic commentary. Legislative statements are read under the assumption that they possessed relevance apart from what scholastic commentators were prepared to make of them. And in the same vein, a vast majority of scholarly investigations have not hesitated to adopt current language to write about interactions between late medieval rulers and those ruled, between theory and practice, and between norm and power, often overlooking that indispensable ingredients of the Western experience such as state monopolies on violence and justice did not arise until the Middle Ages had come to an end. What, to put it differently, remains of our word "law" if it no longer reflects the will of a single and superior authority, backed up by permanent police and salaried agents of enforcement? And what will it mean for the expression of "lawyer" if it refers to trained experts who received normative texts and interpretive assignments from their own colleagues instead of sovereigns? With the respective functions of jurisprudence and political intervention all but reversed, risks of anachronism run high if we use current vocabulary in hopes of creating an accurate account of the driving factors that, from about 1140 onward, transformed abortion, among many other things, into crime.

In his monograph on records of judicial prosecution from fourteenth-century Marseille, the American historian Daniel Smail has attempted to overcome the explanatory dilemma.[31] To capture the late medieval legal

---

31. Daniel L. Smail, *The Consumption of Justice: Emotions, Publicity, and Legal Culture in Marseille, 1264–1423* (Ithaca: Cornell University Press, 2003), 1–28.

experience, he has invoked words and imagery from a seemingly distant semantic field. The above identification of scholastic jurisprudence with something resembling private entrepreneurship rather than the extended arm of government is in line with his observation that the workings of justice in the 1300s call not for a description in juristic terms but for vocabulary and rationales that in modern English are associated with the world of commerce. The remainder of this chapter builds on Smail's approach by arguing that from our vantage point, marked by five to nine centuries of hindsight, the events propelling Gratian and his successors are best understood in the language of business. The striking freedom of full-time lawyers from state control, for example, reflects the circumstance that systematic law arose from the interplay between changing societal needs and individuals who sought to exploit new market opportunities. By establishing schools that promised to impart knowledge in an unprecedented "scholastic" format, intellectuals carved out a highly lucrative niche for themselves. To attract a paying clientele, they exercised their academic craft in core areas of urbanization. The convergence of supply and demand in places like Bologna points to an exceptional degree of compatibility between normative arrangements favoring townspeople and those promoted by the law professionals.

The advance of jurisprudence was intimately tied to the fortunes of merchants, artisans, and city dwellers. It highlighted the innovative quality and transformative potential of legal expertise, which in the determination of just and unjust proposed a radical departure from the modes of adjudication that had been in place for more than half a millennium up to the 1100s. Scholastic law introduced a method of discerning right from wrong that perfectly matched the concerns of the "commercial revolution." The decisive contribution of Gratian and his colleagues to the prospering of urban interests can be seen in the simultaneous obsolescence of early medieval customary Leges. Celtic and Germanic "manuals for mediators" had proven perfectly sufficient in the past, when overall mobility had been limited and the average person encountered relatively few incentives to leave the security of his or her protective network and area behind. Common mechanisms of conflict settlement had privileged considerations of status and interlocking personal bonds, within which members were expected to be loyal (that is, partial) and vouch for the innocence of allies and friends. By the same token, judicial guidelines were woefully inadequate as instruments extending effective tutelage to traders and travelers, the prototypical upstarts of the eleventh century. Concentration on the measure of clan solidarity did not offer reassurance to anonymous foreigners passing through distant lands. No less disturbing from a business point of view was the lack of stringency in traditional procedures.

A successful defense depended on the availability of backing from oath helpers or collective bailout in the form of monetary compensation. Acts of violence were not prosecuted as such and the restoration of order remained beyond the capacity of presiding judges, should one of the adversaries decide to resume feuding or simply abandon court.

Older notions of voluntary, open-ended adjudication and communal sentencing posed serious obstacles to the establishment of commerce as a dominant and pervasive feature in society. Uncertainty as to the exact course of legal claims must have discouraged many who wished to take their merchandise on the road. Calculating businessmen required a minimum of predictability, permitting them to strike a reasonable balance between risks of material loss and prospects of profitability. The growing need for calculable conditions and physical protection independent of local or family ties contributed to the popularity of ideas according to which proper governance had to proceed on the basis of universally binding standards. While perennial conflict ensued among warriors, bishops, merchants, and townspeople as to their respective role in the implementation of mandatory precepts, parties increasingly realized that involvement in the task promised great material gain. Soon enough, the nonnegotiable maintenance of public peace and downward dispensation of impartial justice turned into chief concerns of Western political leadership.[32]

The spread of trade-oriented attitudes in the years after 1050 gave rise to cultural ideals that had been foreign to early medieval lay existence. The new mentality advanced in the form of five closely interrelated trends, as concepts of right and wrong sustained by warrior society succumbed to values favoring urban and commercial pursuits. The transformation implied, to begin with, that in the name of unleashing mobility, violent feuds had to be branded as intolerable disruptions of normalcy. Peace became the default mode of social affairs. Second, to render the imposition of mandatory rules realistic and feasible, traditional mediation had to give way to adjudication from above, reliant on principles endowed with extreme precision and ensuring predictability and conformity of conduct everywhere. Growing demand for general norms also required their thoroughgoing systematization, granted

---

32. Attempts to explain the advent of systematic law have typically pointed toward legislators and educational elites, as in Harold Berman, *Law and Revolution: The Formation of the Western Legal Tradition*, vol. 1 (Cambridge, MA: Harvard University Press, 1983); and in works on the abandonment of unilateral ordeals, chap. 1, note 30. More recently, studies have begun to stress economic and grassroots factors; see Susan Reynolds, "The Emergence of Professional Law in the Long Twelfth Century," *Law and History Review* 21 (2003): 347–366; also chap. 2, note 2.

that an uncoordinated mass of regulations would have defied the primary purpose of consistent applicability. Third, to guarantee the actual implementation of absolute, well-defined, and noncontradictory standards, it was necessary to insist on the premise of personal accountability. Those who disobeyed the law would have to face their responsibility individually, without recourse to co-jurors and other procedures designed to gauge group support. Reliance on the proximity of family had to be overcome as well, a factor that persuaded scholastic thinkers and their sponsors to propose a regime of territorial security at the expense of clan-based protection. Finally, a legal order treating each subject without regard for his or her social standing presupposed the creation of powerful agencies in a position to break age-old patterns of local peer pressure and personal preferment. Submission to a single "rule of law" (*ordo iuris*) loomed large behind the centralization and consolidation of governmental functions during the High and later Middle Ages, two developments that, along with commercialization, have strengthened their hold on the West to the present day.

As chief agents of the criminalizing effort, the founders of systematic legal thought at Bologna and, across the Channel, at the Inns of Court in London, took care to offer their services at focal points of Western mobility and literacy. They marketed their skills in environments where strangers were likely to congregate and foster a spirit of normative equality and transparency. Swept up by strong urban demand, they could not, however, count on one feature that constitutes an inseparable component in the reflections of modern jurists. From the twelfth to the fifteenth centuries, law professors and practitioners exercised their craft without firmly established mechanisms of enforcement. Jurisprudence, as early modern historians in particular have agreed, preceded the birth of the bureaucratic state and operated for a long time without regular political assistance. The swift adoption of ideas recommending the treatment of abortion as a capital offense, for example, did not lead automatically to the investigation of suspects. Instead, legal thinkers took for granted that judicial activity would create its own benchmarks of intervention. For centuries to come, theorists did not worry about questions of implementation and relied on daily routine to identify areas where their ideas could be applied. While trial objectives were rationalized and framed coherently, effective recourse to juristic doctrines remained at the discretion of adversaries on the ground.

CHAPTER 4

Principal Arguments in Favor of Criminalization

Twelfth-century scholasticism, whether personified by French theologians, Bolognese professors of Roman law, or Gratian and his decretist successors, was unanimous in its adherence to the theory of successive animation, which, briefly put, divided fetal existence into several phases of development. Central to the reflections of academic lawyers and moralists was the question of when the fetus was joined by the human soul (*anima rationalis*). The event was believed to occur weeks or months after conception, superseding prior and lesser forms of fetal life and sustained first by a vegetative and then by an animal stage of prenatal growth. God, it was also agreed, continuously infused newly created *animae* into preconceived bodies and endowed them with reason (hence creatianism). Inspired by Gratian, Peter the Lombard's fundamental theological textbook again identified this instant with the formation of childlike limbs and contours, whereas civilians in the wake of Azo placed it with apparent numerical precision at the fortieth day of gestation. Early scholastic writers showed little awareness of the fact that their faith in creatianist doctrine represented a peculiar choice, as their authoritative sources, all composed during the ancient period, had contended with at least two alternative embryological models. One of them maintained that humanity was transmitted through the mixing of the parental seed (*ex traduce*) and present from the moment of insemination. The other taught the opposite extreme and delayed full participation in human nature until the time of delivery.

Research has thoroughly investigated the normative statements on abortion from antiquity. Medieval reflections on the subject were exposed, especially through Justinian's *Corpus*, to one strand of thought formulated under Stoic influence. A second position marked the works of Aristotle (d. 322 BC) and soon gave rise to an important tradition of Judeo-Christian writings. The Aristotelian viewpoint was rooted in the assumption that life in the maternal womb did not possess human quality without corresponding bodily features. It inspired a novel precept in the Greco-Jewish translation of the biblical Torah, known as the Septuagint, which expressly inveighed against the homicide of animated fetuses. Among the Latin church fathers, the passage (Exodus 21:22–23) was echoed in particular by Saint Augustine (d. 432), whose impact on the first generation of scholastic teachers such as Anselm of Laon and Gratian proved decisive. As shown in the first section below, their alignment of gradual animation with specific parameters of conduct met with general acceptance at the law schools by 1200. Mindful of embryonic formation, they considered the termination of unwanted pregnancies worthy of capital punishment except for the first six weeks or so of gestation.

The chapter further illustrates how theologians and lawyers again insisted on the wrongfulness of homicidal abortion should a pregnancy entail deadly risks for the expectant mother. In theoretical inquiries discussing medically advised therapeutic attempts to induce a miscarriage, they minimized the appeal of any legal justification to kill the fetus once it had assumed appropriate shape. Scarcely anticipated by late medieval commentators, objections to the effect that not fetal death but the rescue of an adult female patient constituted the doctor's primary objective did not gain prevalence until the early modern period and around the same time as scholastic consensus concerning the simultaneous arrival of physical articulation and humanity in the unborn baby started to be moved from about the fortieth day of gestation all the way back to conception. The growing disenchantment of academic culture with the Aristotelian theory of animation after 1600 is tracked in the last portion of the chapter to a succession of theological and juristic authors who eventually concluded that fetal development in the uterus had to be viewed as human from the very beginning. Although it is impossible to offer an exhaustive analysis of the extant source material, cross-references provided by key witnesses to the intellectual turnaround do suggest that the continuous existence of humanity from one end of the pregnancy to the other was originally proposed by Protestant theologians and jurists before being deemed plausible by Catholic lawyers and medical experts as well. Among the latter, the papal physician Paulus Zacchias (fl. 1650) first recommended the new embryological teachings as scientifically sound.

Successive Animation and Creatianism

From a medieval perspective, the Aristotelian theory of ensoulment found its most important vehicle of transmission in the Greco-Jewish tradition. The Hebrew version of the Old Testament, the Torah, does not mention abortion as a punishable offense but presents the description of a scenario (Exodus 21:22–23) that touches upon the violent death of a fetus. The passage affirms the rightfulness of damage claims by a husband whose wife aborted because of beatings she had suffered from the hands of an outsider. As long as the aggrieved woman did not endure personal physical harm, the Torah states, there is no reason to prescribe retaliation—"eye for eye and tooth for tooth"—apart from monetary compensation for the material loss. The thought of entitlement to normative protection for the fetus on a par with that of a born human being is not expressed. However, the situation changed with the official Greek rendering of the Torah in the third century before Christ. The translators of Exodus 21.22–23 in the so-called Septuaginta did not seek literal accuracy but rather adapted the original to their own embryological understanding:

> If two men litigate and one of them hits a pregnant woman so that she miscarries an unformed fetus, the perpetrator is liable to pay compensation as the woman's husband sees fit; and the former shall give the amount as if it were through arbitration. Was the child already formed, he shall give life for life.[1]

The transformation achieved by the seventy Greco-Jewish interpreters placed the killing of life in the womb for the first time in a punitive context. The fully animated state of prenatal existence is accorded value equal to that of a born individual and specifically to the one whose act the Septuagint clearly defines as homicidal. In addition, the criterion of physical formation, signaling infusion of a rational soul and attainment of complete personal integrity in the victim, is singled out as decisive for the determination of maximum culpability.

Most significant for the future normative development in the West, the rigorous position of the Septuaginta, passed on and disseminated by Hellenistic Judaism, was ultimately embraced by the exponents of nascent Christianity. From the very start, the young religion became a staunch defender of

---

1. Bibliographical references in chap. 1, note 14; also Noonan, "An Almost Absolute Value," 4–9; Kapparis, *Abortion in the Ancient World*, 47–52.

the unborn baby's right to life. The earliest church fathers rallied in unison behind the standpoint that the slaying of a fetus warranted equation with manslaughter. Disagreement among Christians persisted only insofar as certain authors wondered whether or not ecclesiastical discipline should prescribe, along with the Septuagint, distinct retribution depending on the phase of bodily formation. In the Eastern Church, the more rigorous opinion of Basil (d. 380) finally gained acceptance for arguing that, notwithstanding varying degrees of physical articulation, abortion always justified identification with murder.[2] In the Latin world, on the other hand, the patristic camp remained divided, at least initially. Theologians inclined toward the imposition of dual penance quarreled at length with the proponents of "traducianism," in whose estimate the soul joined matter as quickly as conception had occurred and spawned human embodiment. The principal figure among ancient theoreticians to propagate the traducianist view was Tertullian (d. 198), who in one of his literary invectives branded all induced miscarriages as full-fledged homicidia, even if they were performed immediately upon insemination. A famous saying coined by him, "man is he who will be one, just as the whole fruit is already in the seed," was destined to find multiple echoes in the later Western tradition.[3] It deserves to be noted, though, that scholastic writers during the Middle Ages typically ignored arguments ex traduce. Considered heresy, Tertullian's outburst was hardly popular and was generally greeted with silence.

Despite the widespread Hellenistic endorsement of successive animation and regardless of the fact that related ideas of protection for the (animated) fetus received the full backing of Christianity, many people in ancient society appear to have subscribed to contrary beliefs. They rather embraced teachings of the Greek Stoa, which posited that humanness would presuppose delivery and for the newborn to have inhaled his first breath. The Stoic point of view won particularly fervent allies among professionals whose written expertise far outlived their original pagan environment, the representatives of Roman jurisprudence. The works of classical lawyers active during the second and third centuries preserve numerous references to the juridical status of the fetus (partus), describing it as "part of the entrails" (portio viscerum),

2. Nardi, Procurato aborto, 512–522, 640–649; Spyridon Trojanos, "The Embryo in Byzantine Canon Law," in Analecta Atheniensia ad ius Byzantinum spectantia, ed. Spyridon Trojanos (Athens: Sakkroulas, 1997), no. 3.

3. Apologia 9.6–8, in CCL, 1.102–103, discussed in Nardi, Procurato aborto, 93–115, 154–159; Noonan, "An Almost Absolute Value," 12–15.

as "maternal womb" (*venter*), as "man in the making" (*spes hominis* or *spes animantis*), "not really man" (*homo non recte*), or "not yet man" (*nondum in rebus humanis*).[4] Correct interpretation of these expressions is complicated by the presence in Roman law of regulations that attributed to the fetus rights identical to those of a newborn. One particular field of equality concerned the rules of inheritance, where entitlement to succession was routinely interpreted as including children barely conceived at the time of their father's death. Jurists did not always clarify that in similar cases lack of differentiation between live offspring before and after birth rested on a legal fiction and was not meant to reflect matters as they were in nature.

The Stoic refusal to grant human quality to prenatal existence must have struck leaders of ancient Roman jurisprudence as completely self-evident, since only occasionally did they make statements expressly recognizing the underlying philosophical premise. At least one formulation offered by the jurist Paul and eventually incorporated into the Digest (1.5.7) resembles what he and his peers adopted as the general rule. The brief fragment explains that the partus enjoys legal personality whenever discussion focuses on advantageous property rights (*de commodis ipsius partus*), implying guarantees "as if" the fetus "were already part of man's affairs" (*ac si in rebus humanis esset*). Some Christian civilians commenting upon Paul's statement about a millennium afterward sensed that they had detected a contradiction between the sheltering of material benefits (*commoda*) on behalf of an unborn heir and the simultaneous Roman betrayal of his most fundamental interest in self-preservation by arguably allowing abortion.[5] In antiquity, on the other hand, the parallel drawn between pre- and postnatal hereditary rights related solely to the provisional reservation of commoda during pregnancy. Actual application of Paul's proverbial phrase occurred, as mentioned, when a property owner had died and the conceived offspring was treated alongside children who had already been born. Premature death of the *conceptus* through spontaneous or deliberate miscarriage prevented realization of the pending claim and did so in entirely lawful fashion. Paul's younger colleague, Papinian (Dig. 35.2.9.1), reassured Roman audiences that a fetus "not yet born can-

---

4. Cod. 7.4.14; Dig. 5.4.3 pr.; Dig. 11.8.2; Dig. 25.4.1.1; Dig. 35.2.9.1; Dig. 37.9.1 and 7 pr.; Dig. 38.8.1.8; Dig. 40.5.24.4; Dig. 44.2.7.1 and 3; see Anne Lefebvre-Teillard, "Infans conceptus. Existence physique et existence juridique," *RHDFE* 72 (1994): 499–503, reprinted in Lefebvre-Teillard, *Autour de l'enfant. Du droit canonique et romain médiéval au Code civil* (Leiden: Brill, 2008), 53–58.

5. Details above, chapter 3. Interestingly, the Accursian *Glossa ordinaria* (cf. *Die Abtreibung*, 50n99) made no attempt to contrast Paul's qualification of inheritance rights with the humanity of the "formed" fetus in Bolognese opinion.

not be properly called human," and the most famous among classical jurists, Ulpian (Dig. 25.4.1.1), observed that the partus formed but "a portion of the mother and her intestinal tract."

For half a thousand years, the juristic quotations contained in the Digest fell into total oblivion. Professional lawyers ceased to exist in the Western hemisphere and faced an altogether different moral and intellectual climate as they reemerged in the twelfth century. By then, higher learning was engaged in the assemblage and elaboration of guidelines for conduct in a Christian society, defining among other things proper behavior relative to the question of abortion. Gratian based his reflections on the patristic model of Saint Augustine. Peter Lombard consulted the Decretum to compose his textbook for aspiring theologians, and Bolognese glossators working on Justinian's compilation supplied their treatment of fetal death as a capital offense with succinct references to the Mosaic Law. All three disciplines relied in their conclusions on Exodus 21:22–23 as interpreted by the Septuaginta, which Gratian encountered through Augustinian and pseudo-Augustinian writings, the Lombard's *Sentences* through Gratian, and the civilians by way of canonistic sources identifying Exodus with "the law" contained in the second book "of Moses."[6] Scholastic advocacy for Greco-Jewish theories of successive animation as well as the spiritual and criminal condemnation of fatal attacks on unborn life arose, in other words, from a single *auctoritas*. Biblical in appearance, it was historically a product of interpolation, launched in pre-Christian antiquity by students of medical science and Aristotelian philosophy.

The founders of medieval scholasticism accepted the version of the Septuagint without hesitancy. It confirmed their assessment of abortion and was adopted in an atmosphere of great intellectual serenity. Independent of patristic or quasi-scriptural support, university teachers displayed utter faith in the validity of Greco-Jewish creatianism, a notion they seem to have classified among the basic theological premises in matters of right and wrong. A demonstration of the belief that God's creation and infusion of rational souls into conceived and still shapeless bodies during gestation constituted an absolute truth can be seen, for instance, in the way academic jurists and theologians negotiated the presence of a conflicting passage in their arsenal of canonical auctoritates. Apart from allusions to the Septuaginta in Gratian's work (C. 32, q. 2, c. 8–9), the scholastic dossier also included the common vulgate text of Exodus that circulated as part of the Western Bible (Vulgata).

---

6. Cf. chap. 1, notes 4, 12; Bolognese teachers were most likely inspired by the Decretum, C. 32, q. 2, c. 8, known and cited in the twelfth century by its opening word as Moyses.

Saint Jerome had rendered it directly from the Hebrew original of the Old Testament, where it did not feature remarks on successive animation or the penalty of death for induced miscarriage of a formed fetus. Over a brief period, canonists contemplated discussion of the discrepancy, invited by Bernard of Pavia's attempt of 1191 to complement the Decretum with a second set of normative materials published under the title *Breviarium extravagantium*. In placing the Vulgata alongside the decretist reading, however, the *Breviarium*, known today as the *Compilatio prima* (1 Comp. 5.10.2), posed no more than a short-lived challenge. The quote again disappeared from ordinary lectures in 1234, when Raymond of Penyafort's *Decretales,* with the approval of Pope Gregory IX, superseded Bernard's collection definitively. Indifference among colleagues in the intervening period certainly added to Raymond's disregard. A brief gloss by Ricardus Anglicus, written around 1200, is fairly characteristic of their minimal interest. For Ricardus, the chapter figuring in 1 Comp. 5.10.2 dealt only with the unformed partus, while, in his words, "elsewhere [*alibi*], in Gratian's Decretum, there is a well-made distinction" about different stages marking the development of unborn life. By "elsewhere," Ricardus meant the Septuagint.[7]

By glossing over the two renderings of Exodus 21:22–23, late medieval canon lawyers expressed their assurance that the doctrine of gradual animation was solid enough to withstand doubt arising from textual variants. Their conviction stood on especially firm grounds as it coincided with the dogmatic definitions of early scholastic theologians, who in tackling the question of creatianism had charted a single orthodox path that Western Christians were increasingly obliged to follow. Canonistic statements on Exodus in fact repeated what the twelfth-century Ordinary Gloss on Holy Scripture had already stated. And two hundred years later, around 1350, a second standard supplement, written by Nicolaus de Lyra and referred to as the *Postilla*, reiterated the view of older scriptural annotators and canon lawyers that Jerome's vulgate text on Exodus 21:22–23 needed to be understood in the light of the Septuaginta.[8] Throughout the academic establishment, then, the Greco-Jewish proposition of capital punishment for the killing of a fetus served as a normative model, not because it could claim intrinsic validity for being biblical but because it was thought to convey the correct understanding

---

7. Ricardus Anglicus, *Apparatus in* 1 Comp. 5.10.2, s.v. *expecierit maritus* (Paris, BN, lat. 149, fol. 68vb), quoted, with contemporary commentary to the same effect, in *Die Abtreibung*, 28n55.

8. *Glossa ordinaria in* Exodus 21:22–23, in *Biblia Sacra*, vol. 1 (Lyon: Vincent, 1545), fol. 168va, 169ra–b; Nicolaus de Lyra, *Postilla in* Exodus 21:22–23, s.v. *et abortivum* and s.v. *sin autem mors,* in *Biblia Sacra,* vol. 1, fol. 168vb.

of fetal growth. By the same token, the Bolognese canonist Huguccio did not assume that preference for successive animation would be a matter of personal opinion. *Fides nostra* (our faith) alone, he exclaimed around 1188, would teach whose position students had to embrace. The main reason for rejecting alternative speculation on the origins of the human soul including traducianism was that it had been invented by heretics, who were damned in eternity for their disrespect of true religion.[9]

Until the age of the Reformation in the 1500s, Huguccio's observation accurately reflected scholastic attitudes toward theories of prenatal development. That newly created immortal souls would enter the womb as the embryo assumed human shape was deemed beyond debate, an accepted truth, and an attestation of proper faith. Lawyerly reflection would stay firmly and safely within these preestablished parameters. Along similar lines, the mid-1300s witnessed the formation of an important minority opinion among Bolognese teachers who, inspired by the doctrinal conclusions of Signorolus de Homodeis and Baldus de Ubaldis, maintained that lay judges in Italian cities were not necessarily bound by conventional academic wisdom and its identification of abortion with homicide. Instead, the objectors argued, the killing of the unborn called for treatment among the lesser offenses, considering that Roman criminal law had denied the partus legal status equal to that of born children. It was, to be sure, one thing for jurists like Signorolus and Baldus to point out that through close and literal reexamination they had uncovered in Justinian's *Corpus iuris civilis* the consistent rejection of creationist ideas; it would have been another to prefer the Roman position because of a belief in heretical Stoic philosophies that did not accord to human life physical existence before delivery. Chapter 3 has highlighted how lawyers of the Ius commune tacitly accepted the difference between legal and dogmatic statements and steered clear of challenging contemporary orthodoxy. They cited the relevant leges attributed to Paul, Papinian, and Ulpian for authoritative and juristic support but refrained from showing approval or even recognition of their ancient forerunners' views concerning the fetus.

Dogmatic insistence on the tenet of creationism informed believers about the unquestionable succession of events from insemination to the entry of an immortal soul and simultaneous delineation of the human physique. Meanwhile, determination of the way in which growth in the womb unfolded on a timeline was left entirely to experts from the field of medicine, the

---

9. Huguccio, *Summa*, C. 32, q. 2, c. 9, s.v. *cum semine;* printed above, introduction, note 14; *Die Abtreibung*, 24n43.

fourth academic discipline to arise in the twelfth century. Its representatives were perfectly positioned to strengthen orthodoxy, as their learned activities concentrated on the exposition of creatianist ideas, transmitted through the ages by the Hippocratic *Corpus* and by Aristotelian science. Full doctrinal consensus among the four branches of higher learning and neat separation of their respective areas of competence also enabled twelfth-century juristic thinkers to quote patristic authors whenever they wished to speak generically about the ensoulment of embryos and consult *medici* to establish in more specific terms what would have been, for example, the length of the interlude between conception and formation. Writing in 1164, the Bolognese decretist Rufinus directed readers of his *Summa* on Gratian to the *physici* for additional instruction as to why the process would last twice as long in a female as in a male fetus, over a period of eighty versus just forty days. His fleeting remark is characteristic of how legal thinkers relegated in-depth embryological inquiries to the physicians and their superior knowledge of medical authorities such as Hippocrates and Galen.[10]

To supply a rationale for the criminalization of abortion, jurists of the formative period garnered authoritative support freely and across disciplines from legal, theological, and medical sources. Beginning with Gratian and over the next four hundred years, consensus about physiological fundamentals ruled supreme at the law schools. To illustrate the point, there is the instance of ecclesiastical tradition as part of which popes, councils, and church fathers furnished canon lawyers with a bewildering variety of words to denote the decisive moment when the conceptus was joined by the human soul. Gratian's leading auctoritas, Saint Augustine, had used expressions deriving from the noun *formatio,* whereas Innocent III in 1211 preferred the term *vivificatio.* Still others described the fetus as "alive" (*vivus*) or simply "animated" (*animatus*), potentially adding to the confusion.[11] For the later Middle Ages, however, major juristic debate as to the exact significance of the existing terminology has not yet been tracked in the records. Nobody seems to have seized the opportunity and disputed specific legal outcomes by exploiting, in typically lawyerly fashion, the persistence of approximate vocabulary. On

---

10. Rufinus, *Summa,* D. 5, c.1, s.v. *In lege namque precipitur,* ed. Heinrich Singer (Paderborn: Schöningh, 1902), 17. On medical embryology, see chapter 6; concerning the rise of schools for physicians, Nancy Siraisi, "The Faculty of Medicine," in *A History of the University in Europe,* vol. 1, *Universities in the Middle Ages,* ed. Hilde de Ridder-Symoens (Cambridge: Cambridge University Press, 1992), 361–387.

11. C. 32, q. 2, c. 8 speaks of *animatus* and *formatus,* X 5.12.20 of *vivificatus.* Controversy regarding such varied language does not predate the 1500s; cf. below, notes 21–22.

the contrary, professors agreed wholeheartedly that *viv(ificat)us, animatus,* and *formatus* always implied the presence of an *anima rationalis.*

A parallel phenomenon can be seen in the way interpreters of Justinian's *Corpus* approached the quandary of animation. From the very start, their explanatory endeavors brought them into contact with contemporary theological and medical discussion, as civilian lawyers, in disregard of canonistic habits, gauged the arrival of humanity in the uterus not by focusing on physical shape but by measuring the process in length of time. The oldest glosses concurred that "forty days" prepared the fetus for transformation into a human being. Although canonists showed awareness of the figure and ascribed it readily to "the expertise of physicians" (*peritia physicorum*), it took them until the 1400s to integrate numerical information directly into their own treatments of criminal abortion. Earlier on, the omission established a curious divide between civilian comments trying to determine the duration of inanimate existence quantitatively and canonistic glosses that stressed the qualitative criterion of bodily consolidation. In addition, commentary on Justinian's *Corpus* accommodated an ever-greater array of numbers from authors lecturing, or being read, at the medical schools. The renowned civil lawyer Bartolus of Sassoferrato (d. 1356) once observed that the Ordinary Gloss on Marcian's Dig. 47.11.4, the conventional "location," or *sedes materiae,* for pertinent explications, alluded to a relatively brief period of "forty days" prior to animation, a total Bartolus considered correct at least with regard to the unborn male. "I also hear voices claiming that the partus be animate after sixty days," Bartolus continued, "a variation I will leave for further inquiry to the natural philosophers."[12]

Bartolus touched the tip of an interpretive iceberg that he and his colleagues were keenly aware of. Several decades earlier, his teacher, Cinus of Pistoia (d. 1317), had asked Gentile da Foligno, a celebrated professor of medicine, to provide jurists with a detailed embryological treatise. Most of the consilium Gentile wrote in response focused on the question of the greatest possible distance between intercourse and birth, a problem that affected many cases of hereditary succession in which paternity had been cast in doubt. Incidentally, Gentile addressed the issue of formatio as well. He repeated established views according to which the male fetus developed faster than the female and supplied an approximate time range for the process that he thought extended

---

12. Bartolus de Saxoferrato, *Commentaria, in* Dig. 47.11.4 (Munich, BSB, lat. 3634, fol. 181rb); canonists and civilians quoted numbers furnished by the physici from as early as the 1160s and 1170s; see above, note 10 and chap. 1, note 12.

from thirty to a maximum of fifty days after insemination. In subsequent years, Gentile's conclusions reached many readers among the teachers and students of Bolognese jurisprudence through the insertion of his consilium into various commentaries on the Digest.[13] Concurrently, demand for medical instruction was satisfied by yet another *tractatus* on fetal development that originally came from the pen of the celebrated physician and theologian, Giles of Rome (ca. 1280). The work of Giles reached larger law audiences from about 1350, when it was transcribed into Albericus de Rosate's massive compendium on the *Digestum vetus*. Having reproduced the reflections of Giles almost word for word, Albericus acquainted jurists with an array of biblical, philosophical, medical, and theological *auctoritates* devoted to determining the chronological lapse between procreation and arrival of the human soul. Through his efforts as a compiler, Albericus attested to the fact that precise numbers and timetables invited endless scholastic ruminations, whereas dogmatic consensus about successive animation united, at long last, everyone involved in the debate.[14]

Legal and Theological Assessments of Therapeutic Abortion

In another demonstration of how evaluations of abortion as crimen hinged upon the aspect of bodily formation, late medieval commentators pondered the admissibility of medically induced miscarriages. In the formative years of Bolognese jurisprudence, law teachers established various categories of guilt that since their first articulation around 1200 have left a permanent mark on Western notions of legal responsibility. Besides proposing fundamental distinctions between sin and crime, penance and punishment, juristic thinkers also measured the severity of individual misconduct in what they called cases of *perplexio*, real-life situations in which normative obligations collided with one another. In his lectures on pastoral theology delivered at Paris during the 1190s, Peter the Chanter contemplated the dilemma of a physician who was asked to prescribe contraceptive drugs in order to protect a woman of

---

13. Hermann Kantorowicz, "Cino da Pistoia ed il primo trattato di medicina legale," *Archivio storico italiano* 37 (1906): 115–128, reprinted in Hermann Kantorowicz, *Rechtshistorische Schriften* (Karlsruhe: Müller, 1970), 287–297. Later on, Gentile's consilium as reported by Cinus was often incorporated into juristic expositions of Dig. 1.5.13 or Dig. 28.12.29.

14. Albericus de Rosate, *Commentarii, in* Dig. 1.5.7 (Venice: Societas Aquilae Renovantis, 1585; repr., Bologna: Formi, 1974), fol. 47rb (no. 10–11); cf. M. Anthony Hewson, *Giles of Rome and the Medieval Theory of Conception* (London: Athlone Press, 1975), 166–178.

delicate condition from certain death in a pregnancy. Christian duty prohibited the administration of sterilizing medication and branded it as a form
of homicidium by design. But what if the doctor knew that the patient's
husband would demand from her fulfillment of the marital debt through
sexual intercourse, a request that she, according to lawful and sacramental
standards, could not refuse without falling prey to an alternative count of
mortal sin? The spousal *debitum*, canonical and lethal, versus uncanonical
and life-saving contraception: How was the *medicus* supposed to resolve the
conflict? With canonistic doctrine concurring, Peter the Chanter settled
the matter by advancing a simple formula. Believers, he stated, should never
commit evil acts so as to attain an ulterior good. Differently put, the preven-
tion of conception would burden one's conscience to the point of forsaking
paradise, whereas the threat posed by the insistence of a married partner on
carnal favors did not diminish chances of salvation apart from those of the
unrelenting spouse.[15]

More than a century after Peter the Chanter's speculations on perplexio
in connection with the marital debt, Johannes de Regina, a theologian and
professor at the Dominican convent of Naples, reached similar conclusions
when he debated, around 1320, a closely related scenario focusing on the
figure of the perplexed physician. The "miscellaneous academic inquiry"
(*quaestio quodlibetalis*) of Johannes provided late medieval scholasticism with
perhaps the first monographic treatment of "therapeutic abortion." As a
pupil of Thomas Aquinas, Johannes de Regina's approach to the issue was
thoroughly theological in the sense that he used citations from Aristotle
instead of canonical textbooks to back up his line of reasoning. In the end,
though, his quaestio fully coincided with established canonistic views on the
matter. Aided in particular by a biblical quote from the Roman Epistle of
Paul in the New Testament (Rom. 3:8), Johannes produced a faithful echo
of the very maxim his Parisian colleague, Peter the Chanter, had employed
long before, reasserting that "evil must not be done to accomplish something
of merit." Johannes went on to argue by analogy that a pregnant woman who
risked death if she chose delivery over an abortion did not necessarily have
the right to expect expert assistance. A doctor called in to induce a miscarriage would stay on the safer side of salvation if he accepted her death as

---

15. Petrus Cantor, *Liber casuum conscientiae* 350, ed. Dugauquier, 463. The decretist analysis
of perplexio has been summarized by Kuttner, *Kanonistische Schuldlehre*, 257–298. On the virtual
(*voluntatis*) rather than actual (*actus*) homicidium of contraception, ibid., 3–62; Gründel, *Die Lehre von
den Umständen*, 102–257; Noonan, *Contraception*, 157–159. About the carnal debitum in canonical
marriage, James Brundage, *Law, Sex, and Society* (Chicago: Chicago University Press, 1987), 150–156.

caused by an agent other than himself, be it in the form of disease or through complications during childbirth. At this juncture, however, the Neapolitan theologian was careful to invoke a distinction of normative consequences based on whether the ailing mother's fetus had already passed the threshold of complete animation. For assuming that the body in the womb had not yet acquired human features, it seemed permissible in his eyes to have an abortion performed on grounds of necessity. The inanimate embryo lacked an immortal soul, and interrupting gestation prematurely implied the sacrifice of a lesser good for a greater one, the demise of a future instead of an actual person. As a result, the situation called for diametrically opposed outcomes depending on which phase of embryological growth had been attained by the time the possibility of therapeutic intervention was broached.[16]

After 1450, the quodlibet composed by Johannes de Regina started to engage a wider circle of spiritual and legal consultants. His text was included in the confessional *Summa* of Antoninus, Archbishop of Florence, and again taken up by one of the last comprehensive works in the late medieval penitential format, the *Summa summarum* of Sylvester Prierias published in 1518.[17] While this tradition affected especially the literature on penance, a second set of writings on the permissibility of therapeutic abortion was handed down at the canon law schools, with a *lectura* authored around 1365 by Simon de Bursano serving as the fountainhead. The original remarks of both Simon and Johannes de Regina have barely survived, and they caught the attention of their medieval colleagues mostly by way of indirect testimony, either through Antoninus Florentinus or, as with Simon, in the form of a brief account Marianus Socinus the Younger (d. 1467) incorporated into his lectures on the Gregorian *Decretales*. Heightened interest in the treatments of Johannes and Simon, it turns out, did not develop until the passing of three or four generations. Still, the two authors and their fifteenth-century followers arrived at nearly identical conclusions. They permitted clinically induced miscarriages prior to fetal formation in the womb and were inclined to reject surgical or medicinal intervention at any time thereafter. Simon de Bursano, to be sure, briefly wondered in his lecture

---

16. Johannes de Regina, *Quodlibet* 10.27, fully transcribed (from Naples, BN, VII B.28, fol. 29va-b) in *Die Abtreibung*, 75n144; cf. Peter Biller, "John of Naples, Quodlibets and Medieval Concern with the Body," in *Medieval Theology and the Natural Body*, ed. Peter Biller et al. (York: York Medieval Press, 1997), 3–12; Francesco Migliorino, "La parola e le pieghe della Scrittura. I Libelli di Pietro Geremia," in *La memoria ritrovata. Pietro Geremia e le carte della storia*, ed. Francesco Migliorino et al. (Catania: Maimone, 2006), 89n78, has identified a second medieval copy of the quodlibet in Palermo, San Domenico, Libellus I di Pietro Geremia, fol. 224r.

17. Antoninus Florentinus, *Summa maior* 3.7.2 (Lyon: Cleyn, 1506), no. 2; Sylvester Prierias, *Summa*, s.v. *medicus* 4.2 (Strasbourg: Grieninger, 1518), fol. 334va.

whether prenatal manslaughter could be excused in light of Gratian's chapter *Ipsa pietas* (C. 23, q. 4, c. 24), which stated that pursuing a good thing was licit as long as the ill that arose from it was only accidental. Marianus Socinus Junior contrasted Rom. 3:8, the much-quoted biblical maxim condemning acceptance of evil in view of ulterior gain, with a phrase he borrowed from the Roman law. In his mind, it held the opposite by suggesting that "in between negative outcomes one must opt for the minor one" (Dig. 9.2.51). Content to hint at the challenge from Justinian's *Corpus*, Marianus did not launch an all-out attack on established opinion. For the moment, he promised to "leave the whole issue undecided and discuss it, so God will, on some future occasion."[18] As far as we can tell, he never did.

The scholastic assessment of conflict between multiple duties, cast into relief by the quandary of therapeutic abortion, revealed confidence in the possibility of accommodating incidents of perplexio. Late medieval analysts agreed that they needed to concentrate first and foremost on the problem of immediate responsibility, which in their opinion outweighed additional considerations, particularly those that misled individuals toward what they perceived of as greater or final rewards. Accordingly, the slaying of a human fetus for reasons of health preservation warranted charges of actual homicide, even when a trained physician had intervened for the sole purpose of saving the mother's life. What figured next in the reasoning of normative thinkers was scrutiny of the legal issues at stake. Homicidium of a shapeless embryo was deemed less damnable than manslaughter "in effect" (*actu*). By implication, a doctor who prescribed medication to stop growth of a future existence and secure the survival of someone already alive was viewed as justified, provided, of course, that nobody except the medicus himself removed the deadly peril. The scenario would change altogether if the advantage obtained through medical intervention were canceled out by something equally valuable but destined to perish in the process. Quite paradoxically, it was the theologian Johannes de Regina who alone elaborated on the question of where the respective boundaries would run between sinful killing on the one hand and on the other classification of the act as punishable in the lay courts. Surpassing the vague assertions of canonists like Simon of Bursano and his followers, Johannes emphasized the legal (*temporalis*) rather than pastoral (*spiritualis*) criterion of animation. The presence of real

---

18. Marianus Socinus, *Lectura super* X 5.12.5 (Lyon, 1559), fol. 162rb. Simon de Bursano's *Summa* is known in two mss. (Florence, Biblioteca Laurenziana, Aedilium 55, fol. 123r–266v; Barcelona, AC, 40, fol. 1r–134r); see Domenico Maffei, "Addenda et Corrigenda," in Domenico Maffei, *Studi di storia dell'università e della letteratura giuridica* (Goldbach: Keip, 1995), 535*–537*. For a transcription of Simon's relevant passage, *in Clem.* 5.4.1, and that of Marianus, see *Die Abtreibung*, 66–67n125–126.

crime in therapeutic abortion, he suggested, would presuppose the victim's full humanity, whereas expulsion of an "inanimate" fetus never deserved retribution beyond the confines of the penitential forum.

Historians who limit their overview of arguments for the criminalization of abortion to the years before 1500 will miss what arguably constituted the most conspicuous accomplishment of late medieval academic culture. For several centuries, university lawyers, theologians, and scholars of medicine created and sustained a remarkable level of doctrinal convergence that rested especially on shared ideas about the process of fetal growth. To explain the high degree of unanimity and harmony among the learned, it seems plausible to surmise that orthodox demands and the threat of prosecution for heresy discouraged attempts to challenge the fundamental premise of creationism. Yet the dramatic surge of disagreement in subsequent embryological debate calls for a different explanation. Until 1650, Catholic belief in creationist theories survived wholly unshaken and intact. Simultaneously, almost every other facet of the traditional consensus on fetal development and normative protection provoked major intellectual dissent and led to the revision of common opinion among Protestants and their confessional adversaries alike. That the Age of the Reformation was marked by an unprecedented spirit of controversy in relation to questions of prenatal homicide can also be deduced from discussions concerning the admissibility of therapeutic miscarriage. They certainly intensified and led to the formulation of multiple if not mutually exclusive positions.

Early modern opinion on the perplexed physician who induces an abortion to save the life of a pregnant woman can be said to have yielded three different responses, two of which plainly disagreed as to whether criminal punishment should be meted out against the doctor. Several juristic authors wrote that the medically advised termination of a pregnancy never merited legal prosecution as long as the procedures were undertaken because of serious health reasons. In search for older authority arguing along the same lines, jurists after 1500 frequently invoked Marianus Socinus Junior, despite the fact that, historically, the latter had maintained a fairly uncommitted point of view. The misunderstanding was caused by the canonist and archbishop of Lucca, Felinus Sandaeus (d. 1503), whose decretal commentary cites Marianus as having declared approvingly that, yes, "the medicus is altogether excused" from sentencing.[19] Medieval jurisprudence was consequently believed to

---

19. Felinus Sandaeus, *Lectura super* X 5.12.5, in Felinus Sandaeus, *Opera* 1 (Lyon: Moylin, 1514), fol. 184va; his misrepresentation of Marianus provoked a marginal comment by the Lyonese editor of 1514, who wrote that "theologians hold the contrary view"; for additional coverage of sixteenth-century sentiment, *Die Abtreibung*, 115–117.

have witnessed dissent between the likes of Marianus and Antoninus Florentinus, when in reality contention had been markedly absent. Apart from a third series of statements that perpetuated Johannes de Regina's insistence that penal liability or indemnity ought to hinge upon the presence or absence of a rational soul in the womb, a thorough and qualitative reorientation in the way academic discourse framed the question of perplexio would not occur until the Jesuit theologian Thomas Sanchez reassessed the matter as part of a lengthy *disputatio* on matrimony in 1617.[20]

The fourteenth-century contributions of Johannes de Regina and Simon de Bursano had assumed that not the unborn child but fatal disease or physical dysfunction was responsible for the mother's tragic predicament. Either cause left no room for arguments of self-defense that tried to excuse the sacrifice of an innocent life. While sharing previous objections, Thomas Sanchez called for greater leniency and an important change in perspective. His own assessment, Thomas explained, would rather depart from the doctor's obligation to rescue the patient, an objective physicians were entitled to pursue insofar as the means they used were chiefly aimed at recovery. If adequate cures did not augment the danger of stillbirth except indirectly and by collateral effect, the conscientious medical expert would never have to appear in a public trial and face punitive charges. The shift in emphasis away from perplexio, characterized by equal interest in, and worth of, the two potential victims, toward distinguishing primary and secondary goals of therapeutic intervention was soon greeted by the mainstream of Western thought as the best response to an otherwise intractable dilemma.

Tentatively proposed by Simon de Bursano several centuries earlier, the solution offered by Thomas met with surprisingly quick and widespread acceptance, which showed that he was part of a larger intellectual transformation heralding the definitive abandonment of animation as the principal criterion for norms against abortion. Many contemporary theoreticians had begun to write learned expositions in which they sought to present new rationales for reducing the duration of gestation prior to arrival of the anima rationalis until, finally, the chronological lag separating the two events turned into a wholly negligible quantity. As the perceived presence of humanity in the maternal womb gradually expanded to maximum length, Thomas Sanchez addressed the resulting imbalance by minimizing legal liability for medically induced miscarriages. In tune with epochal trends, he further swayed

---

20. Thomas Sanchez, *Disputatio de sancto matrimonii sacramento* 3.9.20 (Antwerp: Heredes Martini Nutii & Joannes Meursius, 1617), 224a–b.

his audience at a time when juristic authors first combined reflections on the subject of perplexio with a second argument hardly ever figuring in works written before the latter half of the sixteenth century. By following lawyerly example, Thomas admonished readers to have complications arising from a pregnancy inspected by none other than officially approved experts in the field of medicine. Their competence alone was regarded as beyond prosecutorial suspicion.

The Demise of Late Medieval Embryology

Generic indications in the scholastic textbooks and commentary as to how animation would operate became a source of significant concern in the sixteenth century. For generations, legal interpreters had combined references to the fetus with adjectives such as "live," "alive," "formed," or "animated." From the beginning of the early modern period, however, several new theories emerged that each favored greater differentiation between the stages of prenatal growth. Academic discourse now discerned a maximum of five phases running from conception through animation, formation, and viability (vivificatio) on to birth. It remains unclear to what extent the most elaborate analyses in this regard at the hands of Antoninus Tesaurus (1590) and the Spaniard Franciscus Torreblanca Villalpandus (1618) were written in order to subvert the traditional association of criminal law with the embryological teachings of high medieval scholasticism.[21] Both Villalpandus and Tesaurus justified lay punishment in ways that resemble the logic of current Western legislation far more closely than the original canonistic and theological preoccupations of Gratian and Peter Lombard, whose intention it had been, above all, to protect the bodily and spiritual integrity of immortal souls. Villalpandus and Tesaurus instead sought to determine the exact moment at which the ability to survive outside the maternal womb had grown sufficiently to equate killings with those of an autonomously existing homo. A starting point for their reflections was provided by Signorolus and Baldus, who urged reconsideration of Stoic assertions by ancient Roman jurists and especially the famous statement of Papinian that nobody can claim human nature *antequam sit natus*, "before he is born" (Dig. 35.2.9.1).

Tesaurus and Villalpandus took the prerequisite of being *natus* to mean that for full participation in humanity a fetus had to be capable of independent

---

21. Antoninus Tesaurus, *Novae decisiones sacri senatus Pedemontani* 12 (Venice: Hieronymus Polus, 1591), fol. 12va–16va; Franciscus Torreblanca Villalpandus, *Epitome delictorum* 2.43 (Seville, 1618), fol. 148rb–149va (no. 12–38).

survival. The determining criterion was not identifiable with animation, which in juristic opinion occurred early during gestation—or after "forty days," as the *Glossa ordinaria* of Accursius tersely states—but rather later, in an instant they identified with embryonic formation. The authors' distinction between animatio and formatio may have appeared to contemporaries as firmly rooted in older textbook tradition. Their late medieval predecessors, on the other hand, would have been startled by it. Upon introducing the standard of viability as distinct from the entry of the human soul, Tesaurus and Villalpandus went on to look for argumentative support in passages from the Hippocratic *Corpus*, comforted by the knowledge that Justinian's Digest, on at least two occasions (Dig. 1.5.12 and Dig. 38.16.3.12), expressly recommended juristic recourse to the auctoritas of the Greek doctor. As they delved into ancient medical wisdom, the Spanish and the Piemontese lawyer finally parted company. Villalpandus concluded that some children born prematurely and more than four months into the pregnancy would live on their own and beyond the limit of twenty-four hours, which a royal Castilian law of 1505 had set for the partus to be formally considered among the nati. Antoninus Tesaurus for his part tried to gauge the age beyond which death no longer constituted the inescapable consequence of an untimely delivery. He denied such possibility prior to the ninth month, citing Hippocrates, who even for the eighth had predicted minimal chances of endurance in the outside world.[22]

In keeping with older scholastic doctrine, the two jurists proposed dual punishment, correlated the aggravated form of killing with homicidium, and repeated the Accursian gradation of penalties into exile and execution. For the rest, their reliance on established modes of thinking was admittedly slight. Tesaurus and Villalpandus concurred, for instance, with the analysis of Signorolus and Bolognese minority opinion by acknowledging that the Roman *Corpus iuris civilis* did not subscribe to the canonistic identification of abortion with manslaughter. In addition and prompted by the realization that canon law offered no specifics on the question of timing, they felt free to improve upon the guidelines of the Ius commune. The narrowing they postulated for incidences of veritable homicide in the maternal womb from previously forty or eighty days to the fifth or even the ninth month of gestation reflected their exclusive concern with physical viability. By dismissing admonishments to the contrary as purely spiritual in motivation, they refused to share the objectives of late medieval jurisprudence, which had defended

---

22. Tesaurus, *Novae Decisiones* 12, fol. 14rb–vb (no. 5, 7). Villalpandus, *Epitome* 2.43, fol. 148rb–149rb (no. 14, 25–26, 31–32); cf. *Las leyes de Toro glosadas* (Burgos: Juncta, 1527), fol. 46va (*ley* 13).

the right of unborn human beings to receive infant baptism, lead a Christian life, and seek eternal salvation. Moreover and given the obvious discomfort of Tesaurus and Villalpandus with the legacy of scholasticism in general, it is surprising to note that their critical acumen left the matter of successive animation completely untouched. In this respect, their reflections remained firmly anchored in the sixteenth century, a period when lawyers were not yet inclined to challenge basic theological notions that from the days of Gratian had inspired the criminalization of abortion in the West, be it in the form of creatianist premises or through insistence on a delay between conception and infusion of the rational soul.

Growing skepticism toward late medieval theories of *animatio successiva* was first conveyed to legal experts by a revised commentary on Justinian's *Institutiones* that Johannes Harpprecht, professor of jurisprudence at the University of Tübingen, published in 1603.[23] The author of the work was greatly intrigued by traducianism, a philosophical concept his colleagues had dismissed for centuries, condemning it time and again as utter heresy. Upon careful inspection of orthodox as well as unorthodox views, Johannes Harpprecht argued that the variety of numerical calculations among medical, philosophical, and theological *auctoritates* allowed him to determine on his own at which time the fetus transformed into a human existence. The traducianist standpoint, he felt, was the most plausible in that it assumed the presence of a rational anima from insemination (*in semine*) and rendered a sole agent responsible for every aspect of fetal development. To supporters of creatianism, the German law professor offered prospects of reconciliation by leaving it undecided whether the presence of humanity at conception had to be understood as merely virtual (*potentia*) or as concrete and real (*actu*). He was, however, unwilling to accept another creatianist assertion, long shared by theologians and canon lawyers, according to which divine creation and embodiment of the anima rationalis did not occur until the fetus assumed proper shape. To account for it, scholastic medicine had attributed earlier manifestations of prenatal growth to a succession of vegetative and sensual animae, which steered the more primitive biological mechanisms also present in plants and animals.[24]

---

23. Johannes Harpprecht, *Tractatus Criminalis: Commentaria in* Inst. 4.18.5 (Frankfurt/M.: Bitsch, 1603), 382–389 (no. 11–31); a 1598 edition of the *Tractatus* still lacks the critical passages; cf. *Die Abtreibung*, 153–160.

24. On creatianism and the traducianist challenge, see Hewson, *Giles of Rome*, 4–18; Maaike van der Lugt, "L'animation de l'embryon humain dans la pensée médiévale," in *L'embryon, formation et animation. Antiquité grecque et latine, traditions hébraïque, chrétienne et islamique*, ed. Luc Brisson et al. (Paris: Urin, 2008), 234–243.

Johannes Harpprecht's rehabilitation of traducianist ideas struck a blow at the normative edifice Bolognese jurisprudence had founded on its unquestioned belief in the theory of threefold animation. Harpprecht openly conceded that further modification of traditional embryological doctrine might undercut the intrinsic validity of the criminal laws on abortion. For the time being, though, he assured readers that juristic practice, the weight of common legal opinion, and the speculative nature of his newfound objections justified the continued reliance on existing norms. The stipulations of the Ius commune, he wrote, did not have to be adjusted to the superior logic of traducianism just yet: "The crucial distinction between formed and unformed, or animate and inanimate fetal life will persist as long as the wiser among men find a difference between something destined to be formed and actually formed [actu], or destined to be animated and actually animated."[25] In order to substantiate his doubts concerning the unfolding of prenatal existence by way of formation and simultaneous infusion of the human soul, Harpprecht went against usual habits and did not quote legal authorities, in obvious recognition of the fact that he had reached intellectual territory still uncharted by the jurists. Given the absolute originality of his approach, he looked toward neighboring disciplines and mustered argumentative support from the protagonists in recent theological debate. The most explicit anticipation of his traducianist leanings occurred in treatises written by some of his countrymen, as it was in Germany that the scholastic condemnation of animation ex traduce had been submitted to intense revisionist scrutiny. Harpprecht referred in particular to the opinion of Martin Luther, who reportedly had maintained that a rational soul animated the fetus right from conception. Additional references in Harpprecht's commentary of 1603 suggest that the "divine" reformer's alleged position enjoyed great popularity among the Lutherans, with Johannes Harpprecht notably coming from their midst.[26]

Marking the high point of embryological controversy, a compilation of theological treatises under the Greek title of *Psychologia* was printed at Marburg in 1590. One of the contributors to the volume, Petrus Monavius Lascovius from Hungary, tried to explain why it was that Catholic opinion, faced with mounting support for the tenets of traducianism, had abstained from offering any vigorous responses. For Petrus, the restraint was motivated, above all, by

---

25. Harpprecht, *Tractatus criminalis*, 388–389 (no. 31).

26. Ibid., 387 (no. 27), where Martin Luther is said to have favored traducianism "in private"; also ibid., 385 (no. 21), citing one Protestant theologian under reference to the "Psychologia Goclenii" (see next note).

respect for centuries of church tradition. Eminent men like Thomas Aquinas and other representatives of scholasticism had determined that fusion of the human soul with the fetus did not take place until physical articulation of the limbs. In the categorical terms of dogma, they had excluded the possibility of tying previous fetal growth to a single agent already active in the semen. In their wake, canonists had put the fortieth or eightieth day after conception as the probable date for definitive animation to occur.[27] Around 1600, then, initiatives aiming at reconciliation with Protestant ideas needed to exploit the confusing array of timelines for the transition from one prenatal stage to the next. And indeed, it was at this juncture that the Belgian physician Thomas Fienus succeeded in breaking new ground. In a book of 1620, he argued at length that the *infusio* of immortal *animae* was achieved no later than three days after insemination. Anticipating criticism of his dramatically shortened schedule for its incompatibility with Roman orthodoxy, Fienus claimed that concrete, physiological signs of intervention by a rational soul could be seen as early as upon appearance of the first embryonic membrane.[28]

In reexamining Catholic teachings, Thomas Fienus took pains to demonstrate his detachment from traducianist theories. He shared the attitude of late medieval theologians for whom human souls present in semine were automatically regarded as elements of the parental seed. Twelfth-century interpreters had stated that seminal transmission ex traduce squarely contradicted accepted teachings about the soul and its origins. In their view, only the physical body bore the blemish of original sin, and God did not infuse the immortal element of humanity until some time after procreation. Scholastic thinkers had also accounted for fetal growth in the absence of a rational anima, from conception to formation, by identifying the principle shaping prehuman development with Aristotle's two states in which the embryo was inhabited first by a vegetative and then by a sensitive soul. At this juncture, Thomas Fienus sought to be radically innovative. By associating the process of formatio with a single force governing each phase of plant-, animal-, and manlike existence, he dramatically reduced the interlude between insemination and final infusio, from traditionally at least forty days to no more than three.

That prenatal human life was supposed to be driven by a unique and constantly evolving rational essence endowed Catholic opinion, in the mind of Daniel Sennert, professor of medicine at Wittenberg, with a previously unmatched

---

27. Petrus Monavius Lascovius Ungarus, "Dissertatio," in *Psychologia*, ed. Rudolphus Goclenius (Marburg: Egenolphus, 1590), 201–202.

28. Thomas Fienus, *De formatrice foetus liber* (Antwerp: a Tongris, 1620), 7.8, 8.9, and 8.11.

degree of simplicity. A Protestant who wrote his medical *Hypomnemata* around 1630, Sennert readily identified himself as a sympathizer of traducianism and assumed that animae rationales would be present in the semen. He was prepared, however, to supplement personal views on the matter with theological clarifications designed to accomplish, in questions of animation, a workable settlement of differences between Catholic and Protestant Christians. Sennert suspected that the early occurrence of animate embodiment, which his Belgian colleague Thomas Fienus had proposed for as soon as the third day after procreation, formed the mere concession of someone overly concerned with dogma. Had it not been for fear of being labeled a traducianist, the Catholic Fienus would not have hesitated to move the soul's origins as far back as the procreative act. Sennert urged his confessional adversaries to consider the possibility that traditional fusion and confusion of two separate issues such as the presence in semine on the one hand and ex traduce on the other would not withstand renewed and closer inspection. Sennert solicited creatianists to acknowledge that they did not betray orthodoxy by perceiving divine creation and the entry of an immortal soul as coincidental with the moment of conception.[29]

Before long, Daniel Sennert's amenable remarks were cited approvingly in a *quaestio* written by Paulus Zacchias, the celebrated papal physician. Although the high-ranking author and member of the Apostolic Curia, in imitation of canonists like Hugucccio several hundred years earlier, branded the traducianist tendencies of his Protestant colleague as outright heresy, Zacchias accepted without reservation Sennert's invitation to scrutinize whether the instant of full animation might not coincide with the very beginnings of fetal life. The quaestio asserts that presence of the immortal soul at insemination does not necessarily imply preexistence in semine and as a result does not compromise dogmatic belief in divine creation. Before sending his conclusions to the publisher, moreover, Zacchias was careful to submit the quaestio, printed for the first time in 1650, to ecclesiastical censure, aware that he was placing himself in opposition to a formidable legacy of learned and orthodox consensus. The unqualified recognition of the work by Roman church authorities contributed to the breakaway in Western thought from Aristotelian and scholastic concepts of animatio successiva and further undermined, after half a millennium, their pivotal role in academic debate.[30]

---

29. Daniel Sennertus, *Hypomnemata physica*, 4.10, in Daniel Sennertus, *Opera* 1.4 (Lyon: Huguetan & Ravaud, 1641), 34b–46b, 54a–62a (c. 6–7, 10–14); for the original date of his treatise, *Die Abtreibung*, 157n274.

30. Paulus Zacchias, *Quaestiones medico-legales* 9.1.1–5 (Frankfurt/M.: Bencard, 1688), 728a–749b; first published in Rome, 1650.

Modern accounts tracking the advance of criminalization have paid greatest attention to intellectual developments. The evolution of learned reflection has been presented mostly in isolation from social and judicial realities, creating a narrative of steadily expanding knowledge and conceptual refinement as though professorial opinion grew organically and ever more sophisticated from generation to generation. Chronology, on the other hand, provides a first tool to dispel similar impressions and demonstrate how normative discourse adopted an intermittent rhythm, documenting, for example, particular activity during the formative years between 1140 and 1240, when the fundamentals of criminal abortion were forged into uniform language. Subsequently, there was a considerable period in which juristic and pastoral commentary added but little to the theoretical edifice, typically reiterating the essentials of medical theory, using approximate terms to describe the timing of animation, and showing little regard for the intricacies of embryology. It was, as a matter of fact, not until the 1500s that these and related issues again stoked controversy. From then on, they quickly generated a mountain of erudite analysis, which attained new levels of subtlety and, over the course of just two or three lifetimes, prompted revision of many deeply ingrained assumptions.

CHAPTER 5

Objections to Criminalization

In the prescriptive sources of the later Middle Ages, there is a massive preponderance of statements that treat abortion as a serious crimen. A carefully crafted rhetoric of condemnation, first formulated coherently at the twelfth-century schools of law and theology, spread from the academic centers in Bologna and Paris to places throughout Latin Christendom. Proliferation of the message depended on the professed and ordained ministers of the church. Textual transmission guaranteed that laypersons received uniform instruction about sinning in the form of sermons and penitential manuals, whereas priests, nuns, and monks were further subjected to a streamlined set of disciplinary measures. By 1300 at the latest, the success of canonical instruction was evident. A single normative construct shaped ecclesiastical standards and Christian consciences from one corner of the Western Hemisphere to the next, with individual regulations being marked by a degree of doctrinal consistency that only the culture of scholasticism, highly professionalized and perpetuated institutionally, could ensure at the time. In opposition to this formidable alliance of opinion among the educational, literary, and religious elites, voices of disagreement on matters of prenatal homicide struggled to find enduring written expression, let alone comparable systematic justification that would have been rooted as deeply in scriptural authority and dogma, in Greek and Arabic embryology.

To illustrate the point, even the most potent argumentative weapon in defiance of the Bolognese legal precepts, the authoritative challenge posed by the Roman law of antiquity and preserved in Justinian's *Corpus iuris civilis*, was made into a sophisticated tool by the hands of experts who themselves ranked high among members of the juristic establishment. As noted in chapter 3, ancient lawyers including Ulpian, Paul, and Papinian had embraced Stoic tenets that categorically denied the fetus equality with born human beings. Their unchristian stance influenced a group of fourteenth-century jurists who favored interpretations expressly at odds with canonistic consensus. Led by Signorolus de Homodeis and Baldus de Ubaldis, they rejected the older scholastic classification of induced miscarriage alongside spiritual and sometimes actual manslaughter, maintaining instead and with support from Justinian's *leges* that stipulations in Italian municipal statutes inflicting the death penalty for homicide did not permit extension to cases where the victim had yet to be delivered. Simultaneously, Signorolus, Baldus, and later dissenters were unwilling to pursue Stoic rationales to the point of granting lay perpetrators complete impunity for their involvement in acts of abortion. Although Baldus may have toyed with the idea, his colleagues never went as far as to challenge the basic premise of criminalization. What stopped them in their tracks was in particular a fragment in Justinian's Digest (Dig. 48.8.8) that, at least in the eyes of premodern readers, imposed exile on every willfully aborting woman. Authored by Ulpian, the *lex* seemed to erect an insurmountable barrier to any notion of freedom from punishment.

The surviving records are largely the product of clerical and academically inspired writing and reflect the prototypical views of educated and verbally articulate preachers and teachers, whereas proof for the existence of medieval hostility toward the criminalizing agenda of scholasticism is limited to occasional glimpses in the texts and to clues that arise from readings between the lines. In lay courts subject to the Romano-canonical rules of adjudication described in chapters 7 and 8, discomfort with the official narrative is present mostly in indirect or muted disguises, in oddly intermittent patterns of sentencing, in habits and episodes of prosecutorial indifference, and in procedural safeguards stalling hasty conviction. Hints at moral inertia can also be detected, unless the threshold of explicit recognition is passed altogether and the documentary evidence refers to litigants accused of collusion or laments the widespread connivance of ordinary people. The following sections, on the other hand, focus on two legal cultures that were the most stubborn and vocal in their unwillingness to bring abortion and infanticide into the orbit of secular prosecution. First, we discuss jurors in German-speaking areas, who did not fully accept Bolognese jurisprudence until the later 1400s. And then there is the special case of England, where common lawyers in the years after 1348 excluded fetal homicide from their list of capital crimes. Moreover and historically speaking, it would be misguided to depict negative attitudes toward the advance of canonical and civilian standards as conscious maneuvers to obstruct justice, given that the concept of crimen itself constituted a novel, eminently aggressive and intrusive device. Local societies were rather selective in their treatment of specific wrongful acts as punishable offenses in the modern sense of the word.

Customary Indifference North and East of the River Rhine

Until 1500, Western Christians in many areas encountered the Ius commune of Bolognese origin, with its impersonal criteria of guilt, its written rules of investigation, and its tribunals inflicting bodily punishment, as a recent and frequently precarious invention. Romano-canonical procedures continued to compete with alternative modes of conflict management that typically relied on self-help and lawful protection through friendship and family alliances. In customary trials, evidentiary techniques gauged the solidarity and cohesion within adversarial groups. Arbitrating judges invited defendants and accusers to swear collective oaths or accept judicial battle, revealing a prosecutorial logic that appeared far removed from the recommendations of professional jurists who sought to uncover the factual truth behind allegations. The distance between the downward justice of scholasticism and traditional communal negotiation was enormous. Presented with multiple legal avenues and remedies, the average consumer of the law pursued his agenda quite freely in what for centuries looked like the normal state of affairs. Conduct encouraged or condoned in one court was easily stigmatized or treated as suspect in another. Zealous adherence to the norms of ecclesiastical or lay legislators could prove out of place in a contestant's immediate social surroundings.

Among the laity, the juristic assessment of fetal homicide met with varying responses that reflected the geographical division of western Europe into roughly equal halves along the Rhine and the Alps. In regions lying to the north and east, familiarity with Bolognese canonical norms extended across German and Slavic lands into the Scandinavian, Baltic, and Hungarian peripheries. Attesting to the reach of ecclesiastical jurisprudence, several of the most successful confessional handbooks were produced at some distance from the core areas of the Ius commune. Among them is a pair of *Summae* that John of Freiburg composed in convenient pocket and cumbersome study formats during the 1290s, as well as a rendering of John's minor work in the vernacular a century afterward. The latter was authored by Berthold, a fellow Dominican likewise residing at the convent of Freiburg in Breisgau. In each of these penitential texts, confessors and penitents would find the scholastic regulations faithfully reproduced. In close imitation of Raymond of Penyafort's earlier archetype, abortion was listed under the rubric of *De homicidio*.[1] Hundreds of still-extant manuscript copies indicate that Christian awareness of the relevant norms did not fade as one traveled through the territories of central Europe. Outside the clerical realm, however, the situation looked very different.

In his fundamental study of 1962 on the beginnings of jurisprudence in Germany, Winfrid Trusen underscored the importance of three major phases and trends for the gradual and ultimately successful adoption of scholastic norms.[2] Originating from Bologna and Paris, the first wave of influence affected the practice of ecclesiastical courts, so that by 1250 church adjudication had been transformed in line with developments occurring all across Latin Christendom. As Romano-canonical institutions and terminology shaped discipline and fostered the domestic output of episcopal statutes, sermons, and literary admonishments by the clergy, a second current of juristic inspiration increasingly couched standards regulating the life of laypeople in the technical and procedural language of Roman and canon law. Popularized by the activity of ecclesiastical tribunals and pastoral exhortation at the parish level, scholastic nomenclature and appreciation for the use of written records slowly filtered into the proceedings of municipal and princely justice, a process Trusen referred to as *Frührezeption,* the early phase of German appropriation. The full absorption, or *Vollrezeption*, of Bolognese legal culture unfolded only in the years after 1400 and advanced especially by way of the towns. Outlying places in the countryside or to the north and east of the empire remained untouched until the Age of the Reformation.

Trusen's chronology, his emphasis on the function of ecclesiastical jurisdiction as a model for secular adaptation, and the geographical pattern he discerned with regard to the rise of jurisprudential attitudes in Germany receive ample confirmation from the study of late medieval sources on abortion. They in fact validate his threefold pattern of *Rezeption* in the midst of growing awareness that abortion constituted not just a spiritual but also a worldly offense. The oldest German testimony to emanate from lay authority and prescribe corrective treatment for perpetrators of

---

1. Johannes de Friburgo, *Summa* 2.1 (Paris: Parvus, 1519), fol. 51va (no. 29); Berthold of Freiburg, *Johannes deutsch*, in *Die Rechtssumme Bruder Bertholds*, ed. Georg Steer et al., 5 vols. (Tübingen: Niemeyer, 1987–1993), 3:1629–1630 (s.v. *Manslacht*); also chap. 2, note 9.

2. Winfried Trusen, *Die Anfänge des gelehrten Rechts in Deutschland* (Cologne: Böhlau, 1962).

homicide in the womb seems to have come from Nuremberg, where there is a brief entry in the records of the city court describing the case of a pregnant woman, the beating she had endured from a man, and her subsequent miscarriage. If the accused proves unable to clear himself by oath and secure the assistance of two co-jurors, the text declares, "he shall pay retribution [*puessen*] for the murder [*mort*] in the way the law prescribes."[3] Dating approximately to the second quarter of the fifteenth century, the passage is readily attributable to the second stage of Trusen's Frührezeption. Although the fact is somewhat concealed by the use of dialect, it replicates, within the realm of town jurisdiction, procedural principles and terms that without substantive modification might have been lifted from the canon law. As discussed in chapter 2, Romano-canonical procedures obliged those who had been denounced to appear before their ordinary bishop and overcome anonymous insinuations of crimen through penance or by submitting to compurgation.

The citizens of Nuremberg implemented a parallel set of rules for the town judiciary. Lacking strong coercive capabilities, they assumed that instances of miscarriage by assault were most likely to come to their judicial attention. Only the private initiative of aggrieved parties could provide justice with the necessary prosecutorial momentum. Whether in the English common law of 1200 or in connection with criminal charges brought by A against B at Cremona during the time of Signorolus in the 1340s, downward intervention in early cases of prenatal death catered almost exclusively to plaintiffs in pursuit of monetary compensation. Interestingly, moreover, the Nuremberg scribe adopted the canonical terms of "doing penance" (puessen) and "aggravated homicide" (mort) to denote both the nature of the fatality and its proper penal consequences. Suggesting indebtedness to public rituals of penitential reconciliation, his choice of vocabulary prepared the ground for future semantic expansion. In the age of the Vollrezeption, the two concepts would facilitate attempts by municipal judges to extend jurisdiction from mere damage suits to the criminal prosecution of abortion as such.[4]

---

3. Nuremberg, Staatsarchiv, Rep. 52b, no. 228a, fol. 65r; cited by Karl Roetzer, "Die Delikte der Abtreibung, Kindstötung und Kindesaussetzung im mittelalterlichen Nürnberg" (PhD diss. University of Erlangen, 1957), 25–27. The tradition of Old Frisian Laws on miscarriage is framed in the same way; see Marianne Elsakkers, "Her and Neylar: An Intriguing Criterion for Abortion in Old Frisian Law," *Scientiarum Historia* 30 (2004): 107–154.

4. Writing a couple of generations later, in 1497, the local humanist Conradus Celtis, *Norimberga* 14, in *Conrad Celtis und sein Buch über Nürnberg*, ed. Albert Werminghoff (Freiburg: Boltze, 1921), 194, considered the capital punishment of the Ius commune the ordinary verdict for those convicted of abortion in the city.

The city of Leipzig in Saxony, equally important as a commercial center and located about two hundred miles to the north of Nuremberg, produced around the same time a similar if far more detailed prescriptive statement on violent miscarriage. It first appeared in a compilation of verdicts passed by local lay jurors who served as members of a renowned judicial panel, the so-called *Leipziger Schöffengericht*. The text shows once again how central elements of ecclesiastical denunciatory procedure supplied the *Schöffen* with a blueprint for their own mechanism of inquiry and final sentencing (*Spruch*). They sought, for example, proof by way of oaths, insisted on proper reputation (*bona fama*) as a necessary prerequisite for oath helpers, laced their description of accusatory charges with connotations of aggravated homicide, and held out to accusers the prospect of liability payments. Unlike in Nuremberg, on the other hand, the formal obligation of collective swearing was assigned to the injured party rather than the offenders:

> If peace breakers, by invading a man's home with murderous instruments, have frightened the owner's healthy wife who at the time was pregnant and past one-half of the gestation period, to the effect that the wife became ill and miscarried within three days; and if the owner was able to prove with two oath helpers of good reputation that the wife was so frightened that she fell ill, and with two women of good fame that the stillborn was delivered within three days, the peace breakers shall not be able to deny that the baby was aborted because of the fear they provoked and remedy the situation with [the victim's] full monetary value [wergelt].[5]

Written perhaps as late as 1450, the passage reflects a normative environment in which the integral adoption of Bolognese jurisprudence, associated by Winfried Trusen with the subsequent century, still figured as a distant possibility. Unaware of impending developments, the Schöffen from Leipzig embraced distinctly premodern attitudes by identifying lawful retribution with coverage of the loss caused to an injured family. In addition, they recommended assertive oaths, aided by others who embodied the trust placed in adversaries by respectable members of the community, as the most effective means to assess guilt and innocence. When the Leipzig panelists handed down their Spruch, they also demonstrated allegiance to prosecutorial rationales that in certain regards can be traced back to clerical compilations of the early Middle Ages, to the penitentialia and to tribal Leges, with their tariffs of

---

5. Dresden, Sächsische Landesbibliothek, Cod. M.20, fol. 44r, in *Die Leipziger Schöffenspruchsammlung*, ed. Guido Kisch (Leipzig: Hirzel, 1919), 136 (no. 110).

compensation already defined as wergelt. Several statements by the Schöffen remind us of customary trial formats, including the vague stipulation that limits admissibility of accusations to killings committed during the second half of a pregnancy. Prescholastic concepts of animation and physical formation may have been on the Saxon lay jurors' minds.[6]

To present, in a nutshell, the principal dynamics connecting abortion and crimen in areas of the Frührezeption, modern historians would be hard-pressed to find a better illustration than the elaborate verdict that the Schöffen from the town of Brno in Moravia returned about the year 1353. As noted in chapter 3, the impact of legislation on the issue was negligible in comparison with the role played by church courts and the general appeal of Bolognese jurisprudence. When as a result the Moravian lay jury was informed one day about the arrest of a woman who had been caught in the act of drowning her newborn child in the river Svratka, members of the panel disputed the case vigorously before agreeing at least on a way to document the divided outcome of their deliberations. As John, the municipal scribe, reported in his compilation of Schöffensprüche, the twenty-four jurors had supported conflicting views while, paradoxically, the truthfulness of allegations against the defendant was beyond dispute. To begin with, one of the factions had wished for the sentence to follow the standards of "Old Brno" (iudicium antique Brunne), claiming that young mothers accused of infanticide could count on complete impunity:

> The woman is not to be punished by any means. And this is so because she bore a baby boy and had her own right to him [proprium ius in eum]. Thus, she may kill him and make him perish, for everyone is free to do with what is his, or hers [in re sua], that which he, or she, pleases to do.[7]

Part of the fourteenth-century jury from Brno called for the defendant's immediate release, in keeping with the view of many town inhabitants that reproductive choices were a personal matter. The remainder of John's narrative indicates, however, that by 1353 the tide had begun to turn against traditional lay indifference concerning the fate of unwanted offspring. A good number of the sworn members, John pointed out, believed that the case represented a serious breach of the societal order, regardless of whether

---

6. Collective oaths and compensation point to the influence of German ecclesiastical *Sendgerichte,* first described by Regino of Prüm, chap. 2, note 23; the sixth-century Salic Law features wergelt payments that differ according to the stage of fetal growth, chap. 1, note 26.

7. Flodr, *Právní knih města Brna,* 1:328 (no. 520); Rössler, *Die Stadtrechte von Brünn,* 252 (no. 536): "Dicebant . . . quod ipsa mulier non esset aliqualiter punienda ex eo quod cum infantem genuisset et proprium ius in eum habuisset ipsum perimere potuit et necare; quilibet enim in re sua quod ei placet facere potest."

the casualty amounted to murder for hire or occurred short of interference by an outsider. The municipal record supplies several paragraphs with objections voiced by two groups of dissenters among the Schöffen. One of them had reminded jurors that the drowning of babies warranted the imposition of salutary penance by a spiritual confessor, just as the contracting and dissolution of marriages fell under ecclesiastical competency.[8]

The largest portion of John's account was dedicated to the argument of a third party that commensurate punishment for the act would coincide with what "the Roman law" had stipulated. A woman guilty of having extinguished nascent life at any time following animation in the womb deserved to be executed for homicide. "If she aborts previously and within forty days from conception," John went on, "she must be sent into exile." Both execution and relegation were quoted as extant in legibus, among the norms to be found in Emperor Justinian's sixth-century *Corpus iuris civilis*. In reality, they rested on interpretations offered half a millennium later by the medieval jurists. Almost word for word, the Schöffenspruch repeated the Bolognese glossa ordinaria, read at civilian schools alongside the principal authoritative passage, or sedes materiae, on questions of abortion (Dig. 47.11.4). With the Schöffen in their wake, the original authors of the gloss, Azo and Accursius, had furnished a canonized reinterpretation of ancient Stoic jurisprudence "according to the Mosaic law" (*secundum legem Moysi*), which in their estimate referred to the biblical reading of Exodus 21:22–23 as rendered by the Greco-Jewish Septuagint. Partisans of the rigorist view on the panel at Brno hence justified support for the death penalty by quoting academic communis opinio, in line with contemporary habits, under the disguise of imperial legislation.[9] In addition, they tried to bring future decision makers onto their side, as John, the municipal scribe, was instructed to have the verdict preceded by a rubric that issued an ominous warning to prospective offenders. "In actuality [*opere*]," the text states, capital retribution "has not been inflicted upon the accused. Rather and for the time being [*ad presens*], the Schöffen have ordered that the sentence be put in writing and serve subsequent generations as a lasting reminder."[10]

---

8. Flodr, *Právní knih města Brna,* 1:328; Rössler, *Die Stadtrechte von Brünn,* 252: "Alii autem dicebant quod judicio spirituali esset punienda quia sicut contractio et solutio matrimonii sic et prolis peremptio ad forum ecclesiasticum spectaret. Unde mulier confitendo reatum suum a confessore auctoritatem habente penitentiam deberet consequi salutarem."

9. Flodr, *Právní knih města Brna,* 1:330; Rössler, *Die Stadtrechte von Brünn,* 254. "In legibus" and "secundum legem Moysi," invoke the civilian glossa ordinaria, chap. 1, notes 12–13.

10. Flodr, *Právní knih města Brna,* 1:328; Rössler, *Die Stadtrechte von Brünn,* 252: "Licet poena quam presens continet sententia opere non fuerit completa, tamen jurati ad perpetuam futurorum memoriam ipsam scribi et notari jusserunt."

For all we know, posterity at Brno and in towns to the east where John's collection was consulted did not heed the most intransigent of suggestions made by the jurors. Until 1500, no board of Schöffen is known to have passed a sentence of execution for the intentional slaying of unborn or newborn life. This means that the significance of the Spruch lies not in its immediate practical repercussions but in highlighting how the Bolognese criminalization of abortion came to affect lay justice on the far side of the Rhine and Danube. Official rhetoric described the process as animated by imperial legislation or statutes emanating from high up in the priestly hierarchy. Yet in accurate historical terms, the scholastic law was imported mainly through manuals that, in varied and idiosyncratic arrangements, furnished material norms as well as penitential and Romano-canonical procedures for the pastoral and judicial uses of churchmen. Absorption of the same information by municipal and princely courts was impeded or even halted by protests coming from the local population. Many were accustomed to the idea that it was only families who should be concerned with childbearing and that pregnant women, according to John's formula, were in absolute command of nascent life within their bodies and upon delivery. Interestingly, the scribe from Brno described the mother's power over her baby in language clearly inspired by academic definitions of provisional and full ownership (proprium ius in eum/in re sua).[11] As already emphasized by Winfried Trusen, juristic terminology lent expression to legal affairs in German and adjacent territories long before the comprehensive reception of jurisprudence took hold in the years after 1450.

What renders the Brno verdict so remarkable among the surviving sources is the theoretical justification it offers for lay protest against the Bolognese equation of infanticide with murder. For once, the chorus of uniform and institutionally sustained condemnation did not silence objections raised by a handful of Moravian jurors. By maintaining that the human fetus formed a mere portion of the maternal womb, the final judgment of the Schöffengericht further resembles present-day legal and political arguments that give aborting women an undiminished right to their own bodies, with the qualification, of course, that the dissenters speaking out around 1353 thought of extending the exemption from punishment to the killing of newborns as well. Given the late medieval situation, the text from Brno also appears unusual in that it subjects the fate of nascent offspring to the sole discretion of pregnant mothers, an affirmation that must have been prompted by the specifics of

---

11. On the decretist distinction between *ius in re* and *ius ad rem,* cf. Robert Benson, *The Bishop-Elect: A Study in Medieval Ecclesiastical Office* (Princeton, NJ: Princeton University Press, 1968), 116–144.

the investigated case. The assertion of an individual claim to privacy, not to mention a female one, was unimaginable during the period either for John or for the sworn and male judges. Preservation of autonomous *familiae* in the form of households and clans, on the other hand, constituted a self-evident goal for the protagonists in court and loomed large among the defensive claims permitted to seep into the official documentation.

Published toward 1265 and discussed in chapter 3, lex 7.8.8 of the Castilian *Siete Partidas* provides a piece of royal legislation in favor of reduced sentencing for husbands who in restoring marital discipline beat their wives and caused them to miscarry. In early modern times, town statutes of 1537 and 1553 promulgated respectively at Senigallia and Macerata in central Italy likewise declared the excuse to be legally valid.[12] Meanwhile, social consensus as to the significance of honorability, to be shared and guarded by families, shaped the normative discourse everywhere. The late medieval Apostolic Court of Penance issued formulaic letters of pardon absolving repentant sinners from abortions said to have been performed in anticipation of shameful exposure or to evade the death threats of angered relatives. And as late as 1632, the Italian jurist Laurentius Ursellius argued in theory for the permission to kill a fetus prior to animation, assuming that this was done for the sake of saving fallen daughters, born into households of good reputation, from loss of their standing in the community. Such exceptions from punishment were finally condemned by Innocent XI in an apostolic bull of 1679, after Bolognese juristic opinion had long rejected the idea of diminished liability on account of both public disgrace and spousal correction.[13] Mainstream scholasticism had never granted aborting laypersons freedom from criminal retribution unless the accused could claim to have acted in their capacity as medical doctors, entitled to provoke fetal expulsion for health reasons and under the condition that it ended only the life of an unformed embryo.

---

12. Senigallia (1537), in *Statutorum et reformationum magnificae civitatis Senogaliae volumen* (Pesaro: Concordia, 1584), 3.35; *Volumen statutorum Maceratae* (Macerata: Bini, 1553), 3.48. The two texts are cited by Josef Kohler, *Das Strafrecht der italienischen Statuten vom 12.-16. Jahrhundert* (Mannheim: Bensheimer, 1896), 334–336; for the Castilian *Siete Partidas* 7.8.8, see chap. 3, note 14.

13. Innocent XI, *Propositio* 34 (2 March 1679), in *Enchiridion symbolorum* 2134, ed. Heinrich Denzinger et al. (Freiburg: Herder, 1991), 634, rejecting, among others, the argument of Laurentius Ursellius, *Examen apum* 1.7, 2 vols. (Rome: Plaei, 1632–1637), 45a (no. 11). Letters of pardon from the Apostolic *Penitentiaria* often invoke shame or the fear of relatives as the reason for an abortion, e.g., *Bullarium Poloniae* 6.355 (no. 1656), of 16 January 1450; Rome, APA Reg. div. 2bis, fol. 244r–v (printed in *Die Abtreibung*, 192n336), of 12 July 1450; one mandate to the same effect, dated 30 December 1417, was issued by the papal chancery; cf. Filippo Tamburini, *Santi e peccatori. Confessioni e suppliche dai registri della Penitenziaria dell'Archivio Segreto Vaticano (1451–1486)* (Milan: Istituto di Propaganda, 1995), 39.

The conclusion of the case from Brno is unusual in that the Schöffen presented an articulate rationale, founded on abstract principle, to argue against the classification of abortion and infanticide among the criminal offenses. To defend their position, the jurors relied on forms of legal reasoning with deep roots in the Romano-canonical tradition, accentuated as well by Bolognese law professors like Signorolus de Homodeis and Baldus de Ubaldis, who during the same period challenged established notions of homicide. Yet contrary to the Moravian board, neither Signorolus nor his imitators proceeded to dismiss the underlying idea of criminalization outright. In limiting their opposition to the demand for reduced punishment, they seemed at least somewhat more sympathetic toward popular discomfort with the harshness of penal retribution than the majority of rigorists and older jurisprudence in the wake of Azo and Accursius. In court records from the heartland of the Ius commune, to the south and west of the Rhine and the Alps, there are indeed many allusions to resistance from below against the Azonian standards of sentencing. Resentment appears to have been fueled by the widespread feeling that judges ought to give obligations toward family greater weight than general doctrine was prepared to concede.

Apart from the Moravian verdict, the available sources do not contain any express criticism of the relevant jurisprudential norms. It is rather the privacy of households, the regard for hierarchies tying children and young people to their elders, and the desire to preserve one's bona fama that receive mention here and there as alleviating circumstances or are embedded in pleas requesting a rare exception to the rule. These protestations must have been, despite their fleeting occurrence, recurrent, endemic, and for the most part tacitly understood, as is perhaps best illustrated by a letter of pardon that the French king granted in 1453 to Marion Faudier of Eu in Normandy. Marion's father, Jean, was alleged to have repeatedly raped his own daughter and tried to conceal the resulting pregnancy by forcing her to imbibe a mixture of abortifacient herbs. To address the question of why Marion endured the violence so silently and for a considerable length of time, the letter explained that she had kept her mouth shut "for fear of her father to whom she was subject," at which point, and as if by intuitive afterthought, the text added the words "as reason dictates."[14] Given the preceding graphic description of her brutal and abusive treatment, the invocation of unwavering filial respect

---

14. Paris, AN, JJ 184, no. 303 (March 1453): "Il congneut et habita charnellement ladicte Marion sa fille par force et contre son gre et volente et en ce dampnable propos et volente continua par mou temps pendant lequel icelle Marion . . . de ce ne se osoit plaindre ne douloir par la crainte et doubte de sondit pere auquel elle estoit subiecte comme raison est."

may seem oddly out of place. It was, however, directed at fifteenth-century audiences, who were imbued with an overpowering sense of duty toward small-scale, intensely personal and patriarchal relationships.

Rejection in the Royal Courts of England (1327–1557)

What separates the English history of prenatal homicide from the rest of Latin Christianity is that, at some point in time, the common law of the crown transformed popular disapproval of criminalization into an ordinary feature of lay justice. After Edward I had died in July of 1307, it still looked for a while as though royal justices traveling on their circuits would keep prosecuting the offense among the felony cases. Whenever a dead fetus was at hand, neighborhoods were obliged to undertake a public inquest, and where battery followed by miscarriage had occurred, it was usually the injured women themselves who came forward and launched a private appeal against the perpetrators. Judicial records continue to report the flight of individuals and carefully note the value of their confiscated belongings. It is true that very few accusations culminated in physical punishment, but low conviction rates do not suggest diminishing prosecutorial zeal if compared with figures from the previous century. Unchanged adherence to the punitive standards of Bracton and the canonistic identification of homicidium with the slaying of a formed fetus were again confirmed by a mandate summoning Thomas of Chobbeham, who in 1320–21 approached the king's justitiarii at the Middlesex eyre. A plea role asserts that Thomas angrily threw Agnes, the pregnant wife of Thomas Aleyn, out of his house during an altercation over questions of debt. In her retreat, Agnes stumbled over a stone lying in the doorway and fell to the ground. Within four days, she miscarried, about fifteen weeks before her child was due. The chain of events bore a striking resemblance to the situation of Maude de Haule, who a generation earlier had been hanged on account of identical charges. Yet for one reason or another, Thomas of Chobbeham was luckier, and the jurors acquitted him without further ado.[15]

In his dissertation on the law of felony in medieval England, Harold Schneebeck concluded that public indictments targeting attacks on life in the maternal womb remained common until the last years of Edward III's reign (1327–77). The most recent case he cited dates nevertheless to the

---

15. Kew, TNA, Just. 1/547A, m. 19d (Crown v. Thomas of Chobbeham; Middlesex eyre, 1320–21); on Maude de Haule's execution of 1283, chap. 2, note 37; cf. also chap. 2 for a discussion of criminal abortion in English common law prior to 1327.

Middlesex eyre of 1329.[16] Subsequently, felonious accusations grew rare and soon ceased to occupy the royal courts altogether. Their gradual disappearance from among the capital pleas occurred without any hint at legislative intervention, and so investigations into the abandonment of older judicial routine must inspect the juristic handbooks for clues. Two pedagogical treatises written around 1290 in fact voice opposition to Bracton and the canonized understanding of criminal homicide as extending to death inflicted after fetal formation. A single manuscript, the so-called *Mirror of Justices*, maintains that killings of children before and during the first year of life would always fall under church jurisdiction. The unknown author of the idiosyncratic work, chided for his inclination to "lie unblushingly" by the famous nineteenth-century legal historian Frederick Maitland, argued in addition that nobody could be called an infant before emerging from the mother's body. In tackling the issue from a more technical and procedural angle, a second, frequently copied manual circulating under the title of *Britton* criticizes the habit of admitting appeals by women who suffered a miscarriage by way of percussio. Similar complaints deserve to be rejected on formal grounds, *Britton* states, because unborn victims do not fulfill the legal requirement of a proper name, conferred through baptism.[17] As the affirmations of both authors related to judicial practice, it turns out that they tried to modify rather than describe legal reality.

An intriguing entry in the roll of an Oxford coroner shows that the revisionist remarks of the *Mirror* and especially *Britton* cannot be dismissed out of hand as poorly informed about English felony proceedings. On April 23, 1300, the forensic expert of the crown (coronator) examined the corpse of a baby boy, in whom local witnesses believed they recognized Emma of Hereford's youngest son. The royal official managed to ascertain that the pregnant Emma had previously participated in a festive gathering sponsored by the archdeacon of Buckshire where, in the midst of considerable commotion, bystanders had pushed her back and forth until she slid and smothered her child "in the mother's womb." Were it not for the comment in *Britton*, historians today would struggle to understand why the coroner's record, on no less than four occasions, refers to the stillborn by the name of Roger.[18]

---

16. Kew, TNA, Just. 1/548, m. 4; Schneebeck, "Law of Felony," 237–238.

17. *Britton* 1.24.7, ed. Francis Nichols (Oxford: Clarendon, 1865), 114; *The Mirror of Justices*, ed. W. Whittaker (London: Quaritch, 1895), 139, with Maitland's disparaging comment, ibid., xxvi; also D. J. Seipp, "The Mirror of Justices," in *Learning the Law: Teaching and the Transmission of Law in England, 1150–1900*, ed. Jonathan Bush and Alan Wijffels (London: Hambledon Press, 1999), 85–112.

18. Oxford, Record Office, Twyne Coll. IV.146, in *Oxford City Documents, Financial and Judicial, 1268–1665*, ed. James Thorold Rogers (Oxford: Clarendon, 1891).

In a similar vein, the significant change in juristic attitudes toward felonious miscarriage during the first few decades of the fourteenth century is stressed by a learned summary that the common lawyer William Staunford wrote on the subject in 1557. Staunford's treatise *The Pleas of the Crown* argues in essence that the killing of the unborn had never warranted intervention by the king's courts and did not fit secular categories of crime at all.[19]

Staunford relied on four pieces of precedent with origins reaching far back into the past. They belonged to the relatively short period from 1313 to 1348, when charges of felonious *homicidium* underwent a thoroughgoing legal reassessment. None of the texts had been drawn from among the brief and often monotonous entries in the plea rolls. Staunford had spotted them in the *Graunde Abridgement*, a widely used tome compiled by his older colleague Anthony Fitzherbert as a comprehensive digest of late medieval common-law doctrine.[20] First published in 1514, Fitzherbert's guide consists mainly of excerpts from the "year books," a type of literature that, not unlike *Britton* and the *Mirror*, was conceived in the service of professional education. The year books began to circulate during the reign of Edward II in the 1290s and eventually formed repertories of single notes taken by trained and perhaps specifically appointed legal observers at trials or while attending the oral deliberations of royal judges. Dedicated in particular to the propagation of procedural novelties, the uniformity and extensive textual tradition of the year books further indicates that they were edited in a central location of learning and appeared, as the title suggests, in regular annual installments. Their mode of production and function as expert training tools furnished readers for centuries with sophisticated technical information that ordinary methods of record keeping were ill suited to communicate.

Staunford's oldest corroborating item offers details that the compiler of his original source, the year book of 1313–14, must have privileged over other pieces of information. The anonymous reporter's succinct prose is characteristic of the literary genre as a whole: "A presentment was made because a woman, while on her way to the chapel, gave birth to a baby boy. She immediately cut his throat, threw him in a pond, and

---

19. William Staunford, *Les plees del corone* 1.13 (London: Societas Stationariorum, 1607), fol. 21r–v. The evidence presented by Staunford underlies much of the modern discussion on abortion in medieval common law, including Schneebeck, "Law of Felony," 232–243; and Barbara Kellum, "The Female Felon in Fourteenth-Century England," *Viator* 5 (1974): 253–268; an exception is Butler, "Abortion by Assault."

20. Anthony Fitzherbert, *La Graunde Abridgement* (London: Tottel, 1577); Staunford cited titles *Corone*, pl. 146, pl. 263, pl. 418, and *Enditement*, pl. 4.

took flight. Therefore, she be compelled to appear and outlawed."[21] The passage includes a reference to the precise historical whereabouts of the incident, the "Kent circuit" (*Iter Cancie*), and thus modern historians can contrast the year book version with fuller data available from the pertinent eyre roll.[22] Differences between the two amount in large part to the names of litigants, the indication of places, and the victim's gender. Interestingly, however, the shorter narrative of the year book does not mention the final verdict of guilt (*malecreditur*) returned by the jury, as neither Fitzherbert nor his late medieval predecessor seem to have quoted the case because of its ultimate outcome. They mentioned only the threat of outlawry, which coincided with the conventional treatment of contumacious defendants in English common law. As a result, continuous repetition of the entry must have depended on its illustration of a different legal concern. Given the revisionist bent of several juristic commentators writing around 1300, the significance of the Kent precedent rested very likely on the exact description of events from the moment of birth to the act of killing. Infanticide committed immediately upon delivery and prior to baptism, the text implies, required, in actual practice and contrary to the recent theories of *Britton* and the *Mirror*, classification among the felony pleas.

In moving forward, Staunford adduced from Fitzherbert's *Abridgement* a pair of entries that had been prompted by the same judicial affair. The first figured originally in the year book of 1327. The second excerpt was lifted from the so-called *Liber Assisarum*, a parallel set of notes assembled in the reign of Edward III. Compared with the year books, the *Liber* recorded fewer arguments from the central court of the King's Bench and more issues that arose from sessions (*in assisis*) held by itinerant justices in districts along their circuit. For the third year of Edward III's rule, in 1329, the *Liber* recounts the following episode:

---

21. Fitzherbert, *La Graunde Abridgement*, tit. *Corone*, pl. 418 (erroneously dated to 8 Edw. II [1315]): "Presentatum fuit quod mulier eundo versus capellam peperit filium et statim abscidit gulam et proiecit in stagnum et fugit; et ideo exigatur et utlagetur." Fitzherbert's source, the year book of 1313–14, has been edited by Frederick Maitland et al., *The Eyre of Kent, 6/7 Edw. II* (London: Quaritch, 1910), 83; most of the manuscripts use the correct *weyveatur* (for women) instead of *utlagetur* (for male defendants). In addition, see D. J. Seipp, "Crime in the Year Books," in *Law Reporting in England*, ed. Chantal Stebbings (London, OH: Hambledon Press, 1995), 15–34.

22. Kew, TNA, Just. 1/383, m. 55 (Crown v. Juliana Wellyweld; Kent eyre, 1313–14): "Juliana filia Roberti Wellyweld *eundo versus cap*itulum tentum apud Sydyngbourne *peperit* quandam *filiam* apud Chercheseche *et postea scidit gulam* eius *et proiecit* eam *in* quoddam *stagnum* iuxta Watton in borgha de Sedon; *et* predicta Juliana statim post factum *fugit et* malecreditur; *ideo exigatur* et weyveatur. Nulla habuit catalla"; the words in italics also appear in the year book version (note 21, above).

A man was indicted at the King's Bench and brought before Geoffrey Scrope, for having beaten a certain A, wife of J and pregnant with two children; shortly thereafter, one of the children died and she gave birth to the other; the infant was baptized by the name of John and died within two days on account of the injuries suffered earlier on; the indicted man was taken into custody, appeared in court, and pleaded not guilty; and because the court believed that there was no felony, the justices released him temporarily and against sureties.[23]

The narrative of events in the year book of 1327 depicts the alleged offense with little variation but gives extensive coverage to successive developments. Upon dismissal of the defendant, the case was by no means considered closed. Instead, Justice Geoffrey Scrope decided to resume his inquiries and ordered that the accused be arraigned again. The year book also mentions that the king's court received a written response to the summons, explaining that the suspect was unable to appear because he had been imprisoned by the mayor of Bristol. The reason for the defendant's capture by town authorities, the year book informs us, remained entirely (*penitus*) unknown.[24]

At this point, the information conveyed through annual reporting ceased. It was typical among authors of the year books to concentrate on doctrinal novelties or shifts in juristic opinion without explaining how individual trials unfolded from stage to stage. Sometimes it was found worthwhile to record even viewpoints that had been refuted by the justices in court. Staunford's oldest reference from the Kent eyre of 1313–14 shows that the moment of birth was crucial for the admissibility of felony charges. His next two quotes, concerned with accusations brought to the King's Bench in 1327–29, take the issue to new extremes by alleging that a single act of violence killed before as well as after delivery. Of injured twins, one had perished in the mother's womb. The other had succumbed as a born infant and after baptism by the name of John. The reporters were careful to mention that the official investigators had doubted the criminal nature of the plea and questioned the appropriateness of capital indictment. Had their formal scruples been confined to specifics, or had they wondered whether the protection of unborn

---

23. *Le livre des assises* (London: Atkins, 1679), 4 (pl. 2), repeated in Anthony Fitzherbert's *Abridgement,* tit. *Enditement,* pl. 4; this is the famous "Twin-Slayer Case," translated by John Baker in Rafferty, "Roe v. Wade," 514.

24. *Year Book* [Michaelmas], *1 Edw. III,* fol. 23r (London: Yetsweirt, 1596), fol. 19r; cf. Anthony Fitzherbert, *Abridgement,* tit. *Corone,* pl. 146, translated in Rafferty, "Roe v. Wade" 512–513, and in Dellapenna, *Dispelling the Myths,* 145.

life was altogether beyond the reach of the English common law? Allowing for greater historical accuracy, several rolls from the King's Bench supplement Staunford's material with testimony about the way the proceedings went forward and came to a definitive conclusion.

For the Easter session of the King's Bench in 1327, the court register mentions that a man called Richard of Burton from Bristol was summoned to appear and answer criminal charges that on September 11 of the previous year he had feloniously killed Jo., the child of the tailor William Carles. Proof demonstrating that Richard is the defendant called D. in the year book of 1327 derives from a letter of arraignment sent to the sheriff of Gloucester on July 14. Copied word for word into the records of the King's Bench, the text reproduces each of the accusations against Richard. At variance with or in addition to information presented by the annual reports of 1327–29, it states that A., the mother of the two injured babies, bore the full name of Alicia and that the born and baptized infant was a girl, Johanna, rather than John, a boy. Particularly significant from the lawyerly perspective, the complete rendering of Richard's indictment reveals that the felonious quality of the case derived not only from Johanna's demise but from the slaying of her previously miscarried twin as well. The justices of 1327 apparently did not assume that human life prior to birth enjoyed lesser legal value than an individual outside the maternal body.[25] The rolls do not confirm the impressions left by both the year book and the *Liber Assisarum* that the inquest was eventually abandoned and did not furnish any concrete result. Four letters of summons, it is true, were insufficient to haul Richard into the highest royal court. On one occasion, he was said to have been impeded by imprisonment at the hands of John le Taverner, the mayor of Bristol, according to the year book. When Richard finally arrived at the bench early in the summer of 1328, he proved that he had not spent his absence in idleness. Toward the end of May 1327, he had joined the king's troops near York in preparation for war against the Scots and managed to secure a royal pardon for his alleged criminal offenses. One year later he presented the king's letter in London, and the trial against him ground to an immediate halt.[26]

---

25. Kew, TNA, KB 27/270, m. 9 (Rex Roll); printed in *Die Abtreibung*, 303n517, translated in Rafferty, "Roe v. Wade," 514–515, and in Dellapenna, *Dispelling the Myths*, 147–148.

26. Kew, TNA, C. 66/167, m. 17 (cf. *CPR* [1 Edw. III] 113); the text of Richard's pardon and references to the four summonses (from Kew, TNA, KB 27/270, m. 9; KB 27/272, m. 9; and KB 27/273, m. 12d) are translated in Rafferty, "Roe v. Wade" 516–530, and in Dellapenna, *Dispelling the Myths*, 148–150. On military pardons, a fourteenth-century novelty, see Lacey, *Royal Pardon*, 100–106.

Staunford's fourth and last precedent, attributed by his immediate source, Anthony Fitzherbert's *Graunde Abridgement*, to the year book of 1348, briefly cites the indictment of a man who had provoked a miscarriage through *percussio*. The presiding justices had declined to set a court date for the defendant, arguing, first, that it was difficult to ascertain whether he had been responsible for the child's death. The other reason motivating their unwillingness to open criminal proceedings complemented the position presented half a century earlier by the anonymous author of *Britton*—that the lack of a name for the victim precluded not only private appeals of homicide but also public inquiries launched by royal officials. In the context of Staunford's own allegations, this second criterion for the bringing of felonious charges did not square with his citation from the *Iter Cancie* of 1313–14, which had tied the criminal quality of attacks on nascent human life to birth rather than baptism.[27] The internal contradiction did not escape Staunford, who combined his conclusion with an explicit refusal to view the baptismal act as paramount for the admission of capital cases. In the end, however, he rejected the idea of inserting prenatal manslaughter among the punishable offenses in favor of a third and decisive juridical formula. To qualify for *homicidium* in the common-law courts, he summed up, the slain had to be born and "in the nature of things" (*in rerum natura*).[28]

Somewhat perplexingly, none of the four passages from Fitzherbert's compendium anticipated Staunford's final verdict. Yet in light of the technical language he adopted, sixteenth-century colleagues must have been aware that his solution merely reiterated conventional legal thinking. Staunford's summation in effect echoed doctrine that the *Liber Assisarum* had proposed as early as in 1348. Given that the murder of nameless strangers would elude criminal prosecution should the requirement of baptism be applied consistently the anonymous reporter of the *Liber* had favored a different rationale

---

27. Above, note 21. Staunford's quote is from Anthony Fitzherbert's *Abridgement*, tit. *Corone*, pl. 263: "Un fuit endit de ce que il tua enfant en le ventre sa mere et l'opinion que il ne serroit arraigne sur ce eo que nul nosme de baptisme fuit en l'enditement et auxi est dure conustre s'il occist ou non etc." Fitzherbert claimed to have lifted the passage from the *Year Book* [Mich.], *22 Edw. III*, although it is absent from the printed version (London: Tottyl, 1585) of the year book for Michaelmas term, 1348; English in Rafferty, "Roe v. Wade," 594–595, and in Dellapenna, *Dispelling the Myths*, 150.

28. William Staunford, *Les plees* 1.13, fol. 21r: "Queux choses sont requisites a faire homicide? Est requisit que le chose occise soit in rerum natura; et pour ceo si home tua enfant in le venter sa mier ceo n'est felony ne il forfetera ascun chose."

which, from a systematic perspective, seemed certainly more compelling and equitable:[29]

> Nobody is obliged to answer to a felonious appeal, if the private accuser has not named the killed individual. In public indictments of homicide committed against an unknown person, one is required to respond, as in the case of W. Chamble and K. Burgeis, who were summoned for having killed a foreigner near Lok. They were brought before the King's Bench, forced to plead and found not guilty. This poses the question of whether someone who kills a child in the mother's womb shall suffer capital punishment. I do not think so, for neither does the victim possess a name, nor was he or she present in the nature of things [*in rerum natura*].

The entry from the *Liber Assisarum* demonstrates that Staunford was not alone in his opinion. Rather than being a revisionist, he adhered to theories that were more than two hundred years old by the time he wrote. Unwillingness among common lawyers to prosecute induced miscarriage as a crime did not rest on the whims of a single court reporter. Instead, the solution advanced in 1348 could count on many sympathetic minds in the profession. This is suggested not only by the prosecutorial hesitation expressed in Staunford's sources of 1327–29 but also by the fact that he felt comfortable in omitting the one precedent that fully supported his own conclusion. Did he stop short of invoking the passage from 1348 because he failed to find the critical, final part of it in Fitzherbert's *Graunde Abridgement?* Or did he just assume his colleagues would be as accustomed as he was to ranking in rerum natura among the operating principles of English lay justice?

For the period from 1348 to the publication of Staunford's *Les plees del corone* in 1557, there is no evidence that royal justices went on to prosecute prenatal homicide as a punishable act. The numerous official investigations and private appeals initiated on account of felonious miscarriages throughout

---

29. *Le livre des assises* (22 Ass. pl. 94), 106: "Nul home est tenu a responder al appelle de felonie ou le plaintif ne fait pas nosme le nosm mort un home; mes al enditement de la mort un home disconus doit home responder sicut accidit de W. Chamble, K. Burgeis queux furent endites de la mort un home disconus occis a Lok dont ils fuerent arraines en Bank le Roy et mis a responder et troves de rien culpe etc. Quaere: Si home occist un enfant deins le ventre sa mere s'il pour cel suffrire mort? Credo quod non quia non nominabitur occisus nec umquam fuit in rerum natura," translated in Rafferty, "Roe v. Wade," 595–601. Anthony Fitzherbert's *Abridgement* (above, note 27) omits the latter portion of the text (from "sicut accidit"), first printed in digest format by Robert Brooke, *La Graunde Abridgement* (London: Tottel, 1573), tit. *Corone*, no. 91 (fol. 183v).

the thirteenth century no longer had an equivalent in the later court rolls. To explain the fundamental change, the coincidence in chronology between signs of judicial indifference and the appearance in the *Liber Assisarum* of the formula in rerum natura is readily at hand. Its success in opposing the canonical criminalization of abortion, however, did not lead to the complete disappearance of fetal killings from the legal documentation. Some defendants who risked physical punishment were still mentioned in connection with percussiones, although the references now served as a mere backdrop for conduct considered truly damnable. In 1348, for example, the adjudication of prisoners at York included the case of William of Garton, indicted for having slain a child in the womb of his wife, Elena. Yet William's rage had also been fatal to Elena and, in an earlier incident, to an unnamed stranger. An indictment from Lincolnshire in 1361–62, moreover, concerned the deadly battery of an infant "alive in the stomach" of Elizabeth from Albebarowe, this time in combination with rape and Elizabeth's own tragic demise.[30]

To distinguish pleas of the crown adequately from proceedings aimed at the monetary compensation of injured parties, modern investigators have to look for fleeting mentions of the term *felonice*, which typically indicate whether a court episode decided over questions of life and death. To complicate matters, the recorded indictment of Robert Byllings, jailed at Leicester in 1409, left posterity uninformed about the fact that his adversary, John Cogerell, had demanded satisfaction beyond the restitution of material damages:

> Robert Bylling, vicar of the church at Stonnesby, was captured because, in the night of July 18, 1407, he had, against the will and without permission of John Cogerell, broken into the house of the aforementioned John at Stonnesby, where Robert had pushed John's wife, Alice, with his hand onto the bed so that the baby boy in her womb was killed and she miscarried. He also had had intercourse with her, whereupon Alice had left the house and cohabitation with her husband John for seven weeks, during which John lost goods and cattle worthy about twenty shillings.[31]

John Cogerell's complaints were not framed to reveal his intentions explicitly. The registered plea does not assert a frequently fictitious "breach of peace,"

---

30. Kew, TNA, Just. 1/527, m. 11d (Crown v. Wilhelmus de Garton; Lincolnshire eyre, 1361/62), cited by Schneebeck, "Law of Felony," 240–241; Kew, TNA, KB 27/354, m. 66 (York Gaol Delivery, 1348), transcribed in *Die Abtreibung*, 310n527.

31. Kew, TNA, Just. 1/388, m. 54 (Johannes Cogerell v. Robertus Bylling; Leicester Gaol Delivery, 1409); the original Latin text is printed in *Die Abtreibung*, 311n528.

effected "through the wrongful use of armed force" (*vi et armis*), which would have been the standard formula for pecuniary claims. That his case aimed instead at the infliction of punitive measures is only confirmed by a phrase featuring separately in the original roll. It repeats the jury's decision in favor of the accused along with the clarification that Robert had been arraigned on suspicions of felony (*de felonia*).

The narrative of 1409 does not identify the offense that threatened Robert with the death penalty. The count of miscarriage was probably not at the center of charges, as the English common law expected complaints of this sort to be brought by the injured women themselves, and also because Alice seems to have sided with the defendant, aiding and abetting Robert in his purportedly felonious behavior. Judicial court rolls of the fifteenth century frequently attest to the admissibility of indictments for the remaining accusations. Many records focus exclusively on forcible entry into a home, on the stealing of wives, or on the culpable loss of animals and movable belongings valued in excess of six shillings. Each of them warranted prosecution as a capital case.[32] By contrast, there is little reason to associate deadly retribution with the sole assertion that an adversary had taken human life in the form of an unborn baby.

Available judicial evidence that definitely treats miscarriage as a crown plea consists at the moment of just one indictment. It affirms rather than contradicts the new theoretical guidelines set by the *Liber Assisarum* in 1348. When John Hull, justice of the King's Bench, received orders to proceed against inmates of the prison at Gloucester late in July of 1409, the local sheriff, Richard Mawardyn, hastened to send his records to John and his colleagues in London. A series of annotations by Richard survives to the present day. It includes allegations against a certain Nicholas atte Welle, whom jury members assembled at Grymboldesasch had gravely accused in the previous month of April: "Nicholas atte Welle, *parcarius* from Poculchurch, broke into the house of William Chestrell, near Henfield, the night of February 21, 1403, and beat William's wife, Sybilla. In so doing, Nicholas caused injury and feloniously killed a boy in the womb of Sybilla, who was pregnant at the time."[33] The wording of the public accusation is unambiguous. In the eyes

---

32. *Die Abtreibung*, 312n530, quotes pertinent case material from the years 1400–1401. Alternatively, John Cogerell could have filed charges of abduction, or *raptus,* against Robert; see Caroline Dunn, "The Language of Ravishment in Medieval England," *Speculum* 86 (2011): 79–116.

33. Kew, TNA, Just. 3/20/4, m. 44 (Crown v. Nicolaus atte Welle; Gloucester Gaol Delivery, 1409); the Latin record of the jury inquest is printed in *Die Abtreibung*, 313n531.

of the jurors, the percussio Sybilla had received from Nicholas atte Welle deserved to be punished with death, and the royal justices convening at the castle of Gloucester on July 23 were compelled to express their professional opinion on the matter. It was their task to assess whether or not the common law still classified the killing of unborn human beings as a felony. The answer can already be surmised from a court roll that one of the presiding judges deposited upon his return to London. It does not devote a single line to the defendant's fate. More forthcoming and explicit, on the other hand, is the calendar of the sheriff, in which Richard of Mawardyn listed each of the jailed suspects for later presentation in court. Among the persons he cataloged, there is a brief reference to Nicholas atte Welle, "indicted and imprisoned pending further determination." Above the same phrase, a second remark, written in minuscule letters, informs readers about the way the pretrial against Nicholas came to an end: "Released from jail by way of pardoning; and because the indictment is insufficient."[34] The recorded version of Richard's indictment contains the names of the two spouses affected by the miscarriage, as well as those of the twelve jurors who had pressed charges. The place and exact time of the alleged criminal incident were not omitted either, implying that the objection of formal insufficiency rested on the erroneous use of the term *felonice*. The jury's attempt to present Nicholas's percussio alongside capital crimes such as homicide or robbery was apparently greeted with incomprehension by Justice John Hals and his peers. In accordance with the *Liber Assisarum* of 1348, they declared the plea to be null and void.[35]

In view of learned recognition and prosecutorial indications suggesting that induced miscarriages stopped being a felony in the English common law from early in the reign of Edward III, what factors were responsible for the swift abandonment of judicial rigors after the thirteenth century? At some distance and in a different legal context, lay jurors meeting at Brno around 1353 produced important evidence to the effect that the scholastic equation of abortion with homicidium did not enjoy the unanimous support of ordinary Christians and was resented especially by groups concerned with their honorable status and standing in the community. One faction of the Moravian Schöffen pointed out that, by custom, the killing of unborn and

---

34. Kew, TNA, Just. 3/20/4, m. 45; the justiciar's roll of the Gaol Delivery session, held on July 23, 1409 (TNA, Just. 3/189, m. 32–32d), is silent on Nicholas atte Welle's case.

35. Reliant on the maxim that indictments and appeals "quashed partly, are quashed altogether" (*cassatur una pars, cassatur per totum*); cancellation occurred most typically on the basis of omitted names, places, or dates for the felonious offense, as in the pleas cited in chap. 2, notes 38 and 40.

newborn humans was to be left to the discretion of the delivering mothers. That panel members appointed to return criminal verdicts in England were similarly inclined to regard the death and survival of nascent children as properly pertaining to the domain of parenthood, in spite of the supervisory claims advanced by secular authorities, can also be inferred from a wider selection of court data. In her extensive work on cases of infanticide, Barbara Hanawalt has examined a large number of judicial records from the years between 1300 and 1348. Having sifted through thousands of pleas regarding violent homicide, she did not count more than four incidents alleging the suspicious death of a recently delivered baby. Rolls compiled over the next two centuries have not yielded any *infanticidia*, notwithstanding theoretical clarifications that in 1348 reemphasized the felonious character of fatal attacks on victims in rerum natura.[36] And even earlier, in the 1200s, during the heyday of criminal charges for prenatal homicidia, infanticide does not appear to have preoccupied English lay juries except in the rarest of circumstances. At the eyres of Suffolk in 1240, Sussex in 1255, and Norfolk in 1257, a total of three defendants was convicted and executed.[37] No other incidents of capital sentencing are presently known.

Thirteenth-century accusers were slow to pursue infanticide judicially and eager to bring cases of miscarriage caused by an outsider to the family. Driven by the same logic, lay prosecution never dealt with the death of unborn offspring procured by the hands of natural mothers. Rarely if ever did the prototypical scenario of abortion in modern parlance draw the attention of English secular judges. The opening of a trial occurred routinely on behalf of households whose members had lost a baby as a result of external interference. To secure sufficient leverage for themselves, many among the less affluent in society resorted to the remedy of criminal appeals, invoking purported breaches of the public peace and requiring intervention by the king's officials. Until the reign of Edward I (1272–1307), this common attitude multiplied the incidences of percussiones couched procedurally in the language of capital crimes but aimed primarily at pressuring offenders into compensation payments for the aborted baby. That material damages were at the heart of allegations is explicitly stated by some of the records.

---

36. The latest noted medieval case is from the York eyre of 1348, Kew, TNA, KB 9/156, m. 79 (Crown v. Agnes de Hankeswyk), after the infanticides listed by Hanawalt, *The Ties That Bound*, 154–157; cf. Sara Butler, "A Case of Indifference? Child Murder in Later Medieval England," *Journal of Women's History* 19 (2007): 69–71, 74–76.

37. Cited by Hurnard, *King's Pardon*, 107, 161–163, 169; Kellum, "Infanticide," 373–378; and James Given, *Society and Homicide in Thirteenth-Century England* (Stanford, CA: Stanford University Press, 1977), 61, 144.

For the majority, the motive has to be deduced from hindsight and in light of changes that soon after 1275 prompted the decline of prenatal fatalities among the crown pleas.

Henceforth, a different format of accusations, allowing parties to seek indemnity for infringements of the peaceful order, became widely available to average families. Issuance of the necessary mandate (writ) would cost a generally affordable fee, and poor petitioners received the letter gratis. The writ permitted recipients to bring incidents of violence (*quare vi et armis*) to the knowledge of royal justice and demand monetary rather than physical vindication. In formulaic expressions, the novel procedure pursued harmful misconduct such as the illicit invasion of land, the forced entry into someone's house, injury to the body, and the abduction of cattle and supplied litigants with a viable instrument for claims falling short of capital prosecution. Certainly by the 1290s, the inherent modification of older procedural strategies became manifest in that judicial records started to document percussiones devoid of any reference to felony and increasingly in connection with "trespass," the invasion of property carried out vi et armis. When juristic theory agreed to follow suit by eliminating the killing of a formed fetus from the category of homicidium in 1348, miscarriages caused to pregnant women survived in criminal appeals and indictments only as a narrative device, underscoring that alleged blows to the body had been truly severe.[38]

In his work of 1992, Philipp Rafferty tried to prove that the eventual refusal of the common law to treat the willful killing of unborn human life as a felony did not come about until sometime after the publication of Staunford's treatise in 1557. To support his contention, Rafferty quoted various judicial entries that appeared after the *Liber Assisarum* of 1348. Yet the evidence he mustered in no way matches the slew of recorded accusations from the thirteenth century, in which absolute and exclusive prosecutorial focus is placed on "felonious" prenatal manslaughter. If anything, the case material accumulated by Rafferty serves to show that total impunity of induced miscarriages in the royal courts may not have been endorsed by all. A commentary on a compilation of royal statutes from the 1400s does confirm that its unknown author, in anticipation of statements made by early modern lawyers such as Edward Coke in 1644 and Matthew Hale in 1682, preferred to have wrongful fetal death adjudged at least among the punishable misdemeanors

---

38. Daniel Klerman, "Settlement and the Decline of Private Prosecution in Thirteenth-Century England," *Law and History Review* 19 (2001): 35–47; Meekings, *Crown Pleas*, 78–79, 276.

(*misprisons*).[39] The idea seems to have bypassed late medieval court practice. From the days of Edward III, sources reveal that prenatal existence was not safeguarded except by ecclesiastical judges, who continued to investigate fatal attacks in line with canonical regulations valid across Latin Christendom.

In England and arguably elsewhere, late medieval lay opposition to the criminalization of abortion is as ill documented as it was probably ever present. For the most part, popular resentment toward public interference with the accustomed and family-based control of procreative behavior does not surface in writing. But whenever protestations did transform into literary expression, they conveyed their criticism in uniform fashion. Whether the rejection of capital punishment for prenatal homicide was rationalized by literate circles at the center of scholastic jurisprudence in Bologna, inside the courts of the English jury system, or along the periphery of reception north and east of the river Rhine, proponents always relied on the principal alternative to common juristic opinion provided by Justinian's *Corpus iuris civilis*. Signorolus de Homodeis and his colleagues referred to unborn life with the words of the ancient jurist Papinian as "not properly human"; the anonymous English annotator of 1348 and, two hundred years later, William Staunford invoked Paulus, another Roman lawyer, to conclude that unborn beings were not yet in the nature of things; and jurors serving on the panel at Brno adapted civilian ideas to grant mothers the absolute right (*ius in re*) to dispose of their children both at and prior to birth. In widely different contexts, refusal of the prevailing legal viewpoint hinged upon objections drawn from Bolognese discourse and its foremost academic textbooks.[40]

Equally important, the search for authorities defying the correlation between abortion and physical sentencing occurred with marked simultaneity in areas very distant from one another. Hardly more than a decade separated the *Consilium primum*, written by Signorolus around 1342–43, from the annual installment of the *Liber Assisarum* compiled in 1348 and, finally, the Brno verdict that John, the municipal scribe, incorporated into his collection

---

39. Cambridge, UL, MS E.S. 22, fol. 212r, translated in Rafferty, "Roe v. Wade," 602; contrary to Staunford, two important seventeenth-century lawyers again defined abortion as *misprison*: see Edward Coke, *Institutes of the Laws of England* 3.7 (London: Pakeman, 1644), 50–51; Matthew Hale, *Pleas of the Crown* (London: Atkyns, 1682), 53a–c. According to Rafferty, "Roe v. Wade," 119–195; John Baker, *The Oxford History of the Laws of England* VI: *1483–1558* (Oxford: Oxford University Press, 2003), 555n21–22; and Dellapenna, *Dispelling the Myths*, 185, abortion was a (felonious) lay offense between 1348 and 1557, although they do not cite a single criminal verdict exclusively concerned with the slaying of an unborn baby.

40. Above, note 7; chap. 3, note 23; Francisco Cueña-Boy, "Reflexiones en torno a la idea de rerum natura en la Glosa ordinaria de Acursio," *RIDC* 15 (2004): 201–215.

of Schöffensprüche about the year 1353. As written sources do not explain the obvious chronological convergence, modern historians are left to speculate about what cultural force persuaded local protagonists to embrace parallel ideas and attitudes at exactly the same time. Once again, the church appears to have been responsible for the even spread of innovative scholastic concepts through juridical and pastoral channels. At the beginning, there was the revisionist analysis of Roman legal materials undertaken by Signorolus that soon gave articulation to secular reservations about the criminal prosecution of prenatal manslaughter in outlying places like England and Moravia. It is well known that the two regions did not possess schools of civilian jurisprudence aside from offering rudimentary training to ecclesiastics. Penitential and canonistic manuals, on the other hand, permeated the Western Hemisphere sufficiently so that sophisticated legal theories reached every location near and far. The advance of both canonical and uncanonical teachings depended on the omnipresence of clerical institutions.

CHAPTER 6

Abortion Experts and Expertise

Modern Westerners readily accept the idea that current medical practice differs greatly from the healing techniques of the later Middle Ages. Knowledge about the human body has accumulated in ways that make earlier learning seem less impressive, if not outright primitive. It was not until the mid-twentieth century that scientific and technological advances allowed for the routine termination of pregnancies. Only since the 1950s have operations been conducted in specialized and specifically accredited hospitals, and a wide consensus has built up among practitioners that the physical risk for aborting patients should be minimal. By contrast, women carrying unwanted babies in the years between 1100 and 1500 did not have to resort to abortion to confront rates of mortality in childbirth and average life expectancies that now rank as staggeringly adverse and menacing. From a present-day perspective, late medieval hygienic conditions were altogether unsafe. In cultural terms, however, today's health care systems retain many elements that first developed in the age of scholasticism. Along with the formation of academic curricula for theologians and lawyers, the teaching of medicine acquired permanent features in the 1100s, and society learned to greet university graduates respectfully as "masters" and *doctores*, in open recognition of their ability to offer valued services to affluent clienteles. And while the doctrinal expertise of the era has failed to withstand the test of modernity, the consultation of physicians in possession of a doctoral degree has provided enough reassurance to have demand for their cures increase steadily ever since.

Parallel to intellectual habits in the neighboring disciplines of law and theology, twelfth-century scholastic medicine found guidance in textual *auctoritates* that for the most part trace back to the period of antiquity. In line with Gratian and the early civilian teachers, the pioneers in the field were primarily engaged in a bookish pursuit, distilling from older literature uniform and comprehensive readings for classroom use. Through the elimination of internal contradictions and the careful conceptual analysis of statements attributed to ancient writers like Hippocrates and Galen, they put together a coherent doctrinal edifice and imparted it to students in the typical academic formats of marginal *glossae*, self-standing *summae*, and monographic treatises. Attempts to forge a learned synthesis from previous, widely scattered data further benefited from the contributions of Arabic doctors such as Avicenna (d. 1037) and Averroes (d. 1198), whose expert commentaries on the Hippocratic and Galenic source material were grounded in a tradition that preceded the inception of professional training in the West by many centuries. With an approach that called for philological and interpretive scrutiny rather than experimental autopsy, the university knowledge of abortifacient procedures and prescriptions also relied on imported repertories. The principal trove of pharmacological data survived on parchment as part, or in elaboration, of the *Materia medica* composed between 60 and 78 by the Greek physician Dioscorides. In translation, alphabetized, excerpted, and increasingly rendered in vernacular versions, the *Materia medica* conveyed standard information about the physiological effects of numerous plants and herbs while complicating the endeavor of modern historians to discern medieval scholarly insight from content that by the later Middle Ages had turned incomprehensible or obsolete.[1]

As branches of higher education, jurisprudence and medicine grew out of similar circumstances. The specialized skills they conferred permitted practitioners to carve out niches of opportunity in larger and preexisting service sectors. One catered to the peaceful resolution of conflict between adversaries, the other to physical comfort and recovery. Not very different from the lawyers who concentrated on public mediation and justice, the

---

1. On the rise of scholastic medicine, see Nancy Siraisi, *Medieval and Early Renaissance Medicine: An Introduction to Knowledge and Practice* (Chicago: Chicago University Press, 1990), 60–96; concerning the academic discussion of reproductive health issues, Danielle Jacquart and Claude Thomasset, *Sexuality and Medicine in the Middle Ages* (Princeton: Princeton University Press, 1988), 104–286.

representatives of academic medical doctrine gradually extended their reach and competence into areas long occupied by people whose preparation for the task did not involve certification, literacy, or years of theoretical and full-time training. Scholastic gynecology, for instance, did not assume a commanding role right away and appropriated the entire spectrum of health care for women in a slow and intermittent process. Twelfth-century university expertise saw the intervention of male doctores as being narrowly restricted to female breast conditions; illnesses affecting the reproductive organs were typically left to the cures of neighbors. In the 1300s, when learned monographs began to tackle the problem of infertility as their common point of access into the field of obstetrics, authors continued to address pregnancy and birth only if treatment was needed in connection with serious disorders and emergencies. In Latin treatises on surgery, cases of difficult birth did not solicit discussion prior to the *Chirurgia magna*, completed in 1363 by the celebrated papal physician, Guy de Chauliac, who further reminded his readers that, ordinarily, both gestation and delivery fell under the supervision of licensed matrons. More regular forms of assistance did not warrant description until manuals on midwifery expanded the scope of Western writing from the mid-1400s onward.[2]

The focus of this chapter is provided by occasional references in the judicial and juridical sources to the actual procurement of an abortion. What the texts reveal in particular and consistently is a neat distinction along gender lines between medical expertise furnished by men and health services that were rendered by women. The next two sections illustrate respectively how criminal judges in the years after 1250 routinely consulted "wise matrons" (*matrones sages*) over questions concerning the "secret" or reproductive parts of the female anatomy, while male physicians and surgeons were invited to conduct forensic inspections that involved the rest of the human body. This division of labor, moreover, was accompanied by a deepening rift between the low-end and everyday care in childbirth offered by typically illiterate midwives on the one hand and the text-based and exclusively "masculine" medicine taught at the universities on the other. Given the above-mentioned gradual integration of gynecology and obstetrics into the academic curriculum, the coverage of specifically feminine ailments and physical conditions in

---

2. For the gradual delineation of midwifery and gynecology as distinct occupational fields, see Monica Green, *Making Women's Medicine Masculine: The Rise of Male Authority in Pre-Modern Gynaecology* (Oxford: Oxford University Press, 2008), 91–117, 246–287; cf. also Guido de Cauliaco, *Inventarium sive Chirurgia magna*, ed. Michael McVaugh and Margaret Ogden, 2 vols. (Leiden: Brill, 1997), 1:368.

the learned literature remained for many centuries rather selective, featuring extensive reflections on, say, embryology next to rare and fleeting remarks on abortifacients and their proper administration. What little can be gleaned on the matter of induced miscarriages from the known legal and non-legal documentation is finally gathered and interpreted in the last section.

Evidence of Midwifery

In several publications on the history of contraceptives and abortifacients from antiquity to the Renaissance, John Riddle has argued that during the Middle Ages, the gynecological expertise amassed through readings and the frequentation of lecture halls lagged considerably behind the skills of ordinary females, who over the centuries had developed superior insight into the workings of reproductive health by way of experiment and direct assistance in pregnancies and delivery. Moving on a different and purely theoretical trajectory, students of medical science never really explored the data that the proverbial wise women were passing on orally from one generation of birth helpers to the next. Riddle considered it probable that the pharmacological advice assembled in the *Materia medica* of Dioscorides to impede procreation had its ultimate root in the unheralded teachings of Greek folk medicine. The subsequent copying of ancient prescriptions, he surmised, went far beyond mechanical reiteration and involved constant and gradual adaptation of the materials, necessitated not least by consultation of the *Materia medica* in places outside its original Mediterranean setting that were more familiar with the flora of northern Europe. In seemingly trivial textual changes and additions, Riddle believed he had detected the persistent influence of lay knowledge that, he claimed, circulated most abundantly among nonscholastic and self-taught providers of everyday prenatal and natal care. Modern scientific analysis has confirmed that age-old recommendations in the literature such as highly toxic rue (*ruta graveolens*) or savin juniper (*juniperus sabina*) are somewhat effective if prepared adequately. Both plants, it has been found, are endowed with chemical agents that may provoke expulsion of the fetus, a medical conclusion supposedly reached for the first time in the anonymous and undocumented spheres of midwifery.[3]

---

3. John Riddle, *Eve's Herbs: A History of Contraception and Abortion in the West* (Cambridge, MA: Harvard University Press, 1997), 10–63, 101–108, 132–157; for a critique of Riddle's assertions, see Monica Green, "Gendering the History of Women's Healthcare," *Gender & History* 20 (2008): 498–507.

Court records at least support the idea that pregnancy and birth were concerns consistently entrusted to female specialists, whereas the treatment of other physical conditions and ailments was reserved for male apothecaries, barbers, surgeons, and general physicians. Early recognition of this sexual division of labor comes from the pen of Bartolomeo da Varignana, an illustrious member of the Bolognese medical and political establishment between 1265 and 1311. In a piece of expert testimony he probably wrote sometime after 1277 for the purpose of conveying his academically trained opinion on the bodily state of a certain Gilia to the highest criminal tribunal in town, Bartolomeo explained that Gilia was to be considered pregnant following the report of two wise women (*sapientes obstetrices*) who had examined her at his request and "just as the philosophers of medicine prescribe." It appears that Bartolomeo and his colleague Bertolazzo Saraceno had limited themselves to the discernment of outer signs and symptoms (*signa et accidentia*). Scrutiny by touch (*ad tentandum*) was performed by the unnamed obstetrices.[4]

After Jehannin de Verdelay had been incarcerated by the provost of Paris for the battery of Jehanette de Gagny in November 1338, a learned master (*maitre*) of medicine by the name of Pierre de Largentiere was called in to inspect Jehannette's head injuries. At the same time, it was considered appropriate to summon Emmeline la Duchesse for ascertainment of whether the child in Jehannette's womb had escaped the violence unharmed. Over the course of the 1330s, the criminal registers kept by the Parisian abbots of Saint-Martin-des-Champs addressed Emmeline repeatedly as a "sworn matron" (*matrone juree*), acknowledging that she and her peers were operating with express approval and permission of the authorities.[5] In criminal litigation, their medical findings were held in highest regard. The forensic analyses they

---

4. Bologna, AS, Curia del podestà, Carte di corredo 1bis/22: "Magister Bartholameus de Varegnana et magister Bertholatius Saracenus de precepto et voluntate domini Petri iudicis ad maleficia iverunt ambo ad videndum Giliam et diligenter perscrutati sunt signa et accidentia que erant in ea. Item predicti medici miserunt duas sapientes obstetrices ad tentandum predictam Giliam sicut filosofi medicina precipiunt. Unde perscrutatis signis et accidentibus que vidimus et audimus in ea et relatis omnibus etiam a dictis ostetricibus rationabiliter suspicamus eam esse pregnantem." The autograph refers to Bartolomeo as "magister," a title he obtained in 1278; cf. Stefano Arieti, "Bartolomeo da Varignana," in *Medieval Science, Technology, and Medicine*, ed. Thomas Glick et al. (London: Routledge, 2005), 78–79.

5. Paris, AN, Musée 356, in *Registre criminel de la justice de Saint-Martin-des-Champs à Paris au XIVe siècle*, ed. Louis Tanon (Paris: Willem, 1877), 519, and in Louis Tanon, *Histoire des justices des anciennes églises et communautés monastiques de Paris* (Paris: Larose & Forcel, 1883), 144 (13 November 1338): "Maistre P. de Largentiere a raporte le perilg hors de mort de mehaing . . . ; Emmeline la Duchesse matrone juree a raporte le perilg hors du fruit de ventre de ladicte Jehannette." Emmeline reappears as matrone juree in several entries of the register, see chap. 7, note 7.

presented could determine the outcome of trials, as extant allegations in writing, transcripts of sentences, and letters of pardon reveal on several occasions. When Katherine Baudouine, a resident of la Gavenne in the Loire region told judges in April of 1401 that her baby, secretly conceived and delivered, had been stillborn, a quickly assembled panel of female jurors (*jurees*) maintained to the contrary that the infant had entered the world alive. Caught between her obvious distortion of the facts on the one hand and the lack of eyewitnesses or any full confession of guilt on the other, Katherine had to reckon with preliminary imprisonment of uncertain duration. Only the arrival of a *lettre de remission,* mandated by the king, secured her release from what might have become an unending situation of prosecutorial deadlock.[6] Frequently remembered in the documentary evidence for their services, the matrones jurees were entitled to offer public advice or act as examiners in legal proceedings once they had taken an oath before town magistrates, lords, or representatives of the crown. First recruited, it seems, shortly after 1300 in the Paris region, they soon obtained certified status all across the French kingdom and, by the fifteenth century, in areas eastward into Germany and England to the north. Though it was initially likely for official recognition to hinge upon the recipient's honorable standing and trustworthiness as a legal witness, among the long-term side effects was certainly the professionalization of midwifery and its pertinent skills.[7]

On a summer's day in July of 1383, inhabitants of the small town of Abbéville in Picardy spotted an exposed baby languishing near the Fish-Bridge. After the immediate rescue and conferral of improvised baptismal rites, the newborn died. The tragic incident was treated before an assembly of local jurors whose assignment it was to identify the person responsible for what in all likelihood constituted a punishable crime. As a result, presumably, of female cooperation, suspicions soon closed in on a single individual: "Inquiries progressed and several young women of honorable standing and good reputation, from the town and its environs, were examined, to the effect that they had to bare their

---

6. Paris, AN, JJ 156, no. 54; cf. Bernard Chevalier, *Le pays de la Loire moyenne dans le Trésor des chartes: Berry, Blésois, Chartrain, Orléanais, Touraine 1350–1502* (Paris: CTHS, 1993), 199 (no. 1914). A panel of sworn women is again mentioned in Paris, AN, JJ 66, no. 1137 (December 1332): "Veuilles sages matrones et experts en tel cas . . . les feismes jurer sollempnement que elles bien et dilligament verroient . . . se . . . ladicte Marie eust eu enfant."

7. Monica Green, "Documenting Medieval Women's Medical Practice," in *Practical Medicine from Salerno to the Black Death*, ed. Luis Garcia-Ballester et al. (Cambridge: Cambridge University Press, 1994), 337–340, reprinted in *Women's Healthcare in the Medieval West*, ed. Monica Green (Aldershot, UK: Ashgate, 2000), no. II; Green, *Making Women's Medicine Masculine*, 134–140.

breasts and let the truth be revealed."[8] Members of the community entrusted with physical inspections eventually focused their interest on young Ysabel de Lourmel, a girl they found lactating as if she had just had a child. If she had delivered, why was there no trace of her baby? Overcome by the relentlessness of interrogations, Ysabel finally gave in and admitted her personal involvement in the infanticide. About a hundred years later, in 1507, one of the oldest criminal law books signaling the full reception of scholastic jurisprudence in Germany, the famous *Halsgerichtsordnung* issued for the town and territory of Bamberg, would stipulate that the "milk test" (*Milchprobe*) endured by Ysabel was to be elevated to the rank of "full proof" and merit the automatic application of torture. A few decades afterward, the same article was reedited for the imperial *Constitutio criminalis Carolina* of 1532, and greater inquisitorial caution was enjoined by the legislator. "Numerous doctors," the *Carolina* observed, had opposed the judicial guidelines of the *Bambergensis* by arguing that "due to various natural causes" women might hold liquid in their breasts while not being pregnant at all. Therefore, the *Carolina* concluded, additional information on the medical condition of each suspect, to be gathered by "midwives or otherwise," was needed to corroborate presumptions of culpability before judges could proceed and apply methods of forcible inquiry.[9] The panel of late medieval jurors at Abbéville seems to have been plagued by similar scruples. Had it not been for Ysabel's unqualified confession of guilt, her fate might have hung in the balance much longer. Instead, the town mayor and his sworn panel members (*echevins*), compelled by the rules of Romano-canonical procedure, decided to impose the death penalty. Convicted of murder, Ysabel de Lourmel was burned at the stake.[10]

Wise matrons were again invited to submit their expert opinion when debate was about the precise effects of an attack on unborn or newborn

---

8. Abbéville, BM, MS 115, fol. 146r (July 1383), in Jean Boca, *La justice criminelle de l'échevinage d'Abbéville au Moyen Age, 1184–1516* (Lille: Daniel, 1930), 189–190; at Aalst in nearby Flanders, an equally exhaustive search was conducted in an infanticide case of 1420–21; see Fernand Vanhemelrijck, *De criminaliteit in de ammanie van Brussel van de Late Middeleeuwen tot het einde van het Ancient Regime* (Brussels: AWLSK, 1981), 110–111.

9. *Constitutio criminalis Bambergensis* (1507), art. 44, in *Die Karolina und ihre Vorgängerinnen*, ed. Josef Kohler and Willy Scheel, 2 vols. (Halle: Waisenhaus, 1900–1902), 2:23; *Constitutio criminalis Carolina* (1532), art. 36, in ibid., 1:27. The passage from the *Carolina* has been translated by John Langbein, *Prosecuting Crime in the Renaissance: England, France, Germany* (Cambridge, MA: Harvard University Press, 1974), 277; see also Sibylla Flügge, *Hebammen und heilkundige Frauen. Recht und Rechtswirklichkeit im 15. und 16. Jahrhundert* (Frankfurt/M.: Stroemfeld, 2000), 112–117.

10. Boca, *La justice criminelle*, 190; the rules of the Ius commune for ordinary inquisitorial trials are treated in chapter 7.

life. Teams of female consultants were called in to investigate, for example, scenarios in which the weak physical disposition or excessive workload of an expectant mother rather than intervention by a third party was likely to have caused a spontaneous and unintended miscarriage.[11] In connection with another matter calling for the diagnostic skills of midwifery, French letters of pardon often assessed with forensic exactitude the lapse of time between herbal poisoning and final expulsion of the fetus. Contemporaries did not know of firm measurements with regard to the longest possible interval from the administration of a "dynamic" beverage to its ultimate, fatal outcome. In 1399, Jehannette de Canelesle was thrown into prison at Peronne. She had imbibed a concoction procured by Margot "with the big arms" (aux gros bras) for the purpose of killing the child in her womb. The intended result did not materialize until two months later, but this failed to elicit skeptical comment in Jehannette's written request for leniency. A lettre de remission of February 1392 further noted the death of an embryo whose male or female sex nobody was able to identify. Delivery had occurred prematurely and in the same night the pregnant mother had taken abortifacient substances. Along similar lines, the cases of Alyson Taneurre from Beaune in 1425 and a second trial of 1470 attest to different episodes where stillbirth followed intoxication within an hour and after four days, respectively.[12]

Accusations launched on account of excessive beatings were marked by far greater chronological stringency. If a miscarriage was said to have been inflicted by the blows of an outsider, judicial sources frequently combined indications of cause and effect with more elaborate medical observations. In May 1387, Jehanne de la Porte from Bar-sur-Seine requested from the French king remission of her criminal charges. Incensed by the defamatory words of a neighbor accusing her of arson, Jehanne had been drawn into an open fistfight. There had been mutual pushing, dragging, and shoving, after which her adversary, Jehannette, the wife of Bertin, delivered a stillborn

---

11. Paris, AN, JJ 124, no. 337 (June 1384): "Mesmement que sadicte femme estoit tendre femme a son enfentement car elle avoit eu plusieurs ses enfans mors nez et abortez"; also AN, JJ 130, no. 218 (May 1387), and the English example cited in chap. 2, note 40.

12. Paris, AN, JJ 196, no. 287 (August 1470), cf. Chevalier, Le pays de la Loire, 344 (no. 3318): "Beut lesdiz herbes et incontinent ou environ une heure apres ladicte suppliante en tendant dessendre de dessus le lit ou elle estoit couchee son enffant luy cheut a terre"; AN, JJ 173, no. 244 (October 1425): "Et quatre jours apres ce icelle malade getta et eut une petite germe qui avoit forme d'enfant qui ne ot oncques vie et aussi ladicte malade ne l'avoit oncques senti"; AN, JJ 142, no. 103 (February 1392), in Bologne, La naissance interdite, 287–288; AN, JJ 154, no. 310 (July 1399): "Environ deux mois apres par maladie ou autrement mist hors de son corps un enfant qui n'estoit poins plus gros que une petite pomme."

child some five weeks later. Jehanne's immediate reaction to the news was to take flight. Fears of bodily punishment persisted undiminished, regardless of a forensic inquiry that absolved her of legal responsibility: "According to the workings of nature [selon raison naturele], [Jehannette] would have aborted the child within eight or nine days, had the incident really been provoked by [Jehanne's] battery and oppression."[13] The passage may explain why most royal letters of pardon for percussiones granted to French petitioners during the fifteenth century claim significantly shorter periods of delay from the battery to the miscarriage. That the rule of thumb enunciated by the royal mandate of 1387 reflected common experience at the time is equally suggested by a text in the registers of the criminal court at Manosque, near Marseille. Under the date of June 17, 1314, the entry renders the opinion of several sworn women who, through physical touch and in person, had examined a certain Alsace. They eventually determined that Alsace was pregnant, apparently out of danger after a beating and without visible bruises on her skin. In concluding their statement, the female experts supplied a revealing prognosis. They predicted that "the child in [Alsace's] womb will either be outside her body within nine days," and, as the implication ran, dead and aborted, "or stay alive and well in the mother's belly [intra ventrem]."[14]

It is arguable that the spheres of competence for midwives and academic doctors received their most lasting definition in the century prior to the early 1600s. The result was a clear-cut demarcation of responsibilities, due in particular to restrictions imposed by the legislators. The concealment of pregnancies (recel de grossesse) was progressively upgraded to the highest level of judicial evidence, known as full proof. In Germany, the Bambergensis of 1507 and the imperial Carolina of 1532 took the lead by permitting the automatic application of torture to persons suspected of secretive abortion or infanticide.[15] And in 1556, an edict promulgated by King Henry III of

---

13. Paris, AN, JJ 130, no. 218: "Selon raison naturelle se ycellui fait feust avenu pour ladicte bateure et enserrement l'enfant l'eust mis hors dedenz huit jours ou neuf."

14. Marseille, AD, 56 H 968, fol. 39r–v, in Joseph Shatzmiller, Médécine et justice en Provence médiéval. Documents de Manosque, 1262–1348 (Aix-en-Provence: Publications de l'Université de Provence, 1989), 131 (no. 34): "Que dicte mulieres suo iuramento retulerunt . . . quod infra novem dies infans quem habet in ventre erit extra corpus suum aut remanebit intra ventrem sue matris vivum."

15. Constitutio criminalis Bambergensis (1507), art. 43, and Constitutio criminalis Carolina (1532), art. 35, ed. Kohler and Scheel, in Die Carolina und ihre Vorgängerinnen, 2:23, 1:26–27, translated in Langbein, Prosecuting Crime, 277. For historical context, Catherine Crawford, "Legalizing Medicine: Early Modern Legal Systems and the Growth of Medico-Legal Knowledge," in Legal Medicine in History, ed. Michael Clark and Catherine Crawford (Cambridge: Cambridge University Press, 1994), 89–116.

France ordered with unprecedented intransigence that nothing short of death would suffice as a legal remedy. To escape execution, Henry's statute obliged expectant mothers to declare their grossesse timely and in the presence of respectable witnesses, a procedure that intensified not only the mobilization of sworn female experts in matters of childbearing but also their role as extended arms of criminal prosecution.[16] Henceforth, qualified assistance was viewed as indispensable in normal cases of delivery, whereas physical complications turned into a concern for university-trained personnel. The assignment of tasks represented standard Western experience into the mid-twentieth century, when ordinary births began to call for hospitalization as well. To combat infant mortality rates no longer regarded as acceptable, natal care increasingly abandoned the privacy of homes for the glaring light of public supervision, with specialized clinics conducting routine interventions and generating extensive documentation for research, financial, and legal ends. The extreme visibility of the new medical procedures contributed to a sense of crisis in reproductive ethics and healthcare that since the 1960s has accompanied the liberalization of abortion laws in societies informed by Latin Christianity.

Medical Embryology and Abortion Discourse

The teachers of scholastic medicine employed the same learning techniques as their colleagues in the fields of theology and law. Each of the four medieval university disciplines began by creating an authoritative text base and went on to construct from it a logically coherent doctrinal edifice. For the civilians, Justinian's *Corpus iuris civilis* became the undisputed point of reference. Twelfth-century canonists had a millennium of older canonical rules conveniently assembled in Gratian's Decretum, and interpreters of scripture relied on Peter Lombard's *Sentences*. Academic physicians likewise worked from a set of common teaching materials, attempting not least to facilitate availability and comprehension of the two foremost ancient Greek auctoritates on health issues, Hippocrates and Galen. In addition, they consulted the writings of early medieval Arabic doctors who shared with their Latin successors the goal of systematizing Hippocratic and Galenic thought for

---

16. *Les edicts et ordonnances des rois de France* 3, ed. Antoine Fontanon (Paris, 1611), 671–672 (no. 71); parallel instructions appear in a royal statute for England of 1624 (restricted to infanticide committed by unmarried women), *The Statutes of the Realm* 4.2 (London: HMSO, 1819), 1234–1235 (22 Jac. I, cap. 27).

both educational and practical purposes into handier literary formats. Similar to the experience of Bolognese lawyers and Parisian theologians, the effort exposed them to different habits of reasoning that often resulted from wholly incompatible philosophical and religious premises, be they pagan, Jewish, Muslim, or otherwise. As discussed in chapters 1 and 3, for example, the jurists had to grapple with conflicting embryological ideas, either locating the moment of animation at birth or tying it to fetal formation. The physici for their part were exposed to irreconcilable notions about the inviolability of unborn human life, such as when they pondered the question of whether or not abortions should be permissible for medical reasons. Depending on which of the relevant textbook passages they wished to privilege, they could make a strong argument in favor of as well as against therapeutic intervention.

In 1990 Monica Green published an article on the pioneering translator of Greco-Arabic medical literature, Constantinus Africanus (d. before 1098–99) exploring whether different religious attitudes toward unborn human life in the pagan world of Galen and Hippocrates or in the context of early medieval Muslim and Jewish commentary might have prompted forms of Christian rejection or censorship. What she found was that, by and large, Constantinus and the Latin literature on medicine written in his wake did not seek to manipulate the older source material and transmitted information about contraceptives and abortifacients faithfully to their Western audiences. Warnings to avoid abortion for ethical reasons were included to a degree that did not differ much from the remarks already present in the Hippocratic *Corpus* or, say, in the *Liber Pantegni* of Haly Abbas (d. 994), whose text was particularly well known among scholastic writers of the first generation. If anything, Green detected a certain reluctance to speak about ways to impede procreation or terminate a pregnancy, which she believed to have been inspired by Catholic sentiment.[17]

In what follows, particular emphasis is placed upon the obvious inclination of late medieval scholasticism to compartmentalize intellectual discourse along disciplinary lines. It is already evident from a comparative reading of chapters 1 and 3 that Bolognese Roman and canon lawyers were able to advocate diametrically opposed theories of fetal animation depending on shifts in their preference from one cluster of authoritative textbook assertions

17. Monica Green, "Constantinus Africanus and the Conflict between Religion and Science," in *The Human Embryo: Aristotle and the European and Arabic Traditions*, ed. Gordon Dunstan (Exeter: University of Exeter Press, 1990), 47–69.

to another. The four branches of university learning systematized their data in guildlike fashion and according to criteria that were peculiar to each field alone. Respect for mutually exclusive areas of competence was perpetuated side by side with preoccupation for the logically compelling interpretation of one's own auctoritates. Academic physicians echoed their sources, for instance, by insisting that regular sexual activity was good for human health, notwithstanding theological admonitions that regarded intercourse outside marriage or without procreative intent as entirely against God's wishes and hence sinful. The same coexistence of unreconciled teachings is again noticeable when one looks, first, at appeals to competing doctrines of embryology and, second, at the quandary of the pregnant mother who could only be saved by a medically induced miscarriage.

Early scholastic physicians had an approach to the subject of prenatal growth that distinguished them from their colleagues in theology and law. Briefly put, they imitated their literary models closely and almost never broached the issue of human animation. The medical discussion concentrated on different periods of fetal development and counted a minimum of three separate stages consisting of formation, quickening, and full viability or completion. In addition, the Hippocratic source material supplied quantitative measurements in days for the duration of each phase, which varied further according to sex and the respective end of gestation after seven, nine, or ten months. On the other hand, scarcely a word was written about the arrival of the immortal soul, and it was left to theological debate and, influenced by it, legal doctrine to turn the simultaneous occurrence of formatio and animatio into a centerpiece of late medieval religious and normative requirements. To illustrate the prevailing attitude among the physici, the remarks on the permissibility of therapeutic abortion offered by the Bolognese professor of medicine, Gentile da Foligno (d. 1348), are representative for several reasons:

And hence [Avicenna states] that the doctor must not work on the extraction [of the fetus], if it has already come to pass that the fetus is complete. Dino [del Garbo], however, says that [we must extract], if we believe we can extract the fetus in pieces [membratim] by way of cutting and operating in the intimate parts. Or it is the mother you may fear for. If she is in good health, the doctor must not induce her to miscarry. . . . If she is ill, though, then, by omitting the words of Dino and resorting to what is put more clearly, I say that either there is no use in a miscarriage for her and thus it must not be provoked; . . . or it is useful to her, or what nature herself pushes toward and aims at for resolution [*crisim*] and cannot attain; then the doctor helps himself by provoking the miscarriage.[18]

Guided by Avicenna, perhaps the most prominent Arabic physician in Western eyes and author of the encyclopedic *Canon*, as well as by Gentile's colleague and contemporary Dino del Garbo (d. 1327), the argument grants surgeons permission to abort the fully developed (*completus*) fetus (dead or alive) as long as the carrying women does not have the physical strength to expel it spontaneously.[19] The consilium is phrased throughout as a reminder that abortion constitutes only a remedy of last resort and needs to be avoided except where the pregnant mother herself is on the point of death. Yet it is equally apparent and characteristic of academic conventions in the field that there is no mention of animation as such or of its critical importance for the therapeutic decision-making process and no insistence on the sinfulness of attempts to terminate the life of an unborn human being, as was maintained at all times by both the late medieval canonists and theologians (see above, chapter 4). Although Gentile emphasized in another passage of his *Questio* that induced miscarriages were never licit in legal terms, he had no qualms about considering the matter solely from the perspective of his "art which is directed toward the well-being of human bodies."[20]

It deserves to be noted, moreover, that the preference among medical doctors for embryological information with an exclusive focus on physical growth is somewhat obscured by the rise of a novel intellectual trend in the thirteenth century, namely, the full integration of the Aristotelian *Corpus* into scholastic learning. Of special concern for theologians was the doctrine

---

18. The text of Gentile's *Questio an sit licitum provocare abortum* (from Vatican, BAV, lat. 2470, fol. 240r) has been published twice, by Reinhold Schaefer, "Gentile da Foligno über die Zulässigkeit des artifiziellen Aborts (ca. 1340)," *Archiv für die Geschichte der Naturwissenschaften* 6 (1913): 325–326, and Agostino Amerio, "Alcune considerazioni sulla liceità dell'aborto in uno scritto di Gentile da Foligno," *Pagine di storia della medicina* 10 (1966): 89–92.

19. Monica Green and L. Mooney, "The Sickness of Women," in *Sex, Aging, and Death in a Medieval Medical Compendium: Trinity College Cambridge MS R.14.52. Its Texts, Language, and Scribe*, ed. M. Teresa Tavormina, 2 vols. (Tempe, AZ: Center for Medieval and Renaissance Studies, 2006), 2:455–568, lines 679–681, quote an anonymous author on medicine from fifteenth-century England who held the same opinion. For the passage attributed by Gentile's *Questio* to Avicenna, see his *Liber canonis* 3.21.12: *De regimine abortus et extractione fetus* (Venice: Paganini, 1507; repr., Hildesheim: Olms, 1964), fol. 367rb–vb. The reference to Dino remains unidentified; cf. A. de Ferrari, "Del Garbo, Dino," *DBI* 36 (1988): 578–581.

20. "Cum autem queritur an sit licitum aborsum provocare non queritur an sit licitum per legem quod non est, sed an sit licitum secundum artes intendentes ad salutem corporum humanorum." Gentile, *Questio*, in Amerio, "Alcune considerazioni," 91, and Schaefer, Gentile da Foligno," 325.

of successive animation, which, according to the ancient Greek philosopher, would progress from a "vegetative" soul governing fetal existence from the moment of conception to an intermediate "sensitive" one and, finally, to the arrival of an immortal and "intellective" anima in connection with formation. Confronted with this tripartite scheme, theological discourse soon crafted its own explanations as to what precisely occurred during gestation in the womb and propagated them in treatises circulating alongside others written on the same subject by professors of surgery and medicine. An example of great importance for the law schools and legal notions of unborn life was the work published by Giles of Rome around 1280 and mentioned in chapter 4. Later physicians and surgeons, however, did not follow his lead and continued to discuss embryological issues without particular emphasis on questions of human ensoulment.[21]

Abortifacient Prescriptions

According to Monica Green, original instruction as to how to terminate a pregnancy is rare in the late medieval medical literature. As if to underscore the general reticence of Latin authors on the matter, she has discovered, aside from more numerous mentions in the works of antiquity and in translations from the Greek and Arabic, only two texts that provide recipes and techniques to remove a live baby from the womb. The first appears in William of Saliceto's *Summa* on practical medicine of 1268 and is accompanied by a warning concerning the morally suspect nature of contraception and abortion. The other, entitled *Breviarium* and written around 1320 by Arnold of Naples, informs readers in straightforward fashion about appropriate means to expel the fetus.[22] Court records from before 1500 display similar characteristics. Concrete information about methods to induce a miscarriage is uncommon, but if relevant details are presented by the judicial scribes, they suggest trust in the ability of experts to produce the intended physical result. The known legal documentation does not allude to health risks and presumes

---

21. Acknowledged in passing by Siraisi, *Medieval and Early Renaissance Medicine*, 109–114; Romana Martorelli Vico, *Medicina e filosofia. Per una storia dell'embriologia medievale del xiii e xiv secolo* (Milano: Guerini, 2002), 63–84; van der Lugt, "L'animation de l'embryon," 242–250.

22. Green, "Constantinus Africanus," 51–60. On William of Saliceto and his *Summa conservationis,* Helen Lemay, "Human Sexuality in Twelfth- through Fifteenth-Century Scientific Writings," in *Sexual Practices and the Medieval Church,* ed. Vernon Bullough and James Brundage (Buffalo: Prometheus, 1982), 200; see also Arnold of Naples, in Arnaldus de Villanova (misattributed), *Breviarium* 3.5: *De extractione fetus mortui et de mola et ad faciendum aborsum* (Venice: Baptista de Tortis, 1494), fol. 220va–221ra.

the ubiquitous availability of herbs and potions to prevent conception or the birth of an unwanted child.

Some clues about the quality of medical assistance available to women during a pregnancy can be gleaned from the judicial registers of the late medieval French crown. They illustrate, for instance, the approximate nature of diagnostic assessments, in that maladies usually figure under the names of local saints. Behind the illness of Saint Eutrope, interpreters may discern dropsy, or *hydropisia*. But there was also the ailment of Monsieur Saint Quentin, which at a few miles' distance from the homonymous Norman town must have defied easy recognition.[23] Around 1443, Ozanne Boisselelle was reported to have killed a newborn child after the successful concealment of her pregnancy from both husband and relatives. Near term and unable to continue working in the fields, she had justified her weakened physical condition by claiming that she had contracted the disease of Monsieur Saint Fiacre. A combination of geography and hagiography helps to explain the reference. Across northern France, the sixth-century Irish martyr was widely remembered as a heavenly intercessor for Christians afflicted with venereal infections. There was in addition a cluster of shrines dedicated to Saint Fiacre in locations throughout Brittany, not far removed from Montaigu in Poitou, south of Nantes, where Ozanne, by January of 1446, had spent almost three years in a prison cell. Then as now, her ailment lacked specificity in the minds of many, except for those who came from Ozanne's immediate vicinity.[24]

With regard to basic notions of anatomy, French judicial sources addressed health complications in the digestive and reproductive tracts as if they were indistinguishable from one another. Lettres de remission attest to the fusion of physical functions by recounting the story of petitioners who sought to obtain an abortifacient while pretending to require it for different medical purposes. Instead of telling the physician, Guillem Masson, about the actual state of Katherine Armant, her future sister-in-law, Jehanne Collette from Clermont l'Hérault in the Languedoc region, first asked Guillem late in 1466 for a means to alleviate the grave illness affecting Katherine's uterus. Jehanne

---

23. Paris, AN, JJ 148, no. 233 (October 1395), copied into AN, AB XIX 205A, no. 180/250; further AN, JJ 178, no. 257 (July 1447), cf. Yves Dossat et al., *Le Languedoc et le Rouergue dans le Trésor des chartes* (Paris: CTHS, 1983), 375 (no. 3694): "Tant qu'elle peut cela sadicte groisse et dist a sondit oncle qu'elle doubtoit estre malade de ladicte maladie de saint Ytrope"; item AN, JJ 197, no. 1515 (January 1473), ed. Paul Guérin, in *Archives historiques de Poitou* 38 (1909): 343–346.

24. Paris, AN, JJ 177, no. 137 (January 1446), ed. Guérin, in *Archives historiques de Poitou* 29 (1898): 239–241 (no. 1084): "Saichant icelle suppliante estre pres de son terme de avoir enfant ce qu'elle avoit tousjours cele a sondit mary disant qu'elle estoit malade du mal monsieur saint Fiacre et soubz umbre d'icelle maladie avoit fait difficulte d'aller aux champs."

wished to terminate a pregnancy that threatened to heap shame upon her parents and family. Katherine's appointed bridegroom was Jehanne's brother, who risked finding out that his fiancée had conceived a baby while he was traveling abroad. When it became clear that the medication recommended by Guillem Masson was ineffective, Jehanne urged her husband, André, to take the matter to a second healer, the apothecary Pierre Delala. Katherine's condition was now described as that of a poor woman plagued by persistent constipation. To cure her, André received potions and wraps from Pierre, who operated under the assumption that they would purge a patient he had not seen in person.[25] A similar blend of confusion and deception was at work in Brittany, where a court case of 1464 implicated Jehanne Gaudu. After learning that she was expecting a baby, Jehanne confided with her mother, Marie, who in turn approached a neighbor known to have suffered from obstinate stomach ulcers. Against all expectation, the woman's ailments had ended. In telling the unsuspecting "expert" about Jehanne's situation, Marie introduced her daughter as being stricken with "a similar disease."[26]

In October 1425, royal councillors conferred about a pardon for Alyson Taneurre from Beaune in the Isle-de-France region, a woman whose request showed considerable diagnostic ambiguity. Over a period of nearly twenty years, Alyson had offered help and relief to women with serious internal dysfunctions, bringing to the task what she had learned from male doctors and as a victim of comparable afflictions. Not equipped with any official certification as a sworn midwife, the self-taught Alyson was held in high esteem around town for her record of competence and successful consultation in health matters. On one occasion, Perrenet le Moyne summoned her to rush to the aid of his infirm wife, who complained about pain in the chest, kidney, and groin areas. Asked by Alyson whether there was reason to suspect a pregnancy, the woman replied, "Not that she knew." The answer persuaded Alyson to proceed with her usual treatment, which the lettre de remission describes step by step and in unaccustomed detail. To reduce the inflammation of the female "nature," a nutlike fruit identified with the words *gros d'une noix de noyer de connin* was enveloped in cloth and administered in the form of a pessary. The next day, hot baths followed. They were infused with herbal ingredients including *herbe terrestre,* fennel (*foeniculum*), celery (*apium graveolens*), and a

---

25. Paris, AN, JJ 200 no. 64 (February 1468), cf. Dossat, *Le Languedoc,* 417 (no. 4110); the next lettre de remission in the royal registers, AN, JJ 200, no. 65, cf. Dossat, *Le Languedoc,* 417 (no. 4111), renders the petition of a barber, Etienne de Linas, who knowingly tried to rid Katherine of her child.

26. Nantes, AD, B 3, fol. 167r; I am grateful to Jean-Pierre Leguay (Rouen) for sharing this excerpt with me.

smattering of *erbe m.ance, espart goute*. Modern scholarship has pored over these terms to establish their current botanical identity, but the attempt has proven successful only in part. Elementary problems of transcription (e.g., m.ance) still defy understanding and compound difficulties, especially with respect to the last couple of medicinal expressions.[27] Failure to reconstruct Alyson's pharmacological arsenal casts doubt on John Riddle's optimistic assessment of late medieval capabilities to communicate teachings of medical folklore across time and space. The absence of written and institutional preservation made it hard to spread the wisdom of midwifery uniformly and permanently. From the start, efforts to re-create Alyson's therapy of 1425 must have been impaired by lack of a fixed nomenclature. Personal oral instruction, it seems, provided the sole tool by which her treatment could have been reiterated.

The study of scholastic sources suggests that in the minds of contemporaries, at least two of the plants adopted by Alyson Taneurre, fennel and celery, possessed great potency as abortifacients. Perhaps as a consequence, it took Perrenet's wife no more than four days to expel "a small mass in the shape of an infant that had not moved within her nor given signs of life." Alyson was arrested on suspicion that she had provided the deadly cause. Her narrative of the facts, however, is circumspect and excludes any hint at premeditation by claiming complete ignorance of the pregnancy.[28] Another supplicant by the name of Mace le Saige, a resident of Ossanon in Maine, adopted a different exculpatory strategy in view of the ill-fated medical advice he had given. Mace's lover, Jehanne, wondering whether she was pregnant, had phrased her request for relief from feelings of sickness in rather evasive fashion. "Can you point me to a remedy that restores my menstruation?" she had asked Mace, according to his letter of pardon issued in April 1480. "Yes," Mace allegedly answered, "I know of one herb that is useful and it is called rue." Upon taking the recommended ingredient as a potion, Jehanne quickly emitted "a formed and wholly lifeless baby" whose existence "she had never sensed insofar as she had been aware of."[29] Although both Alyson Taneurre

---

27. Paris, AN, JJ 173, no. 244 (October 1425), discussed by Roger Vaultier, *Le folklore pendant la guerre de cent ans* (Paris: Génégaud, 1965), 227–228.

28. Paris, AN, JJ 173, no. 244; John Riddle, *Contraception and Abortion from the Ancient World to the Renaissance* (Cambridge, MA: Harvard University Press, 1992), 108–134, mentions Alyson's *ache* and *fenoul* among the most commonly used feticidal plants.

29. Paris, AN, JJ 207, no. 73 (April 1480): "Elle se doubtoit d'estre grosse et demanda audit suppliant s'il luy savoit enseigner quelque remede pour la faire blaider. Lequel suppliant luy dist qu'il savoit bien d'une herbe a ce propice qui s'appelle rue. . . . Et est advenu que icelle Jehanne qui estoit grosse getta et mist hors . . . ung enfant forme qui n'avoit point de vie, dont elle fut bien esbayee et courroucee par ce qu'elle ne l'avoit point encores senty bouger."

in 1425 and Mace le Saige in 1480 claimed that they had not killed willfully as was required by legal theories of criminal manslaughter, their assertions did nothing to remove the threat of punitive sentencing. Discussed in chapter 7, Romano-canonical jurisprudence treated "dynamic" abortions, perpetrated with the aid of harmful beverages, as "extraordinary" offenses because of the aggravating circumstance of poisoning. As *crimina extraordinaria,* they necessitated the maximum punishment regardless of homicidal intent.

Apart from herbal recipes that were administered as liquids or in solid form, infused into baths, or applied locally, some of the juridical sources also mention the employment of surgical instruments, external physical pressure on the womb and intestines, or leaps from great height. Around 1466, Jehanne Colette and her husband did not seek the assistance of Guillem Masson and Pierre Delala, alluded to earlier, until they had personally tried to end the pregnancy of Katherine Armant, their prospective sister-in-law. With closed fists, they had directed repeated blows at her kidneys. In another case, the lettre de remission of 1404 for Jehan Guillereau refers vaguely to a long and needlelike device (*touaille ou longiere*) that political enemies accused Jean of having employed to extract a fetus from the body of his chambermaid, Agnes Durande.[30] And finally, there is the implicit statement of a barber, Etienne de Linas, whom the two Collettes from Clermont l'Herault had consulted as their third expert to prevent the embarrassment Katherine Armant was about to bring upon her family. Master Etienne's request for pardon signed in February 1468 recalls that he had initially been hired to purge the vessels of Katherine's intimate parts (*mere*), whereupon he made her bleed from both hands, feet, and, acknowledged only in passing, her *veines de la mere.* At a later stage, Etienne was invited to furnish the patient with a means to abort. To do as he was told, the barber abandoned his previous medical approach in favor of various "potions and powders," an indication that, for a *maitre* like him, bloodletting did not rank very high on the list of abortifacients.[31]

The number of pharmacological agents mentioned in judicial records of the French kingdom is barely augmented by information from other legal writings. Court documents elsewhere refer to pincushion flower (*scabieuse*) and mustard seed (*sednave*), while savin juniper figures in a widely read piece

---

30. Paris, AN, JJ 158, no. 293 (March 1404), ed. Guérin, in *Archives historiques de Poitou* 26 (1896): 25–32 (no. 893): "Guillereau avoit fait avoir a Agnes Durande sa chamberiere qui estoit grosse d'enfant de lui comme disoit icellui Thomas icellui enfant et fruit en sang par lui estraindre le ventre d'une touaille ou longiere;" AN, JJ 200, no. 64 (October 1425); cf. Dossat, *Le Languedoc,* 417 (no. 4110): "Ledit Collet suppliant frappa plusieurs foiz icelle Katherine du poing cloue sur les reins."

31. Paris, AN, JJ 200, no. 65 (February 1468), cf. Dossat, *Le Languedoc,* 417 (no. 4111).

of legal advice provided by the Italian jurist Johannes de Anania (d. 1445).[32] Sources devote hardly any space to questions of proper administration, aside from a letter of remission for Jehanne Dusolier, a widow from Puy la Roque in the Rouergue. Issued in July of 1447, it quotes Jehanne's paramour, the priest Raymond Robert, as having prescribed rue or plain alcohol "among the things in the world that overcome a child in the womb most effectively." The text also relates how Robert scrupulously instructed the pregnant Jehanne to take two mouthful of the pulverized plant together with wine on each of the following three days. The plan imposed on Jehanne was not upheld for more extended periods. She adamantly refused further collaboration, especially after Raymond urged her to supplement the abortifacient diet with scabieuse and hard liquor (*eaue ardente*) as well. Eventually, the baby was born secretly and in a deplorable physical state. Before the mother suffocated and buried her offspring in a nearby stable, she performed emergency baptism in accordance with the regulations of canon law. Raymond's purported words supply rare evidence from the late medieval court registers for medication that involved specific dosage instructions.[33]

Testimony provided by juristic texts and the lettres de remission indicates that the divide between literary and popular knowledge of abortion techniques was not very deep or pronounced. Judicial records repeatedly illustrate how peasants and small-town inhabitants resorted to the same herbal ingredients that high-end pharmacological manuals lauded for their effectiveness. Neither medicinal repertories compiled after Dioscorides' *Materia medica* nor illiterate men and women among the laity distinguished sharply among remedies believed to affect the sexual, the digestive, and other organs.[34] When

---

32. Johannes de Anania, *Consilium* 1 (Venice: Rubini, 1576), fol. 3r–v (no. 10): "Sabinam seu aliam herbam pestiferam dedit ut suffocaret partum"; Lille, AD, B 1686, fol. 27v (May 1455), in *Documents nouveaux sur les moeurs populaires et le droit de vengeance dans les Pays-Bas au XIVe siècle*, ed. Charles Petit-Dutaillies (Paris: Champion, 1908), 19–22 (no. 5): "Pour eviter generacion souventesfois elle avoit mengie du sednave"; Toulouse, AD, B 1984, fol. 47r (March 1454), in Jean Louis Gazzaniga, *L'église du midi à la fin du règne de Charles VII (1444–1461). D'après la jurisprudence du Parlement de Toulouse* (Paris: Picard, 1976), 310–312: "Et a mange d'une herbe appellee de gatapuissa pour la fere avortir"; the reading of *gatapuissa*, perhaps related to *scabieuse*, is uncertain.

33. Paris, AN, JJ 178, no. 257 (July 1447); cf. Dossat, *Le Languedoc*, 375 (no. 3694): "Il molut icelle rue et la destrampa de vin en une escuelle et par trois jours ensuivans en fist boire a icelle Jehanne chacune foiz deux boires ou environ."

34. To assume clear distinctions would be anachronistic, given that most abortifacients mentioned in the court records also functioned as wonder drugs, or "repositories of occult powers . . . that could not be accounted for solely on the basis of their physical or chemical properties." Francis Brévart, "Between Medicine, Magic, and Religion: Wonder Drugs in German Medico-Pharmaceutical Treatises of the Thirteenth to the Sixteenth Centuries," *Speculum* 83 (2008): 2.

the situation is viewed from this angle, John Riddle may have been right to argue that, in matters of reproduction, late medieval adaptations and copies of the ancient *Materia medica* coincided in content with folkloristic knowledge. Yet his second claim that the grassroots expertise of wise women greatly exceeded medical insight in the surviving literature is unconvincing. Sources tied to litigation do not confirm that the matrones sages worked from an organized set of obstetrical data, transmitted orally and perfected over generations. Instead, mothers expecting unwanted children received recommendations at random and by word of mouth from acquaintances in the vicinity who gladly shared what they had experimented with on their own bodies. Some prescriptions may trace back to times immemorial. Generally speaking, though, midwifery in the years up to 1500 could not count on a solid educational framework, books of instruction, and a language disseminating gynecological learning across lands with multiple idioms and dialects. The sharing of information precise enough to be replicated from place to place, let alone from century to century, was unimaginable away from the world of university-trained medical and male professionals. In the long run, they were the ones to exploit the advantages of a uniform and sophisticated terminology, gaining competitively against all nonacademic health practitioners. Late medieval clients invested a great deal of trust as they enlisted neighbors, barbers, apothecaries, and physicians for assistance in birth-related matters, gradually preferring skills based on scholastic analysis to amateur teachings reliant on local hearsay. The extant historical material depicts pregnant women as if they had no doubt in the availability of qualified specialists and ways to intervene, through potions, infusions, and powders, whenever nascent life was considered unwelcome.

Historians would also like to determine whether late medieval reports on the performance of abortions afford conclusions about the health risks mothers faced in the process. At first glance, sixteenth-century criminal laws, frequently inveighing against the figure of the pregnant woman who cunningly awaits birth before murdering her child, seem to indicate a general preference for infanticide, just as common sense today surmises that attacks on life within the womb must have been more dangerous to the parent than those on a newborn baby. Analysis of the evidence, however, reveals that no such distinction was made by premodern writers. With regard to lay and canonical norms, it has been illustrated that the conceptual divide between pre- and postnatal homicide rested on the continued use of ancient terminology. It was not a reflection of substance, as those convicted of either crime had to confront identical legal punishment. In case material describing the behavior of suspects, moreover, attempts to kill an unborn baby through medication or mechanical means do not dwell on delivery as a crucial juridical or medical marker. The lettre de remission requested by Jehanne Dusolier in 1447, for instance, mentions consumption of several abortifacient potions and later her suffocation of the newborn, as though the two acts represented a perfect continuum not just in the literature of scholastic jurisprudence but in her own subjective thinking as well.[35] And while the statistically higher incidence of trials investigating *infanticidia* could be interpreted as a sign of the greater frequency of such crimes, the rules of Romano-canonical procedure suggest instead that the disparity had to do with judicial factors. Chapter 7 illustrates how the opening of criminal proceedings in the lay courts demanded the presence of a dead body. Official discovery of a slain fetus was, however, far less likely than that of a born child. Unless aggravating recourse to dynamic poisonous beverages waived the obligation to produce a corpus delicti, rapid termination of a pregnancy constituted the safer option for perpetrators—if not from an obstetrical standpoint, at least from a prosecutorial one.

In current political debate, health concerns concentrate on the aborting mother, in stark contrast with the indifference toward her in late medieval case descriptions. During labor and in childbirth, the principal worry of the judicial reporters was the welfare of the offspring, albeit in a purely spiritual sense. Provided the miscarried or delivered baby was still alive, records state whether killing or abandonment ensued after application of the canonical formula for baptism. A very high percentage of the accused maintained that they had conferred the sacrament in person. Where graphic accounts of pre- or postnatal *homicidium* focus on the distress of defendants who typically acted in utter secrecy without personal assistance and away from adequately appointed bedchambers, compassion hardly inspired the language of the court scribes. An elaborate rhetoric of pain was employed when French petitioners like the widow Jehanne Bruneau claimed in 1452 that "owing to great feebleness at birth she suddenly fainted and fell, thereby smothering her newborn child." An hour later, the infant was dying, although not until Jehanne had duly baptized it. A drama of similar proportions involved eighteen-year-old Guillemette from Louviers in Languedoc, whose petition of November 1414 relates that one day around midnight she found herself in greater agony than ever before. She put a piece of cloth in her mouth to

---

35. Paris, AN, JJ 178, no. 257 (July 1447); in a scene narrated at great length, Jehanne had unsuccessfully taken feticidal potions (above, note 33); following birth, she baptized the child, "laquelle chose faite elle l'eteigny et ce fait l'apporta dedans ladicte estable ou elle l'enterra et sevelit."

avoid crying and lost consciousness, discovering about half an hour later that she had brought forth a lifeless boy.[36]

Appeals to the empathy of readers for the intense suffering of Jehanne, Guillemette, and others were not at the forefront of medieval documentary concerns. As noted in chapter 4, scholastic jurisprudence adopted an extremely unrelenting position toward aborting women, whose entitlement to physical self-preservation was consistently outweighed by the absolute right to life of the human fetus. Physicians for their part had to abstain from therapeutic intervention if it implied the certain death of a formed fetus in exchange for the mother's recovery. Given the uncompromising teachings of theologians and canonists, French female petitioners seeking mercy would have been ill advised to try to sway royal authority by soliciting pity for their own severely impaired condition.

Crises associated with gestation and delivery loomed large in the judicial narratives so as to conjure up images of diminished legal responsibility. To be pardoned, one of the most promising strategies consisted of excuses reinforcing doubt in the presence of culpability. Guillemette in 1414 and Jehanne Bruneau in 1452 each magnified in their stories their mental disorientation and bodily depletion in order to underscore that they had not acted with willful intent. If malice was sufficiently proven, Romano-canonical norms of due process accepted it as justification for maximum punishment. Where emotionally charged passages in the French lettres de remission seem to permit an unencumbered look at the actual experience of ordinary people through the ages, authors in effect lent a formulaic voice to apologetic schemes and procedural exceptions. Individuals may have been sensitive toward the emotional effects of procured fetal death and concealed childbirth. Criminal records, however, were not meant to broadcast health-related anxieties and never present them plainly for what they were.

---

36. Paris, AN, JJ 168, no. 51 (November 1414; copied into AN, AB XIX 205A, no. 180/251): "Ne l'oissant plus crier ne plaindre et que son fait ne feust descouvert elle prist son chapperon et en estouppa son bouche et de la grant douleur qu'elle ait s'esvanoy . . . l'espace de demie heure ou environ et puis se remit et trouva que pendant lesdiz evanoissment et pamaison elle avoit eu enfant male lequel quant elle l'apperceut n'avoit point de vie"; AN, JJ 181, no. 63 (April 1452), cf. Chevalier, *Le pays de la Loire*, 287 (no. 2771): "Elle cheut dessudit enfant et froissa et bleca ledit enfant qui estoit tout mal et tendre tellement que a une heure d'ilec environ icellui enfant ala de vie trespassement; mais avant qu'il mourust ladicte mere lui donna batesme."

CHAPTER 7

Abortion in the Criminal Courts of the Ius Commune

For wrongdoing defined as crimen, twelfth-century jurisprudence provided four different procedural remedies to choose from. Two of them, sacramental confession and penitential denunciation, addressed sin as crime in the abstract (interpretative), directed against God and the community of the faithful. The other two, accusation and inquisition, instead served to prosecute crimina that were verifiable (actu) and entailed breaches of peace to the detriment of earthly society. From a modern perspective, trials brought via confessionis or denuntiationis do not qualify as criminal because inquiries depended on voluntary revelations to a priestly confessor or responded to vague rumors that someone had committed a punishable act. Scholastic lawyers would have agreed in that they, too, saw the principal objective of confessiones and denuntiationes as penance and redemption rather than punishment and restoration of the public order. Neither format assessed guilt by way of investigations into the factual truthfulness of charges. Penitents admitted sinful behavior under the seal of secrecy, and clues indicating whether a person had been denounced justly or unjustly did not rest on accurate reconstructions of the incriminating event but on collective oaths or recognition of culpability in the spiritual realm only. Where works of satisfaction ordered by the absolving priest took the form of flogging or permitted conversion into monetary offerings, average onlookers may have regarded them as indistinguishable from fines and physical sanctions. In the lawyerly mind, however, they always symbolized justice as it was tied to the forum of conscience.

Accusatorial and inquisitorial proceedings were devised for the prosecution of crime in the current sense of the word. Whenever exile or execution—the penalties imposed by Bolognese theorists on those responsible for prenatal death—affected judicial practice in the lay sphere, implementation had to meet requirements that figured under the scholastic labels of *accusatio* and *inquisitio*. This chapter is exclusively dedicated to their investigation. It deals with them, first, in their respective full formats, intended to follow to the letter the rules of due process put forth by Romano-canonical doctrine. In the concluding section discussion turns to the so-called extraordinary variety of intervention by inquisitors, which allowed for the disregard of many procedural safeguards normally protecting criminal defendants and did so for the sake of facilitating the speedy termination of trials. Modern legal historians have studied the rise of summary procedures for qualified or especially heinous offenses, above all those in connection with charges of "heretical depravity" and witchcraft. Yet late medieval demands for swifter sentencing also concerned allegations of poisoning and magic and soon met with the intensifying efforts of secular judges to prevent recourse to abortifacients and abortion as it is commonly understood today.

Ecclesiastical tribunals, to be sure, subscribed to a different set of regulations in dealing with ordinary criminal suspects. As discussed in chapter 2, church jurisdiction in this regard was limited to clerical persons and objected in principle to the shedding of blood. The inquiry of facts was typically bypassed in favor of exculpatory oaths (compurgationes), performed by the defendant and a preestablished number of character witnesses. If the slain fetus had been animated at the time of death, clergy found guilty of miscarriage did not have to face lasting bodily harm but lost eligibility for altar service and their income from benefices. Sentencing could also result in payments or incarceration, each functioning as penance and again reminding modern observers that "criminal" justice for members of the spiritual hierarchy guilty of abortion was primarily a sacramental and disciplinary matter. Laymen were not exposed to punitive measures from sacerdotal hands unless religious corporations sat in judgment over them as feudal or territorial overlords. Persons convicted of fetal homicide in secular courts, however, became automatically irregular and unfit for sacred ordination into the priesthood, just as someone who had killed a spouse and wished to wed another was instantly barred from the blessings of a canonical marriage.[1] Prenatal man-slaughter, on the other hand, never incurred such marital *irregularitas*.

Criminal Accusationes and Inquisitiones

Because of the omnipresence of ecclesiastical institutions, by 1250 every cor-ner of Latin Christendom was confronted with the fundamentals of four-fold Romano-canonical procedure. The common law of England, it is true, shunned the Bolognese model of litigation in favor of a jury-based judicial system. As noted in the last section of chapter 2, however, English crown justices embraced the scholastic concept of fetal homicide and became the first lay jurisdiction in the West to prosecute the offense as a capital crime. On the Continent, the practical implementation of accusationes and inqui-sitiones fared very differently depending on region. Prior to the 1450s, areas north of the Alps and east of the river Rhine were eclectic in their adoption of the new standards. Full reception for purposes of criminal prosecution in the secular sphere remained largely restricted to Mediterranean cities and important princely territories, most notably the kingdom of France. Its rul-ers gained greatly from the promotion of a juristic culture that stood for centralized government, growing mobility, and the preponderance of urban lifestyles and interests. By the same token, the techniques of conflict resolu-tion proposed by the Ius commune met with strongest resistance in the rural hinterland, away from centers of trade and busy roads, where public affairs continued to be dominated by local warriors and feudal custom. That the two criminal trial formats of jurisprudence would eventually prevail in alli-ance with the increasing monopolization of justice by sovereign lords was a historical outcome nobody could have foreseen at the time.

Among laity, competing jurisdictional claims and customary rituals of dispute processing acted as typical counterweights to the advance of Romano-canonical procedures from the 1200s well into the early modern period. In connection with attacks on nascent human life, persistent dif-ficulty in establishing institutional hierarchies for the handling of crime is evident from a series of dossiers compiled between 1270 and 1340 by a number of Parisian abbeys. The texts were written to supply the king

---

1. On the *impedimentum criminis*, Wolfgang P. Müller and Gastone Saletnich, "Rodolfo Gonzaga (1452–1495). News on a Celebrity Murder Case," in *The Long Arm of Papal Authority*, ed. Gerhard Jaritz, Torstein Jørgensen, and Kirsi Salonen, 2nd ed. (Budapest: CEU Press, 2005), 157–163.

with proof of long-standing judicial prerogatives. Pressure to submit capital offenses including murder, rape, and miscarriage through battery (percussio, or in French, *encis*) as *cas royaux* to royal authority was in conflict with the pretensions of local authorities, ecclesiastical and secular, who regarded all adjudication as firmly within their feudal and property rights. From their perspective, crown officials in the vicinity appeared to be interlopers, responsible for the disruption of established power arrangements. In defiance of ancient usage, the king's *prevots* and other officials had issued arrests in pursuit of defendants from the lands of Saint-Maur-des-Fossés or Saint-Martin-des Champs rather than leaving suspects to the judgment of either monastery.[2] In response, the monks at Saint-Maur recorded one incident that involved an individual by the name of Guillelmus Renaudi. The prevot of Paris, Reginaldus Barbo, had summoned him in 1271 to answer charges by another man whose wife Guillelmus had reportedly beaten and induced to miscarry. When Guillelmus found himself imprisoned at the Châtelet, Abbot Peter requested his immediate release and transfer into monastic custody, which the prevot rejected by arguing that serious breaches of the peace such as encis fell outside Peter's competency. What followed was an inquiry among inhabitants of Nogent, who confirmed the traditional role of Saint-Maur as their tribunal even in capital matters, whereupon the prevot gave in and handed Guillelmus Renaudi over for definitive sentencing. The king "never had any rightful claim [*usus*] to cases occurring in the above-mentioned area," the registrar of Saint-Maur concluded, content to keep things as they had always been.[3]

Whereas the creation of judicial hierarchies was slowed by competition among territorial lords, the advance of scholastic criminal concepts went against traditional modes of conflict management. After 1300 as well as earlier, royal judges in France accepted compensatory payment from defendants charged with cas royaux, despite the fact that theory precluded outcomes other than punishment affecting the culprit's body, possessions, or freedom to move about. In 1313, the chancery of Philip the Fair confirmed a document by the *senechal* of the Saintonge, Hugo de Cella, stating that he had

---

2. Paul Viollet, "Registres judiciaires de quelques établissements religieux du Parisis au XIIIe et XIVe siècle," *Bibliothèque de l'École des chartes* 34 (1873): 317–341; Anne Terroine, *Un abbé de Saint-Maur au XIIIe siècle: Pierre de Chévry, 1256–1285, avec l'édition des plus anciens cas de justice de Saint-Maur-des-Fossés* (Paris: Klincksieck, 1968), 40–43, 51–68.

3. Paris, AN, LL 46, fol. 252v; AN, LL 48, fol. 221r; in Terroine, *Un abbé de Saint-Maur*, 167–168; Tanon, *Histoire*, 338. The underlying juristic doctrine is treated by Ernest Perrot, *Les cas royaux. Origine et développement de la théorie aux XIIIe et XIVe siècles* (Paris: Rousseau, 1910).

obtained financial *composicion* from a group of people suspected of encis. The text openly justifies the paid sum as a means to prevent initiation of ordinary proceedings in the Romano-canonical format, accompanied by threats of physical retribution and loss of property.[4] The survival of customary techniques for the discernment of right and wrong is also attested by an inquest from the years around 1343, pitting two branches of the noble family de La Forêt against each other. The head of one party was Marguerite de Beauçay, widow of the late knight Guy, whose armed followers had allegedly pillaged the lands of her adversary, Josselin, causing considerable damage along with an encis. When Josselin proposed to substantiate his complaint in a judicial duel (*gage de bataille*), the Parlement criminel in Paris objected on formal grounds. Being a woman, Marguerite was not entitled to defend herself by taking up arms. It was left unmentioned that the Bolognese procedures usually employed in the king's courts were opposed to the introduction of evidence based on trial by battle.[5]

Jurisprudence created twin instruments for the punitive treatment of criminal charges. Accusationes tapped into preexisting mechanisms of formal litigation, whereby offended parties would bring complaints out of their own initiative to the judges' attention. Chapters 2 and 5 above illustrate the pervasiveness of accusatory impulses by relating how suits aimed at capital punishment for the death of unborn human beings were originally attempted only by spouses who had lost a child through beatings at the hands of someone extraneous to the family. Procedures dealing with secular crimina operated at first in environments that lacked significant law enforcement, where much of the prosecutorial zeal had to be provided by the aggrieved themselves. As the thirteenth century wore on, inquisitiones conducted by publicly appointed and independently investigating personnel grew in number next to cases launched by accusatores, and thus the two procedures, save for the opening stages, ran on parallel tracks. Plaintiffs certainly welcomed the trend because it ensured the mobilization of

---

4. Paris, AN, JJ 49, no. 17, in "Documents relatifs à l'histoire de la Saintonge et de l'Aunis extraits des registres du Trésor des chartes," ed. Paul Guérin, in *Archives historiques de la Saintonge et de l'Aunis* 12 (1884): 88–91 (no. 45); *amende* for *encis* was again preferred in AN, JJ 49, no. 15 (April 1313), in ibid., 83–85 (no. 43); AN, JJ 71, no. 394 (August 1340), cf. Viard and Vallée, *Registres* 3.2, 106 (no. 3875).

5. Paris, AN, X2a 4, fol. 156v; cf. Brigitte Labat-Poussin et al., *Actes du Parlement. Parlement criminel. Règne de Philippe VI de Valois. Inventaire analytique des registres de X2a 2 à 5* (Paris: Archives Nationales, 1987), 219. On the place of duels in criminal proceedings, Louis de Carbonnières, *La procédure devant la chambre criminelle du Parlement de Paris au XIVe siècle* (Paris: Champion, 2004), 508–514.

resourceful officials on their behalf. The advent of inquisitors examining punishable offenses was accompanied by coercive means that ranged from preliminary imprisonment for potentially contumacious defendants to banishment and the confiscation of belongings from suspects in flight. To protect defendants from gratuitous harassment by the adversary, Bolognese jurists thought of commensurate retaliatory punishment (*pena talionis*) for proceedings that had been instigated frivolously. Theoretically, the principle would have required groundless allegations of fetal homicide to result in execution or at least a ban for private accusers. In documented practice, however, failed accusationes of miscarriage by assault nowhere led to the imposition of penae talionis, as presiding judges inspected complaints regardless of their specific provenance. The decision as to whether killings justified a civil damage suit or, in addition, penal treatment as full-fledged crimes was typically reached without complications and on purely evidentiary grounds.[6]

The records of abbatial courts around Paris contain nine incidents of encis registered by the monks of Saint-Martin-des-Champs between 1336 and 1338. Each case was the result of intervention by a private accusator, whose reclamations of guilt were submitted to a panel of sworn matrons examining the injured woman and her baby. Unless the unborn had suffered harm from the alleged percussio, the matter was considered criminally irrelevant and transformed into a civil suit, with payment of compensation (*amende*) looming as the maximum measure of liability.[7] The difference between public penal prosecution and the private pursuit of material damages in court was not made into an issue, as efforts by judicial authorities to draw prosecution of criminal activity toward their own tribunals remained for the longest time dependent on vital support "from below." In 1333, Pierre de Saint-Saornin was asked by the senechal of Melle in Poitou whether he wished to strengthen his accusatio on account of encis with evidence he might have gathered in person. When Pierre declined, the senechal went on to conduct the proceedings unaided. Nobody thought of interpreting the refusal as an act worthy of repercussions, let alone infliction of the pena talionis. To the contrary, the royal official's final sentence put emphasis on the fact that the

---

6. Modern scholarship on criminal accusations and inquisitions has been surveyed by Trevor Dean, *Crime in Medieval Europe 1200–1500* (Harlow: Longman, 2001), 1–29.

7. Paris, AN, Musée 356, in Tanon, *Histoire*, 482; *Registre*, ed. Tanon, 64–65; also Tanon, *Histoire*, 483–484, 486, 487, 489–490, 494–495, 512, 515–516, 519; *Registre*, ed. Tanon, 67–68, 75, 76, 82, 93–94, 131–132, 138, 144.

eventual shift of judicial responsibility had occurred with Pierre's express approval as the original accuser.[8]

The Rules and Safeguards of Ordinary Inquisitiones

Apart from the initial phase, criminal accusationes and inquisitiones proceeded on nearly identical tracks, allowing historical investigations of abortion to treat them interchangeably and as one. At the same time scholarship has urged students not to confuse inquisitorial trials addressing ordinary crime with the Inquisition, which in common parlance stands for rogue justice and the mockery of due process.[9] Following a distinction that medieval jurists themselves made, official investigations of "heretical depravity" and the politically charged offenses of magic as well as witchcraft differed dramatically from standard criminal proceedings conducted by the inquisitores. Perceived as a threat to the very existence of society, heretics became the first to endure treatment as "extraordinarily" unworthy of rules that, in everyday accusations, endowed law with complex judicial checks and balances and consistently extended to the accused the benefit of the doubt (*in dubio pro reo*). Since the early 1200s, in other words, jurisprudence in the West has devised intricate procedural safeguards to shield average defendants from factually and formally flawed allegations. In confronting wrong considered intolerably dangerous, however, many of the same exceptions were eliminated, whether the rationale for doing so was treason, heresy, or sorcery in the remote past or, in more recent times, Communism, hate crimes, or terrorism.

According to the prosecutorial guidelines of the Ius commune, the ultimate penalty of death for prenatal homicide could not be implemented unless either of two evidentiary standards had been met. Inquisitors needed to secure from the accused full admission of their guilt. Alternatively, capital conviction had to rest on the testimony of two eyewitnesses in good standing, capable of confirming the accusation by oath. Circumstantial inferences suggesting liability were accepted only to detain suspects over periods of uncertain length while never permitting the infliction of maximum

---

8. Paris, AN, JJ 66, no. 1264, ed. Guérin, in *Archives historiques de Poitou* 11 (1881): 425–429 (no. 180): "Pierre dist et respondi que non et qu'il ne s'en vouloit de riens faire partie contre euls ne denoncier ne aucune chose maintenir contre euls sur le cas diz a present. Et sur ce fust jugiez. Et fu jugiez de son consentement."

9. Edward Peters, *Inquisition* (New York: Free Press, 1988), 1–22; and note 25, below.

punishment known as *pena ordinaria*. Prosecutors were instead confined to lesser forms of retribution called *penae extraordinariae* or *penae arbitrariae,* which by definition excluded permanent physical harm or mutilation of the convict. Verdicts imposed extraordinarie, moreover, still required the existence of exceptionally strong presumptions. Concerning cases of abortion in late medieval court practice, their list contained no more than three items. The first clue pointing to penal responsibility consisted of mortal remains discovered in the defendant's immediate vicinity. The second indicated knowledge of a concealed pregnancy in the neighborhood, and numerous inquisitores regarded milk in the breasts of women without a baby as a third marker of foul play, again justifying inquiry and eventual punitive measures. The rigid formalism by which proceedings were not permitted to go forward except where at least one of the above triple criteria was in evidence meant that discretionary data of a different kind were altogether inadmissible as legal proof and did not warrant ordinary investigations. In this way, criminal prosecution was often discouraged. With scenarios of birth normally unfolding in the privacy of homes and surrounded by an intimate circle of family and friends, it must have been easy for the respectable to conceal vestiges of pre- and postnatal infanticide forever from outside scrutiny.

For the core areas of scholastic jurisprudence in late medieval Italy, the Spanish kingdoms, and France, records show how the judicial determination of guilt and innocence adhered closely to the restrictions envisioned by Romano-canonical procedure. Prosecutors time and again attributed the decisive impetus for their intervention to revelations made by eyewitnesses. The exceptional significance of testimony available from onlookers is more than manifest considering the wealth of documentation referring to cases of battery, in which a miscarriage was said to have been provoked by someone other than the parents. Precisely because the event occurred in the presence of bystanders, variations of it frequently found their way into the courtroom. In June 1384, the sixty-year-old Jehan Affilet had to confront an awkward situation after he had come to blows with Arnoulet Toupel over aggravating questions of ownership. In the midst of their altercations, Arnoulet's pregnant wife had attempted to mediate. Three weeks later, she bore a dead baby and soon succumbed in childbed herself. A priest who administered the last rites heard her say that Jehan was not responsible for the tragedy. The previous struggle had done nothing to hurt her. Arnoulet Toupel, the husband, also agreed and did not wish to press charges. But Jehan, declared innocent by his immediate adversaries, could not avoid being thrown into prison at Laon. Neighbors claimed to have seen with their own eyes how Affilet's fist squarely landed on the unfortunate woman's body.[10]

About 1404, Bertran Bruneau, the feudal lord of la Mote Fouquerant in the Poitou region, exploited the tight procedural requirements of the Ius commune in yet another fashion. After repeated conflicts with Jehan Guillereau, a neighboring noble and *chastellain,* he decided to bring about the destruction of his personal enemy. Resorting to a carefully crafted conspiracy, Bertran persuaded two dependents of Jehan's household to accuse their patron of involvement in a pair of violent miscarriages. According to statements that both accomplices filed with the criminal court, Jehan had beaten his pregnant wife seven or eight years earlier, causing her baby to be stillborn. He allegedly had been plagued by suspicions that the offspring was not really his. In addition, the chastellain was said to have procured an abortion for one of his chambermaids, Agnes Durande, upon conceiving the child with her in the first place. Each of the charges relied on rumors circulating in Jehan's environment. Yet Bertran in his vindictiveness knew that the prosecutors were looking for more solid evidence. He therefore told his hirelings to present Jehan's *crimina* not merely as facts based on hearsay. Judicial authorities needed to know that the offenses had played out under the accusers' own eyes. Bertran's precise instructions betray his awareness that multiple witnesses were among the few prerequisites securing inquisitorial intervention.[11]

Court proceedings likewise opened following the appearance of a dead body. Investigators often turned the discovery into a highly publicized event, reflected in the rhetoric of scribes who underscored the breach of the human and heavenly order. "In God's own words," a Florentine record of 1426 reads, "nothing is hidden that will not be revealed." Hence "it is believed to have occurred by divine judgment . . ., that shortly after the baby's death a dog passed by the boy's grave and dug up his mortal remains."[12] The gruesome

---

10. Paris, AN, JJ 124, no. 337: "On dit que aucuns virent ferir ycelle femme par ledit exposant [Jehan] du poing . . . laquelle en presence elles son mary et le prestre de la ville a ce appelle pour curer et descharger sa conscience dit et afferma en sa verite et conscience que . . . de tant que on l'en avoit accuse ou denoncie a justice c'estoit et avoit este mal fait."

11. Paris, AN, JJ 158, no. 293 (28 March 1404), ed. Guérin, in *Archives historiques de Poitou* 26 (1896) 25–32 (no. 893): "Et pour ces choses dire et deposer avoir veu de fait . . . avoit promis icellui Bertran a faire beaucoup de bien aus diz tesmoings." For the doctrinal background, Yves Meusen, *Veritatis adiutor. La procédure du temoignage dans le droit savant et la pratique française (XIIᵉ–XIVᵉ siècle)* (Milan: Giuffrè, 2006).

12. Florence, AS, Giudice degli appelli 76, fol. 282v (March 1426), cited in *Die Abtreibung,* 234n407. For parallel formulations, see AS, Giudice degli appelli 99/3, fol. 144v–145r (2 March 1415), cited by Samuel Cohn, "Sex and Violence on the Periphery: The Territorial State in Early Renaissance Florence," in *Women in the Streets: Essays on Sex and Power in Renaissance Italy,* ed. Samuel Cohn (Baltimore: Johns Hopkins University Press, 1996), 101.

find frequently materialized where people had easy access, on cemeteries, at ponds, rivers, and in ditches. On occasion, the tangible traces were hidden at home, "in the private chambers," in a bed chest, the wardrobe, or in latrines. Female servants in particular ran the risk of being detected by watchful employers.[13] For the rest, the severity of punishment was typically determined from the moment the corpus delicti came to light. The Ius commune prescribed that the ascertainment of manslaughter would not hinge on birth but rather on physical formation in the maternal womb. As scholastic theorists agreed, the entry of the rational and immortal soul coincided with the articulation of limbs in the unborn. Because inquisitors of abortion rarely encountered the vestiges of a less than humanly shaped fetus, practically everyone responding to charges of prenatal homicide was subjected to the threat of execution.

Modern commentary dwells on the use of torture as emblematic of late medieval criminal prosecutions, and although recourse to coercion during judicial interrogations formed an integral part of legal theory and practice, inquisitores who sought to extract confessions of abortion or infanticide had to act somewhat circumspectly. Under regular conditions excluding qualified crimes such as heresy, the lawful employment of force was predicated on the existence of evidence sufficient to warrant infliction of extraordinary punishment, short of harm to the body. A document drafted in 1339 by Pierre de Pilemer, *sous-prevost* at the secular court of Saint-Ciriac in Provins, illustrates the extent of caution imposed on investigating officials. It was not only because Agnes le Codinet admitted to having delivered a dead child that Pierre decided to proceed by torturous means. His memorandum also speaks of other indicators suggesting the presence of serious wrongdoing. Pierre explained in his final sentence that Agnes, "out of sorrow and for what she had suffered in birth, and due to her fear of shame and defamation by the people, took the baby and buried it in the courtyard, without alerting her brother, sister, or anyone else." He noted in addition that the defendant, not content to do away with the corpus unassisted and bury it in an unmarked grave, affirmed that she had hidden her pregnancy all along. "She never prepared for labor as is customary" and "made things appear as though she

---

13. See chapter 9. Corpora delicti appear "en une fosse," Paris, AN, JJ 142, no. 103 (February 1392), in Bologne, *La naissance interdite*, 287–288; "en ung petit estaing," AN, JJ 196, no. 287 (August 1470), cf. Chevalier, *Le pays de la Loire*, 344 (no. 3318); "une fontaine qui est publique," AN, JJ 197, no. 264 (January 1473), ed. Guérin, in *Archives historiques de Poitou* 38 (1909): 334–337 (no. 1512); "soubs un banc," AN, JJ 148, no. 233 (October 1395); "dedans le ferme de son lit," AN, JJ 168, no. 51 (November 1414); "es chambres privees," AN, JJ 189, no. 165 (May 1457).

had incurred some sickness unrelated to her true physical state." In Pierre's estimate, the conclusion to be drawn was obvious:

> Given the counsel we have had and the presumptions working against her and in consideration of the aforesaid, and again because the child was discovered dead in her courtyard, carried into the open and shown to the public, we have taken the said Agnes twice into questioning under torture. The same Agnes, before, during, and after interrogations, always persevered in her aforementioned confession, not changing, modifying, or confusing details, and without revealing anything else.[14]

Pierre de Pilemer's definitive *sententia* depicts him as a faithful administrator of the Ius commune. The proceedings against Agnes departed from a crucial piece of evidence, the discovery of a dead infant on her premises. As she was brought in for preliminary questioning, a second aspect legally amounting to "semiproof" was established by her admission that she had secretly buried the child after concealment of her pregnancy and delivery. From this point onward, Agnes ceased to cooperate, declaring that the fear of shameful exposure had caused her to act clandestinely. In her words the fatality had occurred spontaneously during birth and without culpable interference on her part. As two strong presumptions persuaded Pierre of his right to undertake forcible interrogations, Agnes insisted on her version of the story by delineating a tragic incident. Her revelations kept the prosecutor's hands firmly tied. Romano-canonical procedure did not permit maximum punishment if impressions of guilt rested on little except circumstantial evidence. Because full responsibility could not be established, jurisprudence held Pierre to the exercise of his "arbitrary" judgment. Favoring leniency, he determined that the known facts did not even merit extraordinary sentencing, that is, pena along the lines of exile or imprisonment. With characteristic conscientiousness, Pierre sent his order of immediate release for approval to the royal Parlement de Paris, stating that Agnes had endured enough hardship through torture and long incarceration as a suspect.[15]

---

14. Paris, AN, JJ 71, no. 304 (May 1339), cf. Viard and Vallée, *Registres* 3.2, 93 (no. 3785). For the juristic limitations ordinarily placed on forcible interrogations, Pennington, "Torture in the Ius Commune," 818–830; John Langbein, *Torture and the Law of Proof: Europe and England in the Ancien Regime* (Chicago: University of Chicago Press, 1977), 117–131; Piero Fiorelli, *La tortura giudiziaria nel diritto commune*, 2 vols. (Milan: Giuffrè, 1953–1954), 2:1–50.

15. Paris, AN, JJ 71, no. 304: "Consideree l'information dessus dicte et ce que ladicte Agnes a touz jours persevere en la confession sans riens varier . . . par notre sentence diffinitive et par droit avons absolu et absolons ladicte Agnes du dit cas"; translated in chap. 8, note 24.

It will probably never be known whether Agnes lied when she claimed to have endured a stillbirth. Late medieval documentation proves that torture was not deemed appropriate without the convergence of multiple indicia, amounting in her case to the threefold admission of concealment with regard to pregnancy, delivery, and burial of a corpus. Court records clearly show that comparable standards governed the applicability of forcible questioning elsewhere. In 1475, Venetian officials arrested Lucia Sclabona, the servant of a Sicilian merchant. A lifeless newborn had been found in her patron's house, and suspicions long harbored by the neighbors finally fell on her. Another maid by the name of Margarita Saracena faced identical circumstances in 1498. Over the course of their preliminary inquests, the women claimed to have delivered children who lacked any vital signs. The decision of the tribunal to expose both Lucia and Margarita to torture occurred in a situation that exactly paralleled the one confronted by Pierre de Pilemer in 1339.[16] Arguably, coercive methods of fact-finding were implemented with some restraint, considering that before 1500, defendants described in the available evidence as having been subjected to painful interrogations never modified their original response to charges of abortion or infanticide.[17]

If persons accused criminally confessed to having killed offspring, the judges were left with little choice except execution. When female convicts were found to be pregnant, actual administration of the sentence was delayed until after childbirth. Offenders could also avail themselves of appeals to a higher court on the basis of legal technicalities, and petitioners from France and England often acted in time to secure a royal letter of pardon.[18] The adjudicating authorities, however, were not in a position to mitigate the *pena legalis,* or maximum punishment, on their own initiative. To the contrary, a suspect's admission of responsibility for prenatal manslaughter in combination with "half proof" such as concealment muted even the most compelling

---

16. Venice, AS, Reg. 3654, fol. 20v (24 April 1475); AS, Reg. 3658, fol. 200r (6 November 1498). For a transcript of the two entries, see *Die Abtreibung,* 237n413, 239n417, 245n427.

17. Ineffective torturing is mentioned again in Paris, AN, JJ 179, no. 226 (May 1448), ed. Guérin, in *Archives historiques de Poitou* 32 (1903): 71–73 (no. 1159). Venice, AS, Reg. 3643, fol. 90v (23 November 1366), is cited by Guido Ruggiero, *Violence in Early Renaissance Venice* (New Brunswick, NJ: Rutgers University Press, 1980), 178, 188. Lyon, AD, 10 G 2639, no. 1 (of 1452), reports at least the threat of duress; cf. Nicole Gonthier, *Délinquance, justice, et société dans le Lyonnais médiéval* (Paris: Arguments, 1993), 117–118.

18. Postponement for the length of gestation marks an infanticide case of March 1447, Paris, AN, JJ 178, no. 134, ed. Guérin, in *Archives historiques de Poitou* 29 (1898): 419–422 (no. 1132); temporary suspension followed the appeal to higher judicial authority in AN, JJ 197, no. 257 (January 1473), ed. Guérin, in *Archives historiques de Poitou* 38 (1909): 343–346 (no. 1515).

rationale in favor of reduced sentencing. Objections emphasizing the absence of murderous intent, youthful ignorance, or temporary insanity no longer made any difference. The severe restrictions placed on inquisitors and their discretion, consistently transparent in records from the later Middle Ages, were inspired by tight definitions of what constituted lawful, acceptable, and compelling evidence. As one of the key characteristics of the Ius commune and its success, jurists interpreted the need for procedural predictability in peremptory fashion. Court officials were not allowed to tamper with theoretically defined trajectories and outcomes. The confession of homicidium backed up by a specific set of indicators made the result of trials inescapable.[19]

Cases from the fourteenth and fifteenth centuries attest to great awareness among suspects of the automatic link between proven secrecy, admitted abortion or infanticide, and the death penalty. To avoid the gravest of consequences, it was advisable to steer clear of any hint at unlawful involvement. Still, most of the accused were prevented from taking easy escape routes as secular prosecution was not set in motion unless rumors of wrongdoing could be tied to a specific corpus delicti. Arrested individuals had to settle at least for a partial recognition of guilt. In proceedings including the one of Agnes and Pierre de Pilemer in 1339, the line of defense was drawn so that the concealment of pregnancy and birth was not challenged, while participation in what had prompted the fatality was adamantly contested. Judicial narratives further demonstrate how defendants attempted to transfer blame for an alleged miscarriage to another person. In 1381, the laborer Gieffroy le Royer from Le Mans in Maine fled in a hurry after Gervaisote Estrigant told the court that he had tried to rape her in the fields at harvest time and provoked an encis. Gieffroy himself remembered only innocuous and flirtatious encounters. In 1467, Collette Porcheronne, imprisoned at Maulion in Poitou, confirmed that she had been secretive about the baby in her womb. "To be released from jail," her lettre de remission reads, she implicated a former lover for having caused her to miscarry by way of his rude sexual advances. Insinuations made by Margarita Saracena in 1498 to the effect that a girl from the neighborhood was the true mother of the dead child found in Margarita's home fell on deaf ears with Venetian interrogators. Given

---

19. Giorgia Alessi Palazzolo, *Prova legale e pena. La crisi del sistema tra medio evo e moderno* (Naples: Jovene, 1987) 20–41; Fraher, "Conviction According to Conscience," 23–88. Some judges extended imprisonment because of their unwillingness to execute; see Paris, AN, JJ 142, no. 103 (February 1392), in Bologne, *La naissance interdite*, 288: "Yceulz officiers ne l'ont voulu condempner ne juger, par quoy elle est illec demouree en grant povrete et misere et en aventure de fenir ses jours miserablement es dites prisons."

that she managed to escape capital punishment, Margarita must have denied charges of infanticidium to the very end.[20]

The stubbornness of Agnes le Codinet, Lucia Sclabona, Margarita Saracena, and others who steadfastly rejected their implication in acts of homicide deprived late medieval inquisitores of the ability to pass capital sentences. It was not until the appropriation and monopolization of jurisprudence and law enforcement by the early modern state that the prosecutorial constraints of older Romano-canonical procedure were finally overcome. In 1556, Henry III, king of France, proclaimed the new spirit of downward justice when he presented an edict on concealed pregnancies to the members of his supreme court. The opening paragraphs of his provision identify the legislator's main concern by targeting the dubious behavior of female suspects accused of pre- or postnatal killings. On countless occasions, the text asserts, royal officials had investigated the death of a newborn child. More than two hundred years after Pierre de Pilemer, the diligent sous-prevost from the Brie region had passed his sentence, his colleagues still struggled with the curtailment of inquisitorial activities. As Pierre had experienced in his day and the monarch now complained, many women, "apprehended and charged before our judges,"

> excuse themselves by saying that they felt too ashamed to make their vice public, or that their infants were stillborn or deprived of any hope to survive, so that members of our courts of Parlement and other judges, for lack of evidence and anxious to pass judgment in criminal proceedings, have been in disagreement. They either have favored capital punishment or resorted to extraordinary interrogations [with torture], to find out and hear expressly whether a baby issued from the womb had really been dead or alive. And when forcible questioning has finished, the [accused] are often released from imprisonment because they are unwilling to confess anything further, in what has allowed and continues to allow them to repeat their misdeeds incessantly.[21]

For Henry and his juridical advisers, the moment seemed ripe to address what contemporaries increasingly perceived as an inherited dilemma, leading

---

20. Venice, AS, Reg. 3658, fol. 200r-v: "[Margarita] ad torturam deducta falso et contra omnem veritatem inculpavit alias innocentissimas puellas de tali partu"; Paris, AN, JJ 200, no. 132 (July 1467), ed. Guérin, in *Archives historiques de Poitou* 38 (1909), 86–89 (no. 1433); AN, JJ 119, no. 247 (August 1381), in "Documents inédits pour servir l'histoire du Maine au XVᵉ siècle," ed. Arthur Bertrand de Broussillon, in *Archives historiques du Maine* 5 (1905): 267–269 (no. 247).

21. *Les edicts,* 671–672; cf. *Die Abtreibung,* 240 n. 418.

to grave inconsistencies in the daily operations of criminal justice. Prior to the king's initiative, numerous defendants who denied responsibility for an infanticide had reportedly been convicted by their judges to face execution. Others who likewise attributed the death to natural causes had escaped capital punishment because prosecutors felt impeded by the inconclusive evidence and failure to secure more comprehensive admissions of guilt. To reestablish equity and eliminate the procedural imbalance, Henry in 1556 prescribed a radical remedy. His edict ordered that henceforth and throughout the kingdom every pregnant female was to bring her condition to public knowledge. Should she neglect to declare her pregnancy and later miscarry, the concealment would amount to full proof and establish legal liability for murder:

> A woman who finds herself apprehended and convicted of having concealed, hidden, and covered up her entire pregnancy and delivery, without having declared one or the other and without having called in witnesses sufficiently attesting to one or the other, or the death or life of the child at the moment when the newborn was delivered, and whose child is left indigent of the holy sacrament of baptism and public and customary burial, shall be held and considered responsible for having slain her child as a homicide and in retribution be sentenced to death and execution with the rigor warranted by the particular quality of the case.[22]

By a stroke of his pen, Henry III removed decisive procedural safeguards that the courts of the Ius commune, contrary to his complaint about incoherent sentencing, appear to have respected for centuries. Presently available documentation does not suggest that the king's depiction of widespread judicial confusion accurately reflects the late medieval situation. Prior to 1500, not a single case, from France or elsewhere, attests to Romano-canonical proceedings in which the admitted concealment of a pregnancy (*recel de grossesse*) and miscarriage of a corpus would have sufficed to justify capital punishment. Whenever the inquisitors were confronted with partial confessions, they preferred the injunction of penae extraordinariae, which following juristic opinion remained at the judges' personal discretion (*arbitrium*). Also defined as arbitrary, or penae arbitrariae, they did not permit physical harm and did not equal or exceed maximum retribution as envisioned by the academic theorists. In April 1401 Katherine Baudouine swore that after her recel she

---

22. *Les edicts*, 672; *Die Abtreibung*, 128n229.

had delivered a stillborn baby, an assertion that the matrons examining her came to view as an outright lie. Execution was nevertheless regarded as an impossibility. Katherine's confession of secrecy kept her culpability at the level of half-proven homicidal intent, weighing, in abstract terms, no more than the killing of an unformed fetus.[23]

Accusatorial and inquisitorial trials of abortion and infanticide recorded during the period from 1250 to 1500 consistently attest to a narrow range of prosecutorial options. The start of an ordinary criminal inquisitio always presupposed discovery of a corpus delicti, and the death penalty required from suspects an unqualified confession of their guilt. The concealment of gestation did not deserve capital retribution because the charge of homicide fell short of being adequately proven. Soon after 1500, attempts by modern legislators to put the admission of recel and ensuing miscarriage on a par with definitive or absolutely compelling evidence turned out to be all the more incisive. The *Halsgerichtsordnung* from Bamberg of 1507 and the imperial *Carolina* of 1532 became the first statutory texts to threaten women hiding their pregnancies with automatic submission to torture, whereas Henry III's edict of 1556 went to the extreme and demanded their immediate execution.[24] In this way, important procedural safeguards shielding presumed killers of nascent life from the unfettered use of judicial powers by Romano-canonical inquisitores were cast aside. What appeared to be a minor correction of investigative techniques implied that the transition toward modernity was accompanied by change of truly epochal proportions.

Extraordinary Inquisitiones

Despite the mounting introduction of legal evidence in the years after 1500, acts considered so heinous as to warrant the suspension of fundamental procedural principles were not an invention of early modern times. When twelfth-century scholastic jurisprudence began to devise ordinary Romano-canonical procedure, lawyers instantly wondered about possible exceptions to the rule. The acknowledgment of certain extraordinary offenses led to the creation of special provisions to detect, investigate, and punish them. In the eyes of the Bolognese teachers, the figure of the heretic posed the most

---

23. See chapter 1. Concerning Katherine's case, see Paris, AN, JJ 156, no. 54; Chevalier, *Le pays de la Loire*, 199 (no. 1914): "Et jasoit que . . . les jurees qui par commande de justice ont visite ledit enfant ont depose que il avoit eu vie, ladicte Katherine a este prinse et encores est detenue prisonniere."

24. The passages from the *Bambergensis* and the *Carolina* are discussed in chap. 6, note 15.

terrifying threat to society. In order to combat heretical depravity, jurists reduced the standard prosecutorial guidelines of the Ius commune to their barest essentials. They eventually agreed that allegations of heresy did not have to exceed the level of anonymous defamations and that suspects would be denied instruction about the exact source and nature of the incriminating testimony. Whereas ecclesiastical courts normally shunned forcible questioning in cases under their competency, someone believed to have betrayed Christian orthodoxy could be submitted to torture for verification of the charges. Likewise, the prospect of capital punishment for second-time and obdurate offenders was without parallel in regular church proceedings.

If a presumed heretic emerged from his trial relatively unscathed, he owed the final release to judicial caveats that continued to be applicable. Recourse to torturous means in order to elicit a confession, for example, was restricted by theory to three attempts, none of which was supposed to last longer than a day. Doctrine did not permit the breaking of bones and insisted that information obtained by force required "spontaneous" confirmation following at least one night of rest for the defendant. Sentencing was also subject to limitations. Typical of the Romano-canonical process in general, interrogations concluded without any admission of guilt made dismissal of the case mandatory. Confessed culprits who, on the other hand, were prepared to renew their allegiance to the articles of faith by swearing a public oath of abjuration obliged the presiding judge to impose spiritual penance, with works of satisfaction that excluded lasting injury to the body. Only those whose previous judicial record showed them to have relapsed into earlier heretical error and individuals who obstinately defended unorthodox beliefs faced delivery to the secular arm for execution. In formal recognition of the maxim that "the Church does not thirst for blood" (*Ecclesia non sitit sanguinem*), lay tribunals took it upon themselves to inflict the prescribed death penalty and have "incorrigible" offenders burned alive at the stake.[25]

In current perception, the special procedures of scholastic law for the persecution of heretical depravity loom sufficiently large to figure under the all-encompassing label of the Inquisition. Although, historically speaking, the vast majority of late medieval punitive charges brought via inquisitionis

---

25. For regulations concerning *inquisitiones haereticae pravitatis,* see Ian Forrest, *The Detection of Heresy in Late Medieval England* (Oxford: Oxford University Press, 2005), 197–230; Feuchter, *Ketzer, Konsuln und Büßer,* 307–343; Christine Ames, *Righteous Persecution. Inquisition, Dominicans, and Christianity in the Middle Ages* (Philadelphia: University of Pennsylvania Press, 2009), 169–181. It is technically incorrect to describe ecclesiastical penalties for heresy as "punishment" instead of "penance" even where they assumed the form of flogging, payment, or (perpetual) incarceration.

stayed within the same parameters as the cases of infanticide and fetal percussio described in the previous section, premodern jurisprudence did recognize a small group of extraordinary offenses besides heresy. As discussed in chapter 1, the ecclesiastical equation between willful killings of the formed fetus and homicide was read into Justinian's *Corpus iuris civilis* from very early on. The interpretive parallel struck by twelfth-century commentators encouraged the criminalization of abortion in the lay sphere and left a lasting mark on the Western legal tradition. Inspired by notions of proper Christian conduct, Bolognese glossators also distilled from their textbooks references that seemed to condone laxer prosecutorial standards with regard to one particular category of attacks on nascent human life.

Justinian's *Corpus iuris civilis* transmits several injunctions against the use of drugs to manipulate the natural course of procreation. Concerned with the risk of side effects, one lex (Dig. 48.8.3.2) disallows the administration of "medicine affecting fertility" (*medicamentum ad conceptionem*) by imposing exile in the event of deadly consequences. The Digest further condemns the preparation of "abortifacient or love potions" (*amatorium aut abortionis poculum*), threatening those responsible for resulting fatalities with capital punishment (Dig. 48.19.38.5). The text goes on to state that perpetrators who "do not act maliciously" (*etsi id dolo non faciant*) are nevertheless to be executed. When civilians of the twelfth century started to comment upon the passage, their most daunting intellectual challenge lay in the suggestion that even in the absence of murderous intent the killing of a human fetus would warrant maximum sentencing. Given that Justinian's fragment clearly rejects excuses based on the lack of homicidal premeditation, what criteria of liability were to be applied instead? In search of an answer, scholastic jurists realized that they were poorly advised by the Roman sources. Excerpts written by their pagan predecessors proposed a bewildering quantity of terms alluding to penal culpability, from negligent and casually committed acts to a fourfold gradation along the lines of *culpa levis, culpa lata, culpa latior,* and *culpa latissima.* At the same time, systematic statements explaining the array of vocabulary, let alone the exact significance of malice (dolus), were nowhere to be found.[26]

The canonistic doctrine of guilt combined consistency with the advantage of being firmly rooted in prevailing religious and theological assumptions. In analyzing criminal intent, late medieval church lawyers adhered to principles that sinners again encountered in the confessional context. Whereas

---

26. On the ancient Roman understanding of culpa and dolus, cf. Engelmann, *Die Schuldlehre der Postglossatoren*, 14–33.

penitential and punitive discipline assessed both the quality of evidence and the tangible effects of wrongdoing differently, discrepancies did not affect the evaluation of inner motivations, given that a tight correlation existed in terms of purpose between divine redemption and the operations of earthly justice. Most important, retribution in either sphere served medicinal rather than vindictive ends. For the attainment of afterlife, orthodoxy demanded that spiritual advisers conduct their analyses of unchristian behavior "on the safer side" of salvation. "Well disposed minds," a much quoted passage from Gratian's Decretum (D. 5, c.4) reads, "presume fault where there is none, as things that come about without fault often do so because of fault." Later decretists and decretalists followed this logic and formalized the procedures of the penal *forum contentiosum* in accordance with the "salutary" goals pursued by the confessors. It was commonly taught that responsibility in God's eyes exceeded the narrow limits of willful transgression. The unexpected consequences of incriminating behavior had to be considered as well. For ecclesiastical judges, in other words, the Roman reference to deadly abortionis pocula, requiring capital punishment regardless of verifiable murderous intent, did not pose any difficulty of comprehension. Abortifacient potions that inadvertently killed a formed fetus still reflected the highest degree of culpability. As homicides resulting from the distribution of prohibited drugs were already compromised by their occurrence "under illicit circumstances" (*in re illicita*), they figured as consciously attempted and deserved capital punishment.

In efforts to supply Justinian's lex with a rationale that despite the absence of dolus justified infliction of the death penalty, the leading representatives of civilian jurisprudence eventually realized that the straightforwardness of the canonistic solution exerted an irresistible pull. Church lawyers from Laurentius Hispanus (around 1215) onward invoked Dig. 48.19.38.5 in order to show that "dynamic" abortion through beverages formed an aggravated, or qualified, crime, long before Bartolus, the eminent fourteenth-century commentator on the Roman law, set an example by embracing without qualification the interpretive position of his colleagues across the divide between "the two laws" (*ius utrumque*): "Someone who has given [an abortifacient drink] deserves execution," Bartolus tersely remarked in his discussion of various types of pocula, "because he gave it to procure a miscarriage and, therefore, with an illicit purpose in mind [*causa rei illicite*]."[27] Undoubtedly, the words of

---

27. Bartolus de Saxoferrato, *Commentaria, super Digesto novo* 48.8.3.2, s.v. *Adiectio* (Milan: Scinzenzeler, 1510), fol. 184rb. The opinion of Laurentius Hispanus circulated widely as part of the canonistic *Glossa ordinaria* on Gratian's Decretum, chap. 1, note 20.

the renowned teacher from Sassoferrato constituted more than a brief aside. Among lawyers of the Ius commune, the ecclesiastical understanding of guilt incurred in re illicita furnished anything but a vague definition of ill will. The term reminded readers that, in the situation at hand, measurements of homicidal intent were entirely superfluous.

While the civilian interpretation of pocula abortionis continued to foment debate until and beyond the end of the Middle Ages, practice seems to have shared the position of Bartolus all along. Lay judges conducting inquiries into cases of dynamic abortion followed the canonistic definition of penal responsibility at least in spirit, and late medieval judicial records confirm that disregard of dolus in the Digest allowed criminal prosecutors of the Ius commune to dismiss questions of volition altogether. By attributing the status of an extraordinary offense to charges of magic and poisoning, courts were also prepared to lower the benchmark for admissible evidence. As with heresy, slander and anonymous allegations sufficed for the opening of a trial. To illustrate the extent to which accusations involving the use of abortifacient potions undercut the strict formalism of ordinary inquisitorial procedure, the story of Marion Faudier is worth telling. In 1453 the young woman from Eu in Normandy sought sanctuary on church grounds to avoid imprisonment and the impending "rigor of justice." Marion's father, Jehan, prior to his execution for murder had made a confession of guilt that implicated her in a sequence of disturbing events. Jehan admitted to having raped his daughter repeatedly, until Marion alerted him to the fact that she was pregnant. Greatly concerned about the family's honor and reputation, Jehan and his wife urged Marion to abort the child before her state would become public knowledge. When she resisted and implored them to consider the danger to their souls, parental determination grew to the extreme: "[Jehan] said to his wife that she had to find a way, by herbal drink or otherwise, to expel the baby from their daughter's womb, so that he would not run any risk of discovery and shame. . . . They then mixed a potion and forced Marion to take it. And when she refused to do so, her father put a stick in her mouth to keep it open."[28] Marion's fear of serious legal consequences was not unfounded. Once a concoction brewed and imbibed to kill the unborn baby had been mentioned in her father's deposition, she could no longer count on a line of defense that centered on desperate resistance to his murderous schemes. Lack of intent to use pocula abortionis did little to frustrate prosecution or

---

28. Paris, AN, JJ 184, no. 303 (March 1453); cf. *Die Abtreibung*, 255n440.

help her secure an easy verdict of innocence. The lay officials of Eu had already accepted testimony from a convicted criminal. Following Bartolus and the canonical notions of culpability in re illicita, inquisitorial proceedings and Marion's incarceration were imminent notwithstanding the absence of respectable eyewitnesses and a corpus delicti. Like other seekers of ecclesiastical asylum, Marion faced prospects of confiscation and permanent exile unless she could obtain a royal lettre de remission. To be completely restored, she decided to write to the king, humbly requesting from him a mandate of pardon. The surviving registers document the end of her plight. The petition was granted.[29]

Besides magic and sorcery, abortion by way of poisoning ranked among the few offenses enabling prosecutors of the Ius commune to initiate criminal investigations without regard for the origins and quality of allegations. Persistent anonymous rumors or denuntiationes were deemed on a par with full-fledged accusationes and inquisitiones, and malicious intent did not have to be proved, circumstantially or otherwise, to warrant conviction. Whenever a defendant confessed to having made use of pocula, his plain admission called for legal punishment. Depending on the actual effect, it would amount to pena extraordinaria or ordinaria, to lesser or capital sentencing. In this fashion and by facilitating the judicial prosecution of wrongdoing categorized as particularly heinous, scholastic jurisprudence catered as well to periodic demands for swifter retribution, arising from obscure social and political forces and predating the twelfth-century law schools, if not the Western legacy of written norms in general. As especially the work of David Nirenberg has shown, individuals and groups in late medieval society often suffered exposure to violent acts that appeared to be blind and arbitrary but from an anthropological perspective functioned as rather purposeful rituals, reinforcing ties of solidarity within communities, redefining the public identity of members, and retracing the borderline between insiders and outsiders.[30] The intermittent outbreak of defamatory campaigns targeting specific persons or minorities as scapegoats formed a perennial phenomenon that in the literary traditions of Roman and canon law, from late antiquity to the eve of early modern times, was rationalized and justified in the pursuit of

---

29. Paris, AN, JJ 183, no. 303; *Die Abtreibung*, 209n365, 233n406. Flight into sanctuary incurred expulsion from the French kingdom and the loss of belongings, except where refugees were able to secure a lettre de remission; see Claude Gauvard, *De grace especial. Crime, état et société en France à la fin du moyen âge*, 2 vols. (Paris: Publications de la Sorbonne, 1991), 1:177–204.

30. David Nirenberg, *Communities of Violence: Persecution of Minorities in the Middle Ages* (Princeton, NJ: Princeton University Press, 1996).

criminals epitomizing the utmost harm. The suspects were labeled administrators of spells and charms or received summonses for the brewing of love
potions and pocula abortionis.

In the procedural world of the Ius commune, the societal urge to provide quick, ritualized, and highly visible responses to challenges purportedly
undermining the foundation of the public order soon translated into the
creation of simplified criminal trial formats. Through the elimination of
ordinary safeguards, they aided in the condemnation of individuals believed
to be exceptionally dangerous. Scholastic theoreticians, to be sure, placed
instruments allowing for leaner prosecution next to an array of more traditional, community-based modes of collective cleansing, some of which can
be traced in the extant documentation as well. Particularly in areas wit-
nessing the tardy reception of Bolognese jurisprudence, non- or protosys-
tematic types of justice were employed to investigate generic accusations in
connection with dynamic abortion, sustained above all by adverse popular
sentiment. When the duke of Brabant decreed his peace for Terhulpen (La
Hulpe) in 1230, for instance, he stipulated that women found guilty of fetal
death, murder, arson, or other detrimental activity be burned in a wooden
box.[31] In later centuries, German towns recorded pronouncements against
"people bringing injury to the land" (landschaedliche Leute), including one
Adelheit von Stuogarden, who in 1409 endured three years of expulsion
from Schlettstatt (Sélestat) in Alsace. Commonly known as "the limping
physician," the woman was said to have distributed beverages and roots that
led to miscarriage in a matter of days. Adelheit's relegation to the category
of landschaedlich rested on the ascertainment of guilt by seven respectable
witnesses, who confirmed by oath the existence of persistent rumors against
her. The canonical model of proof by decisory oath, used in church courts
to corroborate damaging penitential denuntiationes, was adapted to local
modes of communal sentencing, as the panel of municipal co-jurors swore
to convict persons they believed to be defamed beyond repair.[32]

31. Brussels, AN, Priv. et exempt. 8, fol. 287v; in Chroniques belges, ed. Jan-Frans Willems, vol. 1
(Brussels, 1839), 633.

32. Sélestat (Schlettstadt), Bibl. Communale, Stadtbuch 1, in Karl Baas, "Gesundheitspflege in
Elsass-Lothringen bis zum Ausgang des Mittelalters," Zeitschrift für Geschichte des Oberrheins 73 (1919):
70. A statute from Parma ordered in 1233 that suspects of abortion be summarily expelled along with
other urban riffraff, Statuta civitatis Parmae digesta ad MCCLV, ed. Amadio Ronchini, Monumenta
historica ad provincias Parmensem et Placentinam pertinentia 1 (Parma: Fiaccadori, 1856), 42–43; on
the political background, Augustine Thompson O. P., Revival Preachers and Politics in Thirteenth-Century
Italy: The Great Devotion of 1233 (Oxford: Oxford University Press, 1992), 179–204.

Scholastic doctrine did not permit mere hearsay to result in ordinary inquisitiones as long as defendants denied the charges outright. In connection with abortifacient potions, however, the chances of criminal investigation improved markedly because evidence confirming the presence of dolus or the actual death of a baby ceased to be necessary. The oldest known judicial instance already points to the application of less stringent procedural standards. In November 1298, the secular court of Manosque, near Marseille, undertook inquiries against Isaac, a Jewish physician, whom ill repute accused of having supplied Uga, the daughter of the late Petrus de Dia, with medical means causing her to abort. While Isaac's prescription was said to have worked as alleged, his judges did not have a corpus delicti or reliable witnesses at their disposal. All the same, they decided to go forward and explore imputations solely supported by public fame. As the scribe of the judicial record noted, Isaac's pursuits were in particular need of correction given that they posed "bad examples" (*mala exempla*), a term that literally echoes a Latin formula in the original Roman condemnation of pocula abortionis. Final sentencing was again in line with juristic interpretations of qualified crime. Although the Jew never conceded any homicidal involvement, he could not dispel suspicions that he had been handling poisonous substances. The payment of fifty pounds faithfully reflected Bolognese insistence on arbitrary—that is, less than maximum, or capital—punishment.[33] Trial episodes from France, including those traceable in the royal pardons for Jehannette Canelesle of July 1399 and for Maiore Bourdine and her daughter of April 1405 resulted in a similar vein from "repeated murmurs," or from "denunciation and the instigation of certain hateful people."[34] Vague insinuations of guilt attained their prosecutorial viability from claims of drug-induced, or "dynamic," abortion.

Since the treatment of pocula abortionis as a qualified secular crime presupposed the import of canonistic teachings into civilian jurisprudence, one would expect that church law also classified the offense as particularly worthy

---

33. Marseille, AD, 56 H 955, fol. 6r–8r, 11v–12r, in Shatzmiller, *Médecine et justice*, 80–85 (no. 10–11), translated by Faith Wallis in Wallis, ed., *Medieval Medicine: A Reader* (Toronto, ON: Broadview, 2010), 380–383 (no. 77); cf. Patricia MacCaughan, *La justice à Manosque au XIIIᵉ siècle. Évolution et représentation* (Paris: Sirey, 2005), 150–151. For a parallel case of 1392 from Mechelen, see Brussels, Rijksarchief, Rekenkamer 15660, cited by Louis Maes, *Vijf eeuwen stedelijk strafrecht. Bijdrage tot de rechts- en cultuurgeschiedenis der nederlanden* (Antwerp: de Sikkel, 1947), 267n1.

34. Paris, AN, JJ 154, no. 310 (July 1399): "Pour lequel cas et renommee qui de ce est couru contre luy la dicte Jehannette a este mis es noz dictes prisons"; AN, JJ 160, no. 19 (April 1405): "Lesdiz mere et fille a la denonciation et pourchaz d'aucun genz hayneux ou autrement ont este accusees prises et mises es prisons."

of retribution. In reality, though, canon lawyers were hesitant to implement in the ecclesiastical courts measures they considered perfectly suitable for the laity. Their ambiguous attitude manifested itself in a twofold approach to the matter. The first prevailed in the law schools and at the Apostolic Curia; the second affected penitential writings and diocesan legislation aimed at the improvement of priestly conduct. In manuals of penance, to begin with, early scholastic authors developed a distinctive habit of juxtaposing authoritative sources so as to suggest that contraception and dynamic abortion each led to harsher punitive consequences. Clarifications to the contrary offered by juristic commentators and especially in the *Summa* of Hostiensis (d. 1271) permeated the works of confessional literature from around 1300. Simultaneously, a string of episcopal statutes branded poisoning in the womb as an extraordinary clerical *crimen*. A council of 1285 convened in the southern French diocese of Riez promised to pursue perpetrators with exceptional severity and published a provision that bishops and higher clergy repeated over the course of the following century in many gatherings held throughout the region:

> He who dares to intoxicate another, assists or offers advice in so doing, or prescribes or sells or else administers poison to kill someone, or gives herbs to cause death or an abortion, shall automatically [ipso facto] incur excommunication from which only the Apostolic See can absolve. And if he turns out to be a cleric with a benefice, he shall be deprived of it ipso facto, suffer the loss of his clerical rank through degradation, and extradition to the lay court.[35]

The conciliar decree from Riez fills several of the blanks left by common canonistic opinion. The question frequently posed by contemporary proceduralists as to who should be entitled to absolve from dynamic abortion was answered in favor of the pope, and lingering perplexity concerning the special heinousness of poisoning received a categorical response in that the charge was tied to the most intransigent forms of repression. Automatic (ipso facto) exclusion from the Christian community mimicked the well-known example of *inmissio manuum,* which from 1139 had reserved the readmission

---

35. Riez (1285), cap. 14, edited by Mansi 24.580–581. About 1236, the *Glossa ordinaria,* in X 5.12.5, s.v. *ut homicida* (Frankfurt/M.: Feyerabend, 1590), col. 1209b, suggested that contraception might deserve capital punishment in the secular sphere, a view shown by Hostiensis (ca. 1250) to be juristically flawed, *Apparatus super* X 5.12.5, s.v. *Nasci* (Strasbourg: Übelin, 1512), fol. 285va. Penitential summae written before 1300 often repeat the *Glossa,* whereas later ones follow Hostiensis; cf. Noonan, *Contraception,* 233–237; *Die Abtreibung,* 4n89, 57n108, 72n136.

of those excommunicated for the physical harassment of churchmen to none other than the Apostolic See. The threat of removal from clerical office and income further recalled the canonical punishment of ordinary criminals, aggravated, as in the case of heresy, with degradation and delivery to the secular arm (*traditio curie*). The statute of 1285, it is true, stopped short of mentioning the death penalty that traitors of orthodoxy faced upon their extradition. Still, the framers of the text did everything to separate lethal intoxication from average killings, as is evident from the fact that jurisprudence in general was silent about *degradatio* and traditio curie except when dealing with the notoriously incorrigible, individuals convicted multiple times and of serial wrongdoing.[36]

While earlier synodal legislation from Narbonne in 1240 had coupled the use of abortifacient potions with contraceptive means and assigned suspension from priestly duties to both of them, the stipulations from Riez served as a precedent for reissuance and modification of the text by several southern French councils in the fourteenth century. Later versions adapted the canonical penalties of immediate excommunication, exclusion from altar services and income, degradation, and relegation to the secular arm in order to exploit a normative loophole, supply more stringent measures against drug-related miscarriage, or juristically accommodate cleansing rituals that every now and then united local society in attempts to counter inadvertent death, famine, epidemics, and festering internal enmity.[37] Interestingly enough, though, efforts by prelates to mark the preparation of toxic beverages as an evil of outrageous proportions failed to impact normative routine as it was practiced at the highest levels of ecclesiastical administration. The extreme scarcity of registered absolutions from the Apostolic Court of Penance (Sacra Penitentiaria) in effect leaves no room for assumptions that the sin of intentional

---

36. *Incorrigibilitas* and *inmissio manuum* are treated by Richard H. Helmholz, "'Si quis suadente' (C. 17 q. 4 c. 29): Theory and Practice," in *Proceedings of the Seventh International Congress of Medieval Canon Law*, ed. Peter Linehan (Vatican City: Typographia Vaticana, 1988), 425–438; Richard H. Helmholz, *The Spirit of Classical Canon Law* (Athens, GA: University of Georgia Press, 1996), 366–393.

37. Riez (1285), cap. 14, inspired the statutes of Cavaillon (1288), cap. 14, edited by Mansi 24.961–962; Avignon (1326), cap. 18, ed. Mansi 25.754–755; Avignon 1337, cap. 22, ed. Mansi 25.1094; and Lavaur 1368, cap. 116, ed. Mansi 26.537; cf. Robert Génestal, *Le privilegium fori en France du Décret de Gratien à la fin du XIVᵉ siècle*, 2 vols. (Paris : Leroux, 1921–1924), 2:156–158. Narbonne (1240), cap. 59, has been edited by Joseph Avril, "Sources et caractère du livre synodal de Raimond de Calmont d'Olt, évêque de Rodez (1289)," in *L'Église et le droit dans le Midi (XIIIᵉ–XIVᵉ siècles)* (Toulouse: Privat, 1994), 245; Lucca (1308), cap. 12, ed. Mansi 25.185–186; Bergamo (1311), cap. 19, ed. Mansi 25.494–495; and Florence (1346), cap. 16, ed. Mansi 26.66, likewise reflect the *Glossa ordinaria* (chap. 1, note 20) and its coupling of contraceptives with pocula abortionis.

fetal death, let alone contraception, was reserved to the pope's exclusive jurisdiction. Petitioners who sought access or readmission to the holy orders after being implicated in an abortion never hinted at any legal distinction between prenatal homicides caused by drink and those caused by mechanical means, in tune with what Hostiensis and other prominent canonists told their academic audiences.[38]

Curial administrators obviously regarded homicidal miscarriage as coinciding with ordinary manslaughter, incurring removal from the sacramental rites and the withholding of clerical revenues. Harsher punitive attitudes can perhaps be discerned in a dispensatory mandate from the pontificate of Calixtus III. Requested in 1456 by a certain Nicolaus, archpriest from the diocese of Isernia, the text advocates his readmission to minor clerical orders below the rank of subdeacon. As Nicolaus stated in the narrative, he had killed an unwanted child of his. The fatality occurred at a time when the victim was "not yet alive" (*nondum vivificatus*), a phrase reminiscent of terminology that Innocent III had employed in his widely copied decretal of 1211 (X 5.12.20). Paradoxically, Innocent's reply also asserted that the slaying of a fetus not yet alive, or unformed and prehuman, did not create an impediment to the exercise of holy orders or any need for special dispensation. Was it therefore significant that Nicolaus confessed to having provoked the premature delivery by way of "some poison"?[39] Officials at the Sacra Penitentiaria did not clarify whether Nicolaus was, canonically speaking, correct when he sought a dispensation, and while the unique character of his petition intimates that his supplication was less than necessary, future research may reveal that he was responding to more stringent diocesan standards insistent on papal intervention.

The Ius commune furnished average criminal suspects with considerable defensive armor. Except for the special offenses of heresy and killing by way of potions, formalities of court conduct limited prosecutors significantly. About the time of the Reformation, on the other hand, inquisitorial powers started to grow to the detriment of the accused. The introduction of legal evidence for greater effectiveness in combating delinquency meant that more and more cases were drawn into the orbit of what, in the later Middle Ages,

---

38. A rare request for penitential absolution appears in Rome, APA Reg. div. 8, fol. 109r (2 January 1460); cf. *RPG* 4.161 (no. 1142). Declarationes and petitions to dispense from abortion are cited in chap. 2, notes 13–14.

39. Rome, APA Reg. div. 5, fol. 317r (6 December 1456), printed in *Die Abtreibung,* 196n343. Innocent's rescript of 1211 is quoted in chap. 2, note 12.

had been a comparatively small number of extraordinary allegations. From the 1430s, the trend was reinforced by the emergence of judicial witch hunts. Based on a newly defined crime, they stood at the conjunction of three allegations that traditionally aided in the persecution of capital offenders. As Richard Kieckhefer has demonstrated in his studies of sorcery in fifteenth-century German-speaking lands, proliferating charges of satanic magic were now expressed in formulaic language that invoked the three counts of association with the devil, administration of harmful beverages, and the slaughtering of offspring before or after birth.[40] The list and its peculiarities attest to the influence of many historical factors. Comparison with ordinary Romano-canonical procedure suggests, however, that the triad of accusations enabled judges to circumvent regulations of due process altogether. Cast into relief was the profile of a perpetrator who figured as the investigator's ideal target. Diabolical conspiracy, because of its heretical nature, rendered restraint as to the admissibility of hearsay obsolete; the administration of abortifacient potions justified murder charges without the need to produce a corpus delicti or examine questions of intent; and charges of intoxication, unlike heresy, allowed for the instant mobilization of secular prosecutors in addition to ecclesiastical ones. The witch, in short, was left completely to the discretion of the inquisitores, who in turn embodied downward justice and early modern statehood on the rise.

---

40. Richard Kieckhefer, "Avenging the Blood of Children: Anxiety over Child Victims and the Origins of the European Witch Trials," in *The Devil, Heresy, and Witchcraft in the Middle Ages: Essays in Honor of Jeffrey B. Russell,* ed. Alberto Ferreiro (Leiden: Brill, 1998), 91–110; also Kathrin Utz-Tremp, *Von der Häresie zur Hexerei. "Wirkliche" und imaginäre Sekten im Spätmittelalter* (Hannover: Hahn, 2008), 383–400.

CHAPTER 8

Forms of Punishment in the Criminal Courts of the Ius Commune

Legal historians today agree that during the later Middle Ages criminal sentencing shared important characteristics, whether in the lay jurisdictions of the English common law (see chapters 2 and 5), or those of the scholastic Ius commune. Maximum penalties affected but a small percentage of cases brought before the courts, and verdicts of death or mutilation were carried out in elaborate public ceremonies, attracting throngs of onlookers and culminating in scenes of exceptional cruelty. To capture the essence of the final judicial act, scholars have spoken of its theatricality and stressed the inclination of medieval judges to punish in graphic and exemplary fashion. Emphasis on the twin features of rarity and ruthlessness can be misleading, though, given that the modern Western mind, shaped by the experience of postmedieval state monopolies on justice and violence, is likely to associate occasional, harsh, and widely advertised rituals of punishment with an administrative apparatus prepared to flex its muscle and use convictions as a manifestation of its all-encompassing prosecutorial might. The exhibitionism, gore, and relative scarcity of physical retribution prior to the sixteenth century followed a different logic. It mirrored societal constraints that hampered top-down adjudication and the application of systematized norms in general.[1]

---

1. For scholarship on the subject, cf. Dean, *Crime in Medieval Europe*, 118–143; Andrea Zorzi, "Le esecuzioni delle condanne a morte a Firenze nel tardo medioevo tra esperienza penale e cerimoniale

Current assumptions about the operations of law and punishment presuppose that the determination of culpability and its penal consequences do not depend on participants other than prosecutors, defense lawyers, juries, and judges who, with the accused in attendance, evaluate and conclude cases on the basis of standards previously established in writing. Everything that affects a trial must be brought to the parties' attention in a designated courtroom, to the exclusion of both political prejudice and the emotionally charged clamor of the streets. In premodern times, on the other hand, the restriction of procedural matters to a body of abstractly formulated rules, oversight by legal professionals, and decision making undertaken solely by the judiciary was a feat far from being accomplished. Although scholastic jurisprudence sought to tie the resolution of conflict to special venues and proposed the relegation of sentencing to select and expert officials, judicial maneuvering continued to involve agents who exercised their influence in court as well as throughout the community. Even in the rare event that capital sentences were imposed, criminal inquisitors had to engage with the public to secure the implementation of their verdicts. Execution always remained somewhat uncertain, as bystanders could decide in the last moment to step forward and ask to marry a woman convicted of prenatal murder or as long as unforeseen incidents like the rupture of a cord during hanging convinced spectators of miraculous and divine interference. In either scenario, the meting out of punishment was halted, often definitively, as a result of popular sympathy with female offenders or the widespread belief that God intervened in mundane matters of right and wrong. Obviously, average people and collective sentiment were capable of derailing the formal course of justice, again underlining that the Ius commune, while envisioning different stages of ordinary criminal proceedings, took for granted not the absolute autonomy of investigations but rather their constant exposure to communal feeling, whether expressed in open gatherings and squares or in the barely visible machinations of adversarial families and local power brokers.

That the gruesome treatment and display of convicts served to reassure judiciaries of sufficient social support for their actions is likewise implicit in the lack of juristic comment on how mechanisms of lawful repression were supposed to unfold. Theorists of Romano-canonical procedure left the tangible aspects of punishment to local custom, and academic lawyers were quick to replace pertinent regulations in Justinian's Digest with abstract and

---

pubblico," in *Simbolo e realtà della vita urbana nel tardo medioevo,* ed. Massimo Miglio and Giuseppe Lombardi (Rome: Vecchiarelli, 1993), 153–162.

purely functional descriptions. From the time of Azo Porticus (d. 1202) and his fellow glossators, criminal doctrine referred to maximum penalties generically as *penae legales* or *penae ordinariae* and uniformly labeled lesser retribution extraordinary or arbitrary. With regard to the secular crimen of abortion, scholastic authors set execution (*pena mortis*) in opposition to other punitive measures, agreeing that *exilium* (Dig. 48.8.8), *exilium temporale* (Dig. 47.11.4, Dig. 48.19.39), and the partial confiscation of property and relegation to the mines (Dig. 48.19.38.5), while mentioned as minor penae in the ancient *Corpus iuris civilis,* did not have to be taken literally.

It has been noted in chapter 2 that scholastic notions of criminal punishment were considerably broader than the current use of the term would permit. Twelfth-century canonists extended the applicability of crimen as a concept all the way to the suspension of individuals from the exercise of their priestly functions, a legal outcome that nowadays would fall under the category of internal and disciplinary measures. Conversely, payments or imprisonment ordered by church courts against homicidal clerics and laypersons strike present observers as clearly punitive, whereas late medieval jurists would have classified both as forms of penitential satisfaction. Further research may establish whether the more intransigent treatment of abortion through poisoning, prescribed by numerous episcopal statutes against academic opinion and papal routine, impacted clerical culprits to the point of extradition to nonecclesiastical authority. In the meantime, the discussion of criminal sentencing in the modern sense of the word must restrict its focus to the laity, as clerics enduring penalties for prenatal homicide at the hands of secular judges have not yet been tracked in the records.

According to Bolognese doctrine, laypersons were to suffer execution for the intentional commission of infanticide or fetal homicidium. The survey of punitive rituals in the following section illustrates how the mode of implementation would vary from place to place. In the case of partial admissions, or half-proof, of liability, arbitrary retribution did not permit the infliction of permanent physical harm and favored bans and monetary fines instead. The procedural guidelines of the Ius commune treated in chapter 7, moreover, did not allow for lesser penalties except where a suspect had admitted his or her concealment of a pregnancy, a birth, or a corpus delicti, a fact that often prevented inquisitors from reaching a guilty verdict altogether. Still, the court episodes examined here suggest that many judges used their discretionary powers of investigation to test the resolve of defendants indirectly. They imposed, for example, preliminary jail time of indeterminate length or resorted to other methods of judicial duress short of formal conviction. Their reliance on heavy-handed intervention was concurrently tempered by communal expectations and the interference of friends, families, and bystanders whose influence, tracked at the end of this chapter, lasted not only as long as definitive sentences had not been passed but also until they had in effect been carried out.

Statutory and Customary Specifications

Late medieval prescriptive sources inform us in detail about secular penalties for the crime of abortion. As discussed in chapter 3, the texts do not reveal their historical inspiration unless they are read in conjunction with the precepts of general jurisprudence. Town statutes and princely legislation modified or supplemented the rules of the Ius commune but never replaced them entirely. The greatest problem for modern scholarship lies in the absence of indications as to which aspect of scholastic doctrine legislators sought to override. It seems possible, for example, to surmise cause and effect in Italian municipal statutes that treat voluntary fetal death on a par with homicide, given that their first appearance occurred shortly after Signorolus de Homodeis and his Bolognese colleagues started to question the equation in the 1340s. By the same token, insistence among communal authorities that the injunction of maximum punishment should always presuppose homicidal intent (dolus) was arguably directed against academic views that wished to eliminate proof of malice aforethought from cases involving the use of abortifacient beverages. On occasion, moreover, conflicting norms embraced by kings on the one hand and juristic consensus on the other would exceed acceptable limits and provoke openly adverse legal commentary. A passage from the royal *Siete Partidas* (7.8.8), composed during the 1260s, was rejected as "unlawful" by the sixteenth-century criminalist Gregorius Lopez, for it exempted from execution husbands whose corrective beatings had gone as far as to have their spouses miscarry. And generations of juristic commentators pouring over the Sicilian *Liber Augustalis,* issued in 1231, read feticidal poisoning back into provisions that originally promoted harsher penalties solely for the administration of amorous or love potions, despite the express juxtaposition of abortionis and amatoria pocula in Justinian's *Corpus* (Dig. 48.19.38.5).[2]

---

2. *Constitutiones regni Siciliae* 3.70, 3.73, ed. Wolfgang Stürner, in *MGH* Constitutiones 2, supplement (Hannover: Hahn, 1997), 430, 437–438. Around 1330, their extension to abortifacients was made explicit by Blasius de Morcone, *De differentiis inter ius Langobardorum et ius Romanorum tractatus* 1.3, ed. Giovanni Abignente (Naples, 1924), 24; and especially by Mattheus de Afflictis (d. 1523), *Praelectiones in Constitutiones Neapolitanas* 1.13, 3.41, 2 vols. (Venice: Guarisco, 1606), fol. 66rb (no. 19), 172vb. On the *Siete Partidas* 7.8.8 and its glosses, chap. 3, notes 14, 17. Signorolus and the statutory responses to his *Consilium primum* are discussed in the second section of chapter 3.

By contrast, scholastic criticism of normative efforts to regulate the technicalities of punishment is nowhere to be found. Gregorius Lopez silently accepted the five years of exile "on an island" that *Siete Partidas* 7.8.8 stipulates for the slaying of a fetus before the entry of the human soul, and glosses on *Constitutio* 3.73 of the *Liber Augustalis* never objected to the prescribed confiscation of property and year-long incarceration, whether these extended to potions stimulating the libido or premature birth. At a comparatively early date, the *Ancient Furs* of Valencia, put together from 1238 to 1271 under James I of Aragon, threatened a person convicted of homicidal manslaughter in the womb with burning at the stake. The law appears to have been inspired by the rigor of older Visigothic legislation that demanded execution or at least blinding for this offense and was just being revived in the Castilian kingdom as part of a vernacular version known as the *Fuero juzgo* (6.3.1–7).[3] Unlike other municipal statutes of premodern Italy, a text from Siena of 1309–10 associated dynamic abortion with harsher punitive measures. In accordance with Bolognese communis opinio, a fine of 200 lire was imposed on the distribution or consumption of abortifacient beverages, even where fatalities did not ensue. A provision passed at Biella on the Lago Maggiore around 1345 likewise stood out in that it prescribed different punishments for men (decapitation) and women (burning) as well as for the killing of inanimate as opposed to animate fetal life. The latter case was defined as applicable from two months into the pregnancy onward, the former warranted a fine of four hundred Pavian pounds. Meanwhile, most of the known Italian statuta shunned subtle distinctions and ordered convicted parties to be handed over to the flames.[4] The description of penae looked toward practical issues that academic doctrine did not address.

The crudity of retribution in one of the northernmost Italian communes at Locarno was probably influenced by the vindictive habits in neighboring German-speaking lands, where the tardy arrival of the Ius commune as a blueprint for secular prosecutors stalled trends toward penal uniformity for a long time. According to a provision of 1588, slayers of children

---

3. *Fori Antiqui Valentiae* 9.7, ed. Manuel Dualde Serrano (Madrid: CSIC, 1950–1967), 243. Inspiration for the *Furs* may have come from the thirteenth-century *El Fuero juzgo,* ed. José Perona Sánchez, 2 vols. (Murcia: Fundacion Seneca, 2002), 2:412, based in turn on the Latin original of the *Leges Wisigothorum,* ed. Karl Zeumer, in *MGH LL* 1.1 (Hannover: Hahn, 1902), 260–262.

4. Kohler, *Das Strafrecht der italienischen Statuten,* 334–336; Garancini, "Materiali," 502–510; cf. especially Biella (ca. 1345), cap. 21, in *Statuta communis Bugellae,* 179; Siena (1309/10) 5.258, in *Il costituto del comune di Siena volgarizzato nel MCCCIX–MCCCX,* ed. Mahmoud Salem Elsheikh, 4 vols. (Siena: Monte dei Paschi di Siena, 2002), 2:366.

before or after birth had to have their backs broken on a wheel.[5] Farther across the Alpine rim, two of the oldest codifications of Bolognese criminal law in the Teutonic kingdom—the *Halsgerichtsordnung* for Bamberg of 1507 (article 158) and, in a literal transcription, the *Carolina* (article 133), passed by Charles V at the imperial diet of Regensburg in 1532—further manifest, albeit belatedly, the spirit of jurisprudence by attesting to the absolute liberty of judicial authorities in determining the modalities of capital sentencing. "Has a live child been intentionally aborted," both constitutions proclaim, male perpetrators of the homicide "ought to be put to the sword," females "drowned or," as the passage continues, "be brought to death in some other way." Cruelty coupled with theoretical disregard for the tangible aspects of punishment figured again as emblematic of the advancing juristic culture.[6]

In the records of adjudication, court cases concerned with criminal abortion spell out the significance of what the Ius commune abstractly defined as extraordinary retribution. Starting in 1324, the activities of public lay prosecution in the city-state of Venice were documented in a run of volumes kept by the so-called *Avogaria di comun.* Its officials consistently adhered to the norms of Romano-canonical procedure, regardless of the fact that the final rulings were entrusted not to a single judge but to a commission of forty (in dialect, *quarantia*) sworn members, most of whom lacked extensive juristic training. In dealing with infant death, the quarantia arrived at verdicts that never departed from the established scholastic standards. The oldest presently identified trial from Italy treating abortion as a secular *crimen* involved Clara de Arbo, a young maid serving in the house of Iohannes de Puteo. On June 16, 1490, a panel of Venetian commissioners decided by majority vote to inflict the pena extraordinaria on Clara. Nearly three months earlier, at the dawn of March 26, a dead baby boy had been found in the latrine of her patron's home, whereupon preliminary inquisitiones were launched and witnesses confirmed that Clara had recently been pregnant. Clara for her part readily admitted that she had conceived offspring with Michael Bergomensis, a guard stationed on Saint Mark's Square, and had miscarried some five or six months afterward. A total of thirty-six jurors cast their ballots, with three undecided, seven against, and twenty-six in favor of fuller investigations.

---

5. Locarno (1588), rubr. 127, in Andreas Heusler, "Rechtsquellen des Kantons Tessin IV," *Zeitschrift für schweizerisches Recht* 14 (1895): 317, reprinted separately (Basle: Helbing & Lichtenhan, 1895), 65. Concerning the customary punishment of the *Rad* (wheel), Ekkehard Kaufmann, "Rädern," in *HRG* 4 (1990): 135–138.

6. *Consitutio criminalis Bambergensis*, art. 158, copied into the *Constitutio criminalis Carolina*, art. 133, ed. Kohler and Scheel, 1:69, 2:64.

After weeks of additional scrutiny, they came to the following conclusion: "Clara is to be beaten in the torture chamber with twenty-five floggings and then to be placed on a podium at the third hour of this Saturday. There she must wear in shame a pointed hat [*mitra ignominiosa*] until the ninth hour, before being locked up in prison for the duration of three months."[7]

Clara's treatment faithfully corresponded to academic assessments of criminal liability. She did not acknowledge guilt apart from having hidden her premature delivery and the secret burial of her baby. Because eyewitnesses attesting to the manslaughter were unavailable, the penalty of death had to give way to arbitrary retribution excluding permanent physical injury. Whippings, public exposure to ridicule, and jail time were in line with the fate of other Venetian defendants whose nascent children were said to have died under parallel circumstances. In 1445, one female suspect confessed to having silently disposed of her stillborn progeny, after which the quarantia, faced with half proof, decided to order three months of "incarceration in the lower quarters" (*in carcere inferiorum*). In 1475, Lucia Sclabona resisted through two sessions of questioning by torturous means, always reiterating her initial admission of having concealed the miscarriage of a previously deceased boy. Lucia was condemned to carry a "crown" painted with devilish images, stand on a raised pole between two columns from the third to the ninth hour of a Saturday, and be flogged and driven from Saint Mark's Square to the Rialto Bridge. The Venetian jurors clearly avoided maximum punishment unless intent and effect could be proven as required by Bolognese jurisprudence. When a second Lucia, the illegitimate daughter of Nicolaus de Neapoli, bore a baby girl in 1451 and allegedly threw her into the latrine, she received only four months in carceribus. What saved her life was that the murderous gesture did not translate into fact and the abandoned creature survived.[8]

Legal theorists identified execution summarily as the ordinary consequence of abortion and infanticide, leaving further definition of the appropriate format to leges and statuta issued by local lay authority. Already widespread in

---

7. Venice, AS, Reg. 3657, fol. 41r, printed in *Die Abtreibung*, 245n429. The registers of the quarantia have been described and analyzed by Ruggiero, *Violence*, 18–26, and by Elisabeth Crouzet-Pavan, *Espace, pouvoir et société à Venise à la fin du moyen âge*, 2 vols. (Rome: École française de Rome, 1992), 1:20–22.

8. Venice, AS, Reg. 3650, fol. 21r–v (27 September 1451); Venice, AS, Reg. 3654, fol. 20v (24 April 1475); AS, Reg. 3649, fol. 95 (22 September 1445); partly transcribed in *Die Abtreibung*, 237n413, 244n426–428; also Claudio Povolo, "Note per uno studio dell'infanticidio nella repubblica di Venezia nei secoli *XV–XVIII*," *Atti dell'Istituto veneto di scienze, lettere ed arti* 137 (1978–1979): 115–131.

Roman antiquity, the differentiation of punishment depending on the sex of offenders also permeated punitive practice in the later Middle Ages, to the point where Jehan Faudier of Eu in Normandy revealed his awareness of gendered penae at a moment of great personal distress. Jehan's daughter Marion, who through forcible and incestuous intercourse had become pregnant by him, strongly resisted his idea of preventing prosecution and public infamy by way of repeatedly imbibing an abortifacient potion. In Marion's lettre de remission of 1453, Jehan was cited as having exclaimed that once he was discovered as the administrator of pocula abortionis, "he would be hanged" and Marion's "mother burned," which indeed marked the common difference in treatment for men and women.[9] After statutory legislation passed by the Italian communes, it almost appears as though burning was reserved to everybody found guilty of homicide associated with birth. Yet testimony from the court records shows that communal lawgivers simply presumed the act to involve female rather than male culprits.

It was the stake that awaited adulterous wives accused of infanticide in three cases registered by the Florentine judiciary in 1390, 1412, and 1433.[10] At Paris, a chronicle compiled by Jean de Roye and dedicated to sensational affairs, reported for 1466 the hanging of a big-bodied Norman who for an extended period had kept one of his children as a lover and killed several babies resulting from the relationship. His filial accomplice was subjected to burning in the village of Maigny near Pontoise. Not much later, Jehanne Hardouyne from la Beliardère in Poitou explained in her request for pardon of 1473 that she had long denied responsibility for the slaying of her newborn. Among various subterfuges, she had told authorities that the fatality was provoked by a disconcerting incident. It involved a group of wandering soldiers who set a bakery afire while she was in the shop and about to fetch flour. After changing her version of the truth several times, Jehanne finally broke down, admitted the killing, and was sentenced to perish in the flames.[11]

It is true that there were numerous exceptions to the rule. By 1300 the judicial habit of burying perpetrators alive had become a rarity in the core

9. Paris, AN, JJ 184, no. 303 (March 1453): "Sesdiz pere et mere lui repondrent que se elle en dist mot qu'ilz la tueroient et murdroient en disant par icelluy feu [pere] que se l'on en savoit qu'il seroit pendu et destruit et sa mere arse."

10. Florence, AS, Giudice degli appelli 100/1, fol. 355r (28 June 1390); ibid., 102/2, fol. 201v–202r (9 July 1433); Florence, AS, Podestà 4261, fol. 2r–v (27 January 1412); cf. Cohn, Sex and Violence, 100–101; Zorzi, "Le esecuzioni," 184–205.

11. Paris, AN, JJ 197, no. 257 (January 1473), ed. Guerin, in Archives historiques de Poitou 38 (1909): 343–346 (no. 1515); Journal de Jean de Roye, ed. Bernard de Mandrot, 2 vols. (Paris: Renouard, 1894), 1:166.

areas of the Ius commune but survived well into the early modern period in some of the more peripheral regions. An inquest into abbatial rights of secular jurisdiction recorded in 1273 by the monastery of Saint-Maur near Paris recounts how people at Ozoir-la-Ferrière still remembered Emelota, "the carpentress" (*fabrissa*), who, formerly wedded to the late Richard, had been charged with fatally submerging her infant. She was condemned by the abbot to have her home razed and suffer death through interment.[12] From times before the full reception of Bolognese jurisprudence in southern German territories, a rural verdict (*weistum*) of 1418 documents the live burial of a female "child destroyer"(*kindsverdilgerin*) at Breuungenborn, near Idar-Oberstein, and a second text from 1497 may allude to the same mode of execution at Kirchheim on the Neckar River.[13] In greater geographical and cultural vicinity to the schools of law, sources highlight a whole spectrum of methods to stage capital retribution. Pardoned on Good Friday of 1395, the confessed infanticide Peronelle Hourie, a resident of Chastelneuf in Angoulême, had been pushed into the Charente to drown with her hands tied to her body. The court of Chauroux in the Loire valley preferred to punish Katherine Meunier, convicted in 1476, with hanging, whereas a book of sentences from Ferrara notes that in September of 1444, Bortolomia, the daughter of Jacomo Mestra, was decapitated for having killed a little girl (*puta*). Exactly a century earlier, Bolognese authorities had sentenced Borghina Cristofori to the same fate.[14] In March 1427, inhabitants from the Tuscan town of San Miniato, then under Florentine governance, witnessed how Lucia de Boninsegna, a young mother found guilty of secretly smothering her newborn, was delivered to the executioner to have her head cut off. Many other women from Florence and its dependent territories must have faced the ax, too, considering that a minimum of two convictions for the fugitives Antonia Pauli Simonis of Valdelsa

---

12. Paris, AN, LL 46, fol. 229r; Paris, AN, LL 48, fol. 105v, in Terroine, *Un abbé*, 139–140; cf. Tanon, *Histoire* 334. Another inquest to assert monastic jurisdiction over infanticide is preserved at Aurillac, Archives Municipales, FF 2, no. 29 (11 May 1284), in Roger Grand, *Le paix d'Aurillac. Études et documents sur l'histoire des institutions municipales d'une ville à consulat* (Paris: Sirey, 1945), 129 (doc. XVIII).

13. Breuungenborn (1418), in *Deutsche Rechtsalterthümer*, ed. Jacob Grimm, vol. 1 (Göttingen: Dieterich, 1828), 794; Kirchheim (1497), in *Sammlung altwürttembergischer Statutarrechte*, ed. [August] Reyscher (Tübingen: Fues, 1834), 528.

14. Bologna, AS, Curia del podestà, Libri inquisitionum et testium 161/1, fol. 18r–v; Bologna, AS, Curia del podestà, Accusationes 50b/16 (September 1344), first indicated by Dean, *Crime in Medieval Europe*, 79; Ferrara, Biblioteca Comunale, MS Cl. I 404, fol. 1v (26 September 1444); Paris, AN, JJ 204, no. 42 (April 1476), cf. Chevalier, *Le pays de la Loire*, 367 (no. 3542); Paris, AN, JJ 147, no. 240 (April 1395), copied into Paris, AN, AB XIX 205A, no. 180/249.

and, from inside the city walls, Clara de Perusio, occurred during the short interval from January to April 1412.[15]

Substitute Penalties

Limiting the description of late medieval crime to the official language of those who adjudicated means that much of what historically determined prosecutions remains unstated. Trial documentation served to stress the adherence to procedural principles, emphasize the absolute centrality of courtroom activities, and extol the capacity of inquisitorial judges and juries to reach unilateral and binding decisions. At the same time, the sources contain remarks that, in the form of brief asides and rhetorical commonplaces, illustrate how events associated with inquisitiones and accusationes were instigated and piloted by forces active in conjunction with tribunals and throughout the community, legally as well as politically. In cases of prenatal and natal death, if not homicide in general, it is therefore important to remember that the vast majority of investigations were initiated by private accusers; that punitive charges of miscarriage by assault manifested the desire of families to harass rivals or prod them into compensatory payments; and that most allegations resulting in repressive action affected the unprotected, the poor, and the marginal, with a strong preference for the sentencing of persons who lived unattached or estranged from respectable households. The better an individual was entrenched in networks of solidarity with peers, relatives, and friends, the less realistic were his or her chances of being discovered and severely punished. In adopting the viewpoint of litigants who, in Daniel Smail's formulation, came forward to act as "consumers of justice," then, modern interpreters have reason to imagine the inquisitores as officers regulating a particular kind of traffic. Empowered by scholastic doctrine, they were supposed to steer social tension away from spontaneous vengeance and toward peaceful resolution rather than behaving as authoritative figures who imposed abstract norms on suspects and adversaries alike.[16]

Plaintiffs launching criminal accusations must have been motivated by hopes of bringing, in the person of the inquisitor, an important ally onto

---

15. Florence, AS, Podestà 4261, fol. 2r9v (27 January 1412); Florence, Podestà 4261, fol. 34r–35v and 104v–105r (7 April 1412); Florence, AS, Giudice degli appelli 76, fol. 282r–283v (3 March 1427); cf. Maria Serena Mazzi, "Cronache di periferia dello stato fiorentino. Reati contro la morale nel primo quattrocento," *Studi storici* 27 (1986): 629–630. Florentine criminal sentences of the period refer to the killed newborn as "viable" rather than animated, *vivens et qui in futurum vivere potuisset,* which may indicate that secular judges were held (by local statute?) to treat infanticide against the Ius commune more rigorously than abortion.

16. Smail, *Consumption of Justice,* 7–22; and chapter 2.

their side. For clans and families at loggerheads with hostile neighbors, the judges of the Ius commune wielded considerable procedural weapons, capable of forcing antagonists into submission or at least of persuading them to adopt a more conciliatory attitude. When trials got under way, the coercive arsenal of Romano-canonical procedure allowed for immediate citation of the presumed culprit. If suspects acted "contumaciously" by refusing to appear in court, theory demanded that their movable property be confiscated; and where, to the contrary, summonses were obeyed, incarceration of unspecified duration, torture, and execution loomed as formidable threats depending on the quality of allegations. Most of the accused did not have to ponder eventual death to be intimidated. What frequently impressed them sufficiently was the likelihood of jail time, application of which rested on a discretionary inquisitorial assessment of the available proof. Jurisprudence did not place firm restrictions on the maximum length of preliminary arrest, which induced many of the arraigned to escape justice at the earliest stage of the proceedings. For the accuser, flight implied that the opening round of altercations had been won, as the prosecutorial mechanisms were beginning to work to the detriment of his opponent. Assuming that both parties, and especially the defendant's, commanded adequate public respect, courtroom activities could also give way to informal meetings at the negotiation table.

Extant references to late medieval abortion and infanticide cases indicate that a considerable proportion of the accused eluded prosecutors by fleeing into sanctuary. Others went abroad. Quick relocation beyond the limits of the secular ban worked best in the fragmented political landscapes of northern Italy and southern Germany, while in more consolidated and larger princely territories church asylum provided the usual refuge from interrogation and punishment. Legal attitudes regarding escape on sacred ground have not been studied very thoroughly except for the two medieval kingdoms of England and France. It is nevertheless obvious that, long before the rise of Western Christianity and jurisprudence, religiously exempt areas invited disputants to settle through peaceful bargaining. By 1200, English common law had formalized the rights and obligations inherent in the matter, with defendants being compelled to accept the criminal verdicts of the crown or forsake their belongings, abjure the realm, and go into exile.[17] Across the British Channel, the French mon-

---

17. Karl Shoemaker, *Sanctuary and Crime in the Middle Ages, 400–1500* (New York: Fordham University Press, 2011) 112–151; Helmholz, *The Ius Commune in England*, 14–58. J. Charles Cox, *The Sanctuaries and Sanctuary Seekers of Mediaeval England* (London: Allen & Sons, 1911), is still unsurpassed for its wealth of documentation.

archy was establishing comparable guidelines, although expatriation was never enforced with equal stringency. A lettre de remission, submitted by Agnes Metars from Paris in April of 1469, mentions in passing her retreat to the consecrated confines of a cemetery. Having confessed the murder of her baby and left the king's jurisdictional reach (*en franchise*), she had to stay put with her legs chained to a block of iron. Without the receipt of a pardon, her uncomfortable situation might have persisted for years to come. Alternatively, she would have endured confiscation and perennial expulsion from the *royaume*.[18]

For those who failed to evade capture, Romano-canonical procedure, especially in the restrictions it placed on admissible evidence, provided safeguards that, as noted in chapter 7, turned final sentencing into an extremely arduous affair. During trial, however, the criminal investigators were not shackled by extravagant formalities. In January 1446, Ozanne Boisselelle, charged with the death of her newborn child, had been jailed for three years at Montaigu, near Nantes. She had intitially offered a partial admission of guilt by confirming the concealment of her pregnancy and delivery, and thus the inquiries against her had come to a grinding halt. Ozanne had encountered a situation of procedural deadlock created by half proof, which for the theorists of the Ius commune did not justify full conviction. There was, on the other hand, no maximum term of incarceration to secure her timely release, and fleeting mention of long detention in Ozanne's personal request for pardon suggests the relative normalcy of her predicament.[19] Many French supplicants in fact maintained that they had sent their petitions to the king after protracted periods behind bars. The discretionary treatment of defendants could become as taxing as for Jehan Valat, whom records identify as having earned his living by running a mill not far from Montmorillon in Poitou. In a lettre of May 1448, Jehan recounted how he had been tied to an iron chain over the winter and endured three sessions of torturing. Accused of encis because he had angrily beaten Perrete Sufferte, the daughter of his wife, with a stick, Jehan was first ordered to cover two months of salary for his own prison guard. Then at last he was able to regain his liberty. The court decided to relent when friends came forward and promised to serve as

---

18. Paris, AN, JJ 195, no. 228 (April 1469), copied into AN, AB XIX, 205A, no.180/254; cf. Brissaud, "Infanticide," 238n34. On the treatment of sanctuary in the royal courts, Gauvard, *De grace especial*, 1:204–227.

19. Paris, AN, JJ 177, no. 137, ed. Guérin, in *Archives historiques de Poitou* 29 (1898): 239–241 (no. 1084); cf. de Carbonnières, *La procédure*, 222–254; Guy Geltner, *The Medieval Prison: A Social History* (Princeton, NJ: Princeton University Press, 2008), 1–10.

his pledges, although he was still left strained financially and unable to travel without permit.[20]

The pardon for Jehan Valat relates several details that undercut the officially intended impression of a case obeying standards of due process always and to the letter. As an owner of property, Jehan likely enjoyed considerable social recognition, which may have persuaded him not to flee arrest. And yet something went wrong for him, given that the prosecutors used relatively weak allegations of prenatal death by way of percussio to initiate full-fledged criminal proceedings. At present, Jehan is uniquely remembered as an individual who in connection with miscarriage by assault was explicitly subjected to three sessions of torture. The investigators further extracted reimbursement for his incarceration, although this was illegal with conviction still pending. Clearly, institutional harassment rather than the ordinary administration of scholastically inspired justice characterized events in the registered version of Jehan's narrative, which went unaltered through a final round of verification by the local authorities.[21] Jehan Valat appears to have been the victim of a scheme devised to rid him of his possessions.

Defendants wary of loyalties within their group could enter a church located in the vicinity, frustrate captors by escaping to foreign territories, or improve their lot by combining the search for sanctuary with long-distance voyages to popular pilgrimage sites. In Jehanne Ternarde's petition for remission of punishment, read to the king during her imprisonment at Soissy on the Loire in 1488, she is described as having hidden her pregnancy from late in gestation to birth. According to her testimony, the baby died shortly after the delivery, whereupon Jehanne went, accompanied by her brother, to the cathedral of Orleans, confessed her sins, and accepted the priestly imposition of "grant penitence." For the rest of her life, Jehanne was told to fast "a certain number of Fridays each year."[22] In response to abortion and infanticide, asylum or imprisonment stood frequently at the end of voluntary journeys by contrite defendants to particular places of worship. Having slain a newborn out of fear her husband might sense the child was not really his, Jehannette Secrestain went annually to the penitentiary of Saint-Hilary at

---

20. Paris, AN, JJ 179, no. 226, ed. Guérin, in *Archives historiques de Poitou* 32 (1903): 71–73 (no. 1159).

21. Royal lettres de remission required that their truthfulness be confirmed by the originally investigating court. Failure to pass the test prompted cancellation of the pardon as *surreptice* in the registers, cf. Gauvard, *De grace especial*, 1: 30–41.

22. Paris, AN, JJ 225, no. 255 (April 1488); cf. Chevalier, *Le pays de la Loire*, 367 (no. 3542): "Duquel cas elle se confessa et luy fut enjoinct grant penitence et de jeuner toute sa vie certaine quantite de vendrediz per chacun an lesquelz elle a accompli jusques a present."

Poitiers to receive absolution, a routine she kept up for several decades. Her guilt did not come to light until 1458, some thirty years past the incriminating act. And about 1400, Jean Durant from Poitou journeyed all the way to Rome for spiritual atonement. He was tormented by the fact of having assisted a woman in the killing of her offspring.[23] According to the lettres de remission, the culprits were restored to righteousness after having shown remorse and undergone certified sacramental cleansing, which prompted the royal addressee to confer judicial grace in imitation of God Himself.

Defensive and prosecutorial tactics carried decisive weight when it came to the determination of late medieval criminal punishment. Judges were permitted to handle questioning with relative arbitrariness, a method many of them used to compensate for the multiple procedural obstacles to definitive sentencing. Preliminary incarceration, for example, provided the inquisitor with a device to force adversarial negotiations in his presence, allowing him to chart the outcome of trials proactively. More easily traced in the historical sources, his wide discretion in the mandating of arrests alleviated the risk of judicial paralysis that, brought on by the lack of coercive capabilities on the part of investigators, discouraged the infliction of punitive measures as long as they were based on little except circumstantial evidence. Short of two eye-witnesses or the defendant's full confession, inquisitors in France, unlike their colleagues from the Venetian quarantia, often let the accused go, whether proceedings strongly suggested the existence of a crimen or rendered it a remote possibility. Instead of resorting to the straightforward imposition of minor penae extraordinariae, they used the rigors and unspecified length of imprisonment during inquiries, if not forcible interrogation, as substitute means of retribution, which amounted to formal penalties in all but name.

In the eyes of Pierre de Pilemer, the sous-prevot from Provins in the Brie region, there were rather strong, if indirect, clues that pointed to willful infanticide in the case of Agnes, the daughter of Colin le Codinet. For months, Pierre had conducted his interrogations, until, on May 2, 1339, he abandoned his quest for maximum punishment and restored the suspect to her freedom. Technically speaking, there was no conviction. But Agnes received a significant discount for the many judicial hardships she had endured:

> Having reviewed and considered the confession of the aforementioned
> Agnes, and the presumptions speaking out vehemently against her, and

23. Paris, AN, JJ 155, no. 126 (May 1400), ed. Guérin, in *Archives historiques de Poitou* 24 (1893): 352–354 (no. 860); AN, JJ 188, no. 3 (November 1458), ed. Guérin, in *Archives historiques de Poitou* 35 (1906): 84–88 (no. 1295).

in view of the torments, interrogations, and long imprisonment she has suffered, and because of the above information and the fact that the said Agnes always persevered in her admissions without ever varying anything . . ., we lawfully and by our final sentence have absolved and absolve Agnes from the case insofar as it befits our duty as the judge.[24]

Discretionary sentencing could further come disguised as a conditional pardon that, not unlike the coercive measures factored in by Pierre de Pilemer, mimicked extraordinary punishment while being sharply distinct from it in juristic terms. A good number of lettres de remission issued by the French crown tied legal rehabilitation to the fulfillment of certain tasks, which on occasion emulated works of spiritual redemption to the point of complete identity. The king's willingness to remit crime was seen as akin to a religious act, already evident from the dating of his interventions that often coincided with high Christian holidays. Instead of following the annual calendar in days and months, royal grace is said to have been granted "the week in which our Savior Jesus Christ suffered passion and death," during sojourns at the grave of an important saint, or as "the period of pious fasting" got under way.[25] Additionally, the lettres combine assurances of impunity with assignments deemed appropriate for the cleansing of tainted souls. Exercises of mortification included the abstention from food and drink other than bread and water, prayer for the victims, and the celebration of masses in memory of the dead.[26] Most common among the quasi-canonical prerequisites for reinstatement were pious pilgrimages. Confessors at sacred destinations located across the realm, but not beyond, were to issue certificates confirming that the pardoned visitor had appeared in person and performed his penance as ordered. Despite the scholastic insistence on a neat separation between the clerical and worldly spheres, nobody suspected that, in this particular instance, any improper blending of secular and ecclesiastical jurisdictions was at hand. Although in June 1390 church superiors had long

---

24. Paris, AN, JJ 71, no. 304 (June 1339); cf. *Registres* 3.2, ed. Viard and Vallée, 93 (no. 3785); also chap. 7, notes 14–15.

25. Paris, AN, JJ 172, no. 430 (March 1424), in *Paris pendant la domination anglaise (1420–1436). Documents extraits des registres de la Chancellerie de France*, ed. Auguste Longnon (Paris: Champion, 1878), 130–133 (no. 65): "Pour ce saint temps de karesme ou nous sommes de present." AN, JJ 208, no. 48 (January 1481); cf. Chevalier, *Le pays de la Loire*, 387 (no. 3742): "En honneur et reverence . . . du glorieux confesseur amy de Dieu Sainct Ylaire de Poictiers en l'eglise duquel ou reppose son precieulx corps nous a este facte ladicte supplicacion." AN, JJ 158, no. 293 (March 1404), ed. Guérin, in *Archives historiques de Poitou* 26 (1896): 25–32 (no. 893): "Pour l'onneur et reverence de la sepmaine saincte en laquelle nous sommes de present."

26. Gauvard, *De grace especial*, 2:904–934, for the various terms of conditional pardon.

absolved Colette Wardevoir from the attempted murder of her baby, the royal remission of the crime compelled her yet again to wander barefoot and in repentance to the cathedral of Chartres. To prove that the visit had fulfilled its purpose, she was told to return with due *certifficacion*.[27]

Repeatedly, pardoning would also depend on qualifications along the lines of lesser criminal punishment. The extreme range of arbitrary penalties, which in the Ius commune precluded only the infliction of permanent physical damage, is illustrated by the two confessed infanticides, Philippe Dandonelle and Antoine Clairhout, whose fate in court could not have been more diverse. In mid-August of 1444, Philippe had married Jehan Meschinot from the village of Pouzauges in Poitou. Shortly after All-Saints Day in November, she delivered a child fathered by someone other than her spouse. Philippe Dandonelle hastily performed emergency baptism on the unwanted newborn. The atrocity of what happened next is barely obscured by the written record: "With one hand, she grabbed the head and with the other the neck, thereby killing the baby girl." As the king's councillors pondered the case, they were unmoved by Philippe's tantalizing description of the homicide. She was absolved without further ado. Not so Antoine Clairhout, who belonged to a noble family from Flanders. Early in 1455, the young lady had cut the throat of her infant and lowered the body into a water-filled ditch. Her petition, which in May of the same year was submitted to the Burgundian chancery of Philip the Good, elaborated that Antoine had subsequently "stayed for a little longer to see if the corpse would sink" to the bottom. To save her life, Antoine was compelled to enter a monastery and accept permanent enclosure. The duke confiscated her landed possessions together with rights and revenues, apart from a modest annual pension Antoine was allowed to retain.[28]

It seems that French monarchs rarely followed Pierre de Pilemer's example and combined absolution with the recipient's immediate release. In 1392, one female defendant did obtain credit for "the long and severe *penitance* she has suffered and is still undergoing in the form of imprisonment."[29] Far more

---

27. Paris, AN, JJ 138, no. 272 (June 1390), copied into AN, AB XIX 205A, no. 180/247: "Pourveu que icelle Colete sera . . . tenu de faire pelerinage a Notre Dame de Chartres piez nuz et en rapportera certifficacion."

28. Lille, AD, B 1686, fol. 27v (May 1455), in Petit-Dutaillies, *Documents nouveaux*, 19–22 (no. 5); Paris, AN, JJ 177, no. 26 (January 1445), ed. Guérin, in *Archives historiques de Poitou* 29 (1898): 197–200 (no. 1522).

29. Paris, AN, JJ 142, no. 103 (February 1392), in Bologne, *La naissance interdite*, 287–288, in imitation of Pierre de Pilemer's logic, above note 24.

frequent, however, were royal pardons that stalled rehabilitation by means of temporary bans and incarceration. Either within or outside the kingdom, exile drove many petitioners away from home. Some were authorized to leave and go no farther than "ten miles from the location of their crime," with the added restriction in a mandate of 1414 that such exile had to last for the duration of a year.[30] Other remissions foresaw jailing at a reduced diet of "bread and water," the length of which did not exceed six months and oddly resembled penalties in fifteenth-century Venetian sentences, passed arbitrarily and on account of half-proven abortion or infanticide. In September 1382, Annette de Busson, an escapee staying en franchise, was invited to leave the sanctuary in exchange for two months *es nos prisons;* Jehanne le Ruyer, accused of *encis* by the prior of Saint-Martin-des-Champs in 1396, was detained for one month; and Jehannette Canelesle from Peronne after allegations of miscarriage through poisoning in 1399 was held for six. A combination of punitive elements characterized the formal exculpation of Alyson Taneurre in October 1425, convicted of fetal homicide by means of abortifacient potions. She was to be freed upon payment of civil damages, permanent expulsion from the town of Beaune, and two months of strict captivity.[31] Evidently a tight correlation existed between princely discretion and that of ordinary *inquisitores*. Whenever scholastic doctrine granted the right to dispense justice arbitrarily, rulers and criminal judges invoked the same moral, legal, and religious standards.

Adjustment Out of Court

Claude Gauvard's analysis of *lettres de remission* from the time around 1400 has shown that suspects of homicide frequently opted for the flight onto safe ground. Upon reaching sanctuary or an undisclosed location, they would await news of possible prosecutorial action against them and stay in close contact with friends and relatives who helped process requests of pardon during trial or as part of a subsequent appeal.[32] French criminal judges conversely sought to imprison defendants for indefinite periods while revealing

---

30. Paris, AN, JJ 168, no. 51 (November 1414), copied into AN, AB XIX 205A, no. 180/254: "Pourveu qu'elle sera un an entier bannye ou regne a dix lieues loing du lieu ou ledit cas est avenu sans y aler ne traverser en aucune manière."

31. AN, JJ 173, no. 244 (October 1425): "Elle sera pugnie civilement et demoura a tousiours bannie de ladicte ville de Beaunes et si demourra deux mois au pain et en prison fermee"; AN, JJ 154, no. 310 (July 1399); AN, JJ 151, no. 9 (December 1396); AN, JJ 121, no. 172 (September 1382); cf. Brissaud, "Infanticide," 238n35.

32. Gauvard, *De grace especial*, 1:214–250, 2:941–955; de Carbonnières, *La procédure*, 5–67.

little desire to rush the passing of punitive sentences. Where the proof of guilt did not exceed circumstantial clues, inquisitors like Pierre de Pilemer prolonged the investigations before releasing the accused in recognition of prior judicial duress. Along the same lines, academic jurisprudence defined the criteria for preliminary detention very loosely but established exacting norms for proceedings to begin and for the implementation of maximum penalties. The proceduralists of the Ius commune were less interested in the swift initiation or conclusion of prosecutions than in keeping accusations, once they had been lawfully brought, under the control of tribunals and fully focused on the individual being charged. Late medieval criminal procedure, in other words, again recommended the work of prescholastic mediators in that adjudication continued to concentrate first, on separating offenders from their support groups and second, on preventing retribution and altercation from relapsing into extrajudicial affairs, with threats of violence and collective revenge erupting in squares and streets. Juristic unwillingness to summon alleged culprits in the absence of private accusers or overwhelming evidence and qualms about the infliction of punishment also point to the lack of leverage among the inquisitores, who rarely found themselves in a position to administer justice unilaterally and from above.

Contrary to the ways in which ordinary criminal cases of abortion and infanticide were treated in France, the Venetian authorities had no particular reservations about imposing capital or lesser arbitrary penalties on those convicted. To explain the discrepancy, it could be argued that within the restricted space of an urban republic the coercive capabilities were greater than in the vast rural hinterland of the French realm. Yet the fact remains that in both communal Italy and areas across the western Alps, the social station of those recorded to have been condemned or pardoned did not differ very significantly. Intense personal profiling must have preceded official inquiries in Venice, given that indictments were based on a majority vote cast by the members of the quarantia, all of whom were chosen from among the well-connected members of society. As a result, the registered incidents of prenatal and natal homicide always implicate unwedded servant girls, parallel to testimony from the lettres de remission that single women without sufficient attachment to local networks of respectability and patriarchy faced exceptionally precarious judicial circumstances.[33] Exposed to the

---

33. Between 1324 and 1500, all known cases of infanticide (ten) and abortion (one) from Venice involved domestic servants, cf. notes 7–8 above, and chap. 9, notes 15, 27 below. Most French lettres address unmarried females; one rare exception not concerned with miscarriage by assault is cited in chap. 6, note 29.

highest risk of prosecution were widows, young domestics, and adulterous wives who secretly bore children not fathered by their respective husbands.[34] Clearly, many legal and extralegal mechanisms were put in place to whittle down, stage by stage, the number of alleged perpetrators until only people acceptable to the community as villains had been selected for sentencing and final humiliation. Judges pressured by solidarity groups had to think twice before keeping relatives in prison for too long; they had to forgo torture when scrutinizing honorable burghers with special privileges exempting them from interrogation by force; and they readily accepted bail from the affluent instead of mandating their instant incarceration. Last, the inquisitors also allowed the wealthy to seek representation by proctors, whose expertise contributed to the recurrent abandonment of judicial suits. Social bargaining, in sum, affected the outcome of proceedings more strongly than any abstract notion of equity in the minds of presiding court officials.

Expressed in the language of economics, late medieval judges employed the procedural formats of the Ius commune to increase market share in an environment that bristled with alternative methods of conflict management. Older historiography has exaggerated the extent of authoritative intervention on the part of criminal judiciaries, because anachronistic ideas of monopolistic enforcement were read back into the past or conclusions rested on highly politicized incidents rather than everyday prosecution. More recently, research undertaken by Massimo Vallerani and others has demonstrated that cities under the influence of academic jurisprudence such as thirteenth-century Bologna and Perugia in northern and central Italy still investigated offenses defined as capital without particular emphasis on "absolute" and nonpecuniary sentencing. By far the greatest percentage of crime litigation concerned, according to their findings, private accusations. These rarely resulted in conviction, let alone full physical punishment, and so they permitted defendants with regularity to prevent the loss of face and incapacitating legal infamy. Inquisitors on the whole were content to transform bodily retribution into payments and had few objections to settlements out of court, provided that they were monitored closely and served as a catalyst for the restoration of civic peace.[35] The containment of proceedings within tribunals, sponsored by governments and staffed with professional

---

34. In Florence around 1400, the accusation of adulterous spouses was commonplace; see note 10, above.

35. Massimo Vallerani, *La giustizia pubblica medievale* (Bologna: Il Mulino, 2005), 75–111; Trevor Dean, *Crime and Justice in Late Medieval Italy* (Cambridge: Cambridge University Press, 2007), 17–51; Sarah Blanshei, *Politics and Justice in Late Medieval Bologna* (Leiden: Brill, 2010), 313–366, 484–497.

jurists, was paramount. Difficulties in promoting scholastic legal expertise at the expense of customary modes of composition, mediation, and self-help are visible as well in the disparity between recorded summonses and final convictions. Hardly any charges of miscarriage by assault led to the passing of a guilty verdict. The pleas instead produced declarations of innocence or agreements between parties or simply petered out. It is impossible to account for the imbalance unless the documented activities were in reference to much broader scenarios of rivalry and strife.

The deeper the resources available to plaintiffs and defendants, the fuller the picture that emerges from the surviving records. To illustrate the impact of extrajudicial schemes, the registers kept by the criminal branch of the Parlement de Paris report for 1340 that a knight named Hugues Adémar was charged by Pierre de Massaut with the enforced abduction of his daughter, the beating of his wife, Helaïs, and her consequent encis. As the proceedings started, Pierre failed to attend a court date set for July 21, not arriving at the Parlement until four weeks later. The delay may not have been due to a fault of his but may have occurred because a mandate to appear had never been delivered to him in person. His adversaries, headed by Hugues Adémar, tried to insinuate all the same that because of Pierre's absence inquiries should be halted, whereupon the royal judges decided to delegate the matter back to the tribunal of the Périgord and have the opponents convene with local officials, originally on March 19, 1341, then postponed twice, to November 1341 and July 15, 1342. It also turned out that the king's senechal in the region was partly responsible for the repeated adjournments, given that the Parlement urged him to intensify his investigations just nine days after the second July gathering. Still, more time had to pass before another order, dated July 8, 1344, was issued at Paris to arrest Hugues de la Barda, a close friend of the principal suspect. The addressee was believed to have suppressed a letter of citation, presumably the one that had made Pierre de Massaut miss his initial arraignment of July 21 some four years earlier. The case dragged on, pro-ducing notices that restricted the freedom of the accused to the limits of the Parisian ban and *citationes* enjoining litigation to continue before the senechal of the Périgord. Once the members of the Parlement had granted Hugues Adémar representation by proxy on May 30, 1346, however, the cumbersome affair stopped leaving traces in the documentation for good.[36]

By picturing constant and open-ended negotiation between officials and the larger community as essential to late medieval criminal prosecutions,

---

36. Paris, AN, X 2a 4, fol. 8r, 55v, 79v, 85v, 110r, 131v, 132v, 136v, 170v; AN, X 2a 5, fol. 15v, 67v; cf. Labat-Poussin et al., *Actes du Parlement*, 123, 149, 165, 169, 189, 208, 210, 213, 223, 246, 270.

modern observers gain perspective on the final act of exemplary capital punishment. Besides deterrence and the visible excitement of moral drama, the theatricality marking infliction of the death penalty afforded one last display and verification of the public consensus. Albeit definitive in a formal sense, the inquisitor's sentence left the door ajar for new rounds of social bartering as long as the defendant's demise had not yet translated into undeniable fact. Surprises at odds with preestablished outcomes always remained a possibility. In 1376, Hermin Bruguet, aged twenty-two, stepped forward to claim Hanriette, just tied to the stake, "out of pity and love" as his future spouse. In the words of Hanriette's lettre de remission, the young man vociferously demanded that she be delivered to him in marriage, whereupon the verdict of burning for infanticide was suspended and Hanriette returned to her prison cell. A century later, it was Martin Flory who urged Katherine Bellemere to become his wife moments after she had been taken to the gallows, except that, in this case, the court denied Martin's pressing request. The tide had turned all the same. "Because of the judge's refusal," Katherine lodged an appeal with the crown and went back to jail to await the king's notice.[37]

The ultimate chance for bystanders to obstruct the workings of criminal justice came when punishment did not produce the intended fatal result. Peronelle Hourie from Chastelneuf in Angoulême had prepared herself well for the agonies of death by drowning. After admitting guilt for the slaying of her baby, she had tearfully besought the Virgin Mary and God for mercy. On the day of execution, Peronelle's brothers had commissioned two masses and various prayers on her behalf in the churches. As she was conducted to a bridge and pushed into the waters of the Charente with her hands strapped tightly to her body, the crowd witnessed how she went under and then lost sight of her in the deep river. Then, as if by divine grace, Peronelle reemerged and began to float, never again dipping below the surface for long. In the end, a strong current carried the woman onto a sandbank. Spectators rushed toward the scene and freed her, nodding in agreement that a true miracle had unfolded before their eyes. "Justice ceased to proceed," the narrative accompanying Peronelle's pardon of 1395 concludes peremptorily.[38] And while modern Western opinion typically shuns public displays of capital punishment as uncivilized and cruel, people of the later Middle Ages

---

37. Paris, AN, JJ 204, no. 42 (April 1476); Chevalier, *Le pays de la Loire,* 367 (no. 3542); AN, JJ 109, no. 226 (September 1376); cf. *Die Abtreibung,* 260n450; Paul Lemercier, "Une curiosité judiciaire au moyen âge. La grâce par marriage subsequent," *RHDFE* 34 (1956): 464–474.

38. Paris, AN, JJ 147, no. 240 (Good Friday 1395), copied into AN, AB XIX 205A, no. 180/249.

would have looked with equal discomfort at the concentration of power in present-day judiciaries and at routine prosecutions reducing communal participation to a mere option, limiting the active influence of nonjurists to a narrowly understood procedural privilege and relegating the application of criminal sentences to hermetic death chambers and high-security penitentiaries. Prior to the 1500s, the judges of the Ius commune would have been ill advised to operate in similar fashion. Of central importance to them was the mood of onlookers, who stood ready to interfere both inside and outside the courtroom walls.

CHAPTER 9

The Frequency of Criminal Prosecutions

It is generally assumed in Western discourse that events of public significance such as intentional homicides enter the written record somehow and somewhere. Crime statistics suggest a tight correlation between actual incidents and cases filed by judicial institutions. For the current purpose, it is irrelevant whether the minimal difference between tangible and officially registered facts constitutes, to a higher or lesser degree, a modern myth. More important, common perceptions are correct in their estimate that administrative reporting today captures a larger proportion of unnatural deaths than ever before in human history. Possibly for the same reason, studies of past criminal behavior have tended to be overly self-referential. Historiography has noted, for example, that in the sixteenth and seventeenth centuries the total of child murderers executed in major towns like Nuremberg or Gdansk reached four to five dozen, respectively, an indication that infanticidal acts were on the rise or not particularly widespread. The count of imposed penalties and initiated prosecutions has been used to gauge the frequency of criminal behavior overall. And yet it is necessary to keep in mind that municipal and princely court registers illustrate wrongful conduct only insofar as narrowly defined procedural categories were concerned. Solely with regard to legal punishment, areas across the Rhine and Danube Rivers can be said to have faced unprecedented conditions in the years from 1550 to 1650, when local city officials hanged, burned, or beheaded convicts of prenatal and natal manslaughter at rates that easily surpassed the number of capital sentences inflicted during the Middle Ages. Whereas assertions that not long after 1500 the slaying of unwanted offspring suddenly increased and became "popular" rest on unfounded and anachronistic inferences, the prosecutorial resolve and policing capabilities certainly grew, and the output of trial documentation soon dwarfed comparable efforts of the immediately preceding era.[1]

This chapter pursues quantitative issues along three different trajectories. The opening section elaborates on observations made in the previous paragraph and questions the validity of statistical analyses that measure the recurrence of crime (as opposed to crime allegations) with greater confidence than the procedural scope of late medieval court records would warrant. In the absence of any fuller documentation on punishable wrongdoing, the following two sections investigate particular patterns of recording and discuss frequency merely in terms of, first, geographical distribution and, second, the triple format of prenatal manslaughter charges successively in evidence in most of the judicial sources. The prosecution of fetal homicidium, while omnipresent in church jurisdictions from the 1200s onward, spread in the lay sphere in close connection with the teachings of the Ius commune and, at least until 1348, the English common law. Simultaneously, there was the progression in criminal caseloads from (private) accusations of miscarriage by assault to those on account of fetal death through poisoning and, still later in time, abortion in modern parlance, undertaken by or with the consent of the child-bearing mother. What marked this prototypical shift was, arguably and above all, slow but inexorable growth in the coercive strength of public prosecutors.

Viable Statistical Queries

Medieval court records rarely speak of violent interference with pregnancies and births. The evidence for discrepancies between experienced and recorded practice is largely circumstantial, and quantitative comparisons in relative or absolute terms remain impossible. The surviving data were not relegated to written memory until they had gone through extensive rounds of screening and filtering. As noted in chapter 2, virtually all cases of felonious

1. For an overview and criticism of older scholarship on infanticide in the early modern period, see Richard van Dülmen, *Frauen vor Gericht. Kindsmord in der frühen Neuzeit* (Frankfurt/M.: Fischer, 1991), 58–75; also Ulinka Rublack, *The Crimes of Women in Early Modern Germany* (Oxford: Oxford University Press, 1999), 142–177.

miscarriage in thirteenth-century England were brought by couples seeking monetary compensation. With the help of private appeals framed as homicidal battery, they successfully dragged their adversaries into the king's tribunals. Chapter 7 further describes how, on the other side of the British Channel, restrictions in Romano-canonical procedure concerning the admissibility of capital charges implied that two eyewitnesses or the discovery of a slain baby formed the minimum requirements for trials even to begin. Partial confirmation by the defendant of a concealed delivery and the child's secret burial was also needed for interrogations to go forward. Because a woman's ability to hide unwanted offspring increased exponentially if she lived with relatives intent on preserving family honor, judges of the Ius commune were bound to investigate socially marginalized suspects far more often than well-established ones.

Just as the information preserved in criminal court rolls from England does not prove that willfully aborting mothers did not exist merely because there is no record of them, the scarce appearance of wealthy, noble, and happily married women in abortion or infanticide proceedings on the European mainland does not imply that the two acts were committed above all by the unwed and downtrodden. As highlighted in chapter 8, the rules and regulations of the Ius commune accommodated multiple mechanisms of social profiling. Despite the fact that, except for the first century of the English common law, judicial sources have not yet been studied very systematically, the available findings already point to fundamental biases in the conducting of formal inquisitiones. The Florentine commune, to begin with, was arguably among the most active of lay jurisdictions in persecuting infanticidium, considering that the cursory consultation of its rich archival depositories has brought to light at least seven capital sentences for the years from 1390 to 1433. While five convictions went against contumacious fugitives, two were followed by properly notarized executions, with each targeting the clandestine death of a baby alleged to have occurred upon delivery. The accused were either young domestic servants seeking to hide the shame of illicit intercourse or wives caught, often along with their lovers, as they were trying to conceal the visible consequences of adultery. Enraged husbands, the material intimates, could confound the protective shell of privacy in the same way as being single and dangerously removed from one's own native household and relatives.[2]

---

2. Two texts that report the actual infliction of punishment have been edited by Mazzi, "Cronache di periferia," 622–630, and Ingeborg Walter, "Infanticidio a Ponte Bocci: 2 marzo 1406. Elementi di un processo," *Studi storici* 27 (1986): 637–648; cf. also chap. 8, notes 10, 15.

Between 1329 and 1498, eleven indictments of infant murder, one perpetrated before and ten soon after birth appear in the registers of the Venetian *Avogaria di Comun*. Excluding suspects of higher social status and greater respectability, the allegations were always directed against young females who worked in a foreign environment. That members of the leading merchant class were not immune from unwanted parenthood and attempts to undo its effects would thus have remained an undocumented assumption had it not been for a joint request submitted to the Apostolic Court of Penance in Rome during the pontificate of Pope Calixtus III (1455–58). One of the two petitions was sent by a noblewoman and attests to her improved chances of keeping homicidal activities successfully from the quarantia, the panel of forty jurors adjudicating lay crime in Venice. On July 27, 1455, she received pardon and absolution from the papal Penitentiary after confessing under the sacramental seal of secrecy that she had betrayed her spouse, conceived in pursuit of an adulterous relationship, and cast the newborn into a latrine. As the supplicant did not trust her ordinary archbishop, she asked to have her case transmitted to another ecclesiastical prelate for final examination. Should the matter come to light, life-threatening scandal was likely to erupt. The lack of proof admissible in the secular courts separated her fate from that of the eleven lower-ranking town dwellers who instead endured pain and exposure as criminal defendants in the modern sense of the word.[3]

When examining the judicial pardons that historians have distilled from the royal and ducal registers of late medieval France, the Florentine and Venetian situations are subsumed into a wider perspective. Written in the time span from 1332 to 1488, dozens of texts dwell on presumed infanticidal behavior. The ones that do not cite charges of encis, or miscarriage by assault, conform to the Italian pattern in that they show the largest cohort of accused people to have come from among unmarried servants and unfaithful wives. In addition, the lettres de remission name allegations involving mature widows, male lovers, and health practitioners, who, as discussed in Chapter 7, attracted investigative curiosity because of special procedural rules that facilitated the opening of criminal trials in connection with abortifacient potions. Whenever suspicions suggested the administration of pocula abortionis,

---

3. Rome, APA Reg. div. 5, fol. 78v: "Mulier nupta nobilis Venetiarum exponit quod ipsa olim eius marito longo tempore absente cum alio viro concubuit ex quo prolem procreavit quam prolem instigante diabolo super latrinam parturiendo et prohiciendo suffocavit . . .; et quod super huiusmodi absolutione eligere possint confessorem attenta suspicione ordinarii et scandalis que sequi possint de periculo mortis." The eleven cases of the *Avogaria del Comun* are listed in chap. 8, notes 7–8; below, notes 15, 27; *Die Abtreibung*, 242–247.

mere participation in the act justified arbitrary punishment short of mutilation, and standards ordinarily regulating the initiation of proceedings were reduced to permit, for example, the admission of witness testimony obtained from convicted accomplices. As a result, even medical graduates and priests were at risk of being summoned by the inquisitores, although unattached and estranged females invariably figured as the prime candidates for sentencing and imposition of the death penalty.

Meanwhile, the best source of knowledge about late medieval reproductive choices has been irretrievably lost. It once existed in the minds of spiritual confessors, who listened to their parishioners in regular penitential conversations. After the Fourth Lateran Council of 1215, Catholic Christians were obliged to reveal sinful conduct annually to their ordinary priest or bishop, who in turn enjoined absolution in accordance with uniform instructions provided by the academic establishment. As mentioned in chapter 2, the scholastic doctrine of abortion as crimen first entered the confessional manuals during the closing decades of the twelfth century, when Peter the Chanter and his pupils were active at Paris as teachers of pastoral theology. With the publication of Raymond of Penyafort's *Summa de penitentia* in the early 1220s, the manuals' contents quickly assumed a standardized format. Guided by increasingly streamlined texts, believers throughout the Western Hemisphere grew aware of the juristic equation between induced miscarriage and homicide. They were instructed about guilt of conscience in opposition to legal culpability and heard of theoretical distinctions that separated formed from unformed fetal existence. The relentless inspection of mind and soul by priestly interrogators went as far as to inform the official attitude of churchmen toward allegations of so-called overlaying—the suffocation of small children kept in the parental bed. Canon lawyers routinely posed the question of whether there could be any mortal offense against God while the perpetrator was fast asleep. The correct response was in the affirmative. Automatic excommunication would await those who awoke to a smothered child by their side. Ecclesiastical authorities sensed that there was always reason to suspect infanticide, even in the quietest hours of the night.[4]

---

4. The condemnation rested on X 5.10.3 in conjunction with the scholastic doctrine of *in re illicita* (chap. 2, note 15), which extended full liability to the collateral effects of illicit activity, such as infant death caused by sharing, against canonical norms, the same bed with the victim; cf. Trexler, "Infanticide in Florence," 103–109; Helmholz, "Infanticide in the Province of Canterbury," 160–164; Roger Aubenas, *Recueil de lettres des officialités de Marseille et d'Aix (XIVe–XV^{e}siècles)*, 2 vols. (Paris: Picard, 1937–1938), 2:95–96 (no. 270).

The sacramental nature of a sinner's revelations implied that they had to be understood as unknown to the public. Priests who listened to private confessions were obliged not to share them with others, and failure to observe the most scrupulous silence led to instant removal from sacerdotal functions. Incriminating behavior that pastoral indiscretion brought to the awareness of prosecuting lay authorities was seen as absolutely inadmissible in court proceedings, to the point where extraordinary investigations of heretical depravity in the later Middle Ages, let alone ordinary criminal trials, consistently refrained from allowing confessional secrets to be used against defendants. Restricted by the same rules, the modern historian is deprived of insight into cases that formerly came to the attention of confessors, apart from exceptional instances in which clerical oversight has permitted shreds of confidential penitential information to acquire written permanence. As a result of scribal error, posterity has been informed about the infanticide of a Venetian noblewoman in 1455. A thick veil of institutionally guaranteed privacy has kept a host of comparable data beyond the reach of scholarly verification.[5]

Public penance, imposed upon persons of ill repute who plainly confessed guilt and abjured or were unable to overcome anonymous allegations of wrong by way of purgatory oaths, formed the characteristic outcome of proceedings initiated via denuntiationis, which dealt with weaker evidence than trials leading up to secular punishment. Juristic theory did not mandate that the charges be put in writing, and they often remained undocumented except where more persuasive proof transformed them into ordinary lawsuits. Lack of study has meant that only for fifteenth-century England have continuous runs of records been found in which laity denounced on account of abortion, infanticide, or overlaying are identified as offenders or as having been obliged to swear to their innocence. Pertinent material from areas across the British Channel has not been searched methodically, although there are two entries in the visitation registers of Archbishop Eude Rigaud reporting for 1256 that Agnes de Ponte had been sent to the hospital of lepers at Rouen in Normandy. Agnes had to do penance by providing care for the sick because fama claimed that she had given herbs to a certain Eustachia in order to kill the child in her womb. Infamy also affected Nicola, a woman from the same town (Rothomagensis). Rumor asserted in 1259 that she had

---

5. Peter Biller, *The Measure of Multitude: Population in Medieval Thought* (Oxford: Oxford University Press, 2000), 178–213, has argued for the widespread existence of contraceptive attitudes, based on the frequent condemnation of them in the pastoral literature.

willfully aborted a fetus just one month old. Eude Rigaud did not prescribe works of atonement for her, as nothing of substance (*probabilis*) resulted from his inquiry in 1264.[6] In areas of the Ius commune, canonical *visitationes* may offer the richest source of information about denunciatory activity that, provided it appeared credible to visiting prelates, warranted further examination upon their return home. Prolonged scrutiny was especially applied to clerics, including the unidentified parish priest of Torrelles in the diocese of Barcelona, who in 1303 faced claims that he had beaten his daughter-in-law until she very nearly miscarried. In 1307 Bishop Ponç de Gualba decided to resume his investigations despite the absolution he had granted four years earlier. Ponç now undertook a full-scale criminal inquisitio against the suspect from Torrelles, with risks for the defendant of suspension from the ministry and loss of his sacerdotal income.[7]

Succinctly put, late medieval sacramental confessions were in principle excluded from writing. Denunciatory charges, recorded and preserved erratically, offered little guarantee that any of the underlying allegations rested on actual fact, and accusationes as well as inquisitiones concerned with crime in the modern sense furnished limited coverage of real events in that the procedural rules restricted evidentiary assessments and reinforced the impact of social screening. The surviving judicial documentation is therefore poorly equipped to provide a comprehensive historical repertory of attacks on nascent human life. Moreover, the search for incidents recorded by court officials has made scant progress, impeding the creation of statistics that show extant legal cases for a specific town or region or for institutional entities such as bishoprics, the papal curia, and lay tribunals. A minimal portion of what the sources still contain has been surveyed and identified, either in this book or in comparable modern studies. At the same time, current knowledge already permits the discernment of prosecutorial habits that future discovery of primary evidence is likely to confirm rather than challenge or dismiss entirely. The inability to determine the frequency of criminal abortion in

---

6. *Regestrum visitationum archiepiscopi Rothomagensis. Journal des visites pastorales d'Eude Rigaud, archévêque de Rouen, 1248–1269*, ed. Théodore Bonnin (Rouen: le Brument, 1852), 255 (dated 1256), 338 (of 1259), and 491 (of 1264). As late as 1516, the archpriest of Wetzlar in Hassia noted in his judicial act book the denunciation of an unfaithful husband who had struck his wife and caused her to miscarry; see Wolf-Heino Struck, "Die Sendgerichtsbarkeit am Ausgang des Mittelalters nach den Regesten des Archipresbyterats Wetzlar," *Nassauische Annalen* 82 (1971): 127n208, quoting from Limburg, Diözesanarchiv, LK E/1, fol. 61r.

7. José Martí Bonet, "Las visitas pastorales y los 'Comunes' del primer año del pontificado del obispo del Barcelona Ponç de Gualba (a. 1303)," *Anthologica annua* 28/29 (1981/1982): 709–711, 720–721.

absolute terms, that is to say, does not prevent discussion of the issue in relation to the three parameters of geography, documentation, and procedural typology. Each addresses questions of recurrence from an angle that better suits the original material and yields insight regardless of whether additional data will come to light or rest hidden in the Western archives.

Geography and Patterns of Record Keeping

The criminalization of abortion can be described as greatly dependent on location, advancing as people drew inspiration from the example of uniform prosecution and condemnation in the ecclesiastical sphere. Academic definitions of the offense as sin and crimen affected Latin Christendom from the early 1200s onward. Pastoral works written by Peter the Chanter and Raymond of Penyafort circulated as literary models for the dissemination of standard penitential doctrine, and clerics faced identical disciplinary treatment everywhere. With regard to the laity, on the other hand, chapter 2 has highlighted the pioneering role of the English common law. Its agents became the first secular officials to follow church teachings and treat fetal homicide among the capital pleas. The insertion of miscarriage by assault under the category of felonies bore the mark of a distinct legal tradition. Between 1200 and 1348, crown justices systematically prosecuted the act and threatened convicts with the death penalty. A second region of speedy adoption comprised the core areas of the Ius commune. These extended across the Italian peninsula and Sicily but encompassed as well the French realm and Mediterranean Iberia with the kingdoms of Aragon, Valencia, and Castile, where centralizing princely and municipal authorities started to embrace Romano-canonical standards in the years after 1250. The remainder of territories tied to papal spiritual leadership, inhabited by Germanic, Baltic, Hungarian, and neighboring Slavic populations, formed a third and peripheral region in which the full reception of criminal abortion by the lay courts constituted more of a postmedieval phenomenon, hardly discernible before the 1450s or 1500s.

As discussed in chapter 5, early criminalizing efforts in the courts of the English common law had been abandoned by 1348, when lawyerly opinion agreed definitively that unborn babies could not be regarded as present in the nature of things and enjoy protection under the law of felony. From the closing decades of the thirteenth century, crown pleas on account of miscarriage lost in attractiveness and completely disappeared soon after the end of Edward II's reign in 1327. Simultaneously, prosecution in the heartlands of the Ius commune across the Channel strengthened in terms of visibility. Many governments secured the continuous registration of their administrative acts, incidentally facilitating the modern study of judicial routine. Older trial documentation is harder to come by, and demonstration that the criminalization of abortion and infanticide in the French kingdom, for instance, had become established by 1300 has to be searched for in disjointed and local legal records, if not altogether in literary testimony such as the *Coutumes de Beauvaisis*. Compiled about 1283 by Philippe de Beaumanoir, the work offers sophisticated illustrations of how scholastic doctrine combined proof of criminal liability with nearly insurmountable procedural restrictions. Philippe once mentioned the case of a woman who admittedly had been pregnant. Nobody, however, knew with certainty what had happened to her child after delivery. The suspect asserted that she had hastened to hand the newborn over to the baby's father, a gesture of which the alleged recipient had no recollection. "There was *grant presumpcion* against the young mother," the juristically trained author commented, but the circumstances were "not clear enough to justify final sentencing." The words of Philippe de Beaumanoir suggest that northern French judges of the late 1200s relied on Bolognese criteria of guilt.[8]

Secular justice in territories located to the north and east of France and Italy took much longer to follow suit. In the imperial city of Nuremberg, leaders did not introduce elements of civilian jurisprudence until a couple of generations prior to the end of the Middle Ages. On July 31, 1439, municipal records witness for the first time, and with a delay of more than two centuries compared with the earliest ecclesiastical and English references, a charge of miscarriage by assault that seems to have been inspired by the Romano-canonical format of criminal accusatio. Given that the affair ended with the accuser's failure to show up in court, only a second entry from the same register, datable perhaps to 1450, sheds light on what might have occurred had the trial of 1439 gone forward as planned. Again presenting a private accusation based on percussio, the text still reflects the prevalence of customary and protoscholastic litigation in that the Nuremberg judges sought to ascertain truth by imposing on the defendant a three-handed oath of compurgation.[9]

---

8. Philippe de Beaumanoir, *Coutumes de Clermont en Beauvaisis* 63.1813–1814, ed. Amedée Salmon, 2 vols. (Paris: Picard, 1899–1900), 2:417–418. Earlier still, a royal inquest of 1247 had charged the former *bailli* of Atois in Poitou with having extorted money from a local couple, based on the false accusation of some fifteen years earlier that they had harbored and concealed their niece's pregnancy and then killed the newborn baby; cf. *Recueil des historiens des Gaules et de la France* 24, ed. Léopold Delisle (Paris: Imprimerie impériale, 1904), 115 (no. 180). Charles de Miramon (Paris) has kindly brought this passage to my attention.

9. Nuremberg, Staatsarchiv, Rep. 52b, no. 206; Nuremberg, Staatsarchiv, Nürnberger Briefbücher, no. 14 (31 July 1439), both cited by Roetzer, "Die Delikte," 27.

Then, about half a century later, the legal climate had changed. In 1497, a servant girl called Agnes Pörtlin was subjected to formal inquisitiones on suspicions that she had strangled her newborn baby. "Had mercy not been imparted upon her," the narrative explains, "she would have forfeited life and her body." Fortunately for Agnes, she was allowed to escape unharmed in return for promises that she would permanently abandon the confines of her hometown. In his literary praise of *Norimberga*, written by the humanist Conrad Celtis in 1495, the identification of child murder committed not only after but also before birth with crime worthy of the death penalty was similarly treated as bordering on the self-evident. Three-hundred-year-old tenets of scholastic doctrine were now being implemented beyond the Rhine and Danube, sustained by widespread enthusiasm for juristic reform.[10]

When addressing questions of relative frequency from the documentary point of view, one must keep in mind that the known number of late medieval abortion cases is small in comparison with what the archival repositories have yet to reveal. Legal historians have focused on tracking the origins of present-day institutions instead of aiming at an even-handed reconstruction of past judicial realities. Guided by top-down and teleological approaches, they have paid special attention to central governments and explored premodern judiciaries only insofar as they contributed to unbroken traditions of data preservation. The two Western monarchies that eventually became nation-states, England and France, have thus been treated with exceptional interest. The sentencing of felonious pre-and postnatal homicides in the English common law has been examined as well, and nobody has discovered crown pleas solely concerned with miscarriage and dating to the period after 1348. The silence of the court rolls cannot be mistaken for lack of scholarly effort to break it or for an indication of material loss. To the contrary, there is reason to believe that from the mid-1300s, the willful termination of pregnancies no longer ranked among the capital offenses.[11]

For the French kingdom, judicial activities have likewise been scrutinized with extreme concentration on the monarchy. Repertories covering court business from the beginnings of regular registration until about 1350 have been published for the criminal branch of the Parlement de Paris, the supreme tribunal of the realm, and letters of pardon from the King's Council have been mined by many generations of scholars. Archivists have produced analytical inventories and volume upon volume of full transcripts, which

---

10. Conradus Celtis, *Norimberga* 14, in Werminghoff, *Conrad Celtis*, 194; Nuremberg, Staatsarchiv, Rep. 15a (S.I.L. 69), no. 2 (dated 1497); see Roetzer, "Die Delikte," 37, 56–57.

11. Against the claims of Rafferty, "Roe v. Wade," 12–58; complete analysis in chapter 5.

often were put together by burgeoning societies of local history at the height of the Belle Époque around 1900. The largest portion of presently known abortion and infanticide cases from France has invited consultation because of the existence of these research tools. On the one hand, they supply enough primary texts to discern the operations of Romano-canonical procedure as adopted by the royal judges; on the other, they tend to document litigation as it arrived at advanced appeal stages or invoked the ruler as a last resort, either to overturn, through remission, a final sentence or to end situations of procedural deadlock. The effect has been that cases initially aimed at capital retribution but soon abandoned or settled financially do not appear among the most readily available sources, in spite of the fact that they must have figured in the bulk of late medieval punitive charges.[12]

That the general preference for records of central governments may distort modern perceptions of the original caseload in favor of relatively rare inquiries leading all the way up to sentencing is confirmed by an unusual publication from the Saintonge region. It reproduces a portion of local judicial registers kept for years by the board of jurors in the *échevinage* of Saint-Jean d'Angély. A pair of entries for 1426 reports that someone by the name of Jehan Coupea had been accused of miscarriage by assault (encis). On February 16, Jehan was granted permission by the *échevins* to post bail in the amount of one hundred pounds and have a proctor plead on his behalf while he attended to mercantile affairs awaiting him in Toulouse. Jehan is never mentioned in the text again.[13] Away from the prism of appellate justice and its records, accusations and inquisitions have not been studied at the level of ordinary prosecutions, conducted by officials who served the crown in the provinces. It is only in connection with jurisdictions around Marseille and Lyon that average incidents of homicidal abortion and infanticide have been investigated in their own right.[14] The frequent use of scholastic concepts by royal adjudicators from the second half of the thirteenth century onward points to the existence of considerable evidence for trials held outside Paris, except that until now very little of it has been brought back to light.

---

12. The largest single compilation of lettres de remission in transcription is the "Recueil des documents concernant le Poitou" by Paul Guérin; for succinct *inventaires,* cf. Viard and Vallée, *Registres* 3.1–2; Vallée, *Registres* 3.3; *Actes du Parlement de Paris, 1254–1328,* ed. Edgard Boutaric, 2 vols. (Paris : Imprimerie impériale, 1863–1866); Labat-Poussin et al., *Actes du Parlement.*

13. Saint-Jean d'Angély, Archives, FF 26, ed. Denys d'Aussy, "Registre de l'échevinage de Saint-Jean d'Angély (1332–1496)," in *Archives historiques de la Saintonge et de l'Aunis* 32 (1902): 395, 398–399.

14. Shatzmiller, *Médecine et justice,* 80–85 (no. 10–11), 131 (no. 94); Gonthier, *Délinquance, justice, et société,* 117–118, 204.

For other central areas of the Ius commune in Italy and along the Mediterranean coast of Iberia, an incalculable quantity of local legal records have yet to be consulted by modern scholars. Perhaps because the unified Italian nation-state is without a direct medieval ancestor and also because present-day Spain did not possess a single government prior to the fusion of the Aragonese and Castilian crowns in 1479, medieval registers of royal administration, whether at Naples, Palermo, or Valencia or in Catalonia, have not been studied nearly as closely as those of France. Where information about ordinary criminal prosecutions of alleged child murder has become available, it has been used rather anecdotally to illustrate broader historical phenomena, for example, the presence of violence and deviancy in Renaissance society. The random inspection of documentation from Venice and Florence has instantly identified accusations of abortion and infanticide, and growing interest in data from Aragon, now deposited at the Archivo de la Corona in Barcelona, promises significant findings that demonstrate how the normative culture of eastern Iberian towns was heavily influenced by teachings of Bolognese stamp and origin.[15] More to the south, Sicilian monarchs also favored the advancement of jurisprudence, with Emperor Frederick II sponsoring a Neapolitan law faculty as early as 1224. Still, even questions concerning the whereabouts of sources on the practice of criminal justice in the *regna* have remained understudied and unexplored.[16]

North of the Alps and east of the river Rhine, secular prosecution of abortion and infanticide as capital crimes did not occur until the wholesale reception (*Vollrezeption*) of Bolognese legal theories in the second half of the 1400s. Henceforth there were signs of a cultural reorientation toward scholastic techniques of adjudication, aided not least by attempts of municipal administrators to institute the regular registration of court business. As early as 1444, fiscal records in Frankfurt refer to a sentence of execution, subsequently rescinded, of a woman for child murder, and an entry from Breslau in Silesia of 1474 appears to have been based on academic norms in that the judges banned a married couple from town for having supplied townspeople

---

15. Povolo, "Note per uno studio," 115–131; Claudio Povolo, "Una sentenza dell'avogaria di comun (1459)," *Archivio veneto* 114 (1980): 109–111; Cohn, *Women in the Streets*, 100–101, 148–160; Marie Kelleher, *The Measure of Woman: Law and Female Identity in the Crown of Aragon* (Philadelphia: University of Pennsylvania Press, 2010), 15–47.

16. Andrea Romano, "Tribunali, giudici e sentenze nel Regnum Siciliae (1130–1516)," in *Judicial Records, Law Reports, and the Growth of Case Law*, ed. John Baker (Berlin: Duncker & Humblodt, 1989), 211–301; Rosalba Sorice, *"Quae omnia bonus iudex considerabit." La giustizia criminale nel Regno di Sicilia (secolo XVI)* (Torino: Giappichelli, 2009), 7–37.

with abortifacient beverages. It is possible to object that both passages do not necessarily suggest the comprehensive appropriation of Romano-canonical procedure in German and Polish towns, especially because prior to the 1490s more elaborate remarks on charges of infanticidium along the lines of allegations against Margarete Höllin of Nördlingen and Agnes Pörtlin from Nuremberg are hard to find in the surviving documentation. Only mercy saved the latter two from the infliction of capital punishment, the one feature that legal historians have regarded time and again as signaling the advent of ordinary inquisitiones and accusationes, in opposition to older communal modes of settlement concluded by way of compensation payments.[17] Gradual preparation of the social environment for new forms of justice, however, did not always require written instruments, as Mathias Jacobi's petition of 1461, seeking papal pardon in a case of homicidal miscarriage, helps illustrate.

The request, recorded by the Apostolic Penitentiary in July of 1461, was primarily concerned with Mathias Jacobi de Godkow, a priest from the archdiocese of Cracow, who wished to overcome a canonical impediment to his exercise of the sacred orders. Mathias had incurred suspension because, according to people in the neighborhood, he had caused a miscarriage to his chambermaid, Helena. He instead claimed that the fatality had ensued inadvertently and without awareness of her pregnancy, thereby securing for himself an official declaration of innocence pending approval of the stated facts by his ordinary, the archbishop. Of particular relevance in the present context is the supplicant's brief allusion to what Helena experienced after her delivery of the stillborn child. "Out of certain presumptions and suspicions," the text explains, she was caught and arrested by the inhabitants of her village, at Radkwo, who interrogated her until she confirmed that Mathias was responsible for the loss of an "already alive [vivificatus]" fetus.[18] The circumstances of her capture may forever elude modern curiosity. Yet it is remarkable that as early as in 1461, somewhere in the rural provinces of southern Poland, a panel of peasants decided to imprison and question a female suspect believed

---

17. Nördlingen, Stadtarchiv, Inquisitionsakte 1495 (Margarete Höllin); Nördlingen, Stadtarchiv, Blutbuch (sentence of 24 February 1497); cf. Alfons Felber, "Unzucht und Kindesmord in der Rechtssprechung der freien Reichsstadt Nördlingen vom 15. bis 19. Jahrhundert" (PhD diss., University of Bonn, 1961), 98. Paul Frauenstädt, "Breslaus Strafrechtspflege im 14. bis 16. Jahrhundert," *Zeitschrift für die gesamte Strafrechtswissenschaft* 19 (1890): 1–35, 237; Frankfurt/M., Stadtarchiv, Bürgermeisterbuch, fol. 23; Frankfurt/M., Stadtarchiv, Rechenbuch, fol. 45; cf. Georg Kriegk, *Deutsches Bürgertum im Mittelalter*, vol. 1 (Frankfurt/M.: Rütten & Löning, 1868), 545–546.

18. Rome, APA Reg. div. 9, fol. 252v–253r (10 September 1461); ed. *Bullarium Poloniae* 6.81 (no. 333); cf. *RPG* 4.47–48 (no. 1803).

to have provoked the death of her own baby. Perhaps her story was reshaped by trained canon lawyers and narrative conventions prevailing at the papal Curia in Rome. Alternatively, it is possible to argue that, far into the Western peripheries, criminal jurisprudence was rapidly gaining ground, with Helena among the first to confront its capacity for unilateral action and repression in the name of secular justice.

A Triad of Typical Cases

By 1200, Bolognese jurists had determined that the intentional procurement of death to a human fetus would amount to criminal manslaughter. The equation started to figure in theoretical and normative writings until it sooner or later reached the lay judges. The spread was conditioned, as noted, by geographical factors and by the relative propensity of local legal cultures to resort to systematized rules and proceedings. In addition, practical application varied depending on the usefulness of the new punitive standards for ordinary consumers. Closer analysis of what prompted recourse to public investigations of abortion as a punishable offense throws into relief a clear-cut, threefold pattern. Typologically speaking, it appears that the earliest wave of prosecutions throughout the West would affect defendants suspected of having caused another man's wife to miscarry. In thirteenth-century England, felonious charges of fetal homicidium involved, as discussed in chapters 2 and 5, indictments or appeals on behalf of women who, often in alliance with their husbands, mobilized royal justice against adversaries alleged to have attacked them during pregnancy, with beatings leading to fatal injury in the womb. In compilations of French customary law (*coutumes*) from the same, incipient phase of criminalization, the technical term of *encis* denotes, yet again, scenarios of violence tied to *percussiones*. The vernacular expression arose long before the *Coutumes d'Artois*, composed toward 1300, became the first prescriptive text to extend the meaning of encis to other forms of so-called *avortis* as well. One has to await publication of the customs for Anjou and Maine in 1437 to encounter explicit recognition that the penalties for encis would also afflict those who killed their own progeny.[19]

Late medieval legislation and statutes occupied a place not nearly as significant as nowadays when it came to the introduction of novel legal criteria. Statutory provisions offer valuable historical insight insofar as they show

---

19. *Coutumes d'Artois,* ed. Ernest Tardif (Paris: Champion, 1883), 11.14–15; *Coutumes de l'Anjou et du Maine,* ed. Charles-Jean Beautemps-Beaupré (Paris: Laurent & Pedone-Lauriel, 1878), cap. 1368; cf. Brissaud, "L'infanticide," 230–231.

how the criminalization of fetal homicide progressed through time and space and how implementation was impacted by practical exigencies. On the other hand, it has been argued in chapter 3 that normative texts of the period have to be read in conjunction with underlying academic doctrine for an accurate understanding of what lawgivers sought to redefine, as jurisprudence and its foremost agents, the university professors, alone wielded adequate communication tools to settle questions of legality for everyone to know. Chapter 1, moreover, has stressed the remote, prescholastic origins of Latin *percussiones* and French *encis* as subjects of formal litigation. Gratian and the Bolognese jurists of the twelfth century repeatedly referred in their reflections on abortion as *homicidium* to the Mosaic *lex* of Exodus 21:22–23, written in the version of the Greco-Jewish Septuagint some 1300 years earlier. The ancient passage had long envisioned complaints about the mistreatment of pregnant women by outsiders as the most typical judicial situation related to prenatal manslaughter, signaling a tradition of regulation that did not require the rise of professional law schools in the West.

In 1211, Innocent III also had a *percussio* in mind when he discussed the canonical implications of abortion for churchmen in a decretal that remains the sole statement of a medieval pope on the subject. Apart from frequent provisions against *encis* in customary compilations from the French kingdom, the oldest secular laws and statutes prohibiting the termination of pregnancies, such as the Castilian *Siete Partidas* of the 1260s, focus on battery as well, notwithstanding that in current perception the act does not offer the most compelling illustration of malicious or murderous behavior. The accusation nevertheless struck premodern audiences as the paradigmatic form of fetal death in the criminal courts. An early ordinance (*fur*) for the town of Valencia, passed in 1271, ordered the payment of compensation plus a fine for convicted persons who "by way of excessive workload, violent *percussio*, or in different fashion have culpably caused a miscarriage."[20] In northern Italy, the influential theoretical objections raised, around 1342, by Signorolus de Homodeis against the common juxtaposition of homicide and killings of a "live" fetus likewise departed from blows administered during a heated argument. The critical incident, with "A hitting the wife of B," was reported in the Milanese lawyer's *Consilium primum* as having played out in the context of a *statutum* passed by the town government of Cremona in Lombardy. In outlying regions of Germany and farther to the north and east, the rise of the offense as a secular crime was delayed until the closing decades of the

---

20. *Fori Antiqui Valentiae* 9.8.27, ed. Dualde Serrano, 249–250, printed in *Die Abtreibung*, 86n158. For the *Siete Partidas,* see chapter 3.

Middle Ages. Still, the pertinent pieces of evidence, whether registered at Nuremberg in 1439 or put in writing about 1450 by a panel of jurors from Leipzig, depict brawls and the external interference with domestic peace as the ordinary setting for prenatal manslaughter, triggering judicial intervention with greater frequency than otherwise imaginable.[21]

Presented in proper chronological order, the second type of criminal suit to occupy the lay courts consisted of dynamic abortions by way of herbal infusion. As was the case with percussiones, the prescholastic roots of formal investigations against people purportedly operating as magicians and sorcerers went all the way back to antiquity, except that the initiative to prosecute did not rest with individuals in pursuit of compensation for damages but with groups and entire communities seeking relief from ominous figures and forces. Collective cleansing campaigns would round up scapegoats and defamed persons charged with vague and accumulative faults often extending to attacks on unborn or newborn life, if not voluntary corruption of the environment and public health in general. In the beginning phases of the Ius commune, recorded accusations typically combined the use of abortifacients with rather generic insinuations of culpability. Over time, however, inquisitiones and accusationes started to focus on allegations of abortionis pocula as defined by Romano-canonical doctrine or inspected serial offenses considered "incorrigible" by the proceduralists. From the 1430s onward, finally, jurisprudence further facilitated the prosecution of heinous crime in that fetal poisoning, heresy, and repeat offenses were lumped together under the new category of "witchcraft" trials.

Persecutions targeting outcasts reveal their political rather than judicial nature in records that attest to the long survival of prescholastic purgation rituals, especially in urban milieus along the Western periphery. As regards Germany in the 1300s and 1400s, chapter 7 has highlighted the habitual expulsion from independent towns of people seen as notoriously "harmful to the land" (landschädlich), whose fault was established by hearsay charges and included harmful prescriptions, infanticide, and the infliction of prenatal death. Earlier, in 1231, a decree issued by the Duke of Brabant had prescribed execution through burning for women responsible for induced miscarriage, murder, arson, and various unspecified offenses. The enactment likely passed in response to outbursts of popular enthusiasm for swift justice that two years afterward, in 1233, spawned the promulgation of a similar statute at Parma, in the immediate vicinity of the Bolognese law schools. Excited religiously by

---

21. Signorolus is discussed in the second section of chapter 3; late medieval German references to abortion are treated in chap. 5, notes 3, 5.

the penitential exhortations of Friar Gerard, town officials rushed to formulate an injunction permitting, within eight days after the *podestà* took office each year, the accusation of individuals said to have distributed abortifacient substances. Those found liable incurred instant banishment from the city and were to be ejected "along with all the other riffraff."[22] A century and a half later, prosecutors in northern Italian communes adopted a more differentiated approach when trying to appease resentment toward "inveterate" evildoers and sorcerers. The judicial registers from Florence report for August 22, 1380, that Laurentius Pini was decapitated following his conviction as a magician, incestuous adulterer, and administrator of deadly potions. That numerous witnesses had charged him with the repeated and sometimes successful administration of drugs "apt to extinguish unborn life" did not prove decisive in the end, as sufficient proof had already been assembled to his detriment. The Florentine entry alludes in the vaguest of terms to "presently unnamed" women who confirmed his participation in acts of dynamic abortion.[23]

Apart from the sentencing of Laurentius Pini, who for his persistent criminal conduct was treated as incorrigible by the Ius commune, the oldest known record of Romano-canonical lay proceedings exclusively concerned with pocula abortionis dates to Manosque near Marseille and the month of November 1298. By any measure, the French orbit seems to have been central to early prosecutions of dynamic abortion. Evidence presented in the final portion of chapter 7 has shown how the offense and its extraordinary legal quality justified the disregard for many requirements ordinarily shaping investigations, including the discovery of a corpus delicti or the need for depositions to be made by honorable, as opposed to infamous and anonymous, witnesses. The definitive release of Aigline Tonnelier, residing at Caux in Normandy, from charges of "venomous and deadly sortilege" on May 23, 1321, concluded a trial that rested on mere hearsay, and a pair of lettres de remission, issued in 1399 and 1405, cited *renommee* and *denonciation* as the driving forces behind inquisitions examining the distribution and consumption of abortifacients.[24] Although similar cases in the registers of Italian and

---

22. *Statuta communis Parmae digesta ad MCCLV,* ed. Amadio Ronchini, Monumenta historica ad provincias Parmensem et Placentinam pertinentia, vol. 1 (Parma: Fiaccadori, 1856), 42–43; also in chap. 7, notes 31–32.

23. "Quarum nomina ad presens pro meliori parte tacentur," Florence, AS, Reg. 1255, fol. 101r–103v; cf. Umberto Dorini, *Il diritto penale e la delinquenza in Firenze nel secolo XV* (Lucca: Corsi, [1923]), 67, 134.

24. Paris, AN, JJ 154, no. 310 (July 1399); AN, JJ 160, no. 19 (June 1405); AN, X1a 5, fol. 108r (23 May 1321), cf. Boutaric, *Actes du Parlement de Paris,* 2:374 (no. 6424).

Iberian courts still await detection, archival study will certainly lead to substantial findings, considering that theorists from the two regions had been
instrumental in shaping the doctrine of fetal death by potion as a qualified
crime, advanced in particular by the noted Bolognese teacher, Laurentius
"from Spain" (*Hispanus*). Printed juristic literature from the fifteenth century
confirms beyond doubt that the harsher treatment of the act first proposed
by Laurentius (fl. 1215) had since become accepted by his Italian successors.
A sequence of four consilia criminalia, composed respectively by Bartholomaeus Caepolla, Franciscus Capitiliste of Padua, Angelus de Castro, and
Antonius de Rosellis from Arezzo, agreed unanimously on applying stricter
criteria of guilt to the administrators of pocula abortionis while debating an
episode of adjudication that probably occurred in 1459. In addition, a piece
of legal counsel crafted by Andreas de Barbatia (d. 1479) discussed the fate
of a man called Bartolotus, accused of having supplied herbal mixtures to a
pregnant Berta with the intent of killing the fetus in her womb. Again relying on the principles laid down by Laurentius Hispanus, Andreas concluded
his consilium by stating that execution could not be meted out against Bartolotus, as nobody had perished from his concoctions.[25]

There is little reason to assume the existence of criminal investigations
focusing on dynamic abortion in territories away from the core areas of the
Ius commune, be it in England or along the peripheries of the Latin West.
Until about 1348, English royal judges limited their prosecutorial attention
to percussiones, whereas subsequently medieval common lawyers denied
humanity to the unborn, and felonious crown pleas no longer included fetal
death except in the form of collateral charges. In regions east of the Rhine
and north of the Alps, on the other hand, criminalization was progressing too
slowly to allow for more than juristically ambiguous mentions of pocula in
the surviving source material, a large proportion of which may already have
been investigated by legal historians.[26] Increasingly, however, the Romance
language-speaking regions primarily exposed to Bolognese jurisprudence
and, from the 1450s onward, German and Slavic towns would share in the
advance of a third and most enduring variety of capital allegations that did
not depend on outsiders aiding and abetting in miscarriages or infanticide
but on biological parents who deliberately terminated the lives of their own

---

25. Bartholomaeus Caepolla, *Consilia criminalia* 34–37 (Lyon: Giunta, 1543), fol. 96va–101ra;
cf. Engelmann, *Die Schuldlehre der Postglossatoren* 86–93; Andreas Barbatia, *Consilia* 2.23 (Venice:
Nicolini, 1580), fol. 74rb–va; his assessment of the charges drew on ideas originally proposed by
Laurentius Hispanus, chap. 1, note 20.

26. See note 17, above, and, with regard to the English common law, chapters 2 and 5.

babies. The *Coutumes de Beauvaisis*, completed by Philippe de Beaumanoir in 1283, contains the oldest known remark to prove application in the lay courts of the scholastic equation between fetal manslaughter and *homicidium* and also that French *inquisitores* employed jurisprudential norms to try women for having performed abortions on themselves. In Italy, Venice reported the execution of a mother found guilty of killing her newborn in 1329, just five years after the inception of continuous registration by the *Avogaria di comun*. Florentine judges of appeals noted the passing of capital sentences from 1390 at the latest, a century before incidents of the same kind appear in the judicial documentation from Germany.[27]

To understand the dynamics of criminalization, it seems to be of secondary importance to determine whether archival discoveries can antedate the lay prosecution of infanticidal and aborting mothers and fathers in France, Italy, or Spain more toward the early 1200s. It is instead significant to note that proliferation of the charge, unlike recourse to justice in connection with *percussiones* or abortion by way of magic and sortilege, did not hinge upon the transformation of specific prosecutorial mechanisms in the secular sphere. Quite to the contrary, the threat of punitive treatment for every slayer of human offspring figured as an original twelfth-century invention of Bolognese jurisprudence, prompting simultaneously the introduction of formal safeguards to alleviate social concern about the dishonorable side effects of top-down investigations. Criminal lawyers curtailed admissible allegations by devising the tight parameters of ordinary Romano-canonical procedure, not permitting the initiation of criminal inquiries except where a dead infant or fetus had been found or where the concealment of a pregnancy could be proved by the suspect's personal admission. For full conviction, the rules insisted on unqualified confessions of guilt or on two eyewitnesses of good reputation, describing under oath how the crime had been carried out.

The tardy appearance of self-inflicted infanticide and abortion in secular criminal courts alongside abortifacient potions and fetal death caused by *percussio* can be tied to yet another development responsible for the advance of the Ius commune, namely, the centralization of government and the judiciary as one of its increasingly inseparable arms. In a drawn-out process that did not become obvious until the early modern period, judges improved their ability to inquire into crime unilaterally. In due time, they opened proceedings independent of the instigation by private parties in search of compensation

---

27. Cf. above, note 17 and, on Florence, chap. 8, note 10, in reference to the earliest known infanticide case from the city of 1390. Venice, AS, Reg. 3641, fol. 78r (20 September 1329).

for the loss of a child and without mobilization by communities anxious to obtain protection against spells and the poisonous impact of "infamous" elements in society. The inquisitores began to scrutinize suspicious activity in private quarters and ultimately on the inside of respectable households. Empowered from the 1500s by sovereign legislation and the rise of permanent bureaucracies, they also acquired the right to dismiss procedural limitations that had long shackled attempts to arrive at the factual reconstruction of alleged events, with the concealment of pregnancy now permitting, for example, the instant application of torture or the straightforward infliction of capital punishment. Still later, in the 1600s, and again attesting to the unabating buildup of state monopolies in the legitimate exercise of violence and adjudication, voices of protest among the intellectual elites grew in volume, exhorting tribunals to use merciful discretion and resort to more humane criteria of sentencing. Since the 1960s, finally, Western legal systems have moved away from the traditional juxtaposition of abortion and homicide in penal law codes. Embracing rationales oddly reminiscent of an age-old jury verdict recorded at Brno in Moravia around 1353, present-day norms concede women far greater autonomy in their procreative choices. And although the traditional connection in Latin Christianity between manslaughter and prenatal killings has been rejected by a majority of lay jurisdictions, ordinary Westerners keep one aspect pertaining to the early modern heritage of criminalization firmly in mind in that they, unlike their medieval ancestors, understand abortion to mean, first and foremost, fetal death induced with the mother's explicit consent.

BIBLIOGRAPHY

Primary Sources

Note that listings in this section are alphabetical by author or title (for works without named authors). Authors are listed by their first names, which usually appear in their Latinized forms; alternative vernacular names are cross-referenced in the index (for example: "Aegidius Romanus. *See* Giles of Rome").

Accursius. *Glossa ordinaria,* in *Corpus iuris Iustiniani,* 6 vols. (Lyon: Societas Typographica, 1612).

Albericus de Rosate. *Commentaria de statutis,* 4 vols. (Frankfurt/M.: Richter, 1606).

———. *Commentarii in Digestum vetus,* 2 vols. (Venice: Societas Aquilae Renovantis, 1585; repr., Bologna: Formi, 1974–1977).

Alexander Tartagnus de Imola. *Commentarii in Digestum vetus* (Lyon: Freis, 1551).

Andreas Barbatia. *Consilia* (Venice: Nicolini, 1580).

Angelus Aretinus. *Tractatus de maleficiis* (Lyon: Giunta, 1555).

Angelus de Ubaldis. *Lectura super Codice* (Lyon: Moylin, 1534).

Anthony Fitzherbert. *La Graunde Abridgement* (London: Tottel, 1577).

Antoninus Florentinus. *Summa maior* (Lyon: Cleyn, 1506).

Antoninus Tesaurus. *Novae decisiones sacri senatus Pedemontani* (Venice: Hieronymus Polus, 1591).

Arnaldus [with the misattribution: de Villanova]. *Breviarium* (Venice: Baptista de Tortis, 1494).

Avicenna. *Liber canonis* (Venice: Paganini, 1507; repr., Hildesheim: Olms, 1964).

Baldus de Ubaldis. *Commentaria in Digesta* (Lyon: Societas Librariorum, 1551).

Bartholomaeus Caepolla. *Consilia criminalia* (Lyon: Giunta, 1543).

Bartholomeus Brixiensis. *Glossa ordinaria* [in Decretum Gratiani], in *Corpus iuris canonici* (Venice: Magna Societas, 1584).

Bartolus de Saxoferrato. *Commentaria super Digesto novo* (Milan: Scinzenzeler, 1510).

Bernardus Parmensis. *Glossa ordinaria* [in X], in *Corpus iuris canonici* (Frankfurt/M.: Feyerabend, 1590).

Berthold of Freiburg. *Johannes deutsch,* in *Die Rechtssumme Bruder Bertholds,* ed. Georg Steer et al., 5 vols. (Tübingen: Niemeyer, 1987–1993).

Bibliorum sacrorum iuxta vulgatam Clementinam versio Latina, ed. Alois Gramatica (Vatican City: Polyglotta Vaticana, 1951).

Blasius de Morcone. *De differentiis inter ius Langobardorum et ius Romanorum tractatus,* ed. Giovanni Abignente (Naples, 1924).

Bracton. *De legibus et consuetudinibus Angliae,* ed. George Woodbine (New Haven, CT: Yale University Press, 1922).

Britton, ed. Francis Nichols (Oxford: Clarendon, 1865).

Bullarium Poloniae, vols. 4–6, ed. Irena Sułkowska-Kuraś and Stanislas Kuraś (Rome: École française de Rome, 1995–1998).

Bullarium Romanum, vols. 8–9, ed. Luigi Tomasetti (Turin: Dolmazzo, 1863–1865).

Capitularia regum Francorum, ed. Alfred Boretius, *MGH* LL 2.1 (Hannover: Hahn, 1883).

Carolus de Tocco. *Glossa in Lombardam,* in *Leges Langobardorum* (Venice: Sessa, 1537; repr., Torino: Erasmo, 1964).

Chroniques belges, vol. 1, ed. Jan-Frans Willems (Brussels, 1839).

Cinus Pistoriensis. *Tractatus* [*de formatione foetus*], ed. Hermann Kantorowicz, "Cino da Pistoia ed il primo trattato di medicina legale," *Archivio storico italiano* 37 (1906): 115–128, reprinted in Hermann Kantorowicz, *Rechtshistorische Schriften,* ed. Gerhard Immel (Karlsruhe: Müller, 1970), 287–297.

Conradus Celtis. *Norimberga,* in *Conrad Celtis und sein Buch über Nürnberg,* ed. Albert Werminghoff (Freiburg: Boltze, 1921).

Constitutio criminalis Bambergensis, in *Die Karolina und ihre Vorgängerinnen,* ed. Josef Kohler and Willy Scheel, vol. 2 (Halle: Waisenhaus, 1902).

Constitutio criminalis Carolina, in *Die Karolina und ihre Vorgängerinnen,* ed. Josef Kohler and Willy Scheel, vol. 1 (Halle: Waisenhaus, 1900).

Constitutiones regni Siciliae, ed. Wolfgang Stürner, *MGH* Constitutiones 2, supplement (Hannover: Hahn, 1997).

Corpus iuris canonici, ed. Emil Friedberg, 2 vols. (Leipzig: Tauchnitz, 1879–1881).

Corpus iuris civilis, ed. Theodor Mommsen, Paul Krüger, Wilhelm Schöll, and Wilhelm Kroll, 4 vols. (Berlin: Weidmann, 1872–1895).

The Courts of the Archdeaconry of Buckingham, 1484–1523, ed. Elizabeth Elvey (Aylesbury, UK: Buckinghamshire Record Society, 1975).

Coutume d'Artois, ed. Ernest Tardif (Paris: Champion, 1883).

Coutumes de l'Anjou et du Maine, ed. Charles-Jean Beautemps-Beaupré (Paris: Laurent & Pedone-Lauriel, 1878).

Daniel Sennertus. *Hypomnemata physica,* in Daniel Sennertus, *Opera omnia medica* 1.4 (Lyon: Huguetan & Ravaud, 1641).

Decrees of the Ecumenical Councils, ed. Norman Tanner, 2 vols. (Washington, DC: Catholic University of America Press, 1990).

Deutsche Rechtsalterthümer, vol. 1, ed. Jacob Grimm (Göttingen: Dieterich, 1828).

Die Leipziger Schöffenspruchsammlung, ed. Guido Kisch (Leipzig: Hirzel, 1919).

Die Stadtrechte von Brünn aus dem 13. und 14. Jahrhundert, ed. Emil Rössler (Prague: Calve, 1852).

The Digest of Justinian, ed. Alan Watson et al., 2nd ed., 2 vols. (Philadelphia: University of Pennsylvania Press, 1998).

Documents inédits pour servir l'histoire du Maine au XVᵉ siècle, ed. Arthur Bertrand de Broussillon (Le Mans: Société des archives historiques du Maine, 1905).

Documents nouveaux sur les moeurs populaires et le droit de vengeance dans les Pays-Bas au XIVᵉ siècle, ed. Charles Petit-Dutaillies (Paris: Champion, 1908).

"Documents relatifs à l'histoire de la Saintonge et de l'Aunis extraits des registres du Trésor des chartes," ed. Paul Guérin, in *Archives historiques de la Saintonge et de l'Aunis* 12 (1884).

The Earliest Lincolnshire Assize Rolls A.D. 1202–1209, ed. Doris Stenton (Lincoln, UK: Lincoln Record Society, 1926).

The Early Assize Rolls for the County of Northumberland, ed. William Page (Durham, UK: Andrews, 1891).

The Eyre of Kent, 6/7 Edw. II, ed. Frederick Maitland et al. (London: Quaritch, 1910).

Edward Coke. *Institutes of the Laws of England* (London: Pakeman, 1644).

El Fuero juzgo, ed. José Perona Sánchez, 2 vols. (Murcia: Fundacion Seneca, 2002).

Enchiridion symbolorum, ed. Heinrich Denzinger et al. (Freiburg: Herder, 1991).

Exercitationes ad Pandectas, ed. Johann Heinrich Boehmer (Hannover: Schmid, 1764).

Felinus Sandaeus. *Lectura super Decretalibus,* in *Opera,* vol. 1 (Lyon: Moylin, 1514).

Fleta, ed. Henry Richardson and George Sayles, 4 vols. (London: Selden Society, 1955–1984).

Fori Antiqui Valentiae, ed. Manuel Dualde Serrano (Madrid: CSIC, 1950–1967).

Franciscus Torreblanca Villalpandus. *Epitome delictorum* (Seville: F. de Liza, 1618).

Gentilis de Fulgineo. *Questio an sit licitum provocare abortum.* Edited by Reinhold Schaefer in "Gentile da Foligno über die Zulässigkeit des artifiziellen Aborts (ca. 1340)," *Archiv für die Geschichte der Naturwissenschaften* 6 (1913): 325–326, and by Agostino Amerio in "Alcune considerazioni sulla liceità dell'aborto in uno scritto di Gentile da Foligno," *Pagine di storia della medicina* 10 (1966): 89–92.

Glossa ordinaria in Exodum, in *Biblia Sacra,* vol. 1 (Lyon: Vincent, 1545).

Gregorius Lopez. *Glossa ordinaria,* in *Las Siete Partidas* (Salamanca: Andrea de Portonariis, 1555).

Guido de Cauliaco. *Inventarium sive Chirurgia magna,* ed. Michael McVaugh and Margaret Ogden, 2 vols. (Leiden: Brill, 1997).

Guilelmus Redonensis. *Glossa ordinaria,* in *Summa sancti Raymundi de Penyafort* (Rome: Tallini, 1603; repr., Farnborough: Gregg, 1967).

Hippolytus de Marsiliis. *Commentaria super titulis Digestorum et Codicis* (Lyon: Crespinus, 1531).

Hostiensis. *Apparatus super quinque libris Decretalium* (Strasbourg: Übelin, 1512).

Huguccio. *Summa decretorum* (Paris, BN, lat. 15396–15397).

Il costituto del comune di Siena volgarizzato nel mcccix–mcccx, ed. Mahmoud Salem Elsheikh, 4 vols. (Siena: Monte dei Paschi di Siena, 2002).

Jacobus Butrigarius. *Lectura super Codice* (first recension, Lucca, Biblioteca Capitolaria, MS 372; second recension, Paris: Parvus, 1516; repr., Bologna: Formi, 1973).

Johannes de Anania. *Consilia* (Venice: Rubini, 1576).

Johannes de Friburgo. *Summa confessorum* (Paris: Parvus, 1519).

Jacobus de Grafiis. *Decisiones aureae casuum conscientiae,* vol. 1 (Venice: Giunta, 1609).

Johannes de Regina. *Quodlibeta* (Naples, BN, VII B.28).

Johannes Harpprecht. *Tractatus Criminalis* (Frankfurt/M.: Bitsch, 1603).

Johannes Teutonicus. *Glossa ordinaria* [in Decretum Gratiani] (Munich, BSB, lat. 14024).

Journal de Jean de Roye, ed. Bernard de Mandrot, 2 vols. (Paris: Renouard, 1894).

Las Siete Partidas (Salamanca: Andrea de Portonariis, 1555).

Las leyes de Toro glosadas (Burgos: Juncta, 1527).

Laurentius Hispanus. *Glossa,* in *Glossa Palatina* [in Decretum Gratiani] (Vatican, BAV, Pal. lat. 658).

Laurentius Ursellius. *Examen apum*, 2 vols. (Rome: Andreas Phaeus, 1632–1637).

Leges Wisigothorum, ed. Karl Zeumer, *MGH* LL 1.1 (Hannover: Hahn, 1902).

Le livre des assises (London: Atkins, 1679).

Les edicts et ordonnances des rois de France, vol. 3, ed. Antoine Fontanon (Paris, 1611).

The London Eyre of 1244, ed. Helena Chew and Martin Weinbaum (London: London Record Society, 1970).

Marianus Socinus. *Lectura super quinto Decretalium* (Lyon, 1559).

Mattheus de Afflictis. *Praelectio in Constitutiones utriusque Siciliae*, 2 vols. (Venice: Guarisco, 1606).

Matthew Hale. *Pleas of the Crown* (London: Atkyns, 1682).

The Mirror of Justices, ed. William Whittaker (London: Quaritch, 1895).

Nicolaus de Lyra. *Postillae*, in *Biblia Sacra*, 8 vols. (Lyon: Vincent, 1545).

Oxford City Documents, Financial and Judicial, 1268–1665, ed. James Thorold Rogers (Oxford: Clarendon, 1891).

Pactum Legis Salicae, ed. Karl Eckhard, *MGH* LL 1.4.1 (Hannover: Hahn, 1962).

Paris pendant la domination anglaise (1420–1436). Documents extraits des registres de la Chancellerie de France, ed. Auguste Longnon (Paris: Champion, 1878).

Paulus de Castro. *Super Infortiato*, 2 vols. (Lyon: Trechsel, 1535).

Paulus Zacchias. *Quaestiones medico-legales*, 3 vols. (Frankfurt/M.: Bencard, 1688).

Penitenzieria Apostolica, *Registra diversorum* (Rome, APA Reg. div. 1–).

Petrus Cantor. *Summa de sacramentis et animae consiliis*, vol. 3, *Liber casuum conscientiae*, ed. Jean-Albert Dugauquier, Analecta mediaevalia Namurcensia 21 (Louvain: Nauwelaerts, 1967).

[Petrus Lombardus]. *Magistri Petri Lombardi Parisiensis episcopi sententiae in quatuor libris distinctae* (Grottaferrata: Collegium Sancti Bonaventurae ad Claras Aquas, 1981).

Petrus Monavius Lascovius Ungarus. "Dissertatio," in *Psychologia*, ed. Rudolphus Goclenius (Marburg: Egenolphus, 1590), 201–202.

Philippe de Beaumanoir. *Coutumes de Clermont en Beauvaisis*, ed. Amedée Salmon, 2 vols. (Paris: Picard, 1899–1900).

Právní knih mĕsta Brna z poloviní 14. století, ed. Miroslav Flodr, 3 vols. (Brno: Blok, 1990–1993).

Prosperus Farinaccius. *Praxis et theorica criminalis*, 5 vols. (Frankfurt/M.: Palthenius, 1610).

Raymundus de Penyaforte. *Summa de penitentia*, ed. Xavier Ochoa and Aloysio Diaz (Rome: Institutum iuridicum Claretianum, 1976).

"Rechtsquellen des Kantons Tessin IV," ed. Andreas Heusler, in *Zeitschrift für schweizerisches Recht* 14 (1895): 259–330, reprinted separately (Basel: Helbing & Lichtenhan, 1895), 1–78.

Recueil de lettres des officialités de Marseille et d'Aix (XIVe–XVe siècles), ed. Roger Aubenas, 2 vols. (Paris: Picard, 1937–1938).

"Recueil des documents concernant le Poitou contenus dans les registres de la Chancellerie de France," ed. Paul Guérin, in *Archives historiques de Poitou* 11 (1881); 21 (1891); 24 (1893); 26 (1896); 29 (1898); 32 (1903); 35 (1906); 38 (1909).

Recueil des historiens des Gaules et de la France, vol. 24, ed. Léopold Delisle (Paris: Imprimerie impériale, 1904).

Regestrum visitationum archiepiscopi Rothomagensis. Journal des visites pastorales d'Eude Rigaud, archévêque de Rouen, 1248–1269, ed. Théodore Bonnin (Rouen: le Brument, 1852).

Regino Prumensis. *Liber de synodalibus causis et disciplinis ecclesiasticis,* ed. Friedrich Wasserschleben (Leipzig: Engelmann, 1840).

Registre criminel de la justice de Saint-Martin-des-Champs à Paris au XIVe siècle, ed. Louis Tanon (Paris: Willem, 1877).

"Registre de l'échevinage de Saint-Jean d'Angély (1332–1496)," ed. Denys d'Aussy, in *Archives historiques de la Saintonge et de l'Aunis* 32 (1902).

Ricardus Anglicus. *Apparatus* [in 1 Comp.] (Paris, BN, lat. 149).

Robert Brooke, *La Graunde Abridgement* (London: Tottel, 1573).

Rufinus. *Summa Decreti,* ed. Heinrich Singer (Paderborn: Schöningh, 1902).

Sammlung altwürttembergischer Statutarrechte, ed. [August] Reyscher (Tübingen: Fues, 1834).

Select Cases of Defamation to 1600, ed. Richard H. Helmholz (London: Selden Society, 1985).

Select Pleas of the Crown, 1200–1225, ed. Frederick Maitland (London: Quaritch, 1888).

Septuaginta, ed. Alfred Rahlfs (Stuttgart: Württembergische Bibelanstalt, 1935).

Signorolus de Homodeis. *Consilia* (Lyon: Giunta, 1549).

Simon de Bursano. *Summa in Clementinas* (Florence, Biblioteca Laurenziana, Aedilium 55; Barcelona, AC, C 40).

Statuta communis Bugellae et documenta adiecta, ed. Pietro Sella (Biella: Testa, 1904).

Statuta communis Parmae digesta ad MCCLV, ed. Amadio Ronchini, Monumenta historica ad provincias Parmensem et Placentinam pertinentia, vol. 1 (Parma: Fiaccadori, 1856).

The Statutes of the Realm 4.2 (London: HMSO, 1819).

Statutorum et reformationum magnificae civitatis Senogaliae volumen (Pesaro: Concordia, 1584).

Summa Bambergensis (Liège, BM, 127E).

Sylvester Prierias. *Summa summarum* (Strasbourg: Grieninger, 1518).

Thomas Fienus. *De formatrice foetus liber* (Antwerp: a Tongris, 1620).

Thomas Sanchez. *Disputatio de sancto matrimonii sacramento* (Antwerp: Heredes Martini Nutii & Joannes Meursius, 1617).

Volumen statutorum Maceratae (Macerata, It.: Bini, 1553).

William Staunford. *Les plees del corone* (London: Societas Stationariorum, 1607).

Year Book, 1 Edw. III (London: Yetsweirt, 1596).

Year Book, 22 Edw. III (London: Tottyl, 1585).

Secondary Sources

Alessi Palazzolo, Giorgia. *Prova legale e pena. La crisi del sistema tra medio evo e moderno* (Naples: Jovene, 1987).

Ames, Christine. *Righteous Persecution: Inquisition, Dominicans, and Christianity in the Middle Ages* (Philadelphia: University of Pennsylvania Press, 2009).

Arieti, Stefano. "Bartolomeo da Varignana," in *Medieval Science, Technology, and Medicine,* ed. Thomas Glick et al. (London: Routledge, 2005), 78–79.

Ascheri, Mario et al., eds. *Legal Consulting in the Civil Law Tradition* (Berkeley: University of California Press, 1999).

Avril, Joseph. "Sources et caractère du livre synodal de Raimond de Calmont d'Olt, évêque de Rodez (1289)," in *L'Église et le droit dans le Midi (XIIIᵉ-XIVᵉ siècles)* (Toulouse: Privat, 1994).

Austin, Greta. *Shaping Church Law around the Year 1000: The Decretum of Burchard of Worms* (Aldershot, UK: Ashgate, 2008).

Baas, Karl. "Gesundheitspflege in Elsass-Lothringen bis zum Ausgang des Mittelalters," *Zeitschrift für Geschichte des Oberrheins* 73 (1919): 27–76.

Baker, John. *The Oxford History of the Laws of England* VI: *1483–1558* (Oxford: Oxford University Press, 2003).

Baldwin, James W. *Masters, Princes, and Merchants: The Social Views of Peter the Chanter and His Circle* (Princeton, NJ: Princeton University Press, 1970).

Bartlett, Robert. *Trial by Fire and Water: The Medieval Judicial Ordeal* (Oxford: Oxford University Press, 1986).

Bellomo, Manlio. *The Common Legal Past of Europe, 1000–1800,* trans. Lydia Cochrane (Washington, DC: Catholic University of America Press, 1995).

Benson, Robert. *The Bishop-Elect: A Study in Medieval Ecclesiastical Office* (Princeton, NJ: Princeton University Press, 1968).

Berman, Harold. *Law and Revolution: The Formation of the Western Legal Tradition,* vol. 1 (Cambridge, MA: Harvard University Press, 1983).

Bertram, Martin, ed. *Stagnation oder Fortbildung? Aspekte des allgemeinen Kirchenrechts im 14. und 15. Jahrhundert* (Tübingen: Niemeyer, 2004).

Biller, Peter. "John of Naples, Quodlibets and Medieval Concern with the Body," in *Medieval Theology and the Natural Body,* ed. Peter Biller et al. (York: York Medieval Press, 1997), 3–12.

——. *The Measure of Multitude: Population in Medieval Thought* (Oxford: Oxford University Press, 2000).

Biller, Peter, and Alastair Minnis, eds. *Handling Sin: Confession in the Middle Ages* (Woodbridge, NY: York Medieval Press, 1998).

Blanshei, Sarah. *Politics and Justice in Late Medieval Bologna* (Leiden: Brill, 2010).

Boca, Jean. *La justice criminelle de l'échevinage d'Abbéville au moyen âge, 1184–1516* (Lille: Daniel, 1930).

Bologne, Jean-Claude. *La naissance interdite. Sterilité, avortement, contraception au moyen âge* (Paris: Orban, 1988).

Boswell, John. *The Kindness of Strangers: The Abandonment of Children in Western Europe from Late Antiquity to the Renaissance* (New York: Pantheon, 1988).

Boutaric, Edgard, ed. *Actes du Parlement de Paris,* 2 vols. (Paris: Imprimerie impériale, 1863–1866).

Boyle, Leonhard. "Summae Confessorum," in *Les genres littéraires dans les sommes théologiques et philosophiques médiévales* (Louvain: Institut des études médiévales, 1982), 271–280.

Brévart, Francis. "Between Medicine, Magic, and Religion: Wonder Drugs in German Medico-Pharmaceutical Treatises of the Thirteenth to the Sixteenth Centuries." *Speculum* 83 (2008): 1–57.

Brissaud, Yves. "L'infanticide à la fin du moyen âge," *RHDFE* 50 (1972): 229–256.

Brown, Peter. "Society and the Supernatural: A Medieval Change," *Daedalus* 104 (1975): 133–151, revised in Peter Brown, *Society and the Holy in Late Antiquity* (Berkeley: University of California Press, 1982), 302–332.

Brundage, James. *Law, Sex, and Society* (Chicago: University of Chicago Press, 1987).

———. *Medieval Canon Law* (London: Longman, 1995).

———. *The Medieval Origins of the Legal Profession: Canonists, Civilians, and Courts* (Chicago: University of Chicago Press, 2008).

Butler, Sara. "Abortion by Assault: Violence against Pregnant Women in Thirteenth and Fourteenth Century England," *Journal of Women's History* 17 (2005): 9–31.

———. "A Case of Indifference? Child Murder in Later Medieval England," *Journal of Women's History* 19 (2007): 59–82.

Caeneghem, Raoul van. "Reflexions on Rational and Irrational Modes of Proof in Medieval Europe," *TRG* 58 (1990): 263–279.

Carbonnières, Louis de. *La procédure devant la chambre criminelle du Parlement de Paris au XIVe siècle* (Paris: Champion, 2004).

Chadwyck-Healey, Charles. *Somersetshire Pleas, Civil and Criminal, from the Rolls of the Itinerant Justices, Close of the Twelfth Century—41 Henry III* ([London,] 1897).

Chevalier, Bernard. *Le pays de la Loire moyenne dans le Trésor des chartes: Berry, Blésois, Chartrain, Orléanais, Touraine 1350–1502* (Paris: CTHS, 1993).

Cohn, Samuel. "Sex and Violence on the Periphery: The Territorial State in Early Renaissance Florence," in *Women in the Streets: Essays on Sex and Power in Renaissance Italy*, ed. Samuel Cohn (Baltimore: Johns Hopkins University Press, 1996), 98–136, 198–216.

Cox, J. Charles. *The Sanctuaries and Sanctuary Seekers of Mediaeval England* (London: Allen & Sons, 1911).

Crawford, Catherine. "Legalizing Medicine: Early Modern Legal Systems and the Growth of Medico-Legal Knowledge," in *Legal Medicine in History*, ed. Michael Clark and Catherine Crawford (Cambridge: Cambridge University Press, 1994), 89–116.

Crouzet-Pavan, Elisabeth. *Espace, pouvoir et société à Venise à la fin du moyen âge*, 2 vols. (Rome: École française de Rome, 1992).

Cueña-Boy, Francisco. "Reflexiones en torno a la idea de rerum natura en la Glosa ordinaria de Acursio," *RIDC* 15 (2004): 201–215.

Dahm, Georg. *Das Strafrecht Italiens im ausgehenden Mittelalter* (Berlin: de Gruyter, 1931).

Dean, Trevor. *Crime and Justice in Late Medieval Italy* (Cambridge: Cambridge University Press, 2007).

———. *Crime in Medieval Europe 1200–1500* (Harlow, UK: Longman, 2001).

Dellapenna, Joseph. *Dispelling the Myths of Abortion History* (Durham, NC: Carolina Academic Press, 2006).

Dölger, Franz. "Das Lebensrecht des ungeborenen Kindes und die Fruchtabtreibung in der Bewertung der heidnischen und christlichen Antike," in *Antike und Christentum*, Kultur-und religionsgeschichtliche Studien 4 (Münster: Aschendorff, 1934), 1–61.

Dorini, Umberto. *Il diritto penale e la delinquenza in Firenze nel secolo XV* (Lucca: Corsi, [1923]).

Dossat, Yves et al., *Le Languedoc et le Rouergue dans le Trésor des chartes* (Paris: CTHS, 1983).

Dubuis, Pierre. "Enfants refusés dans les Alpes occidentales (XIVᵉ–XVᵉ siècles)," in *Enfance abandonnée et société en Europe* (Rome: École française de Rome, 1991), 573–590.

Dülmen, Richard van. *Frauen vor Gericht. Kindsmord in der frühen Neuzeit* (Frankfurt/M.: Fischer, 1991).

Dunn, Caroline. "The Language of Ravishment in Medieval England," *Speculum* 86 (2011): 79–116.

Dutton, Paul. *Carolingian Civilization: A Reader* (Peterborough, ON: Broadview, 1993).

Elsakkers, Marianne. "Her and Neylar: An Intriguing Criterion for Abortion in Old Frisian Law," *Scientiarum Historia* 30 (2004): 107–154.

Engelmann, Woldemar. *Die Schuldlehre der Postglossatoren* (Leipzig: Duncker & Humblodt, 1895).

Felber, Alfons. "Unzucht und Kindesmord in der Rechtssprechung der freien Reichsstadt Nördlingen vom 15. bis 19. Jahrhundert" (PhD diss., University of Bonn, 1961).

Ferrari, A. de. "Del Garbo, Dino," *DBI* 36 (1988): 578–581.

Feuchter, Jörg. *Ketzer, Konsuln und Büßer. Die städtischen Eliten von Montauban vor dem Inquisitor Petrus Cellani (1236/1241)* (Tübingen: Mohr-Siebeck, 2007).

Fiorelli, Piero. *La tortura giudiziaria nel diritto commune*, 2 vols. (Milan: Giuffrè, 1953–1954).

Fischer-Drew, Katherine. *The Laws of the Salian Franks* (Philadelphia: University of Pennsylvania Press, 1991).

Flügge, Sibylla. *Hebammen und heilkundige Frauen. Recht und Rechtswirklichkeit im 15. und 16. Jahrhundert* (Frankfurt/M.: Stroemfeld, 2000).

Forrest, Ian. *The Detection of Heresy in Late Medieval England* (Oxford: Oxford University Press, 2005).

Fournier, Paul. *Mélanges de droit canonique*, ed. Theo Kölzer, 2 vols. (Aalen, Ger.: Scientia, 1983).

———. "Un tournant de l'histoire du droit 1060–1140," *Nouvelle revue historique de droit français et étranger* 41 (1917): 129–180, reprinted in Paul Fournier, *Mélanges de droit canonique*, 2:373–424 (no. 17).

Fowler-Magerl, Linda. *Clavis canonum* (Hannover: Hahn, 2005).

Fraher, Richard. "Conviction According to Conscience: The Medieval Jurists' Debate Concerning Judicial Discretion and the Law of Proof," *Law and History* 7 (1989): 23–88.

———. "IV Lateran's Revolution in Criminal Procedure: The Birth of Inquisitions, the End of Ordeals and Innocent III's Vision of Ecclesiastical Politics," in *Studia in honorem eminentissimi cardinalis Alphonsi M. Stickler*, ed. Rosalio I. Card. Castillo Lara (Vatican City: LAS, 1992), 91–111.

———. "The Theoretical Justification for the New Criminal Law of the High Middle Ages: 'Rei publicae interest, ne crimina remaneant impunita,'" *University of Illinois Law Review* 3 (1984): 577–595.

Frauenstädt, Paul. "Breslaus Strafrechtspflege im 14. bis 16. Jahrhundert," *Zeitschrift für die gesamte Strafrechtswissenschaft* 19 (1890): 1–35, 229–250.

Garancini, Giancarlo. "Materiali per la storia del procurato aborto nel diritto inter-medio," *Jus* 22 (1975): 395–528.

Garcia-Marín, José. *El aborto criminal en la legislación y la doctrina. Pasado y presente de una polemica* (Madrid: Ediciones de derecho reunidas, 1980).

Gauvard, Claude. *De grace especial. Crime, état et société en France à la fin du moyen âge,* 2 vols. (Paris: Publications de la Sorbonne, 1991).

Gazzaniga, Jean Louis. *L'église du midi à la fin du règne de Charles VII (1444–1461). D'après la jurisprudence du Parlement de Toulouse* (Paris: Picard, 1976).

Geltner, Guy. *The Medieval Prison: A Social History* (Princeton, NJ: Princeton University Press, 2008).

Génestal, Robert. *Le privilegium fori en France du Décret de Gratien à la fin du XIVe siècle,* 2 vols. (Paris: Leroux, 1921–1924).

Gilchrist, John. *Canon Law in the Age of Reform, 11th–12th Centuries* (Aldershot, UK: Ashgate, 1993).

Given, James B. *Inquisition and Society: Power, Discipline, and Resistance in Languedoc* (Ithaca: Cornell University Press, 1997).

———. *Society and Homicide in Thirteenth-Century England* (Stanford: Stanford University Press, 1977).

Goering, Joseph. "The Internal Forum and the Literature of Penance and Confession," *Traditio* 59 (2004): 175–227.

Gonthier, Nicole. *Délinquance, justice, et société dans le Lyonnais médiéval* (Paris: Arguments, 1993).

Gordley, James, and Augustine Thompson, *The Treatise on Law (Decretum DD. 1–20)* (Washington, DC: Catholic University of America Press, 1993).

Grand, Roger. *Le paix d'Aurillac. Études et documents sur l'histoire des institutions municipales d'une ville à consulat* (Paris: Sirey, 1945).

Green, Monica. "Constantinus Africanus and the Conflict between Religion and Science," in *The Human Embryo: Aristotle and the European and Arabic Traditions,* ed. Gordon Dunstan (Exeter: Exeter University Press, 1990), 47–69.

———. "Documenting Medieval Women's Medical Practice," in *Practical Medicine from Salerno to the Black Death,* ed. Luis Garcia-Ballester et al. (Cambridge: Cambridge University Press, 1994), 322–352, reprinted in Monica Green, *Women's Healthcare in the Medieval West* (Aldershot, UK: Ashgate, 2000), no. 2.

———. "Gendering the History of Women's Healthcare," *Gender & History* 20 (2008): 487–518.

———. *Making Women's Medicine Masculine: The Rise of Male Authority in Pre-Modern Gynaecology* (Oxford: Oxford University Press, 2008).

Groot, Roger. "The Early Thirteenth-Century Jury," in *Twelve Good Men and True: The Criminal Trial Jury in England, 1200–1800,* ed. James Cockburn and Thomas Green (Princeton, NJ: Princeton University Press, 1988), 3–35.

Grubbs, Judith E. *Women and the Law in the Roman Empire: A Sourcebook on Marriage, Divorce, and Widowhood* (London: Routledge, 2002).

Gründel, Johannes. *Die Lehre von den Umständen der menschlichen Handlung im Mittelalter* (Münster: Aschendorff, 1963).

Hamilton, Sarah. *The Practice of Penance 900–1050* (Oxford: Oxford University Press, 2001).

Hanawalt, Barbara. *The Ties That Bound: Peasant Families in Medieval England* (Oxford: Oxford University Press, 1986).

Hartmann, Wilfried. *Das Sendhandbuch des Regino von Prüm* (Darmstadt: Wissenschaftliche Buchgesellschaft, 2004).

———. *Kirche und Kirchenrecht um 900. Die Bedeutung der spätkarolingischen Zeit für Tradition und Innovation im kirchlichen Recht* (Hannover: Hahn, 2008).

Hartmann, Wilfried, and Kenneth Pennington, eds. *The History of Medieval Canon Law in the Classical Period 1140–1234* (Washington, DC: Catholic University of America Press, 2008).

Helmholz, Richard H., *Canon Law and the Law of England* (London: Hambledon Press, 1987).

———. "Crime, Compurgation and the Courts of the Medieval Church," *Law and History Review* 1 (1983): 1–26, reprinted in Helmholz, *Canon Law and the Law of England*, 119–144.

———. "Infanticide in the Province of Canterbury during the Fifteenth Century," *Journal of Psychohistory* 2 (1975): 379–390, reprinted in Helmholz, *Canon Law and the Law of England*, 157–168.

———. *The Ius Commune in England, Four Studies* (Oxford: Oxford University Press, 2001).

———. "'Si quis suadente' (C. 17 q. 4 c. 29): Theory and Practice," in *Proceedings of the Seventh International Congress of Medieval Canon Law*, ed. Peter Linehan (Vatican City: Typographia Vaticana, 1988), 425–438.

———. *The Spirit of Classical Canon Law* (Athens, GA: University of Georgia Press, 1996).

Hewson, M. Anthony. *Giles of Rome and the Medieval Theory of Conception* (London: Athlone Press, 1975).

Hirte, Markus. *Papst Innozenz III., das IV. Laterankonzil und die Strafverfahren gegen Kleriker. Eine registergestützte Untersuchung zur Entwicklung der Verfahrensarten zwischen 1198 und 1215* (Tübingen: Diskord, 2005).

Hoeflich, Michael, and Jasonne Grabher, "The Establishment of Normative Legal Texts: The Beginnings of the Ius Commune," in Hartmann and Pennington, *The History of Medieval Canon Law*, 1–21.

Honings, Bonifacio. "L'aborto nei decretisti e nei decretalisti," *Apollinaris* 50 (1977): 246–273.

Hunnisett, Roy F. *The Medieval Coroner* (Cambridge: Cambridge University Press, 1961).

Hurnard, Naomi. *The King's Pardon for Homicide before A.D. 1307* (Oxford: Oxford University Press, 1969).

Huser, Roger J. *The Crime of Abortion in Canon Law: An Historical Synopsis and Commentary*, Collected Study Series 162 (Washington, DC: Catholic University of America Press, 1942).

Hyams, Paul. *Rancor and Reconciliation in Medieval England* (Ithaca: Cornell University Press, 2003).

Jacquart, Danielle, and Claude Thomasset, *Sexuality and Medicine in the Middle Ages* (Princeton, NJ: Princeton University Press, 1988).

Jenks, Stuart. "The Writ and the Exception de odio et atia," *Journal of Legal History* 23 (2002): 1–22.

Kapparis, Konstantinos. *Abortion in the Ancient World* (London: Duckworth, 2002).

Kaufmann, Ekkehardt. "Rädern," *HRG* 4 (1990): 135–138.

Kelleher, Marie. *The Measure of Woman: Law and Female Identity in the Crown of Aragon* (Philadelphia: University of Pennsylvania Press, 2010).

Kellum, Barbara. "The Female Felon in Fourteenth-Century England," *Viator* 5 (1974): 253–268.

——. "Infanticide in England in the Later Middle Ages," *Journal of Psychohistory* 1 (1973): 367–388.

Kerr, Margaret. "Husband and Wife in Criminal Proceedings in Medieval England," in *Women, Marriage, and Family in Medieval Christendom: Essays in Memory of Michael M. Sheehan C.S.B.*, ed. Michael Sheehan et al. (Kalamazoo, MI: Medieval Institute Publications, 1998), 211–251.

Kéry, Lotte. *Canonical Collections of the Early Middle Ages (ca. 400–1140): A Bibliographical Guide to the Manuscripts and Literature* (Washington, DC: Catholic University of America Press, 1999).

——. *Gottesfurcht und irdische Strafe. Der Beitrag des mittelalterlichen Kirchenrechts zur Entstehung des Strafrechts* (Cologne: Böhlau, 2006).

Kieckhefer, Richard. "Avenging the Blood of Children: Anxiety over Child Victims and the Origins of the European Witch Trials," in *The Devil, Heresy, and Witchcraft in the Middle Ages*, ed. Alberto Ferreiro (Leiden: Brill, 1998), 91–110.

Klerman, Daniel. "Settlement and the Decline of Private Prosecution in Thirteenth-Century England," *Law and History Review* 19 (2001): 1–65.

Koeniger, Albert. *Die Sendgerichte in Deutschland* I (Munich: Lentner, 1907).

Kohler, Josef. *Das Strafrecht der italienischen Statuten vom 12.-16. Jahrhundert* (Mannheim: Bensheimer, 1896).

Körntgen, Ludger. "Canon Law and the Practice of Penance: Burchard of Worms's Penitential," *Early Medieval Europe* 14 (2006): 103–117.

Kottje, Raymund. *Die Bussbücher Haltigars von Cambrai und des Hrabanus Maurus* (Berlin: de Gruyter, 1980).

Kriegk, Georg. *Deutsches Bürgertum im Mittelalter*, vol. 1 (Frankfurt/M.: Rütten & Löning, 1868).

Kuttner, Stephan. *Harmony from Dissonance: An Interpretation of Medieval Canon Law* (Latrobe, PA: Archabbey Press, 1960), reprinted in Kuttner, *The History of Ideas and Doctrines*, no. 1.

——, ed. *The History of Ideas and Doctrines of Canon Law in the Middle Ages*, 2nd ed. (Aldershot, UK: Ashgate, 1992).

——. *Kanonistische Schuldlehre von Gratian bis auf die Dekretalen Gregors IX. (1140–1234)* (Vatican City: Bibliotheca Apostolica Vaticana, 1935).

——. "Raymond of Peñafort as an Editor," *BMCL* 12 (1982): 65–80, reprinted in Kuttner, *Studies in the History*, no. 12.

——. "The Revival of Jurisprudence," in *Renaissance and Renewal in the Twelfth Century*, ed. Robert Benson and Giles Constable (Cambridge, MA: Harvard University Press, 1982), 299–323, reprinted in Kuttner, *Studies in the History*, no. 3.

——, ed. *Studies in the History of Medieval Canon Law* (Aldershot, UK: Ashgate, 1990).

——. "Urban II and the Doctrine of Interpretation: A Turning Point?," *SG* 15 (1972): 53–85, reprinted in Kuttner, *The History of Ideas and Doctrines*, no. 4.

Labat-Poussin, Brigitte, et al., eds. *Actes du Parlement. Parlement criminel. Règne de Philippe VI de Valois. Inventaire analytique des registres de X2a 2 à 5,* (Paris: Archives Nationales, 1987).

Lacey, Helen. *The Royal Pardon: Access to Mercy in Fourteenth-Century England* (Woodbridge, NY: York Medieval Press, 2009).

Langbein, John. *Prosecuting Crime in the Renaissance: England, France, Germany* (Cambridge, MA: Harvard University Press, 1974).

———. *Torture and the Law of Proof: Europe and England in the Ancien Regime* (Chicago: University of Chicago Press, 1977).

Larrainzar, Carlos. "La ricerca attuale sul Decretum Gratiani," in *La cultura giuridico-canonica medioevale,* ed. Enrique de León and Nicholas Álvarez des las Asturias (Milan: Giuffrè, 2003), 45–88.

Larson, Atria. "The Influence of the School of Laon on Gratian: The Usage of the Glossa ordinaria and Anselmian Sententie in De Penitentia (Decretum, C. 33 q. 3)," *Mediaeval Studies* 72 (2010): 197–244.

Lecacheux, Paul. "Une formulaire de la Pénitencerie Apostolique au temps du Cardinal Albornoz (1357–1358)," *Mélanges d'archéologie et d'histoire* 18 (1898): 37–49.

Lefebvre-Teillard, Anne. "Infans conceptus. Existence physique et existence juridique," *RHDFE* 72 (1994): 499–525, reprinted in Anne Lefebvre-Teillard, *Autour de l'enfant. Du droit canonique et romain médiéval au Code civil* (Leiden: Brill, 2008), 53–86.

Lehmann, Prisca. *La répression des délits sexuels dans les états savoyards. Châtellenies des diocèses d'Aoste, Sion et Turin, fin XIIIᵉ–XVᵉ siècle* (Lausanne: Université de Lausanne, 2006).

Lemay, Helen. "Human Sexuality in Twelfth- through Fifteenth-Century Scientific Writings," in *Sexual Practices and the Medieval Church,* ed. Vernon Bullough and James Brundage (Buffalo: Prometheus, 1982), 187–205.

Lemercier, Paul. "Une curiosité judiciaire au moyen âge. La grâce par marriage subséquent," *RHDFE* 34 (1956): 464–474.

Lopez, Robert. *The Commercial Revolution of the Middle Ages, 950–1350* (Englewood Cliffs, NJ: Prentice-Hall, 1971).

Lucchesi, Marzia. *Siquis occidit occidetur. L'omicidio doloso nelle fonti consiliarie (secoli XIV–XVI)* (Padua: CEDAM, 1999).

Lutterbach, Hubertus. "Intentions- oder Tathaftung? Zum Bussverständnis in den frühmittelalterlichen Bussbüchern," *Frühmittelalterliche Studien* 34 (1995): 120–143.

MacCaughan, Patricia. *La justice à Manosque au XIIIᵉ siècle. Évolution et représentation* (Paris: Sirey, 2005).

Maes, Louis. *Vijf eeuwen stedelijk strafrecht. Bijdrage tot de rechts- en cultuurgeschiedenis der nederlanden* (Antwerp: de Sikkel, 1947).

Maffei, Domenico. *Studi di storia dell'università e della letteratura giuridica* (Goldbach, Ger.: Keip, 1995).

Mansfield, Mary. *The Humiliation of Sinners: Public Penance in Thirteenth-Century France* (Ithaca: Cornell University Press, 1995).

Martí Bonet, José. "Las visitas pastorales y los "Comunes" del primer año del pontificado del obispo del Barcelona Ponç de Gualba (a. 1303)," *Anthologica annua* 28/29 (1981/1982): 577–825.

Martorelli Vico, Romana. *Medicina e filosofia. Per una storia dell'embriologia medievale del XIII e XIV secolo* (Naples: Guerini, 2002).

Mayali, Laurent. "Le notion de 'statutum odiosum' dans la doctrine romaniste au moyen âge," *Ius commune* 12 (1984): 57–69.

Mazzi, Maria Serena. "Cronache di periferia dello stato fiorentino. Reati contro la morale nel primo quattrocento," *Studi storici* 27 (1986): 609–635.

McNeill, John, and Helena Gamer, trans. *Medieval Handbooks of Penance. Translations from the Principal "Libri Poenitentiales" and Selections from Related Documents* (New York: Columbia University Press, 1938).

Meekings, Cecil. *Crown Pleas of the Wiltshire Eyre 1249* (Devizes: Wiltshire Archeological and Natural History Society, 1961).

Meens, Rob. "The Frequency and Nature of Early Medieval Penance," in Biller and Minnis, *Handling Sin*, 35–61.

Meusen, Yves. *Veritatis adiutor. La procédure du temoignage dans le droit savant et la pratique française (XII^c–XIVe siècle)* (Milan: Giuffrè, 2006).

Migliorino, Francesco. "La parola e le pieghe della Scrittura. I Libelli di Pietro Geremia," in *La memoria ritrovata. Pietro Geremia e le carte della storia*, ed. Francesco Migliorino et al. (Catania, It.: Maimone, 2006), 75–95.

Montanos-Ferrín, Emma, and José Arnilla-Bernál, *Estudios de historia del derecho criminal* (Madrid: Dykinson, 1990).

Müller, Wolfgang P. *Die Abtreibung. Anfänge der Kriminalisierung 1140–1650* (Cologne: Böhlau, 2000)

———. "Die Taxen der päpstlichen Pönitentiarie, 1338–1569," *QFIAB* 78 (1998): 189–261.

———. "Signorolus de Homodeis and the Late Medieval Interpretation of Statutory Law," *RIDC* 6 (1995): 217–232.

———. "The Internal Forum of the Later Middle Ages. A Modern Myth?," *Law and History Review* 33 (2015): 787–813.

———. "Violence et droit canonique. Les enseignements de la Pénitencerie Apostolique (XIIIe–XVIe siècle)," *Revue historique* 131 (2007): 771–796.

Müller, Wolfgang P., and Gastone Saletnich, "Rodolfo Gonzaga (1452–1495): News on a Celebrity Murder Case," in *The Long Arm of Papal Authority*, ed. Gerhard Jaritz, Torstein Jørgensen, and Kirsi Salonen, 2nd ed. (Budapest: CEU Press, 2005), 157–163.

Mulchahey, Michelle. *First the Bow Is Bent in Study: Dominican Education before 1350* (Toronto: University of Toronto Press, 1998).

Nardi, Enzo. *Procurato aborto nel mondo greco-romano* (Milan: Giuffrè, 1971).

Neumann, Friederike. *Öffentliche Sünder in der Kirche des Spätmittelalters. Verfahren—Sanktionen—Rituale* (Cologne: Böhlau, 2008).

Nirenberg, David. *Communities of Violence: Persecution of Minorities in the Middle Ages* (Princeton, NJ: Princeton University Press, 1996).

Noonan, John. "An Almost Absolute Value in History," in *The Morality of Abortion: Legal and Historical Perspectives*, ed. John Noonan (Cambridge, MA: Harvard University Press, 1970), 1–59.

———. *Contraception: A History of Its Treatment by the Catholic Theologians and Canonists*, 2nd ed. (Cambridge, MA: Harvard University Press, 1986).

———. "Gratian Slept Here: The Changing Identity of the Father of the Systematic Study of Canon Law," *Traditio* 35 (1979): 145–172, reprinted in Noonan, *Canons and Canonists in Context,* ed. J. Noonan (Goldbach, Ger.: Keip, 1997), no. 4.

Padoa Schioppa, Antonio, ed., *The Origins of the Modern State in Europe, Thirteenth to Eighteenth Centuries,* vol. 4, *Legislation and Justice* (Oxford: Oxford University Press, 1997), 335–369.

Padovani, Andrea. "La glossa di Odofredo agli statuti veneziani di Iacopo Tiepolo del 1242," *RIDC* 20 (2009): 71–111.

Palazzini, Giuseppe. *Ius fetus ad vitam eiusque tutela in fontibus ac doctrina canonica usque ad saeculum xvi* (Urbania, It.: Bramantes, 1943).

Pennington, Kenneth. "Torture in the Ius Commune," in *Mélanges en l'honneur d'Anne Lefebvre-Teillard,* ed. Bernard d'Alteroche et al. (Paris: Presses universitaires, 2009), 813–838.

Perrot, Ernest. *Les cas royaux. Origine et développement de la théorie aux XIIIe et XIVe siècles* (Paris: Rousseau, 1910).

Peters, Edward. *Inquisition* (New York: Free Press, 1988).

Piergiovanni, Vita. *La punibilità degli innocenti nel diritto canonico dell'età classica* I: *La discussione del problema in Graziano e nella decretalistica* (Milan: Giuffrè, 1971).

Poos, Lawrence R. *Lower Ecclesiastical Jurisdiction in Late Medieval England* (Oxford: Oxford University Press, 2001).

Povolo, Claudio. "Note per uno studio dell'infanticidio nella repubblica di Venezia nei secoli XV-XVIII," *Atti dell'Istituto veneto di scienze, lettere ed arti* 137 (1978–1979): 115–131.

———. "Una sentenza dell'avogaria di comun (1459)," *Archivio veneto* 114 (1980): 109–111.

Rafferty, Philip. "Roe v. Wade: The Birth of a Constitutional Right" (Ann Arbor, MI: University Microfilms International, 1992).

Reali, Francesco. "Magister Gratianus e le origini del diritto civile europeo," in *Graziano da Chiusi e la sua opera,* ed. Francesco Reali (Chiusi, It., 2009), 17–130.

Reno, Erik A. III. "The Authoritative Text: Raymond of Penyafort's Editing of the Decretals of Gregory IX" (PhD diss., Columbia University, 2011).

Reynolds, Susan. "The Emergence of Professional Law in the Long Twelfth Century," *Law and History Review* 21 (2003): 347–366.

Riddle, John. *Contraception and Abortion from the Ancient World to the Renaissance* (Cambridge, MA: Harvard University Press, 1992).

———. *Eve's Herbs: A History of Contraception and Abortion in the West* (Cambridge, MA: Harvard University Press, 1997).

Roetzer, Karl. "Die Delikte der Abtreibung, Kindstötung und Kindesaussetzung im mittelalterlichen Nürnberg" (PhD diss., University of Erlangen, 1957).

Rolker, Christof. *Canon Law and the Letters of Ivo of Chartres* (Cambridge: Cambridge University Press, 2010).

Romano, Andrea. "Tribunali, giudici e sentenze nel Regnum Siciliae (1130–1516)," in *Judicial Records, Law Reports, and the Growth of Case Law,* ed. John Baker (Berlin: Duncker & Humblodt, 1989), 211–301.

Rublack, Ulinka. *The Crimes of Women in Early Modern Germany* (Oxford: Oxford University Press, 1999).

———. "The Public Body: Policing Abortion in Early Modern Germany," in *Gender Relations in German History: Power, Agency, and Experience from the Sixteenth to the Nineteenth Century,* ed. Lynn Abrams and Elizabeth Harvey (Durham, NC: Duke University Press, 1997), 57–79.

Ruggiero, Guido. *Violence in Early Renaissance Venice* (New Brunswick, NJ: Rutgers University Press, 1980).

Salonen, Kirsi, and Ludwig Schmugge. *A Sip from the Well of Grace: Medieval Texts from the Apostolic Penitentiary* (Washington, DC: Catholic University of America Press, 2009).

Schilling, Heinz. "History of Crime or History of Sin? Some Reflections on the Social History of Early Modern Church Discipline," in *Politics and Society in Reformation Europe: Essays for Sir Geoffrey Elton on His Sixty-Fifth Birthday,* ed. Erkki Kouri and Tom Scott (New York: St. Martin's, 1987), 289–310.

Schneebeck, Harold. "The Law of Felony in Medieval England from the Accession of Edward I until the Mid-Fourteenth Century" (PhD diss., University of Iowa, 1973).

Schultzenstein, Siegfried. "Das Abtreibungsverbrechen in Frankreich," *Zeitschrift für vergleichende Rechtswissenschaft* 17 (1904): 360–421, and 18 (1905): 266–312.

Schwarz, Heinz. *Der Schutz des Kindes im Recht des frühen Mittelalters* (Bonn: Röhrscheid, 1993).

Scott, Samuel, and Robert Burns, *Las Siete Partidas,* 5 vols. (Philadelphia: University of Pennsylvania Press, 2001).

Seipp, D. "Crime in the Year Books," in *Law Reporting in England,* ed. Chantal Stebbings (London: Hambledon Press, 1995), 15–34.

———. "The Mirror of Justices," in *Learning the Law: Teaching and the Transmission of Law in England, 1150–1900,* ed. Jonathan Bush and Alan Wijffels (London: Hambledon Press, 1999), 85–112.

Shatzmiller, Joseph. *Médecine et justice en Provence médiéval. Documents de Manosque, 1262–1348* (Aix-en-Provence: Publications de l'Université de Provence, 1989).

Shoemaker, Karl. *Sanctuary and Crime in the Middle Ages, 400–1500* (New York: Fordham University Press, 2011).

Silano, Giulio. *Peter Lombard: The Sentences,* vol. 1 (Toronto: University of Toronto Press, 2007).

Siraisi, Nancy. "The Faculty of Medicine," in *A History of the University in Europe,* vol. 1, *Universities in the Middle Ages,* ed. Hilde de Ridder-Symoens (Cambridge: Cambridge University Press, 1992), 361–387.

———. *Medieval and Early Renaissance Medicine: An Introduction to Knowledge and Practice* (Chicago: University of Chicago Press, 1990).

Smail, Daniel. *The Consumption of Justice: Emotions, Publicity, and Legal Culture in Marseille, 1264–1423* (Ithaca: Cornell University Press, 2003).

Smith, Carrie. "Medieval Coroner Rolls: Legal Fiction or Historical Fact?," in *Courts, Counties, and the Capital,* ed. Diana Dunn (New York: St. Martin's, 1996), 93–115.

Somerville, Robert, and Bruce Brasington. *Prefaces to Canon Law Books in Latin Christianity. Selected Translations, 500–1245* (New Haven: Yale University Press, 1998).

Sorice, Rosalba. *"Quae omnia bonus iudex considerabit." La giustizia criminale nel Regno di Sicilia (secolo XVI)* (Torino: Giappichelli, 2009).

Struck, Wolf-Heino. "Die Sendgerichtsbarkeit am Ausgang des Mittelalters nach den Regesten des Archipresbyterats Wetzlar," *Nassauische Annalen* 82 (1971): 104–145.

Tamburini, Filippo. *Santi e peccatori. Confessioni e suppliche dai registri della Penitenziaria dell'Archivio Segreto Vaticano (1451–1486)* (Milan: Istituto di Propaganda, 1995).

Tanon, Louis. *Histoire des justices des anciennes églises et communautés monastiques de Paris* (Paris: Larose & Forcel, 1883).

Tavormina, M. Teresa, ed. *Sex, Aging, and Death in a Medieval Medical Compendium: Trinity College Cambridge MS R.14.52: Its Texts, Language, and Scribe*, 2 vols. (Tempe, AZ: Center for Medieval and Renaissance Studies, 2006).

Terroine, Anne. *Un abbé de Saint-Maur au XIIIᵉ siècle: Pierre de Chévry, 1256–1285, avec l'édition des plus anciens cas de justice de Saint-Maur-des-Fossés* (Paris: Klincksieck, 1968).

Thompson, Augustine. *Revival Preachers and Politics in Thirteenth-Century Italy: The Great Devotion of 1233* (Oxford: Oxford University Press, 1992).

Thorne, Samuel, trans. *Bracton: On the Laws and Customs of England*, 2 vols. (Cambridge, MA: Harvard University Press, 1968).

Trexler, Richard. "Infanticide in Florence: New Sources and First Results," *History of Childhood Quarterly* 1 (1973): 98–116.

Trojanos, Spirydon. "The Embryo in Byzantine Canon Law," in Spirydon Trojanos, *Analecta Atheniensia ad ius Byzantinum spectantia* (Athens: Sakkoulas, 1997), no. 3.

Trusen, Winfried. *Die Anfänge des gelehrten Rechts in Deutschland* (Cologne: Böhlau, 1962).

Utz-Tremp, Kathrin. *Von der Häresie zur Hexerei. "Wirkliche" und imaginäre Sekten im Spätmittelalter* (Hannover: Hahn, 2008).

Vallée, Aline, ed. *Registres du Trésor des chartes. Inventaire analytique* 3.3 (Paris: Archives Nationales, 1984).

Vallerani, Massimo. *La giustizia pubblica medievale* (Bologna: Il Mulino, 2005).

van der Lugt, Maaike. "L'animation de l'embryon humain dans la pensée médiévale," in *L'embryon, formation et animation. Antiquité grecque et latine, traditions hébraique, chrétienne et islamique,* ed. Luc Brisson et al. (Paris: Urin, 2008), 233–254.

Vanhemelrijck, Frans. *De criminaliteit in de ammanie van Brussel van de Late Middeleeuwen tot het einde van het Ancient Regime* (Brussels: AWLSK, 1981).

Vaultier, Roger. *Le folklore pendant la guerre de cent ans* (Paris: Génégaud, 1965).

Viard, Jules, and Aline Vallée, eds. *Registres du Trésor des chartes. Inventaire analytique* 3.1–2, 2 vols. (Paris: Archives Nationales, 1978–1979).

Viejo Ximénez, Javier. "La composicion del Decreto di Graciano," *Ius canonicum* 45 (2005): 431–485.

Viollet, Paul. "Registres judiciaires de quelques établissements religieux du Parisis au XIIIᵉ et XIVᵉ siècle," *Bibliothèque de l'École des chartes* 34 (1873): 317–341.

Vogel, Cyril. *Les 'Libri Paenitentiales,'* Typologie des sources du moyen âge occidental 27 (Turnhout, Belg.: Brepols, 1978), with a supplement by Allen Frantzen (1985).

Wallis, Faith, ed. *Medieval Medicine: A Reader* (Toronto: Broadview, 2010).

Walter, Ingeborg. "Infanticidio a Ponte Bocci: 2 marzo 1406. Elementi di un processo," *Studi storici* 27 (1986): 637–648.

Weigand, Rudolf. "The Development of the Glossa Ordinaria to Gratian's Decretum," in Hartmann and Pennington, *History of Medieval Canon Law in the Classical Period*, 55–97.

Weinbaum, Martin. *The London Eyre of 1276* (London: London Record Society, 1976).

White, Stephen. *Feuding and Peace-Making in Eleventh-Century France* (Aldershot, UK: Ashgate, 2005).

Willoweit, Dietmar, ed. *Die Entstehung des öffentlichen Strafrechts. Bestandsaufnahme eines europäischen Forschungsproblems* (Cologne: Böhlau, 1999).

Winroth, Anders. *The Making of Gratian's Decretum* (Cambridge: Cambridge University Press, 2000).

Wormald, Patrick. "Inter cetera bona . . . genti suae: Law-Making and Peace-Keeping in the Earliest English Kingdoms," in *La giustizia nell'alto medioevo (secoli V–VIII)*, Settimane di studio del Centro italiano di studi sull'alto medio-vevo 42 (Spoleto: Centro italiano di studi sull'alto medioevo, 1995), 963–993.

——. *The Making of English Law: King Alfred to the Twelfth Century*, vol. 1, *Legislation and Its Limits* (Oxford: Oxford University Press, 1999).

Wunderli, Richard. *London Church Courts and Society on the Eve of the Reformation* (Cambridge, MA: Harvard University Press, 1981).

Zoratti, Egidio. *Comparazione analitica degli statuti di Prata con le loro derivazioni legislative* (Udine, It.: del Biano, 1908).

Zorzi, Andrea. "Le esecuzioni delle condanne a morte a Firenze nel tardo medioevo tra esperienza penale e cerimoniale pubblico," in *Simbolo e realtà della vita urbana nel tardo medioevo*, ed. Massimo Miglio and Giuseppe Lombardi (Rome: Vecchiarelli, 1993), 153–253.

INDEX